THOMSON
COURSE TECHNOLOGY
Professional ■ Trade ■ Reference

DIGITAL PERFORMER® 4 IGNITE!

By Eric Grebler

MUSKA & LIPMAN Publishing

THOMSON
COURSE TECHNOLOGY
Professional ■ Trade ■ Reference

DIGITAL PERFORMER® 4 IGNITE!

By Eric Grebler

Digital Performer® 4 Ignite!

Senior Vice President, Professional, Trade, Reference Group: Andy Shafran

Publisher: Stacy L. Hiquet

Credits: Senior Marketing Manager, Sarah O'Donnell; Marketing Manager, Heather Hurley; Manager of Editorial Services, Heather Talbot; Acquisitions Editor, Todd Jensen; Senior Editor, Mark Garvey; Associate Marketing Manager, Kristin Eisenzopf; Retail Market Coordinator, Sarah Dubois; Production Editor, Jenny Davidson; Technical Editor, Mark Abdelnour; Proofreader, Cathleen Snyder; Cover Designer, Nancy Goulet; Interior Design and Layout, Sue Honeywell; Indexer, Sharon Shock.

Library of Congress Catalog Number: 2003114314
ISBN: 1-59200-352-4
5 4 3 2 1

Educational facilities, companies, and organizations interested in multiple copies or licensing of this book should contact the publisher for quantity discount information. Training manuals, CD-ROMs, and portions of this book are also available individually or can be tailored for specific needs.

Muska & Lipman Publishing,
a Division of Course Technology
25 Thomson Place
Boston, MA 02210
www.muskalipman.com
publisher@muskalipman.com

To my parents, Ricky and Victor

Acknowledgments

It took a collaboration of many people to make this book a reality. Todd Jensen and the rest of the Muska & Lipman team were fundamental in bringing this book to life.

I can't say enough about the efforts of Jenny Davidson as copy editor. She spun her magic and took my poorly formatted, barely legible transcript and somehow turned it into this book. Thanks also to Mark Abdelnour who diligently acted as technical editor and was always happy to correct my oversights.

Special thanks to my wife Kara, my parents Ricky and Victor, my brothers Ron, Oren, and Leor, and to the rest of my family and friends for their constant support and encouragement. Thanks also to Carmen Robeson for sharing his passion for music.

About the Author

Eric Grebler is an IT professional, an author, and a certified trainer who has demystified the world of computers for thousands of people. Originally from Ottawa, he currently resides in Toronto, Canada. Eric has developed curriculum and resource material on a wide range of technical topics, including desktop publishing, digital audio sequencing, graphics, XML, and operating systems.

While his first love is vocal music, Eric also spends much of his time delighting audiences with his keyboard and piano performances. He continues to strive toward his lifelong goal of becoming a lounge singer, but if that doesn't pan out, he'll stick to writing books.

Contents at a Glance

Contents

Introduction

This *Ignite!* book from Muska & Lipman will help you understand, use, and explore Digital Performer. Digital Performer is an award-winning audio and MIDI sequencing production system. Historically, Digital Performer has been a very intimidating package, with a complicated, confusing user interface. In this latest version, built specifically for Mac OS X, many changes have been made to simplify the user experience and increase the functionality of different tools.

Digital Performer 4.0 was released in April of 2003. Several months later, a free update became available, which upgraded to version 4.1. The differences between version 4.0 and 4.1 are minimal when it comes to the basic functionality of the program. Any differences in the basic procedures will be referenced in the book.

Obviously, no book can teach you everything there is to know about one topic. The goal of this book is to introduce you to the world of Digital Performer and teach you how to use many of the tools it offers. Along the way, you'll learn tips on how to create your work faster and easier, and some creative tricks to make your music stand out.

Who Should Read This Book?

If you are ready to explore the world of music sequencing on the desktop, this book is for you. Whether you are a seasoned veteran to Digital Performer, or just getting started, you will benefit from this book. New users can take advantage of the step-by-step, illustrated instructions of common tasks, whereas veteran users can use the book as a reference for not only new tools, but also old tools that you might have forgotten.

Some Helpful Hints

In addition to the step-by-step instructions, you'll notice that there are two other elements designed to help you:

TIP

Tips provide you with quick ways or shortcuts to perform certain tasks.

NOTE

Notes provide you with additional information or background on a particular topic.

1

Installing Digital Performer

It has been many years now since the world of computers merged with that of music. Whether you are a veteran of digital audio or you're just getting started, one thing is certain: You won't be able to perform any tasks with Digital Performer until you've got it installed on your computer. Digital Performer 4 is the first version of the software specifically designed for OS X. If you are accustomed to using any of the previous versions of Digital Performer, you'll notice that the way it operates on OS X is slightly different. In this chapter, you will learn how to:

- Confirm your OS version
- Check system RAM
- Install Digital Performer 4

Checking System Requirements

Part of the minimum system requirements of Digital Performer 4 is that you are running Mac OS X version 10.2 or higher. You can quickly check what version you have installed on your computer by using the Apple menu. Depending on the type of tasks you'll be performing, Digital Performer can be quite taxing on the resources of your computer. Your computer's RAM (Random Access Memory) partially controls how quickly software can process information on your computer. DP4 requires a minimum of 128MB of RAM for MIDI sequencing and 256MB for audio recording, but the manufacturer of DP4 recommends 512MB or more. The more RAM your computer has, the faster it will be able to process your recordings.

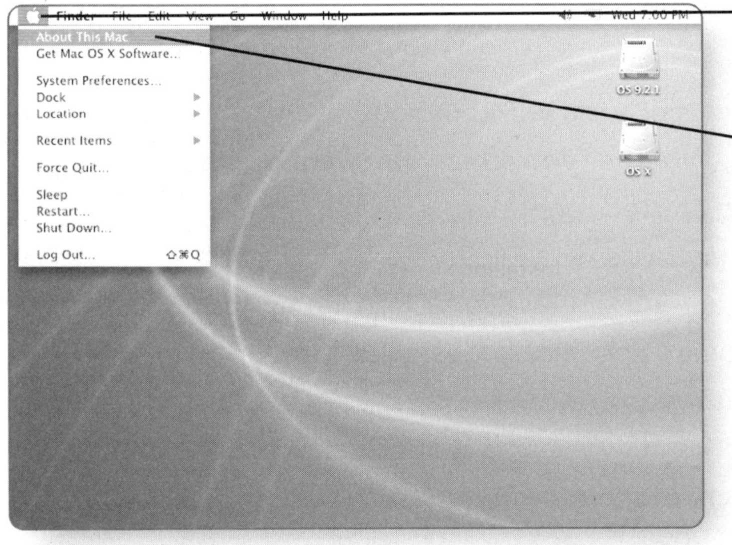

1. **Click** on the **Apple icon** at the top of the screen. A menu will appear.

2. **Click** on **About This Mac**. A dialog box will open that will indicate the version of OS X you are running.

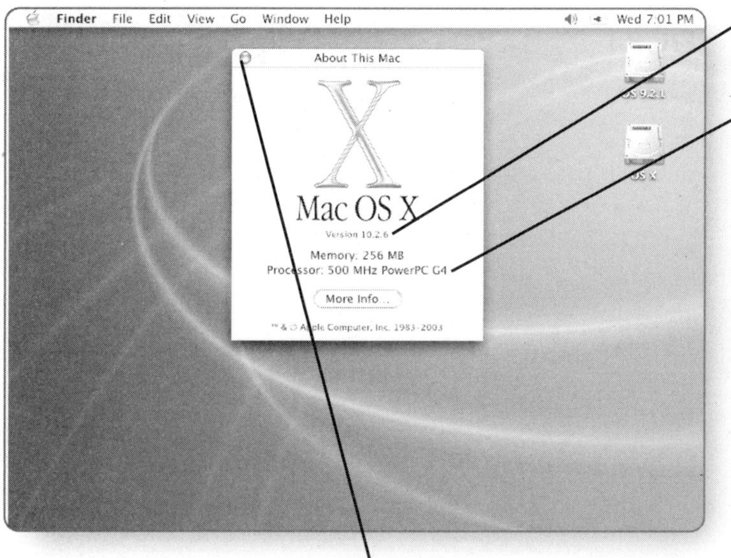

3. Note the **version** of OS X you are running.

4. Note the **amount of memory** you have on your machine.

> **NOTE**
>
> If you are running a version of OS X lower than 10.2, you must purchase an upgrade, which is available through Apple at http://www.apple.com.

5. Click on the **red circle** in the top-left corner of the dialog box to close it.

Installing the Software

Mac OS X makes installing software a relatively simple task. You basically just have to follow the on-screen instructions once the installation process starts.

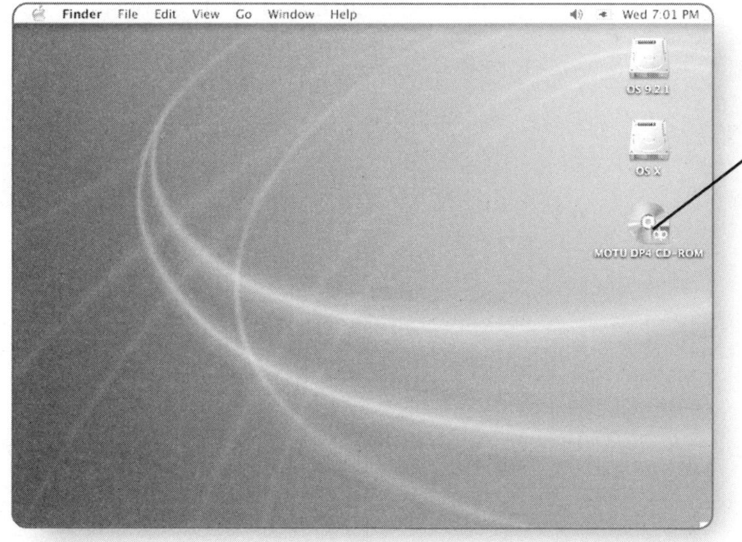

1. Insert the **Installer Disc** into the CD-ROM drive. An icon will appear on the desktop.

2. Double-click on the **MOTU DP4 CD-ROM icon**. A window with several icons will appear.

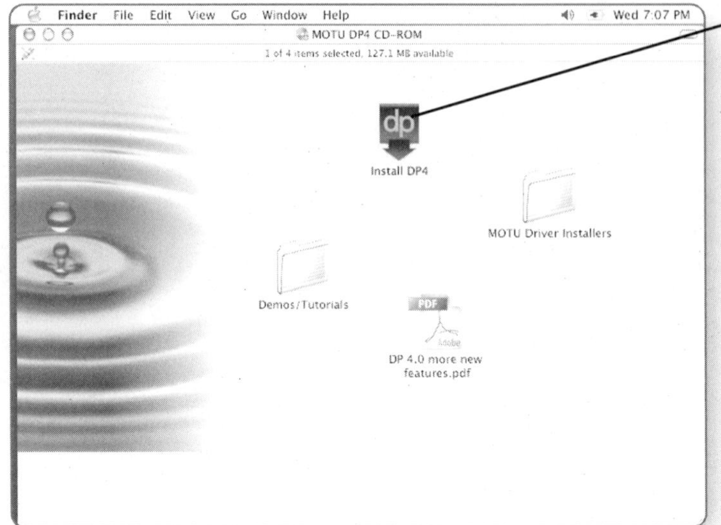

3. Double-click on the **Install DP4 icon**. The installation process will begin.

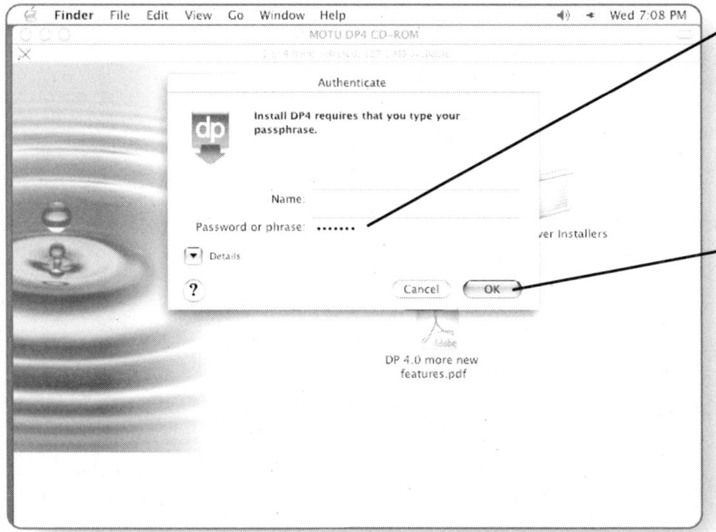

4. Type in your **password**. Depending on how you set up your operating system and how you are logged on, you may or may not be prompted with this dialog box.

5. Click on **OK**. The splash screen for Digital Performer will appear.

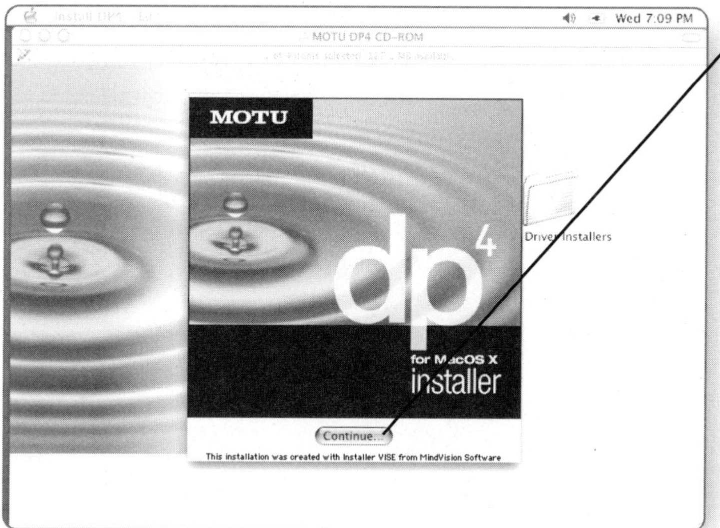

6. Click on **Continue**. The License window will open.

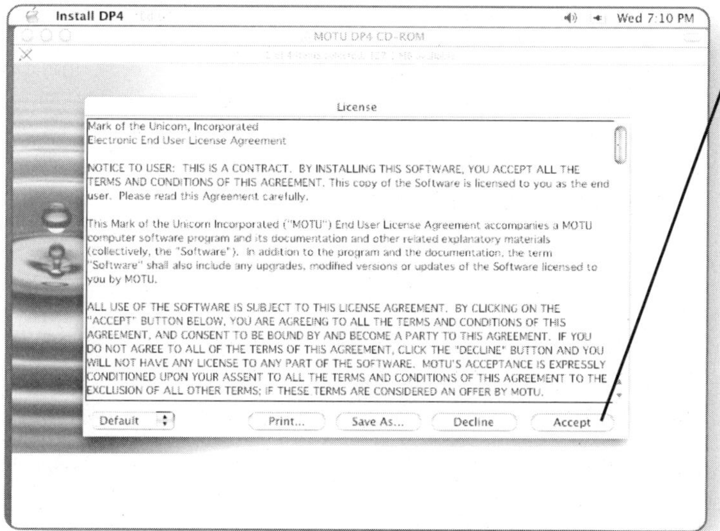

7. Click on **Accept** after you have read the license agreement and if you agree with the terms. A screen will appear, allowing you to select a location to install Digital Performer.

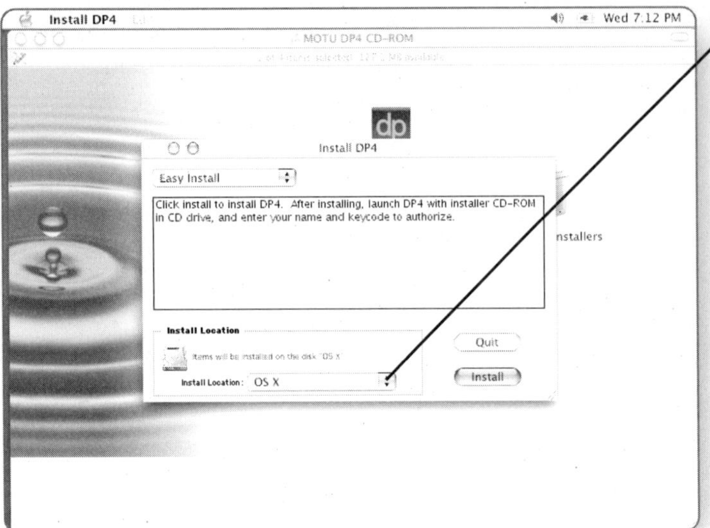

8. Click on the **up-and-down arrow** to bring up a menu of locations to install Digital Performer.

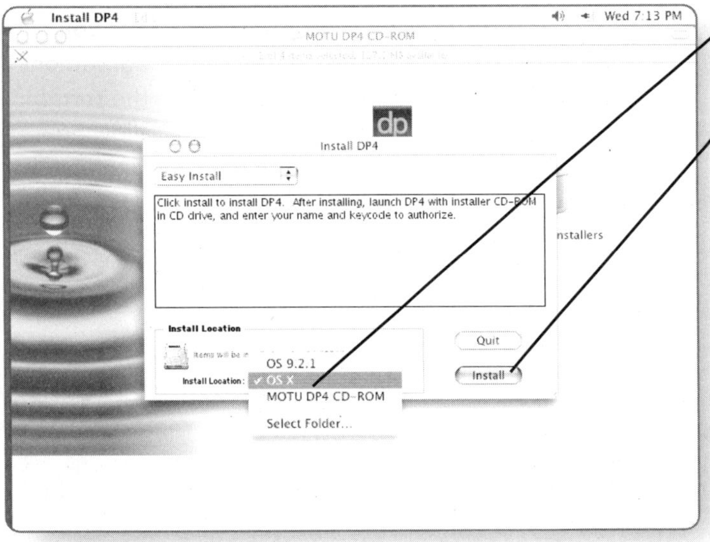

9. Click on the desired **location**. It will be selected.

10. Click on **Install**. The installation will commence.

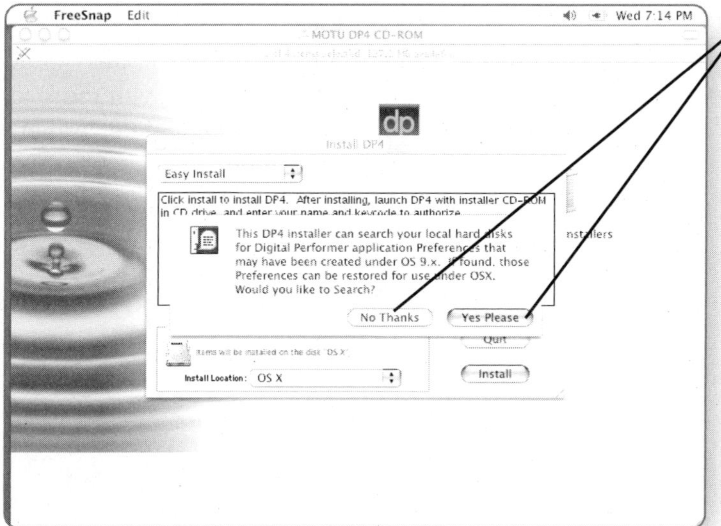

11. Click on **Yes Please or No Thanks**. This dialog box will come up if you had a previous version of Digital Performer and will allow you to keep your old preferences if you so choose.

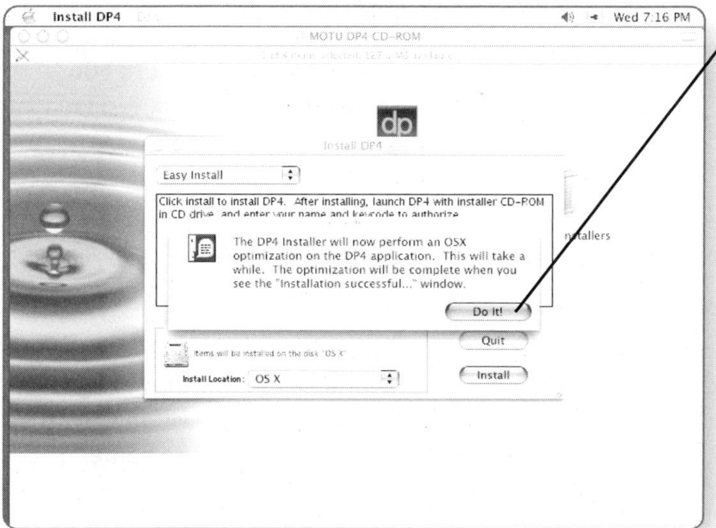

12. Click on **Do It!** to run the OS X optimization.

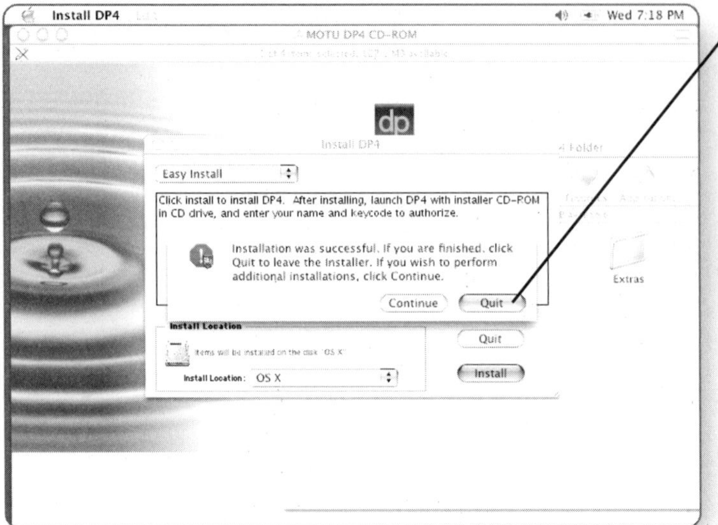

13. Click on **Quit**. The installation process will be complete. A window with the contents of the Digital Performer folder will open.

Creating a Desktop Alias for Digital Performer

If you plan to use Digital Performer often (and I'm sure you will), you might find it convenient to create a shortcut to launch the program on your desktop.

1. Click on the **Digital Performer icon**. It will be selected.

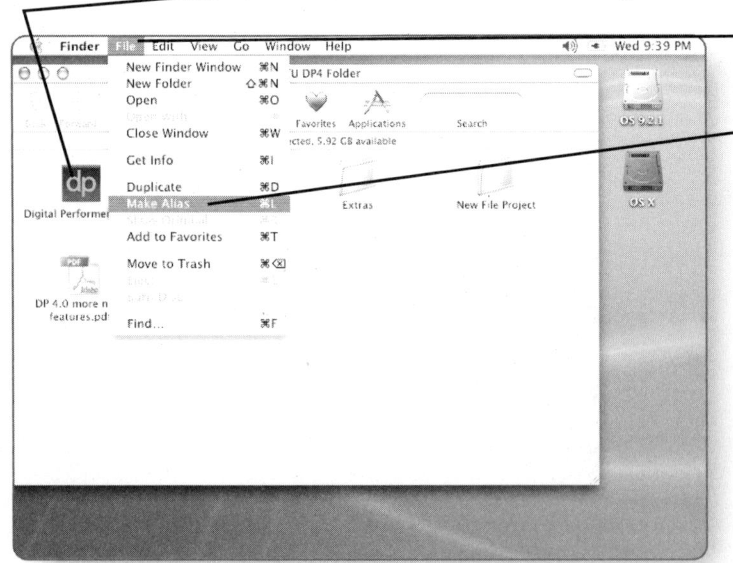

2. Click on **File**. The File menu will appear.

3. Click on **Make Alias**. A second Digital Performer icon will appear in the window, with alias at the end of its name.

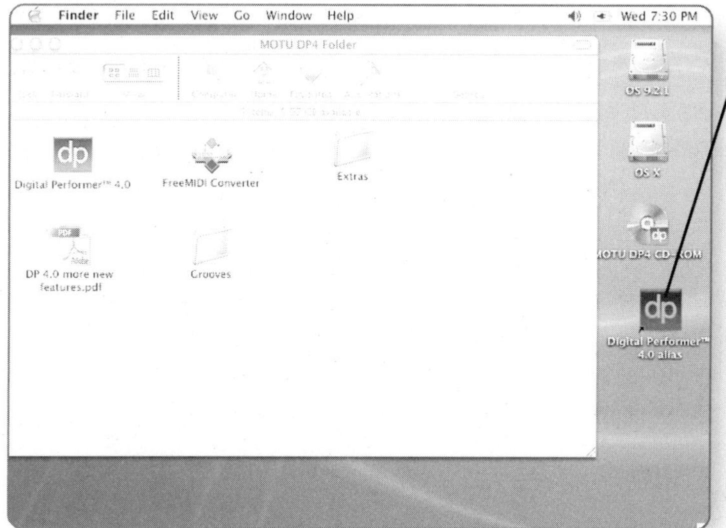

4. **Click** and **drag** the **alias icon** from the window onto the desktop. You will now have a shortcut on the desktop that you can use to access the program.

2

File Basics

If you are anything like me, rather than having specific folders for files nicely organized throughout your computer, you've got everything but the kitchen sink on the desktop. This is one occasion when I do not want you to follow my lead. Life will be so much easier if you just take the time to put things in the right place. Managing where your files are and how they are set up becomes of the utmost importance as the number of files you have on your computer increases. In this chapter, you will learn how to:

- Create a new file
- Open an existing file
- Save a file
- Adjust preferences

Creating a New File

Digital Performer gives you two options when creating a new file. You can either create a new file on startup or from within the program.

Creating a New File on Startup

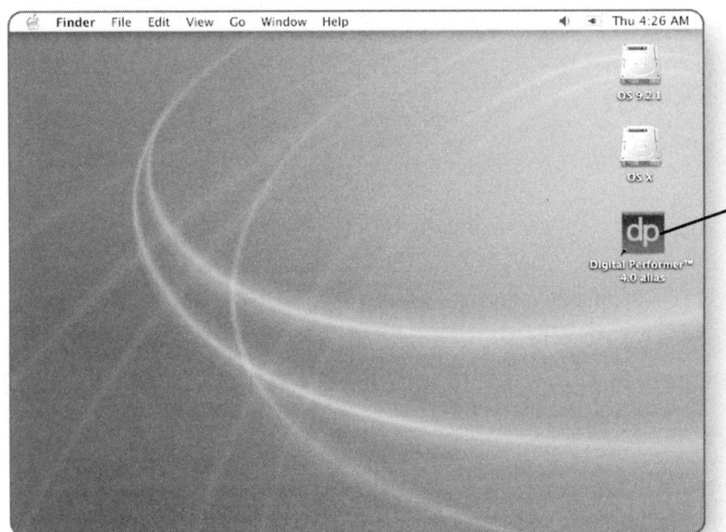

When you launch Digital Performer, a dialog box will appear, prompting you to either open an existing file or create a new one.

1. **Double-click** on the **Digital Performer icon** to launch the program. A dialog box will appear.

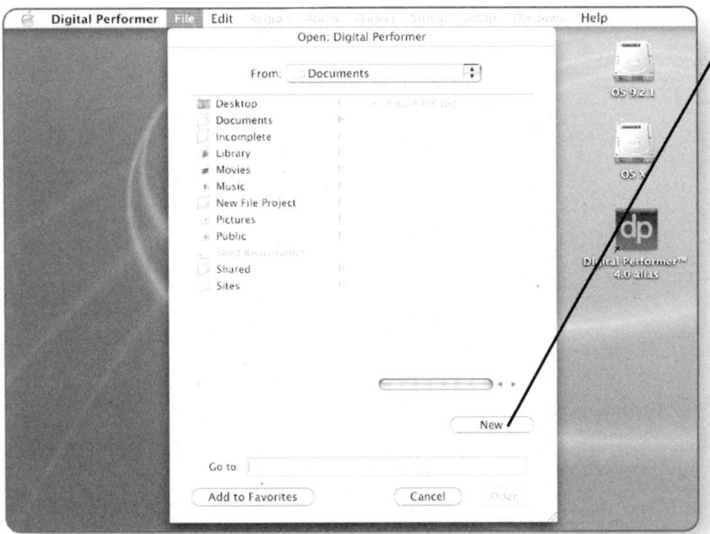

2. **Click** on **New**. A dialog box will appear, prompting you to name your file.

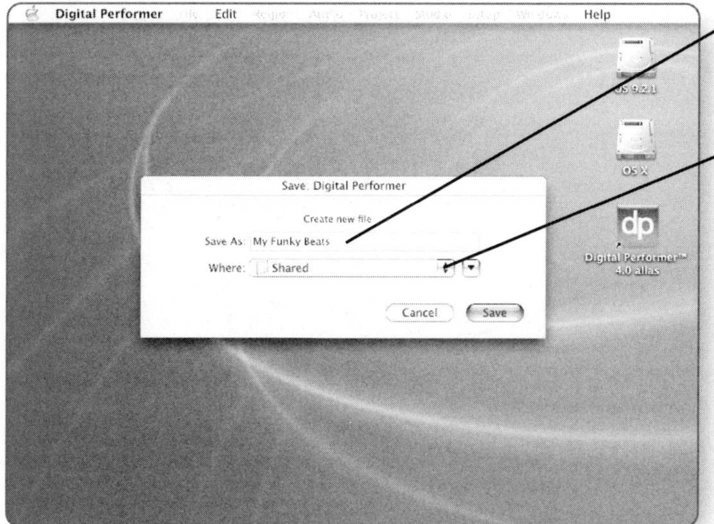

3. Type a **name** for your file. You can give it any name you choose.

4. Click on the **up-and-down arrow** to bring up a pop-up menu that will allow you to choose a location for your file.

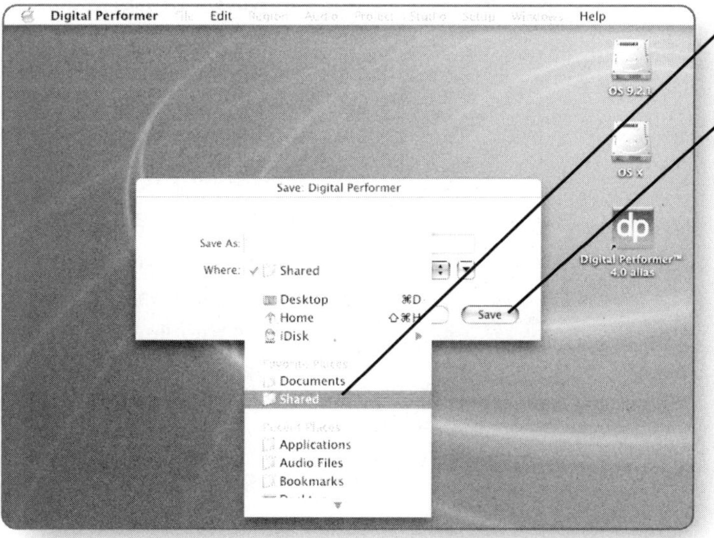

5. Click on a **location** to save your file.

6. Click on **Save**. A file with that name will be created and Digital Performer will open.

Creating a New File within Digital Performer

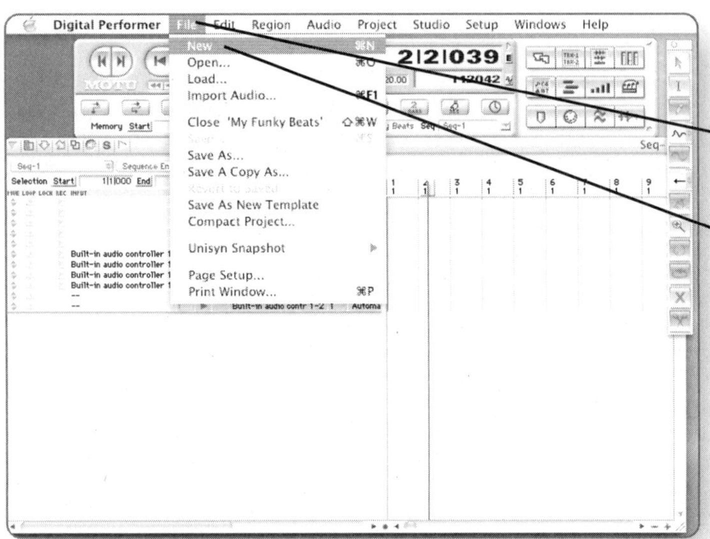

Once you are in the program and begin working, you can always create a new file.

1. **Click** on **File**. The File menu will appear.

2. **Click** on **New**. A dialog box will appear, in which you can select a name and location for your new file.

> **NOTE**
>
> If you are using version 4.1 rather than version 4.0, you will be presented with a submenu when you click on New. Within that submenu, you can click on New again, and the dialog box will appear.

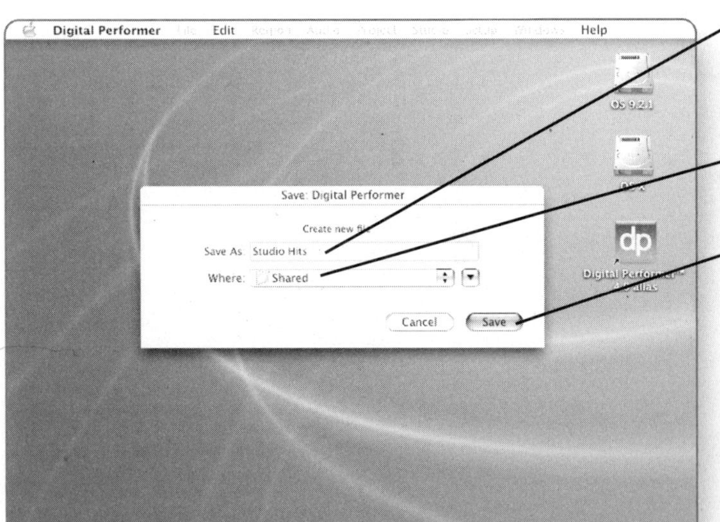

3. **Type** a **name** for your file. You should give it a name that best describes the file.

4. **Click** on a **folder** to save the file.

5. **Click** on **Save**. The new file will be created and you can begin working on it.

Opening Files

Just like when you create a new file, you can open existing files when you launch Digital Performer or when you are already working in the program.

Opening a File on Startup

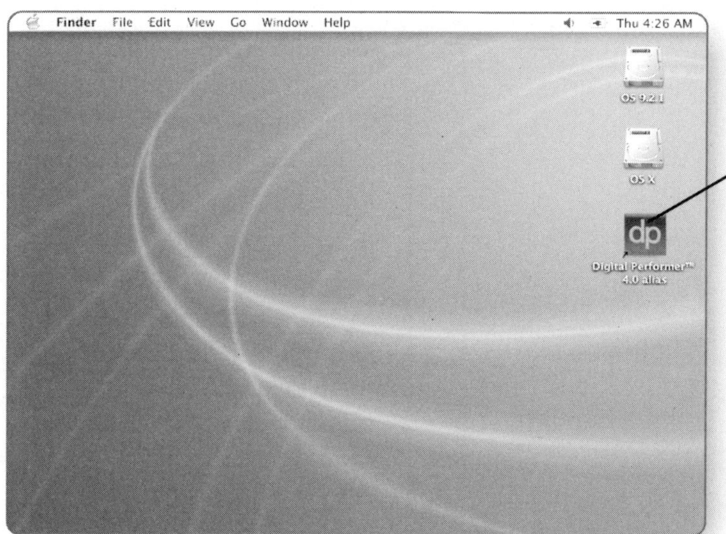

When you first launch Digital Performer, you have the opportunity to select a file to open.

1. **Click** on the **Digital Performer icon** to launch the program. A dialog box will appear.

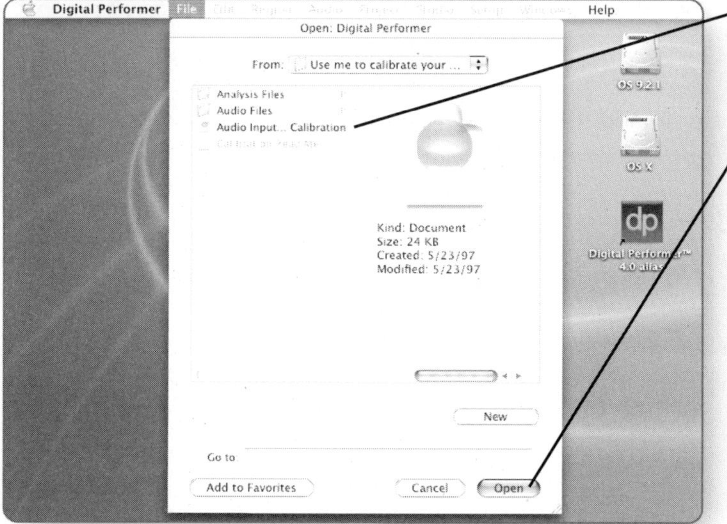

2. **Click** on the desired **file** that you would like to open. It will be highlighted.

3. **Click** on **Open**. The file will open and you can begin working.

Saving Files

The nature of computers is that they do go down, usually at the least convenient time. Once you've started working on a file, it is a good idea to save it periodically so you do not lose any of the changes that you made.

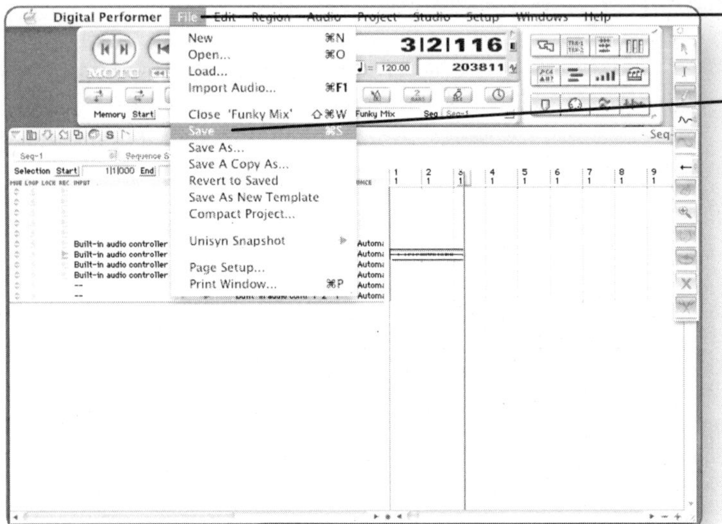

1. **Click** on **File**. The File menu will appear.

2. **Click** on **Save**. The file will be saved with changes you have made up to that point.

> **NOTE**
>
> If you would like to rename the file you are saving, you can use the Save As command under the File menu. When you select this command, the Save dialog box will appear, allowing you to save the file with a new name or location.

> **NOTE**
>
> Command + S is the keyboard shortcut for saving a file.

Closing a File

You can close a file without actually exiting the program by using the Close command.

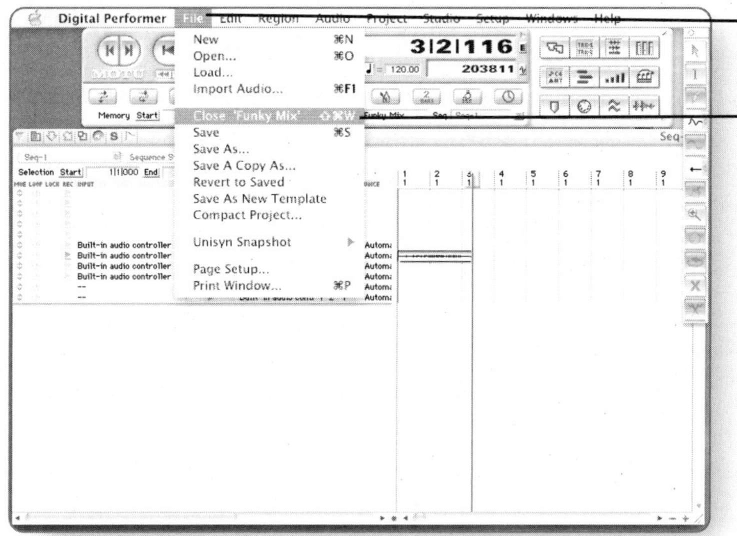

1. **Click** on **File**. The File menu will appear.
2. **Click** on **Close**. If you have saved your work up to this point, the file will close; otherwise, you will be prompted to save your file.

Quitting Digital Performer

When you are finished working in Digital Performer, exiting the program is a breeze. If you have saved your work, the program will automatically close when you choose the Quit command; otherwise, a dialog box will appear, giving you the opportunity to save.

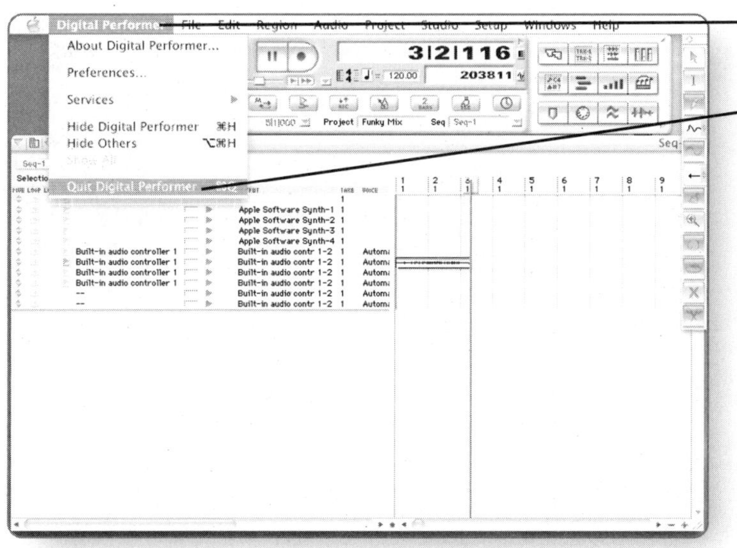

1. **Click** on **Digital Performer**. A menu will appear.
2. **Click** on **Quit Digital Performer**. If you have saved your work up to this point, the program will close; otherwise, you will be prompted to save your file.

Importing Settings with Load

The Load function allows you to take a variety of settings from a saved file and apply them to the file that you are currently working on. This is particularly useful if you are creating a variety of sequences for a project that requires a similar setup.

1. Click on **File**. The File menu will appear.

2. Click on **Load**. You will be able to select the file from which you would like to take the settings.

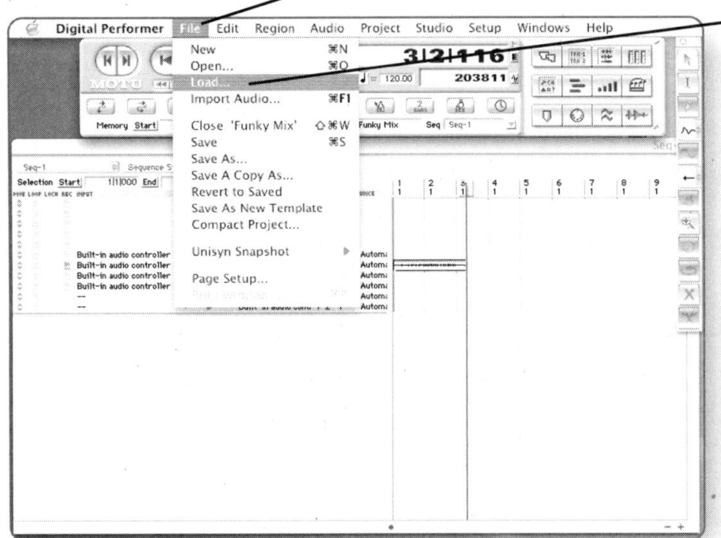

3. Click on the **file** you would like to load. It will be highlighted.

4. Click on **Open**. A dialog box will appear that will allow you to select the settings you would like to load.

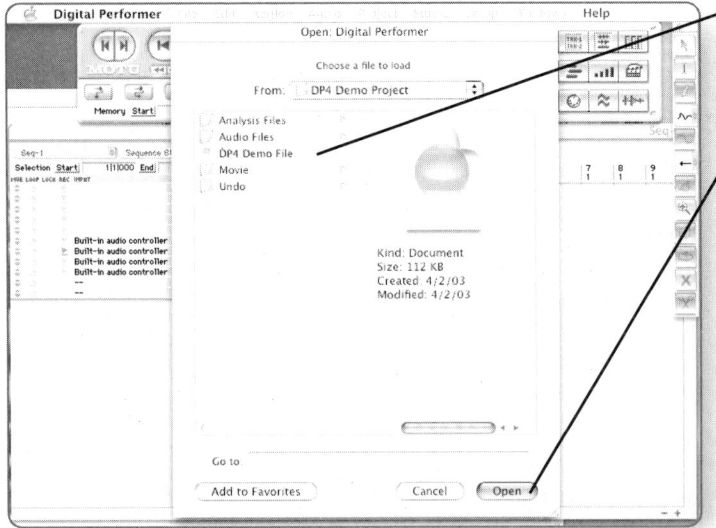

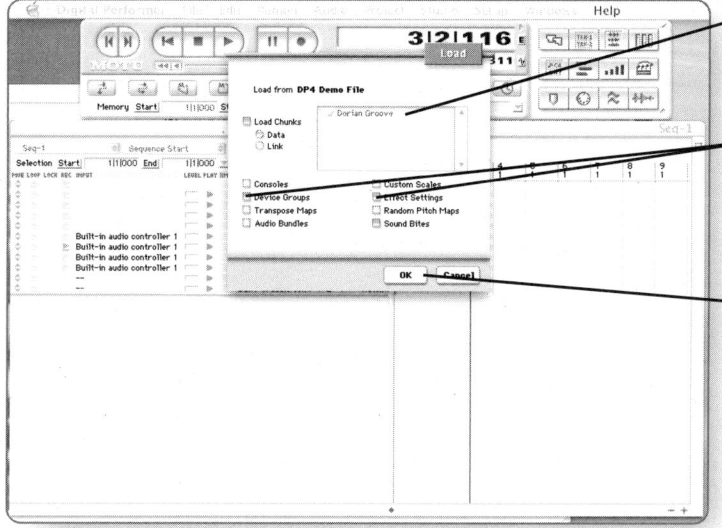

5. **Click** on the **sequence** from which you would like to load the settings.

6. **Click** on the **box** next to each desired load option. The selected boxes will be highlighted.

7. **Click** on **OK**. The selected settings for that file will load into the current file.

Preferences

Digital Performer allows you to customize how the program operates. As you get more familiar with the program, you will find that you use some windows more often than others, and you'd like some settings to always be available. Using the Preferences command, you can select which of the many windows you'd like open when you start the program and what actions you'd like to take place on startup. You can also adjust audio settings and select from a variety of other options.

1. **Click** on **Digital Performer**. A menu will appear.

2. **Click** on **Preferences**. A dialog box will appear, from which you can select your preferences.

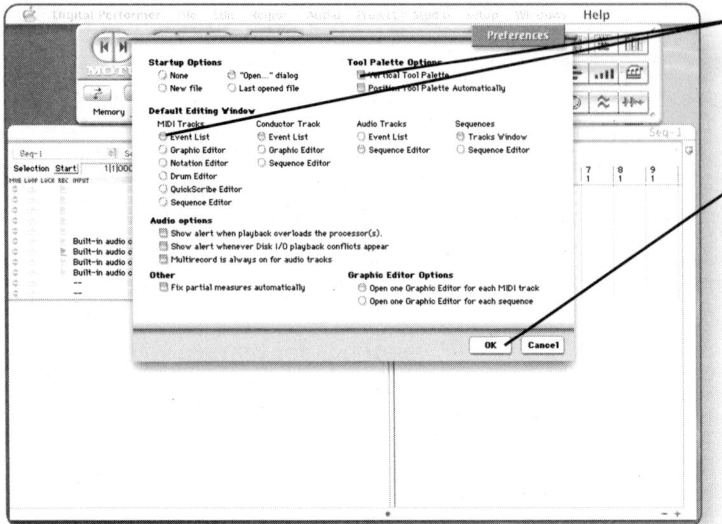

3. **Click** on the **circle** or **square** next to each desired preference. Those options will appear highlighted.

4. **Click** on **OK**. The preferences you have selected will take effect.

Data Display Preferences

The data display preferences allow you to change how musical data, including pitch, time, and tempo, are displayed in the program.

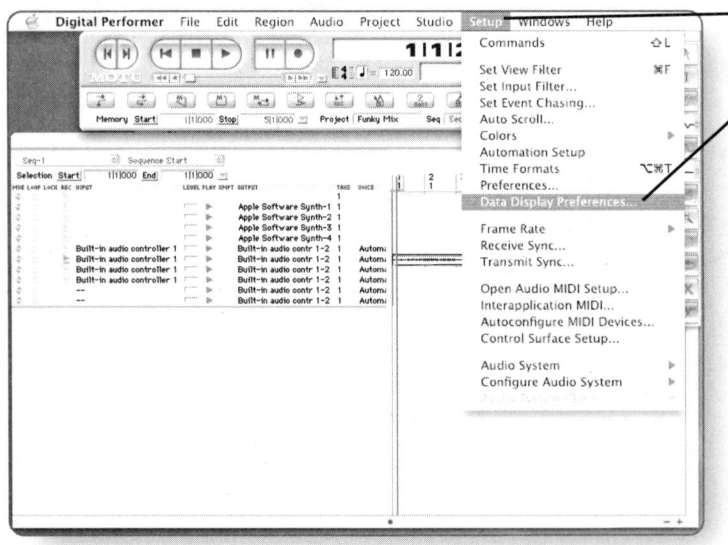

1. **Click** on **Setup**. The Setup menu will appear.

2. **Click** on **Data Display Preferences**. A dialog box will appear, allowing you to set your data display preferences.

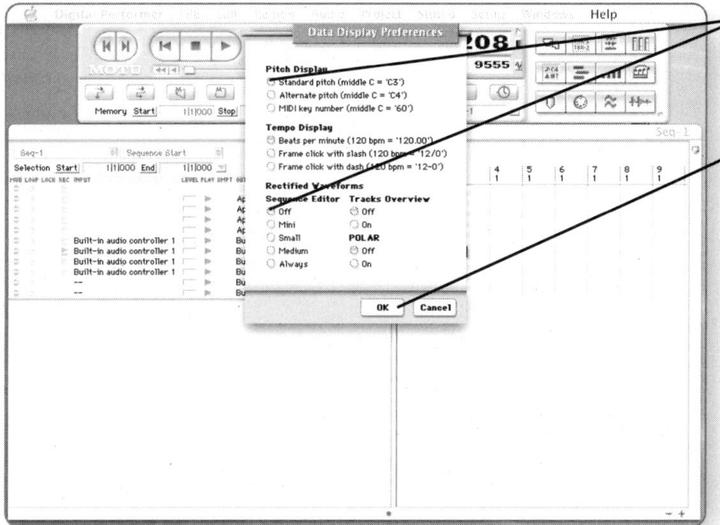

3. **Click** on the **circle** next to each desired preference. The circle will be highlighted.

4. **Click** on **OK**. The preferences you have selected will now take effect.

3

Hardware Setup

In the past, in order for Digital Performer to work properly, you needed to set up a program called FreeMIDI to route your MIDI to and from outside devices. One of the advantages of Digital Performer running on Mac OS X is that it has a built-in program called Audio MIDI Setup that can be used to set up all of your devices, both MIDI and audio. In this chapter, you will learn how to:

- Automatically scan for MIDI devices
- Manually install MIDI devices
- Select audio drivers
- Select audio devices

Adding MIDI Devices

MIDI devices can be connected to your computer directly or through a MIDI interface. Once you have your devices connected and turned on, you can have Digital Performer automatically search for your devices, or you can add them manually.

> **NOTE**
>
> A MIDI device is any device that can convert musical information into digital data. The most common MIDI device is the electronic keyboard.

Automatically Scanning for MIDI Devices

Digital Performer can search your computer for installed MIDI devices and automatically set them up.

1. Click on **Setup**. The Setup menu will appear.

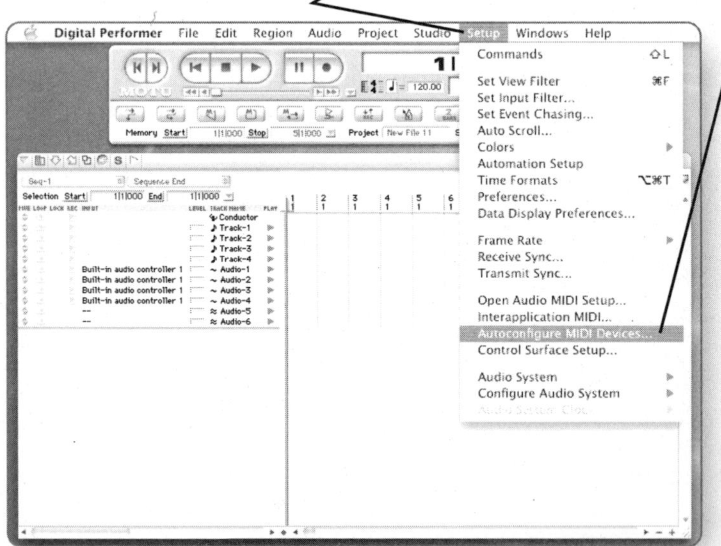

2. Click on **Autoconfigure MIDI Devices**. A small window will open.

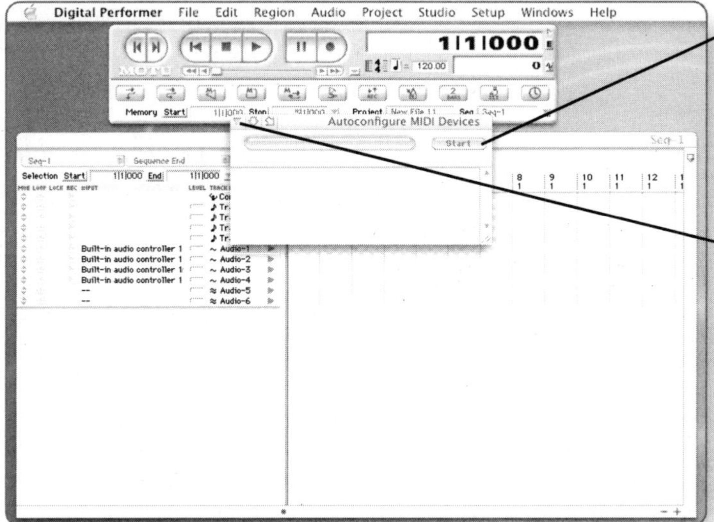

3. Click on **Start**. Digital Performer will search for all of the MIDI devices connected to your computer. As it finds them, it will list them in the window and they will be set up.

4. Click on the **down arrow** in the top-left corner. The dialog box will close.

Manually Installing MIDI Devices

Although the Autoconfigure feature does a good job of finding MIDI devices, there may be some devices it does not find, or you might want to do some fine-tuning. Using the Audio MIDI Setup window you can view, adjust, and install devices manually.

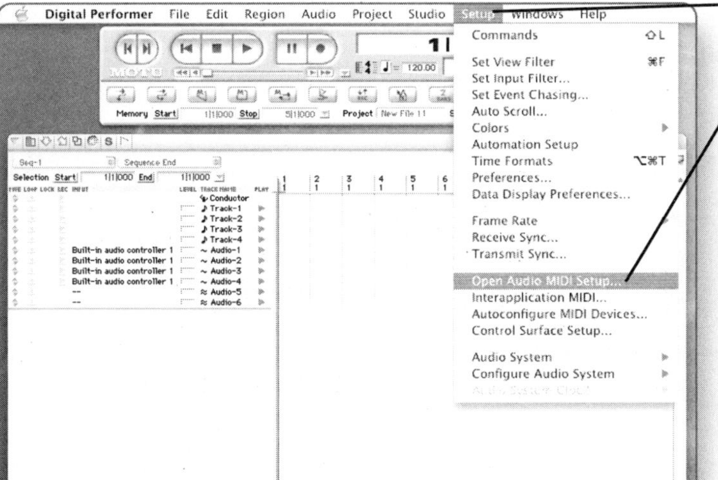

1. Click on **Setup**. The Setup menu will appear.

2. Click on **Open Audio MIDI Setup**. The Audio MIDI Setup window will open.

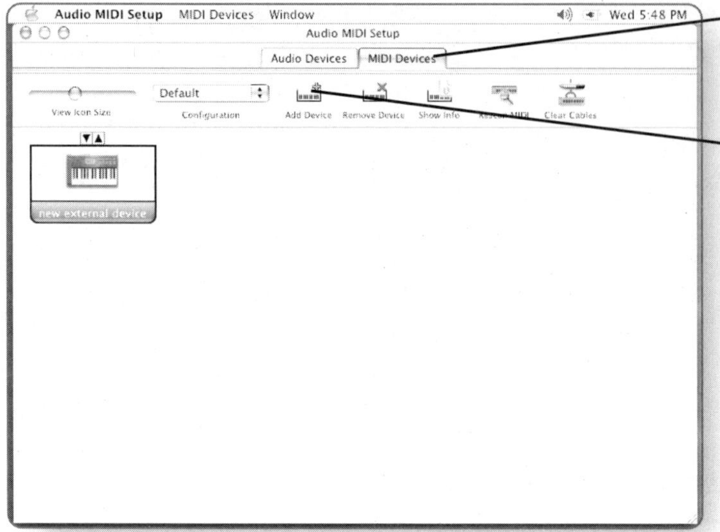

3. **Click** on the **MIDI Devices tab**. You will now have options for your MIDI devices.

4. **Click** on **Add Device**. An icon of a new external device will appear.

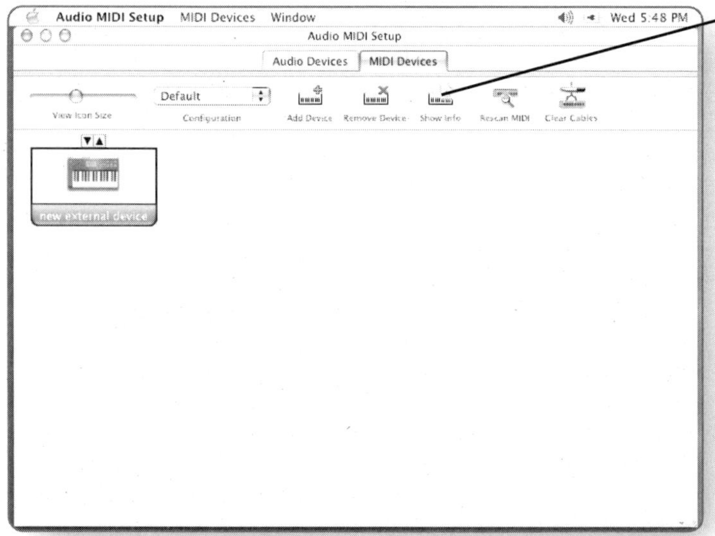

5. **Click** on **Show Info**. You will be able to configure the device.

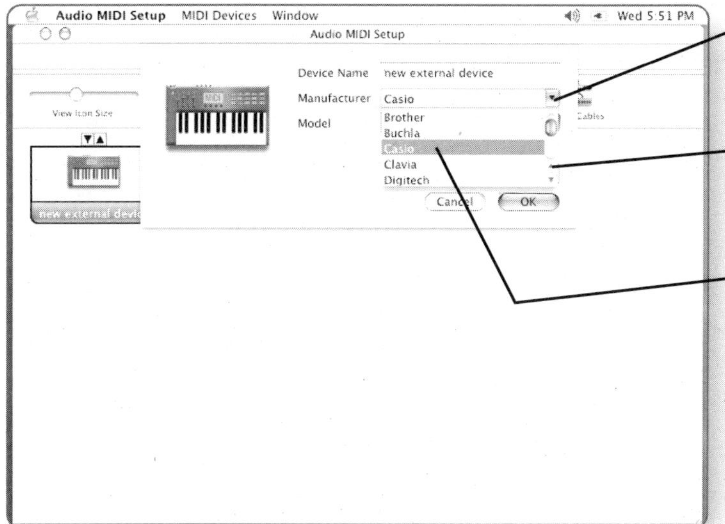

6. **Click** on the **down arrow** beside the Manufacturer field. A list of manufacturers will appear.

7. **Click** on the **scroll arrows** to scroll through the different device manufacturers.

8. **Click** on the **manufacturer** of your device. It will be selected.

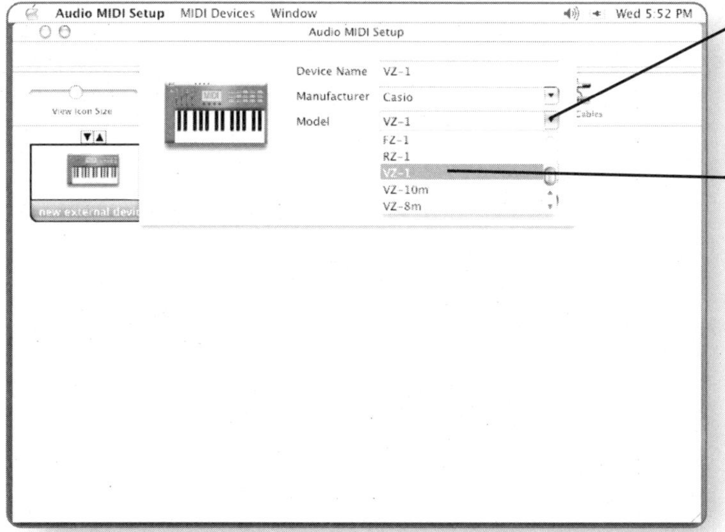

9. **Click** on the **down arrow** beside the Model field. A list of models made by the selected manufacturer will appear.

10. **Click** on the **model** of your device. It will be selected.

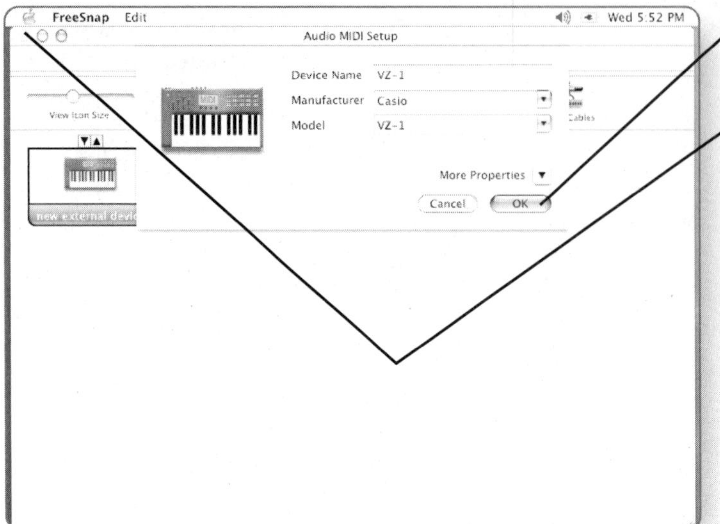

11. Click on **OK**. The device will be configured.

12. Click on the **red circle** in the top-left corner of the window to close it and return to Digital Performer.

Setting Up MIDI Interface Devices

If you are using a MIDI interface, you must first install the software driver that accompanies your MIDI interface. From there, you can assign how your MIDI devices interact with that MIDI interface.

1. Click on **Setup**. The Setup menu will appear.

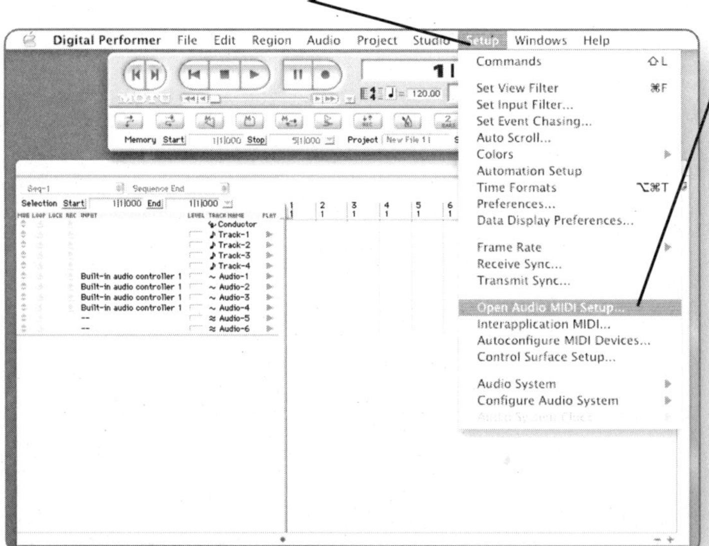

2. Click on **Open Audio MIDI Setup**. The Audio MIDI Setup window will open. Your installed MIDI interface devices and external devices will appear.

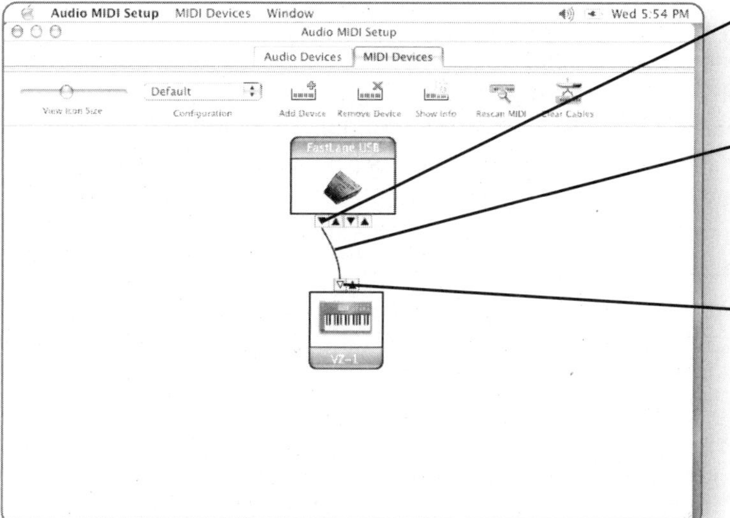

3. **Position** your **mouse pointer** over the output arrow in the interface device.

4. **Click** and **drag** to the **input arrow** of the external MIDI device. A line will appear as you drag.

5. **Release** the **mouse button**. The line will show the connection.

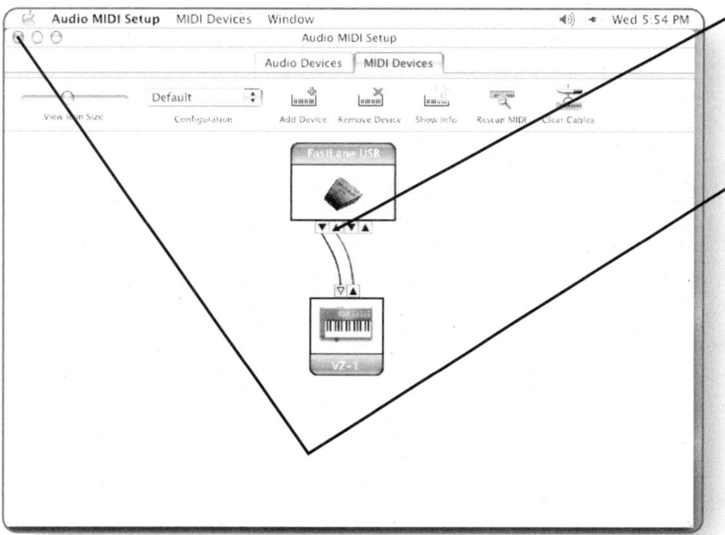

6. **Repeat steps 3 through 5**, this time going from the output of the external device to the input of the interface.

7. **Click** on the **red button** in the top-left corner to close the window once you have finished.

Audio Devices

With Digital Performer, you can begin recording audio tracks instantly using the built-in microphone on your OS X machine. For all other audio devices, you will need to first install the software that comes with the device. Once you have installed the software, you must activate its driver in Digital Performer to access it.

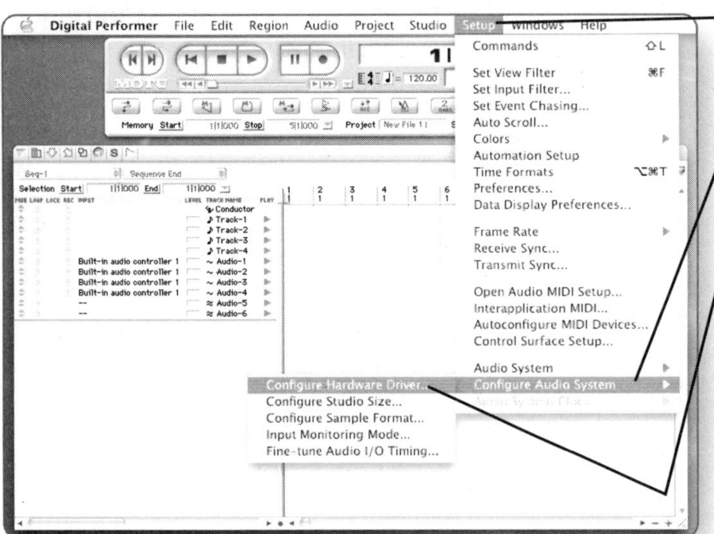

1. **Click** on **Setup**. The Setup menu will appear.
2. **Click** on **Configure Audio System**. A submenu will appear.
3. **Click** on **Configure Hardware Driver**. A window will open in which you can select the driver you would like to configure.

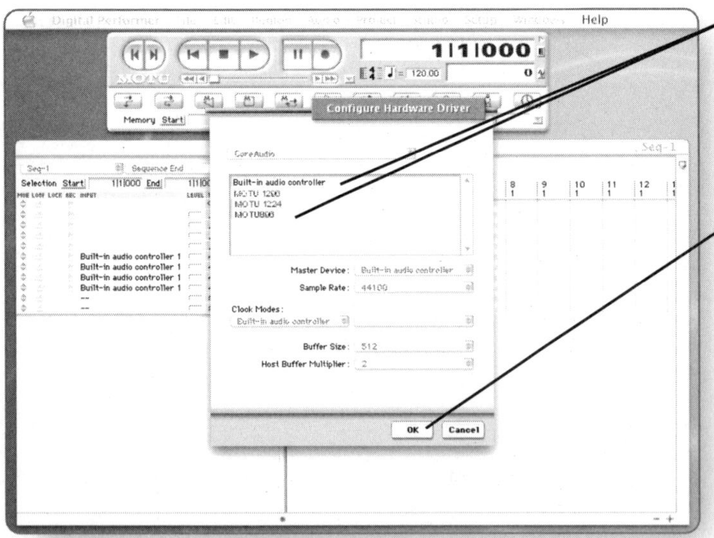

4. **Press** and **hold** the **Shift key** and **click** on the **drivers** you would like to activate. They will appear highlighted to indicate that they are selected.
5. **Click** on **OK**. The audio devices will be configured.

4

Basic Navigation

Your journey into the world of digital audio manipulation using Digital Performer starts with the user interface. User interface is a fancy term that simply refers to what you see on the screen when your program is running. Digital Performer is comprised of a variety of different screen elements with many different buttons and controls, all of which can be used in different ways to help you create and edit audio. In this chapter, you will learn how to:

- Use the menu bar
- Use window elements
- Work with dialog boxes
- Access shortcuts

The Menu Bar

Across the top of the user interface, you will find the menu bar. It consists of a variety of different categories of tools that can be accessed by clicking on the desired category and then selecting the desired task.

Getting to Know the Menu Bar

The menu bar is comprised of eight categories, designed to make finding particular tools easier.

- **File.** This menu contains commands that have to do with managing files that you are working with. Some common commands under the File menu include Open, New, and Quit.
- **Edit.** This menu contains basic editing commands for the program, including tasks like Cut and Paste.
- **Region.** This menu contains a variety of different commands, most of which relate to modifying the sound of your tracks and sequences.

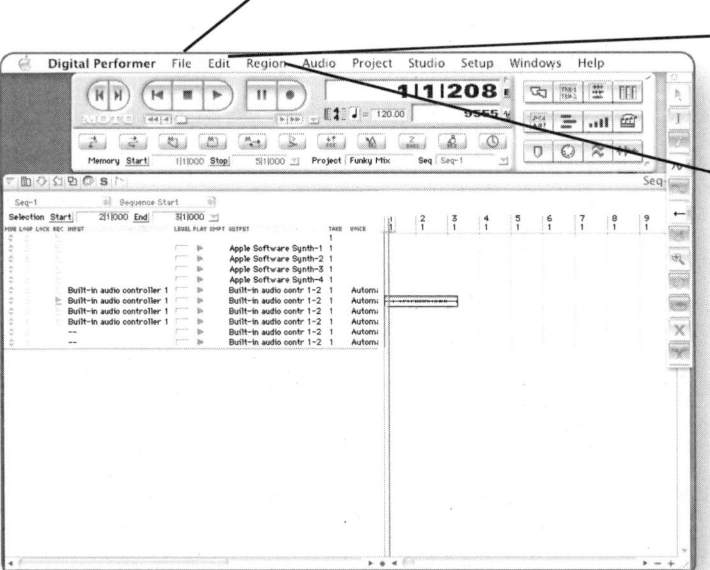

- **Audio.** This menu contains a wide range of commands, mostly dealing with adding sound effects to your audio.
- **Project.** This menu contains many of the commands for advanced editing of your sequences.
- **Studio.** This menu contains functions that will allow you to work with different devices and open certain windows.

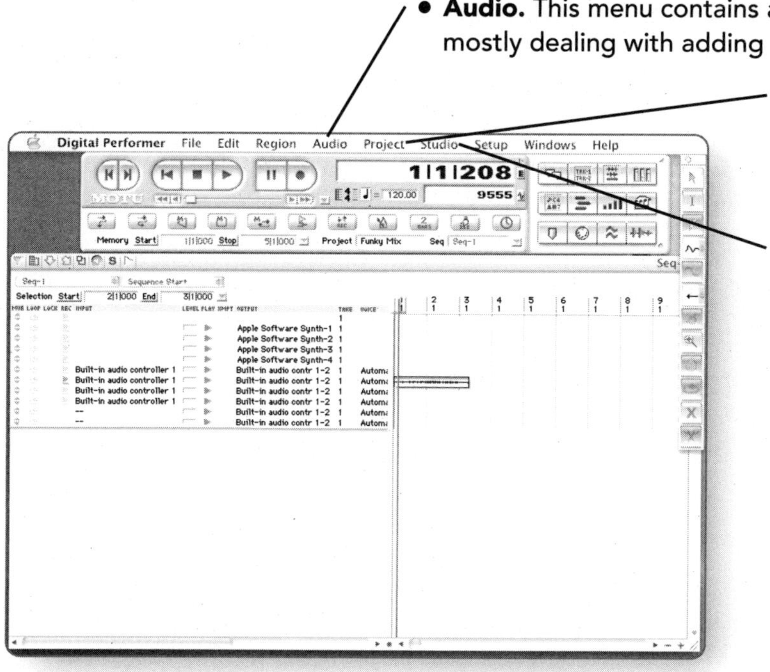

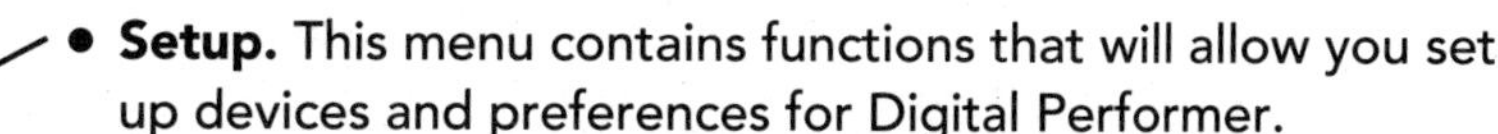

- **Setup.** This menu contains functions that will allow you set up devices and preferences for Digital Performer.
- **Windows.** This menu has commands that allow you to open and control different windows.
- **Help.** This menu will allow you to access the help functionality in the program.

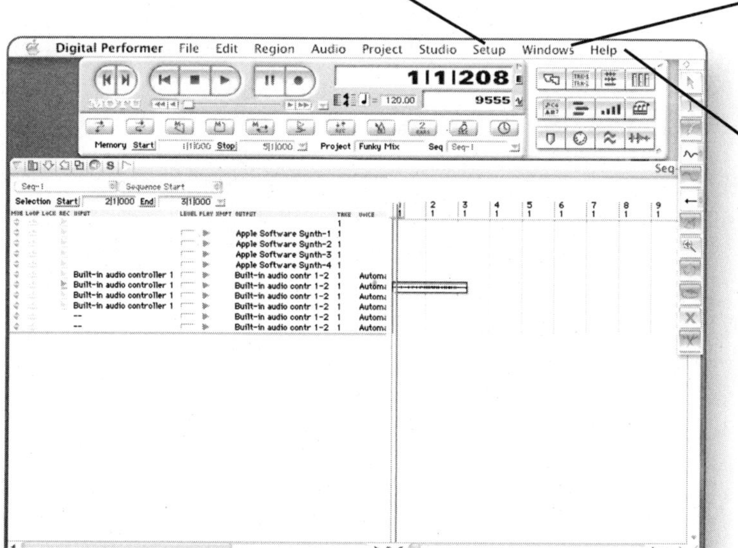

Accessing Menus

Accessing the menus is simply a matter of clicking on the menu and then selecting the desired command.

1. **Click** on the desired **menu category**. A menu of different tasks will appear.

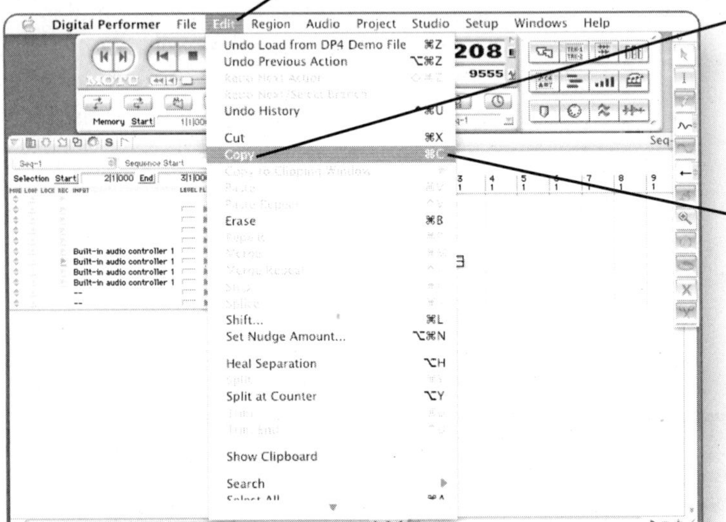

2. **Click** on the desired **menu item**. That task will be initiated.

> **TIP**
>
> Beside some of the menu items, you will notice a series of letters and symbols that show keyboard shortcuts that execute commands. Rather than having to access the command through the menu bar, you can use the keyboard shortcut. In this example, the keyboard shortcut for Copy is Command + C.

Menu Items

Within each menu, there is a variety of different graphical elements.

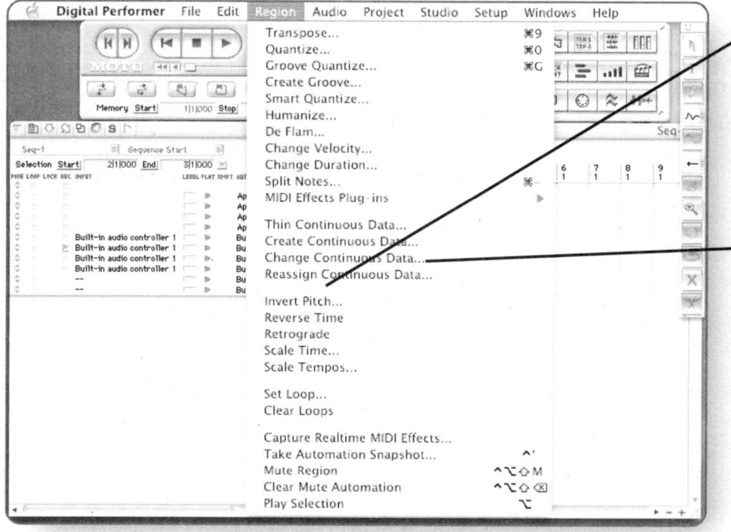

- **gap.** A gap indicates a different category of tasks within a menu. To make life a little easier, Digital Performer groups together logical tasks within menus.
- **ellipsis (three dots).** Three dots after a menu item indicates that a dialog box will open when this menu item is selected.

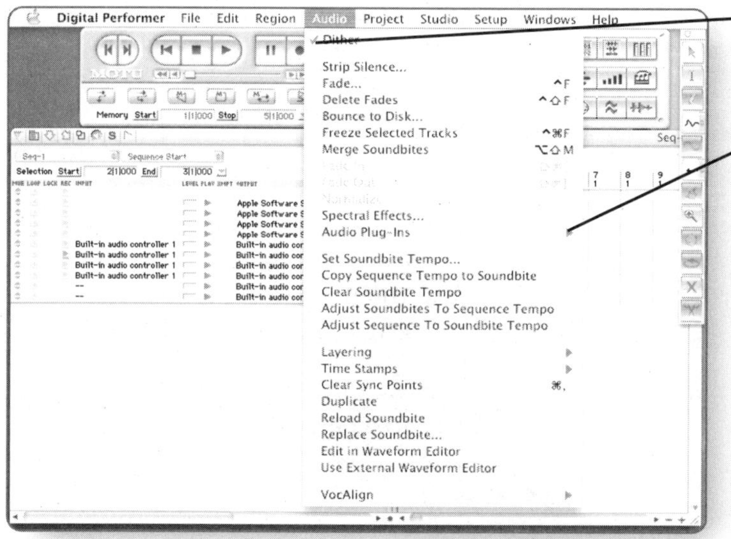

- **checkmark.** A checkmark indicates that the feature is currently open or active.
- **triangle.** A triangle indicates that there is an additional submenu to that menu item.

Working with Windows

Nothing is more detrimental to productivity than clutter. Like most other applications made for the Mac environment, Digital Performer is made up of a variety of different windows. There are literally dozens of different windows that can be open at any given time, which creates the potential problem of having your screen completely cluttered, making it difficult to keep track of what you are doing on-screen. That is why being able to manage open windows is extremely important.

Opening Windows

There are some windows that you will use more often than others, but most can be opened in a similar way. Digital Performer groups windows in sets designed for specific tasks.

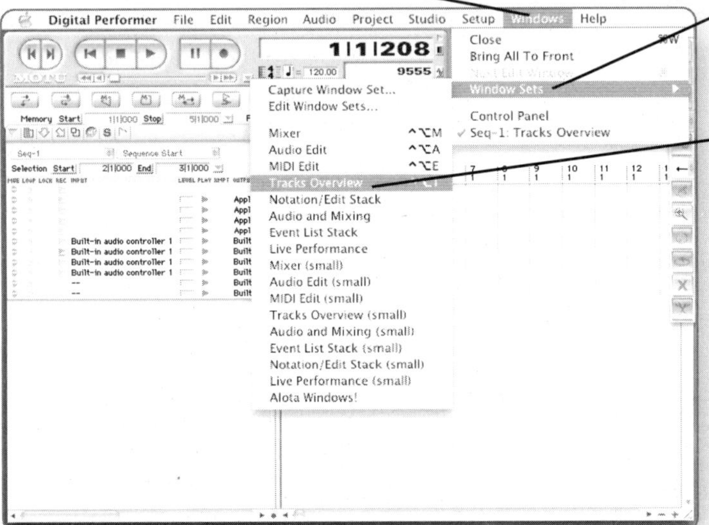

1. **Click** on **Windows**. The Windows menu will appear.
2. **Click** on **Window Sets**. A submenu of different window sets will appear.
3. **Click** on the desired **window set**. The window will open.

Manipulating Windows

Digital Performer allows you to move and change the size of windows in order to help you avoid clutter on your screen and keep your work organized.

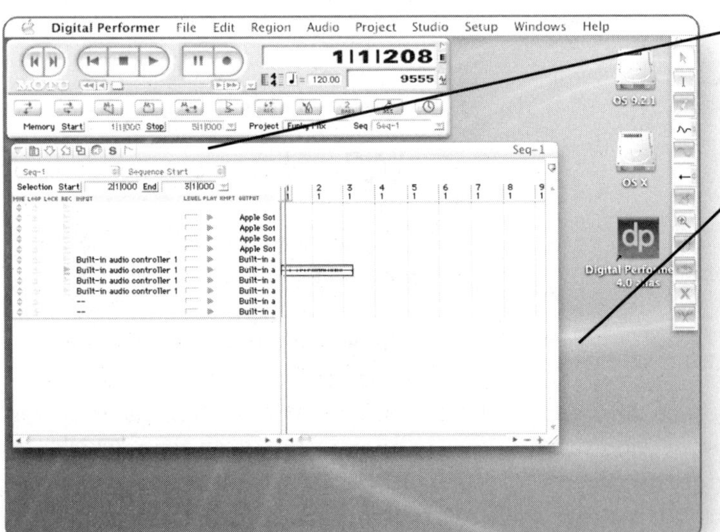

1. **Position** your **mouse pointer** over the title bar of a window. The title bar is the solid bar across the top of a window.
2. **Click** and **drag** the **window** to a new location.

NOTE

The Control Panel, which contains the Stop, Play, and Record buttons, does not have a title bar. You can move it by positioning the mouse pointer in a blank area and clicking and dragging to a new location.

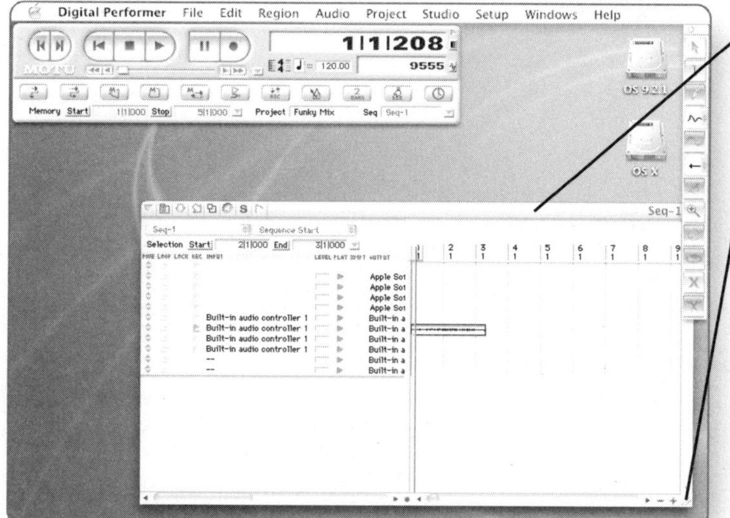

3. **Release** the **mouse button**. The window will be in its new location.

4. **Position** the **mouse pointer** over the three diagonal lines in the lower-right corner of the window.

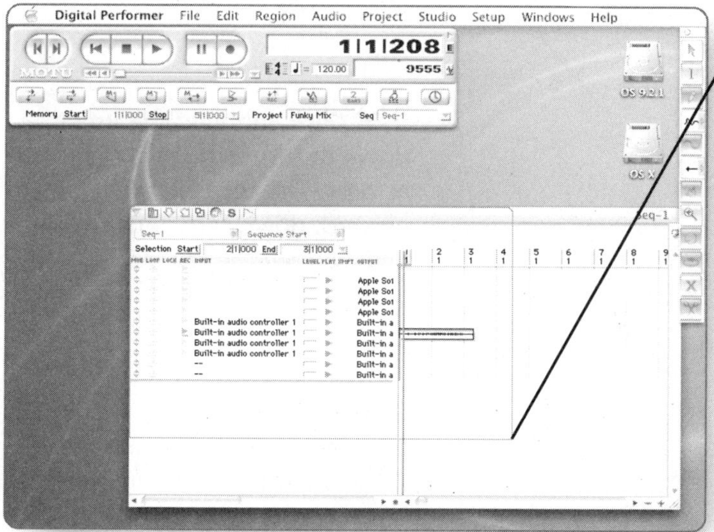

5. **Click** and **drag** in **any direction** to resize the window. As you drag, a line will preview the new size of the window.

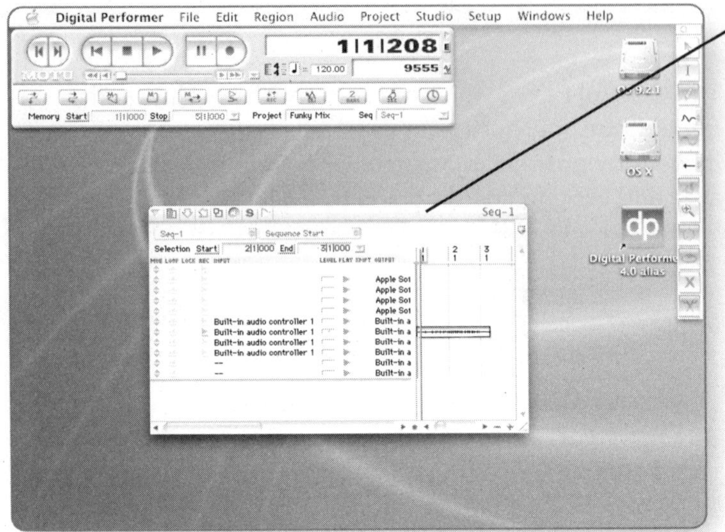

6. Release the **mouse button**. The window will be resized.

Scrolling Through Windows

Depending on the size of a window, there may be more data within that window than can be seen. The scroll arrows allow you to navigate to the data that can't readily be seen.

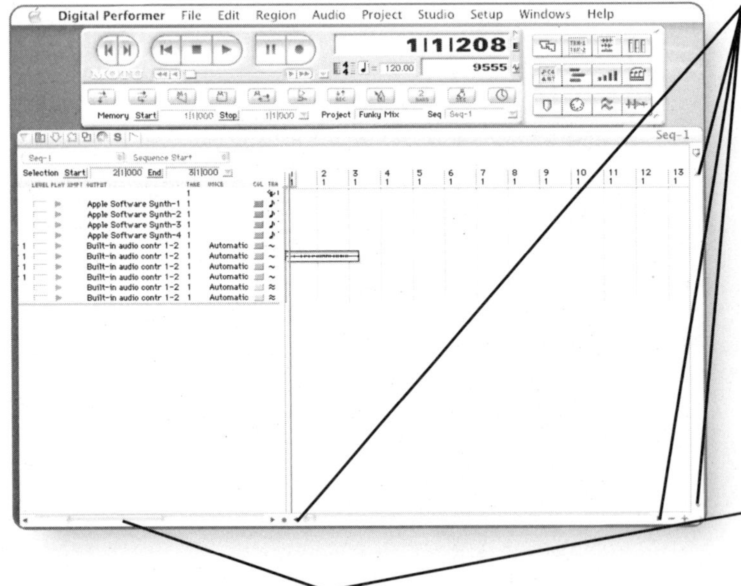

1a. Click on the **up or down** or **left or right scroll arrows**. Each time you click, the data within the window will move.

OR

1b. Click and **hold** the **up or down** or **left or right scroll arrows**. The data will scroll upward, downward, left, or right until you release the mouse button.

OR

1c. Position the **mouse pointer** over the circle in the scroll bar. **Click** and **drag up or down** or **left or right** to quickly scroll through the data.

Window Commands

In the top-left corner of almost every window in Digital Performer, you will notice a series of small icons when you click on the window. These icons represent different commands that you can carry out within that window. Because different windows have different functions, some icons will appear on some windows but not on others.

Closing a Window

Almost every window has a Close button that looks like a down arrow in the top-left corner.

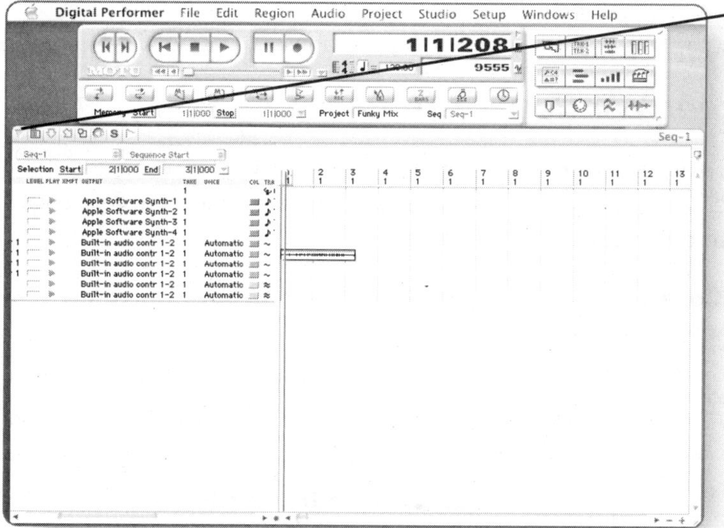

1. Click on the **Close button** in the top-left corner of the window. The window will close.

Mini Menu

Most windows have an icon that represents a mini menu. The mini menu offers commands that correspond with that particular window. Rather than having to search around for different tools, it's a good idea to first check a window's mini menu to see if it has the tool that you are looking for.

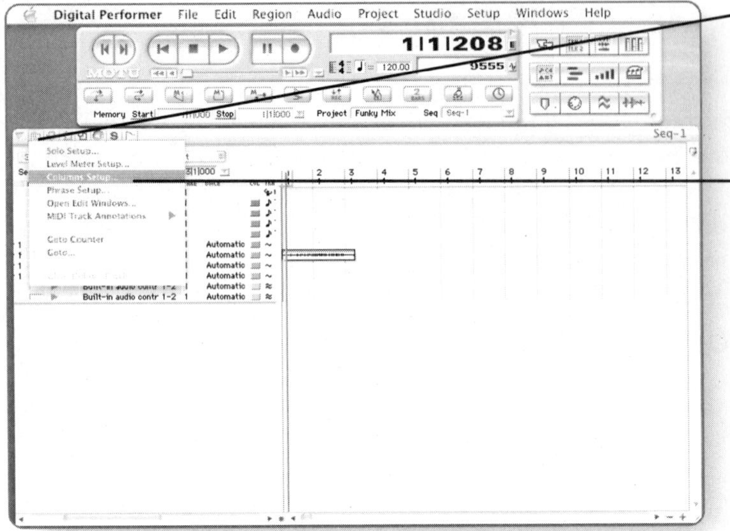

1. Click on the **Mini Menu button**. A menu of different options corresponding to that window will appear.

2. Click on the desired **command**. The command will be executed.

Other Window Commands

There are a variety of other commands available; some are specific to certain windows while others are universal. Some of these other commands include:

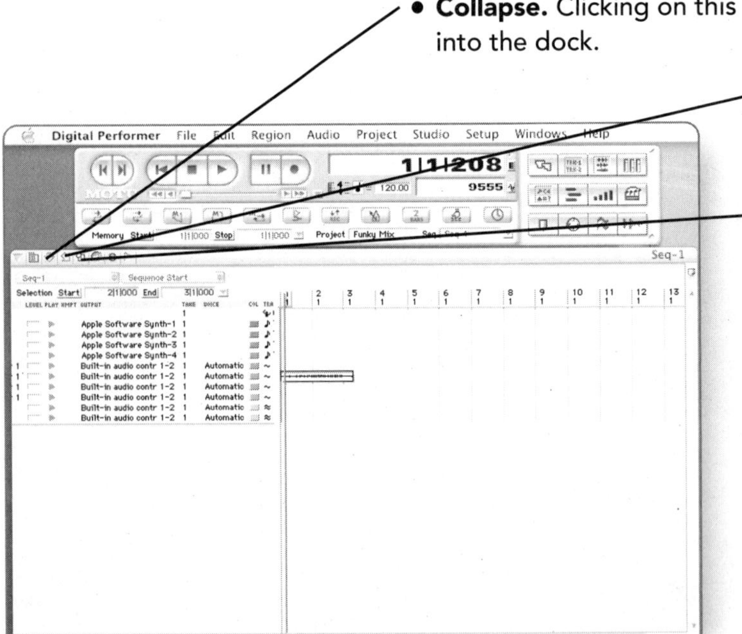

- **Collapse.** Clicking on this button will collapse the window into the dock.
- **Behind.** Clicking on this button will place this window behind all others.
- **Zoom.** This first time you click this button, the window will expand to its largest size. The next time it is clicked, the window will return to its previous size.

- **Audible.** This feature allows you to preview sound bites as well as work with MIDI files.
- **Solo Mode.** Clicking solo mode will mute all tracks. You can then select specific tracks to play.

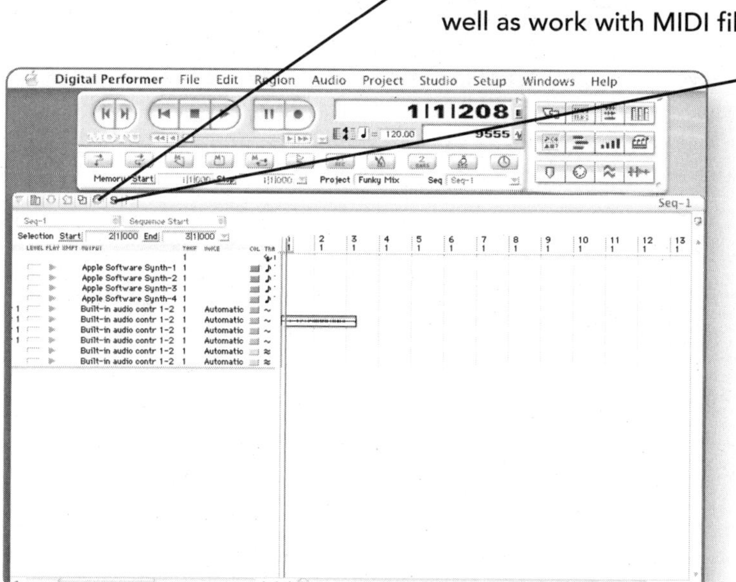

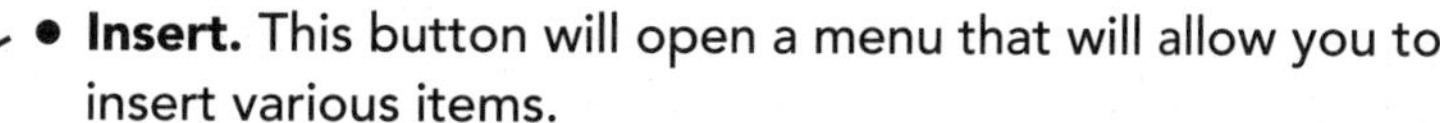

- **Insert.** This button will open a menu that will allow you to insert various items.
- **Snapshot.** In the Mixing window, this button allows you to save all your current settings.
- **Show/Hide Tracks.** As the name suggests, this button will allow you to show or hide your tracks.

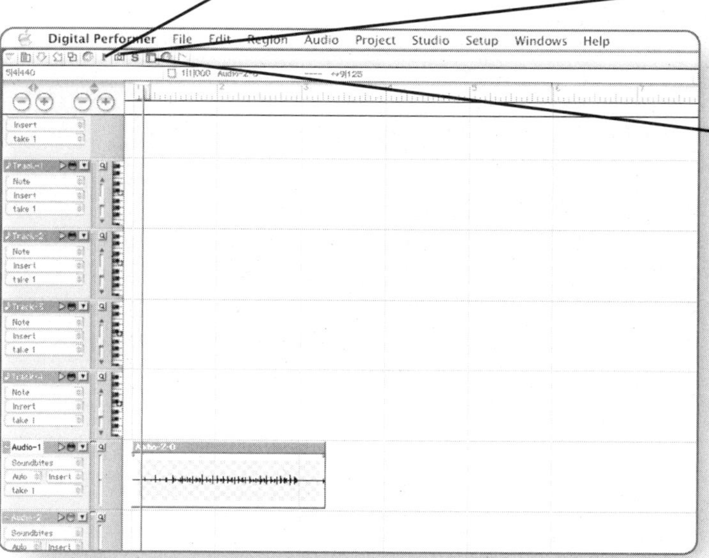

Accessing Windows

Once you've started moving windows around, changing their sizes or placing one behind the others, you may lose track of a window you need to access. The Windows menu allows you to access any window you are looking for.

1. **Click** on **Windows**. The Windows menu will appear.

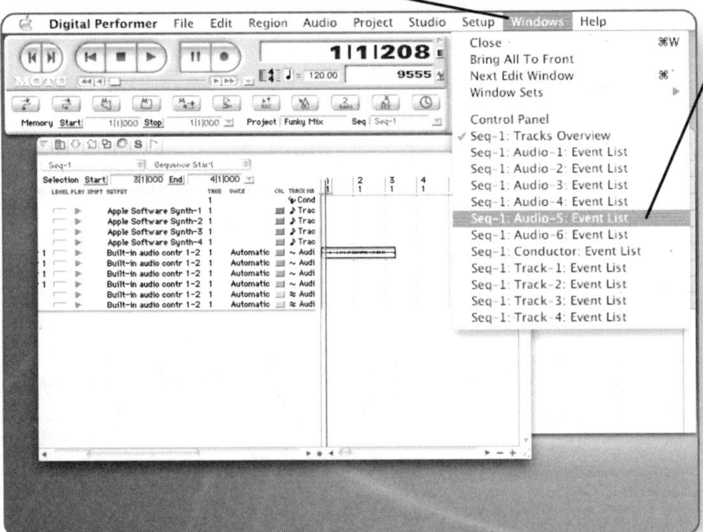

2. **Click** on the desired **window**. If it is already open, it will be brought to the front.

Working with Dialog Boxes

Dialog boxes are one of the easiest ways for you to communicate with the program. In a nutshell, a dialog box asks you for some form of data and offers a variety of different ways to provide the requested information, including checking circles or boxes, inputting numbers, clicking and dragging scroll bars, or selecting from menus.

1. **Click** on **Region**. The Region menu will appear.

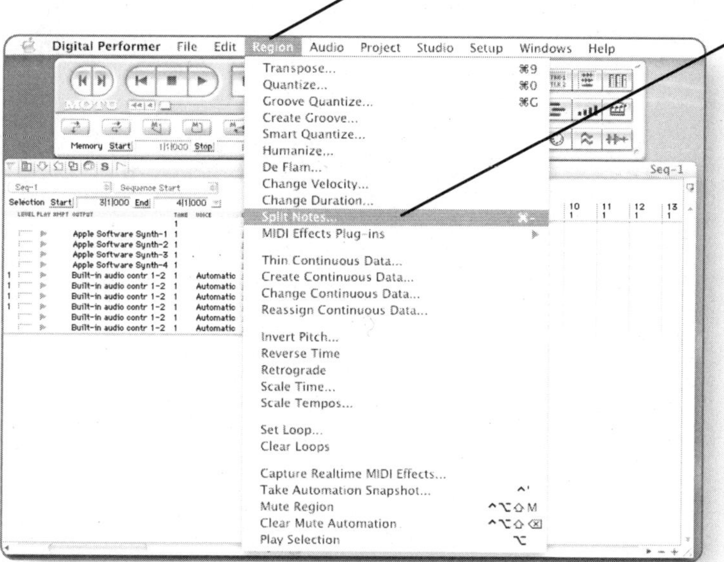

2. **Click** on **Split Notes**. A dialog box will appear. We are using Split Notes as an example; other dialog boxes will work in the same way.

3. **Click** on a **circle** beside an option to select that option. The circle will be highlighted. A circle means that you can only choose one option.

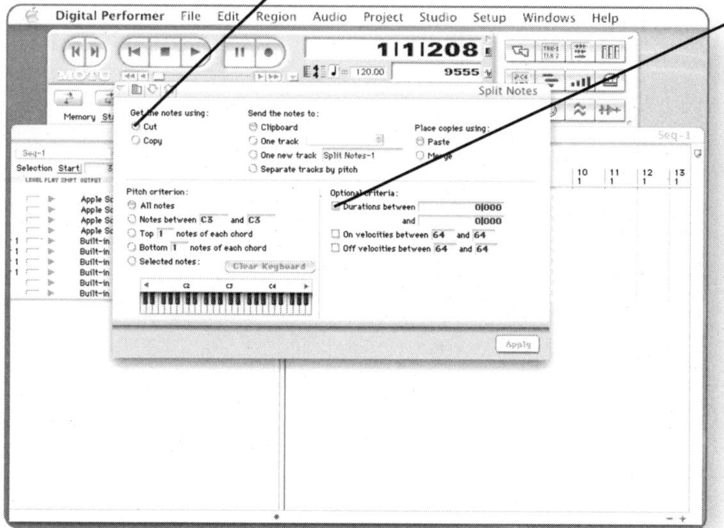

4. **Click** on a **square** beside one of the options. The square will be highlighted. A square means that more than one option can be selected at any given time.

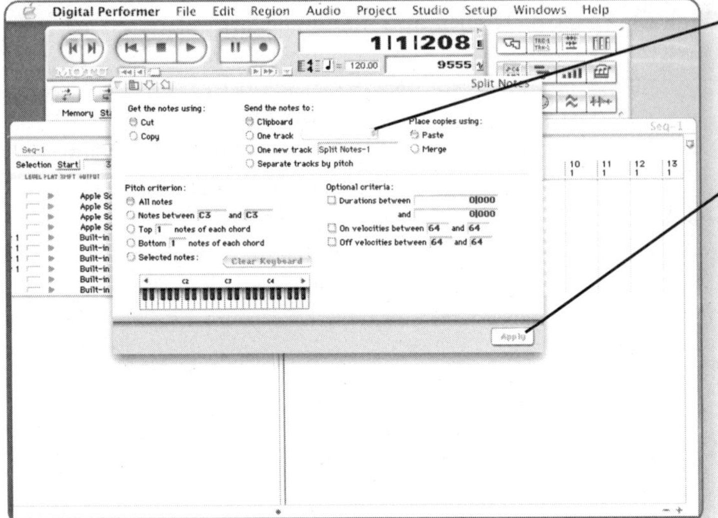

5. Click on the **up-and-down arrow**. A menu will appear. You can then make a selection from the menu.

6. Click on **Apply** to apply the changes and close the dialog box.

> **TIP**
>
> Pressing the Esc key will exit a dialog box without implementing any of the changes that have been made.

7. Click on **Region**. The Region menu will appear.

8. Click on **Transpose.** Another dialog box will open. Again, we are using the Transpose dialog box as an example.

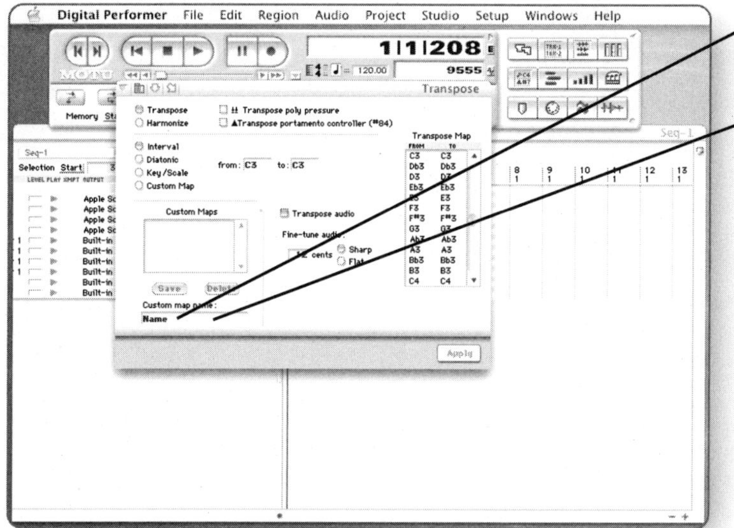

9. **Double-click** in a **field** to highlight the entire field.

10. **Type** in new **data**. It will appear as you type.

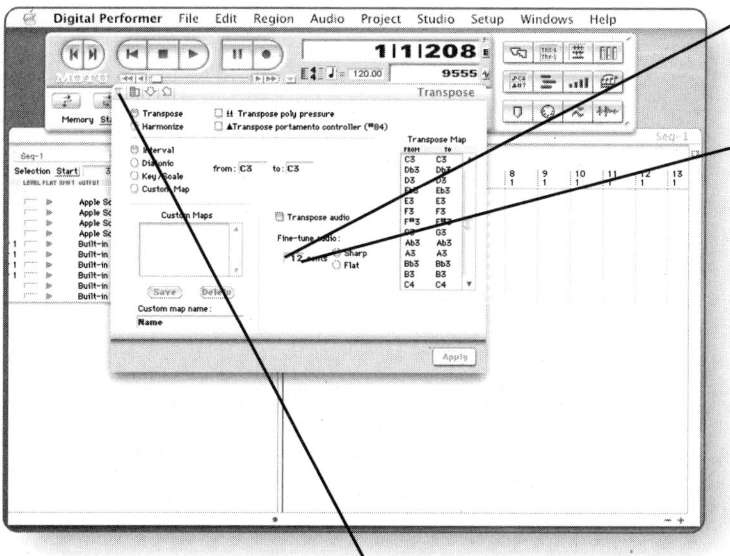

11. **Double-click** on a **number** in the dialog box. The number will be highlighted.

12. **Type** a **new number**. It will appear as you type.

> **TIP**
>
> Once you have clicked in a numerical box, rather than having to type a new number, you can simply click and drag upward or downward to adjust the number.

13. **Click** on the **down arrow** in the top-left corner to close the dialog box.

5

The Control Panel

If Digital Performer were a plane, the Control Panel would be the cockpit. Using the Control Panel, you can navigate to all of the different areas in your sequences. You can manage the playback of your sequences and how they are recorded, in addition to controlling a variety of settings. In this chapter, you will learn how to:

- Use basic controls
- Work with counters
- Use the metronome
- Work with memory bars

Exploring the Control Panel

The Control Panel is the central area used to play back your sequences. It basically looks like any audio player, just with a few more buttons. The Control Panel not only gives you basic control over playing your sequences, it also has some extra features like a counter, metronome, tempo indicator, and more.

The Basic Controls

The basic controls allow you to quickly navigate through your sequence. They work the same as almost any other audio player.

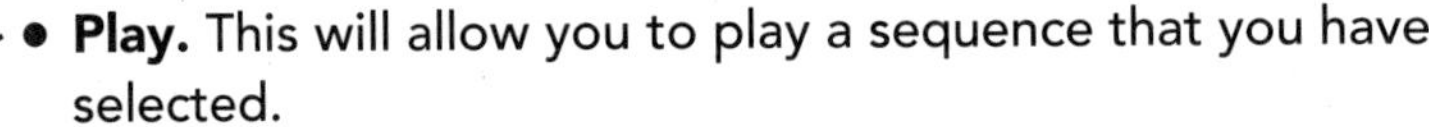

- **Play.** This will allow you to play a sequence that you have selected.

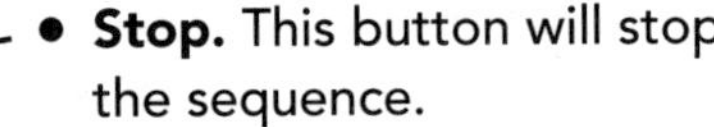

- **Stop.** This button will stop the sequence.

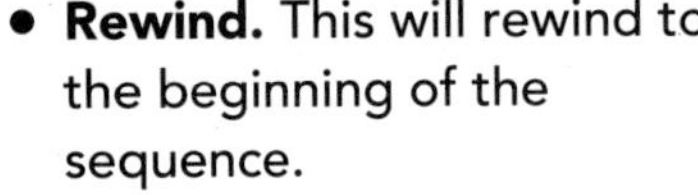

- **Rewind.** This will rewind to the beginning of the sequence.

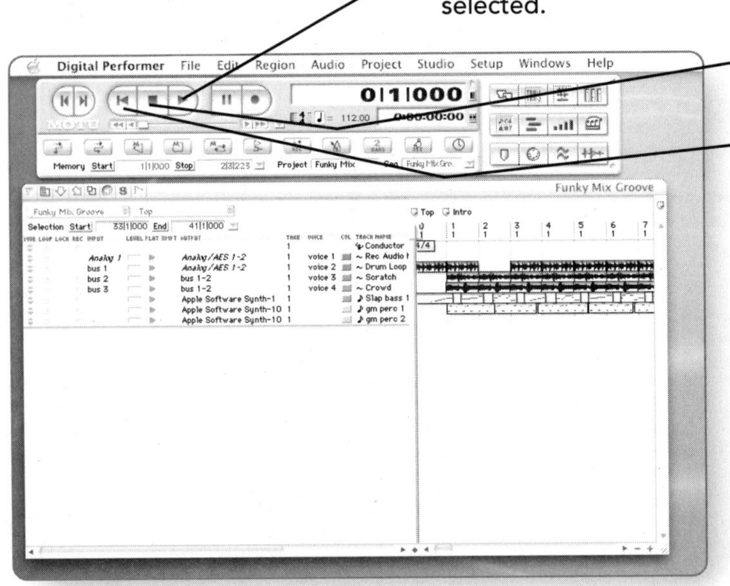

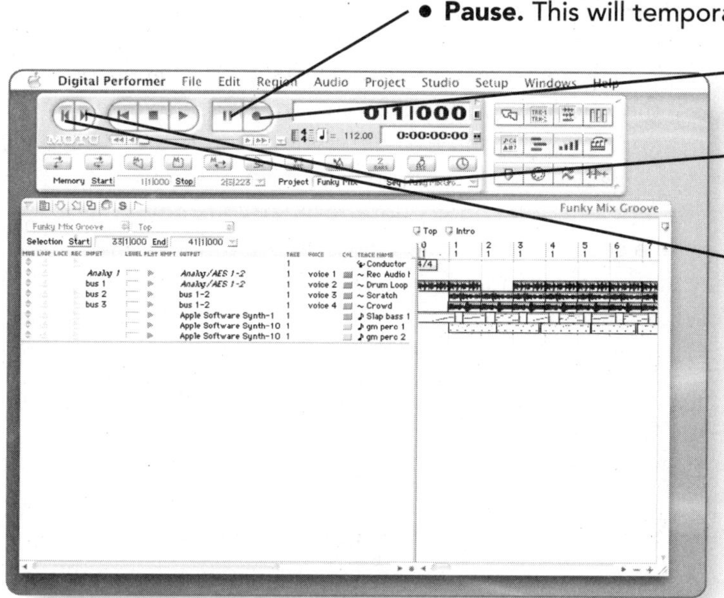

- **Pause.** This will temporarily stop the recording or playback.
- **Record.** This will begin the recording process.
- **Skip Forward.** This will allow you to jump to the next sequence or song in a file.
- **Skip Backward.** This will take you back to the preceding sequence or song in a file.

The Counters

A counter simply lets you know where you are in a particular sequence. There are two different counters displayed on the Control Panel; the larger one is the Main counter and the smaller one is the Auxiliary counter. Other than their size, there is no difference between the two counters.

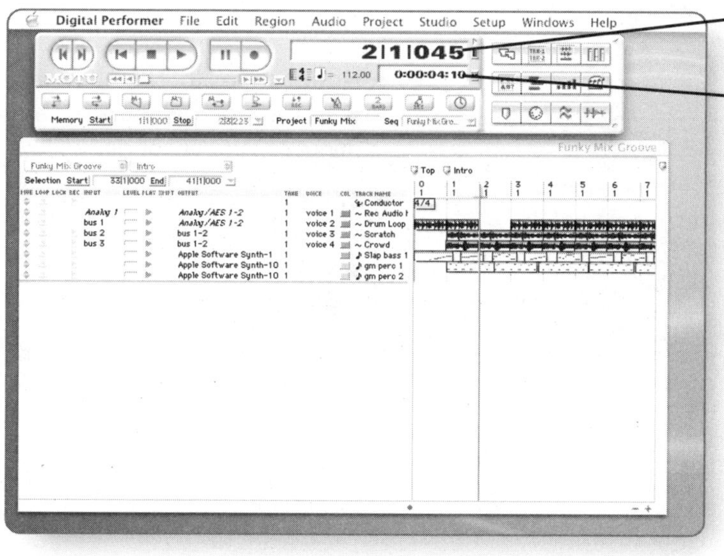

- **Main counter.** This is the larger of the two counters.
- **Auxiliary counter.** This counter offers an alternative counting format.

Counter Display

You can choose the format (measures, real time, frames, or samples) that the Main and Auxiliary counters use to display your location. Basically, the two different counters are available so that you can view your location using two different methods. For example, one counter can let you know where you are in a sequence by measure, while the other counter can display real time. Changing the display is simply a matter of a few clicks.

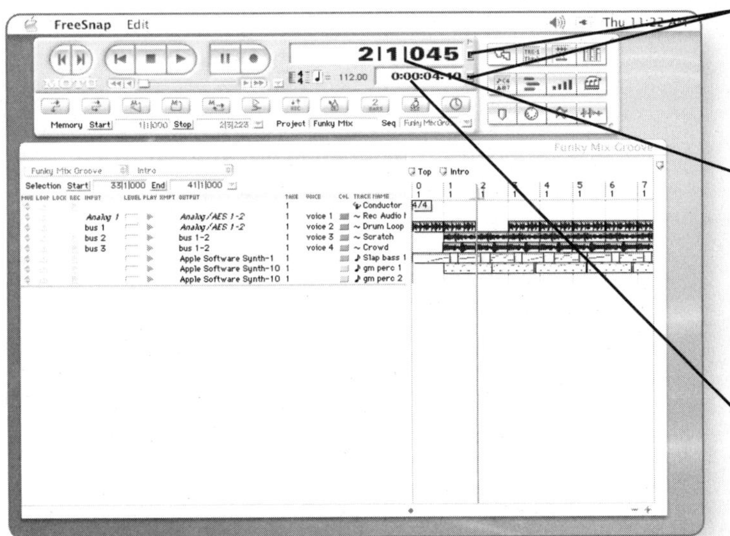

1. **Click** on the **icon** beside a counter. It will change to the next display type. There is a total of four different modes.
   - **Measure counter.** This counter is divided into three elements. The first number indicates the measure, the second number measures beats, and the last number measures ticks.
   - **Real Time counter.** This lets you know where you are in your sequence in real time.
   - **Hours counter.** This shows your location by hours, minutes, and seconds.
   - **Samples counter.** This lets you know where you are by samples since the start of the sequence.
2. **Repeat step 1** until you have reached the desired display type.

> **NOTE**
>
> If you change the Main counter to the same format as the Auxiliary counter, the Auxiliary counter will automatically change to a different format. In other words, the two counters cannot display the same format at the same time.

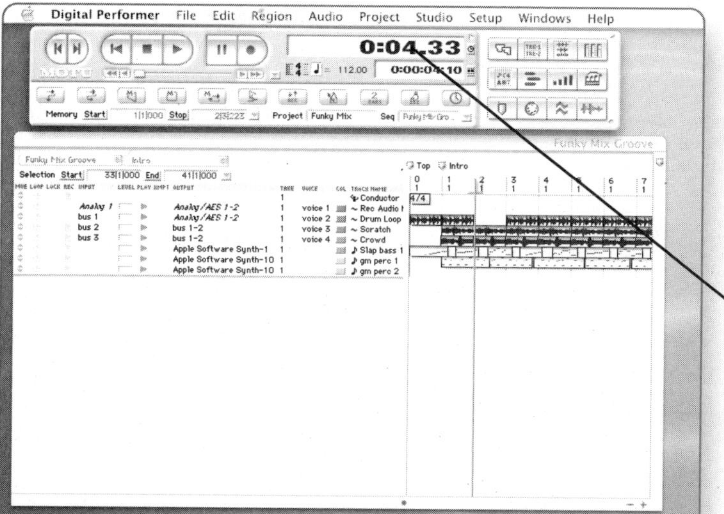

Navigating with Counters

Using the counters, you can jump to different parts of your tracks. You simply have to specify a location and the counter will take you to that part of the track.

1. **Click once** on a **number** in the counter. It will be highlighted.

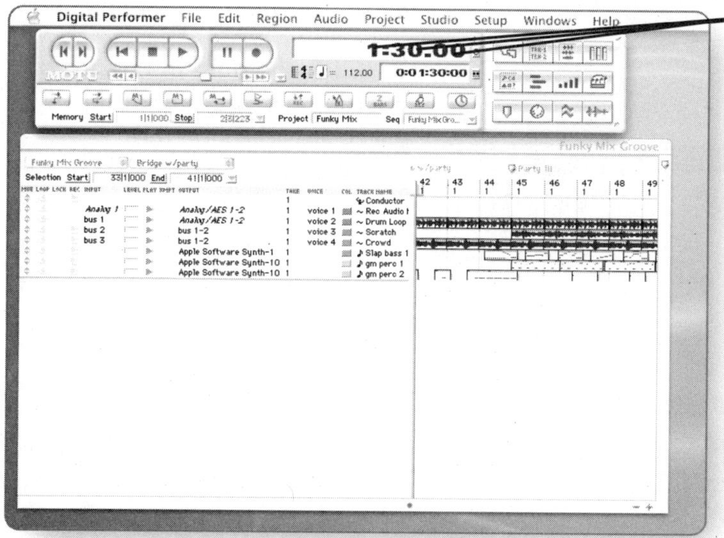

2. **Type** the **location** of where in the track you'd like to be. You have to enter the number for each period of time separately. In other words, if you wanted to go to the 1:30 point, first you would have to enter the 1 and then you would have to select and enter the 30.

3. **Press Return**. You will move to the specified location in the sequence.

The Position Bar

While the counters allow you to move to precise locations in your sequence, the position bar is another alternative for moving to different locations.

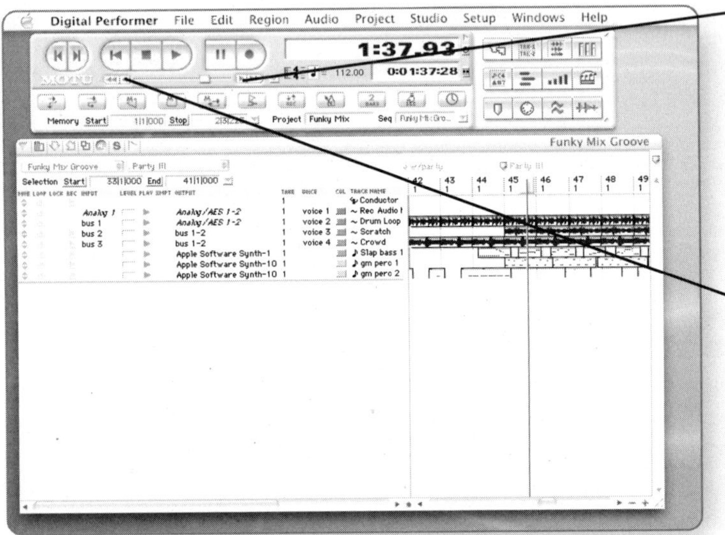

1. **Click** and **hold** the **forward arrow**. The sequence will be cued forward slowly until you release the mouse button.
2. **Release** the **mouse button** once you've reached the desired location.
3. **Repeat steps 1 and 2** with the backward arrow to move backwards slowly in the sequence.

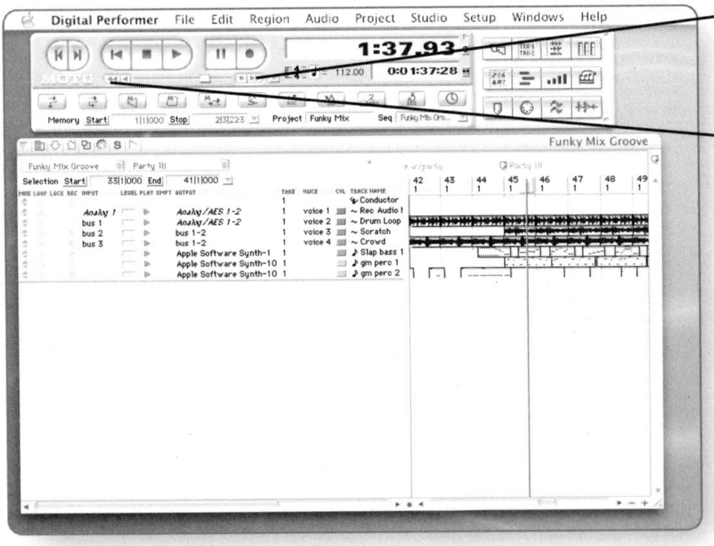

4. **Click** and **hold** the **forward double arrow** to move forward quickly through the sequence.
5. **Click** and **hold** the **backward double arrow** to quickly move backwards through the sequence.

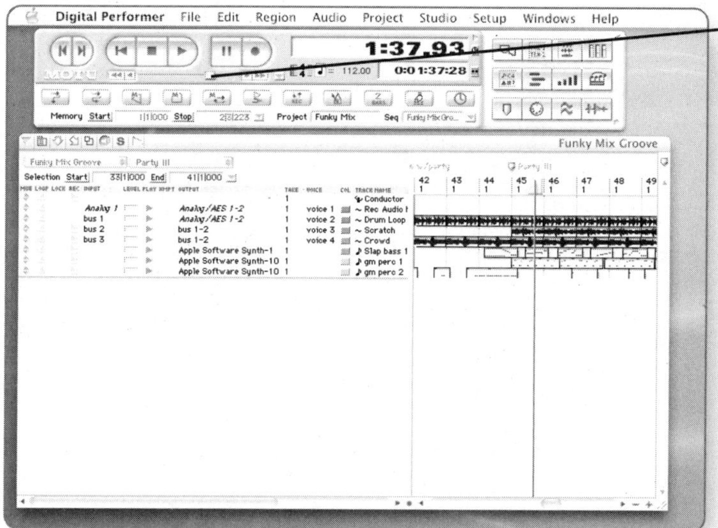

6. **Click** and **drag** the **box** on the position bar to move to any desired location.

The Metronome

Metronomes always remind me of taking piano lessons when I was a kid—that incessant ticking the teacher kept insisting that I follow. Digital Performer has a built-in metronome that can be turned off or on and adjusted to meet your requirements.

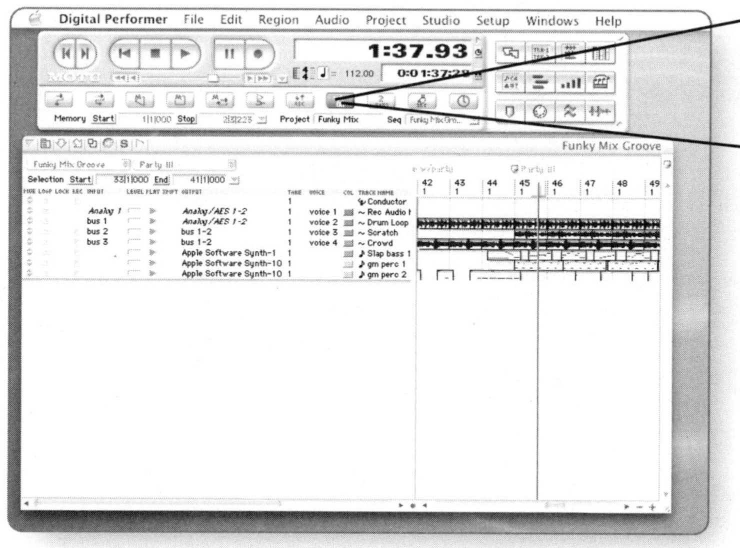

1. **Click** on the **Metronome button**. It will turn on and the button will appear darker.
2. **Double-click** on the **Metronome button**. A dialog box will open in which you can adjust the settings for the metronome.

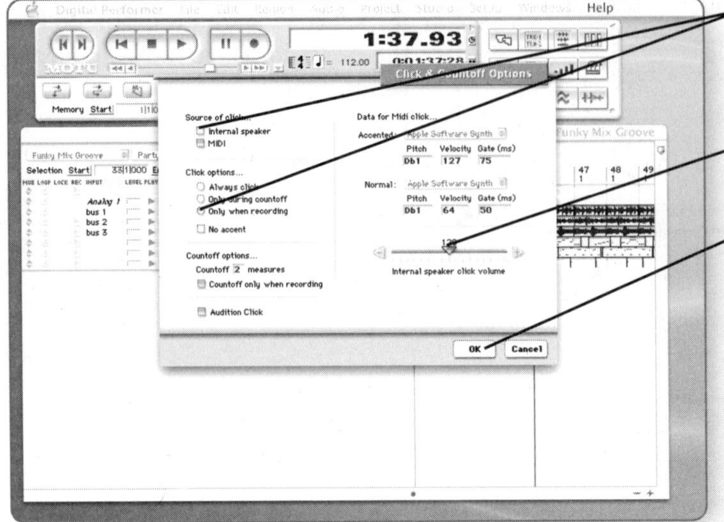

3. **Click** on the desired **options**. Once clicked, they will appear highlighted.

4. **Click** and **drag** along the **slider bar** to adjust the volume.

5. **Click** on **OK**. The settings you have changed will take effect.

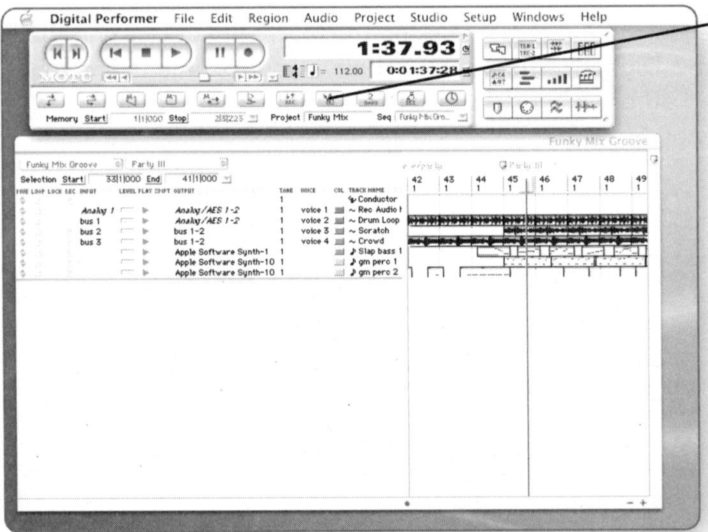

6. **Click** on the **Metronome button** to turn the metronome off. If will appear lighter when turned off.

Countoff

Isn't it cool when the leader of a band counts down "4, 3, 2, 1" before the band begins playing? The Countoff feature in Digital Performer works almost the same way: It counts down a certain number of times using the metronome before it starts to play or record.

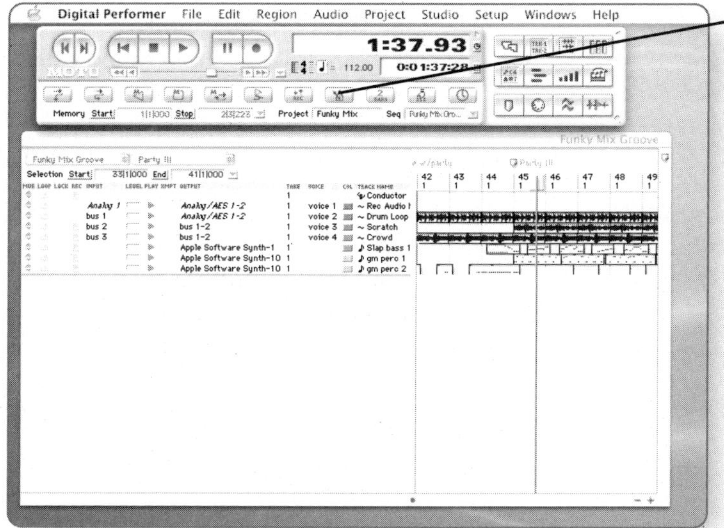

1. **Double-click** on the **Metronome button**. A dialog box will appear in which you can adjust the settings for the countoff.

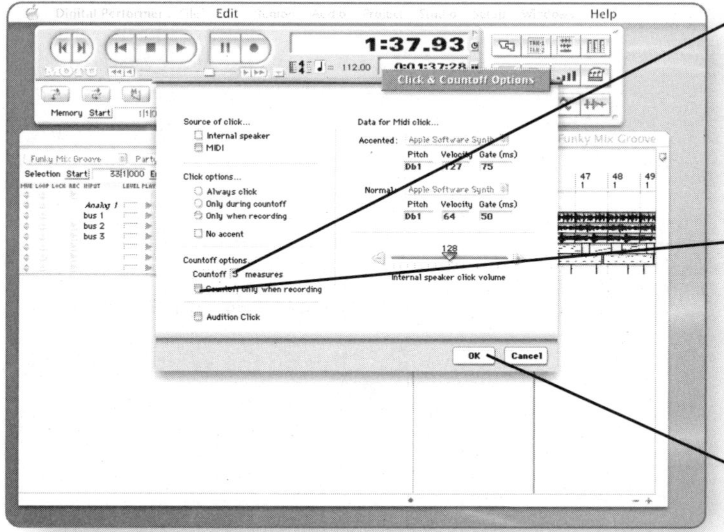

2. **Double-click** in the **Countoff measures box**. The box will be highlighted.

3. **Enter** the desired **countoff number**. It will appear in the box.

4. **Click** on the **box** beside Countoff only when recording, if you do not want a countoff when you are playing sequences. If the box is solid blue, then it is selected.

5. **Click** on **OK**. The settings will take effect.

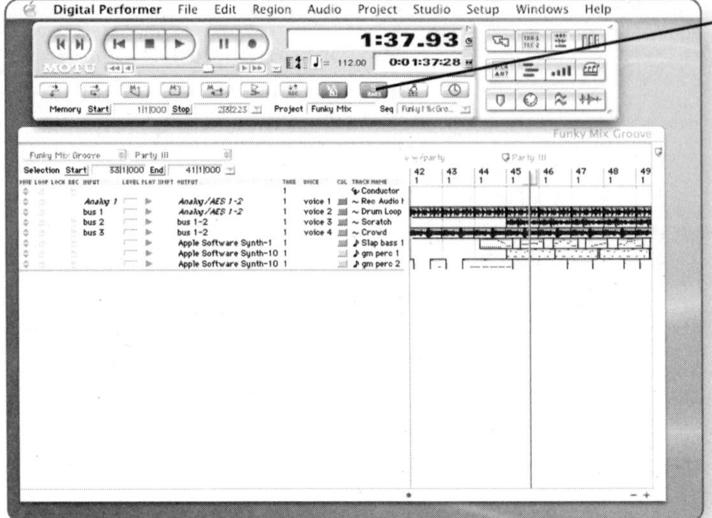

6. Click on the **Countoff button**. It will darken to indicate that it has been activated.

Wait

Wait works in a similar way to Countoff, but rather than providing a countdown, Digital Performer will wait until it receives a signal from either the keyboard or a MIDI device before it starts playback or recording. Using the Wait feature, you don't have to rush between the computer and your instrument; recording or playing only starts when you give the signal.

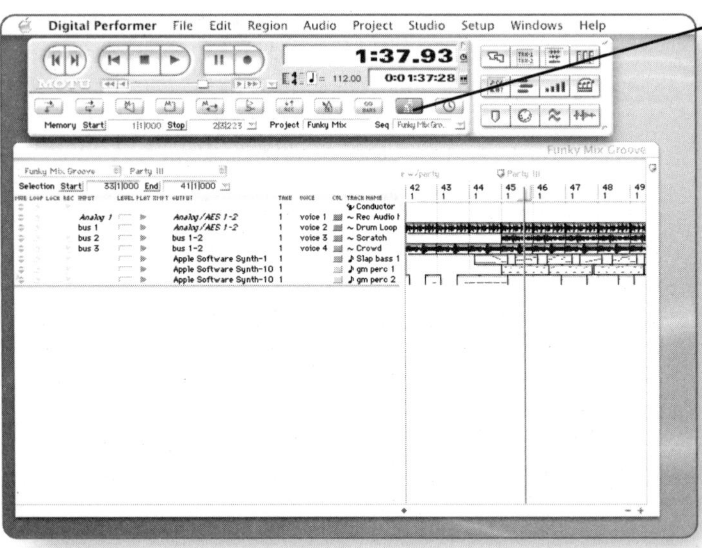

1. Click on the **Wait button** to turn the Wait function on. It will appear darker to indicate that it is on. Once you press the Record or Play button, Digital Performer will wait for a signal from the keyboard or MIDI device to begin recording or playing.

2. Click on the **Wait button** again to turn off the feature.

The Tempo Indicator

Embedded within the Control Panel is the Tempo Indicator, which will tell you what your current tempo is. In Digital Performer, there are two ways to control your tempo—one is through the Conductor Track and the other is through the Tempo slider. When you are using the Tempo slider, you can actually adjust the tempo settings by using the Tempo Indicator.

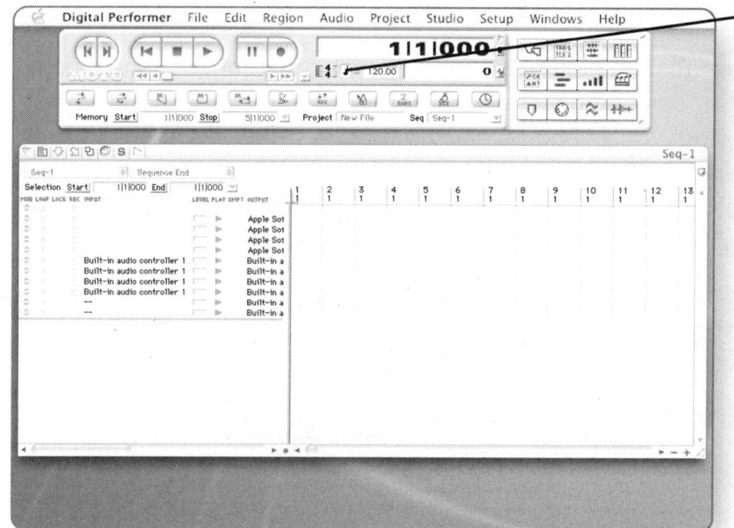

1. **Click** on the **note** beside the Tempo Indicator. A list of different types of notes will appear.

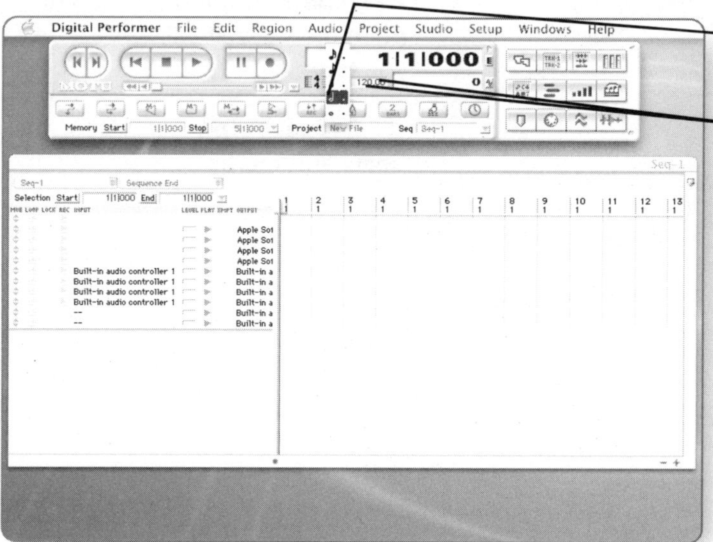

2. **Click** on the desired **note value**. It will be selected.
3. **Click once** on the **Tempo Indicator**. The number will be highlighted.
4. **Type** a new **number** for the tempo. It will appear as you type.
5. **Press Return**. The new tempo will take effect.

The Memory Bar

The memory bar in Digital Performer allows you to control the way a sequence is rewound, stopped, and repeated. Rather than rewinding to the beginning of a sequence, the memory bar allows you to rewind to a specific point. You can also set a point where a sequence will repeat.

Setting Start and Stop Points

Rather than rewinding to the beginning of your sequence, you can set any point in the track to rewind to. When auto rewind is selected, you will be taken to this point rather than the beginning of the track. You can also set a stop point that will stop the sequence at a specific point, or if auto repeat is selected, loop the sequence between the start and end points.

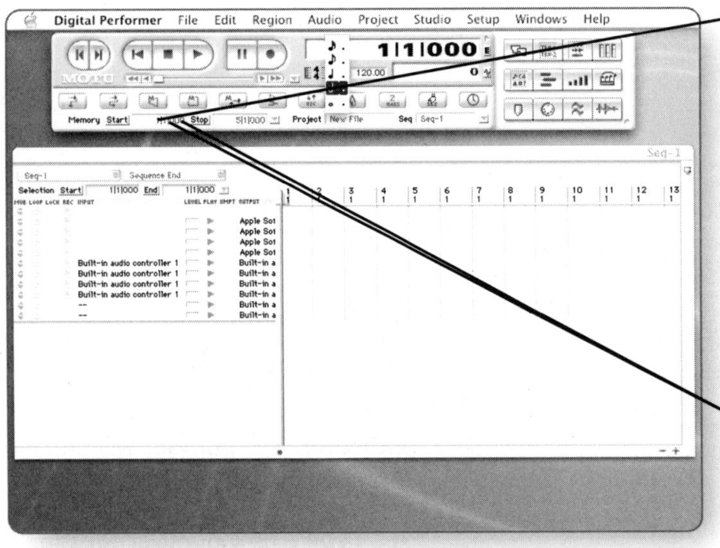

1. **Click** on the **first number** in the Start box. The start point is displayed in the format, measure | beats | ticks. The first number will be highlighted, which will allow you to adjust the measure for the starting point.

2. **Type** a **number** for the start point measure. It will appear as you type.

3. **Repeat steps 1 and 2** for the beats and the ticks.

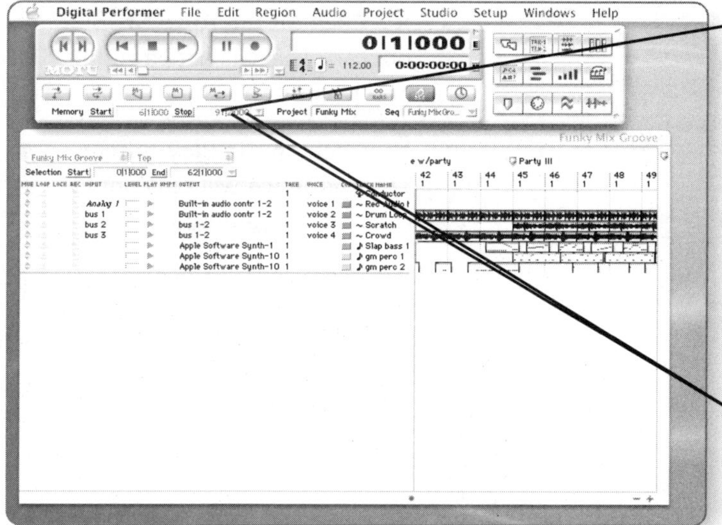

4. Click on the **first number** in the Stop box. The stop point is displayed in the format, measure | beats | ticks. The first number will be highlighted which will allow you to adjust the measure for the stop point.

5. Type a **number** for the stop point measure. It will appear as you type.

6. Repeat steps 4 and 5 for the beats and the ticks.

Using the Memory Bar

Once you have your start and end points defined, you can use the Auto Rewind, Auto Stop, and Auto Repeat buttons to take advantage of your start and stop points.

1. Click on the **Auto Rewind button**. This will activate the start point.

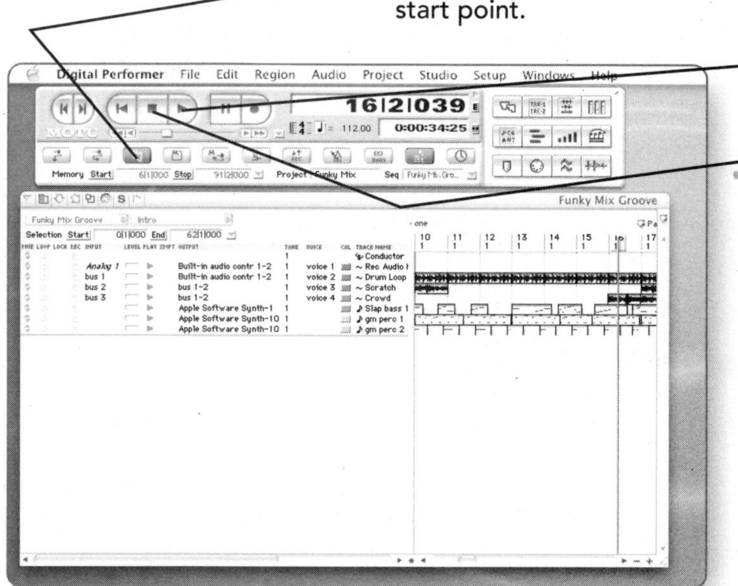

2. Click on the **Play button**. The sequence will begin to play.

3. Click on the **Stop button**. The track will move to the start point.

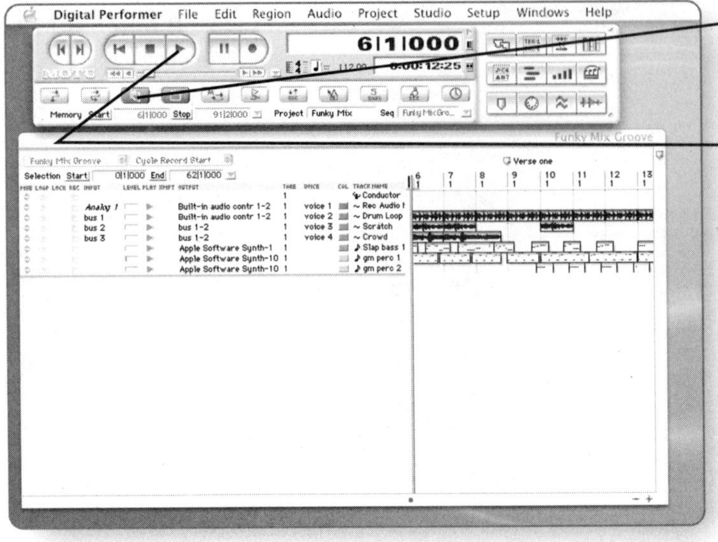

4. **Click** on the **Auto Stop button**. This will activate the end point.

5. **Click** on the **Play button**. The sequence will play until it reaches the end point.

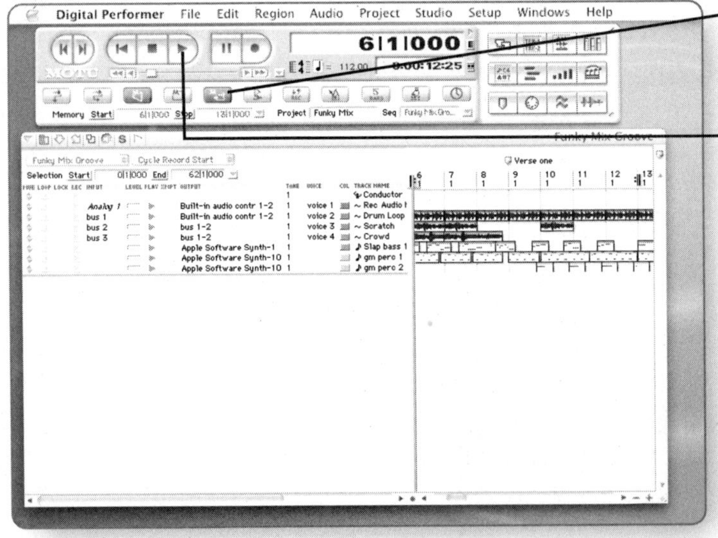

6. **Click** on the **Memory Cycle button**. This will activate looping.

7. **Click** on the **Play button**. The sequence will play until it reaches the end point, at which time it will start playing from the start point.

Receive Sync

Digital Performer allows you to connect a wide variety of hardware and external musical devices to your computer. The Receive Sync button allows you to synchronize Digital Performer with external devices.

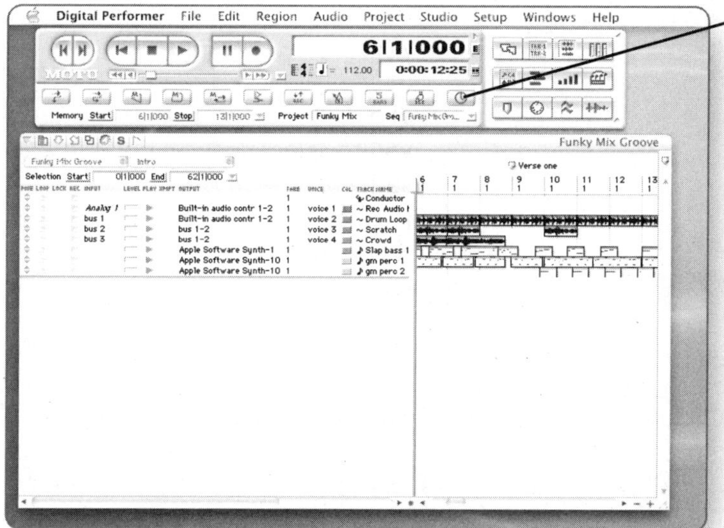

1. **Double-click** on the **Slave to External Sync button**. A dialog box will appear in which you can adjust the settings.

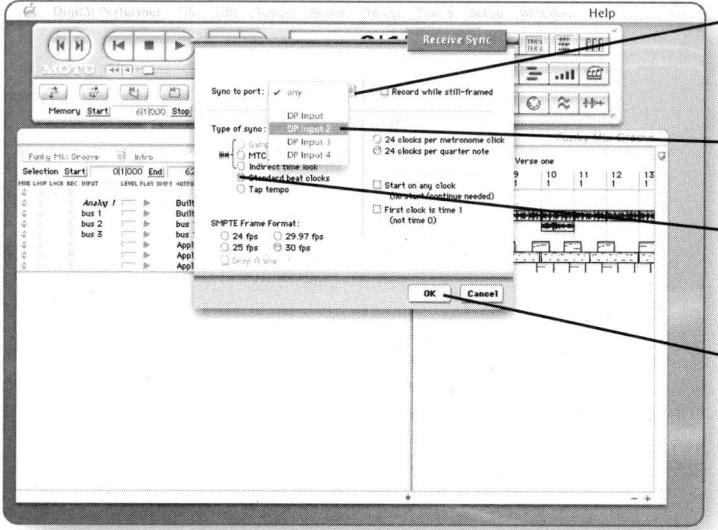

2. **Click** on the **double arrow** beside Sync to port. A list of ports will appear.
3. **Click** on the desired **port**. It will be selected.
4. **Click** on the **circle** next to any of the desired options. The circle will be highlighted.
5. **Click** on **OK**. The settings you have selected will take effect.

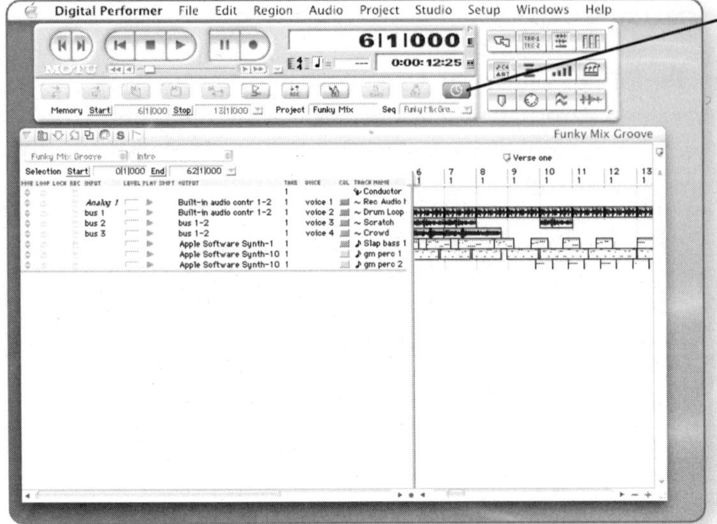

6. Click on the **Slave to External Sync button**. It will appear darker to indicate that it is on and Digital Performer will now synchronize with your external devices.

Auto Record

The Auto Record button allows you to select specific times in a sequence when Digital Performer will automatically start recording. Rather than having to press the Record button, you can use auto record to set specific punch times to start and stop recording within a sequence.

1. Click on the **Auto Record button**. The button will appear darker to indicate it is turned on. The auto record bar will appear, allowing you to enter specific start and end times for the auto record.

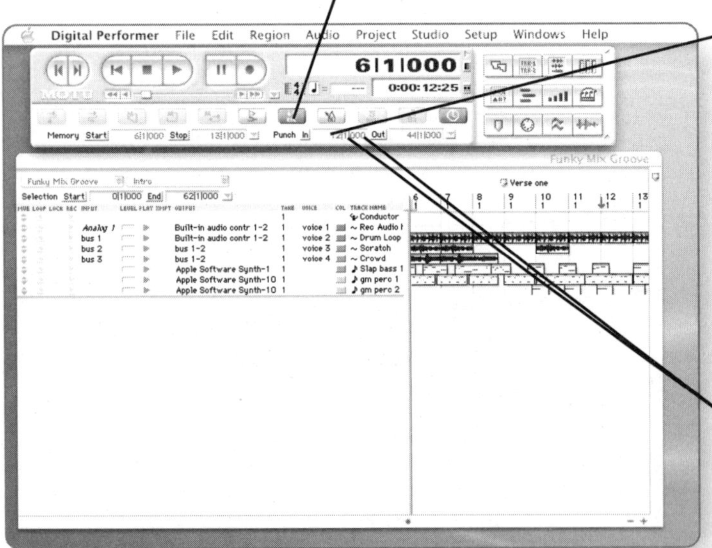

2. Click on the **first number** in the Punch In box. The number will be highlighted. There are three numbers in both the Punch In and Punch Out boxes. The numbers represent the measure, tick, and beat location.

3. Type a **number** for the measure location. The number will appear as you type.

4. Repeat steps 2 and 3 for the tick and beat locations.

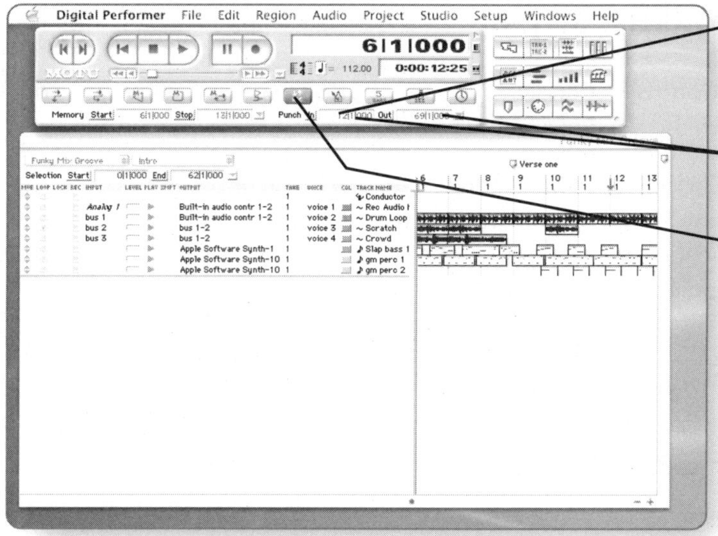

5. **Click** in the **Punch Out box**. This will allow you to specify a location to stop the auto record.

6. **Type** a new **number** for the measure, tick, and beat.

7. **Click** on the **Auto Record button** again when you want to turn the feature off.

Overdub Recording

Overdub recording allows you to record onto a track without deleting the existing information on that track. In other words, you can add to an existing track, rather than deleting or taping over it.

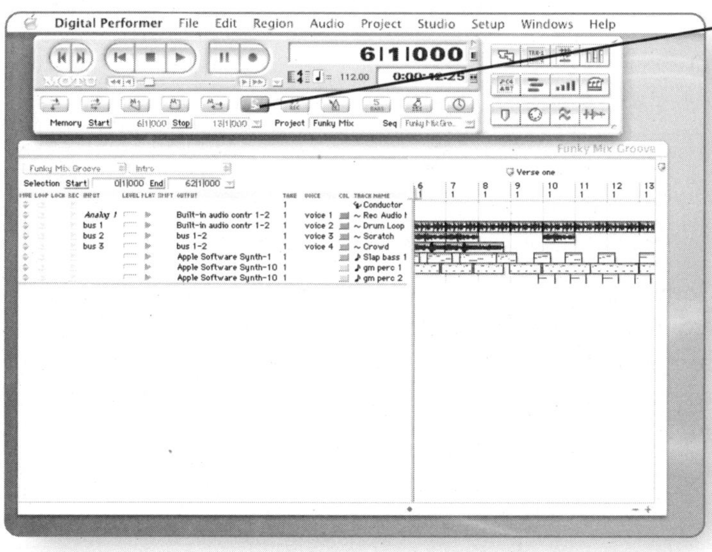

1. **Click** on the **Overdub Record button**. It will appear darker to indicate that it is on.

2. **Repeat step 1** to turn the feature off.

Chunk Controls

The Control Panel gives you two buttons that will allow you to control how chunks of music are played.

1. **Click** on the **Cue Chunks button**. It will appear darker to indicate that it is activated. Activating this button will play the next chunk in the list after the current chunk has reached its end point.

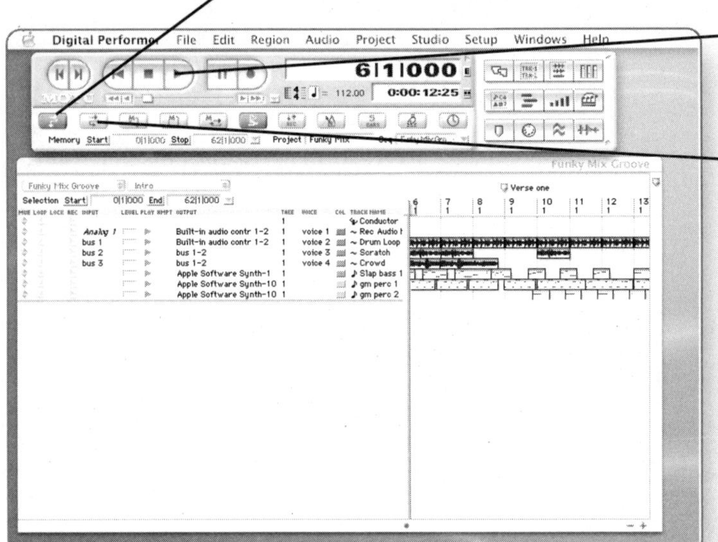

2. **Click** on **Play** once the chunk has reached its end point to begin playing the next chunk.

3. **Click** on the **Chain Chunks button**. It will appear darker to indicate that it is activated. Activating this button will automatically play the next chunk in the list after the current chunk has reached its end point.

Drawers

The Control Panel has four collapsible drawers that can be used to hide or display sections of the screen. With all of the different windows that can be opened in Digital Performer, it's nice to have the ability to hide or display certain parts of the screen.

1. Click on the **arrow** in the top-right corner of the Audio drawer. The drawer will collapse.

2. Click on the **arrow** in the top-right corner of the Tempo Control drawer. The drawer will collapse.

3. Click on the **arrow** in the top-right corner of the Selection drawer. It will collapse.

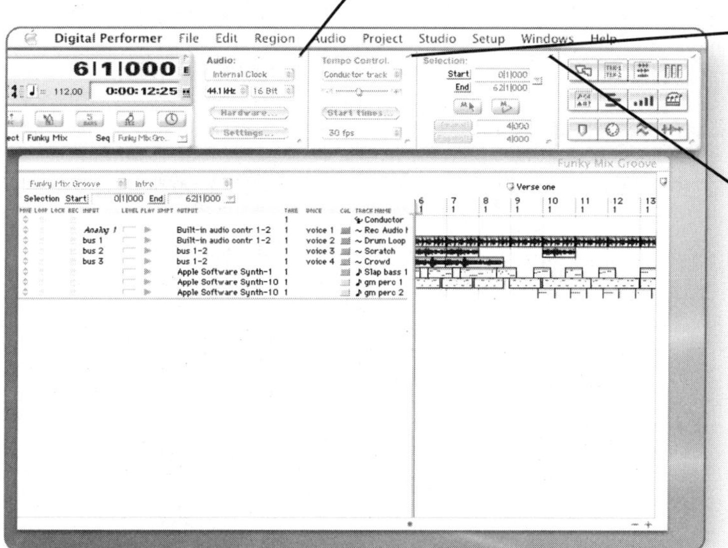

4. Click on the **arrow** in the top-right corner of the last drawer. It will collapse.

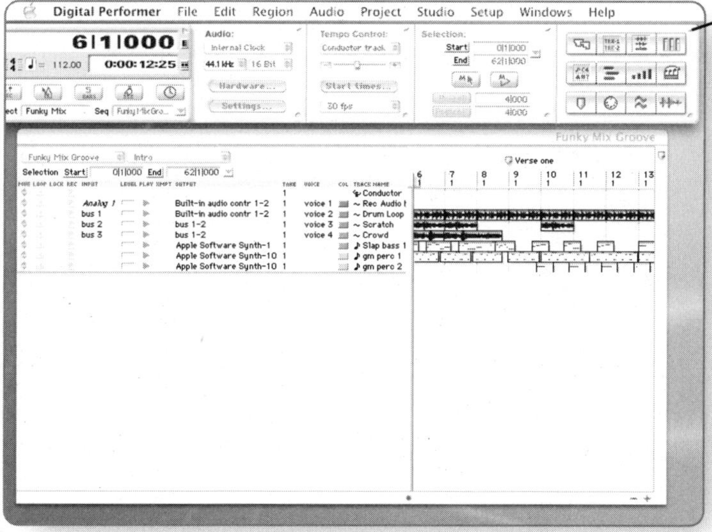

> **NOTE**
>
> When closing a drawer, all drawers to the left of the one being closed will also close.

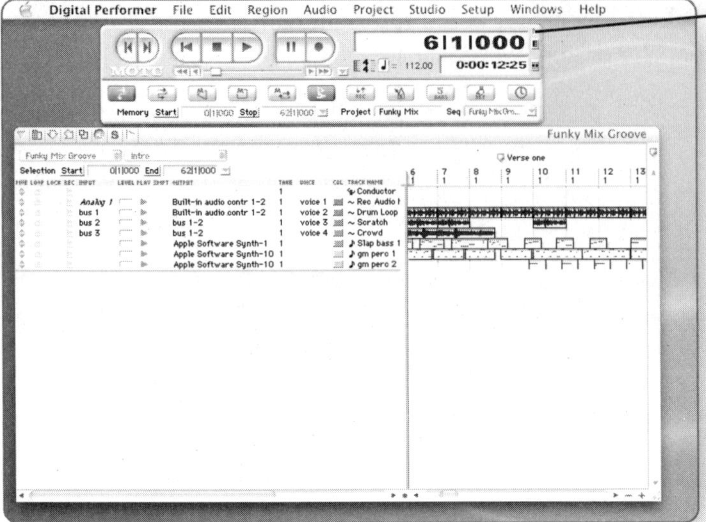

5. **Click** on the **arrow** in the top-right corner of the Control Panel to expand a drawer.

6. **Repeat step 4** until all drawers appear.

Moving Drawers

When you open drawers, they appear in a certain order. You can change the order in which the drawers appear by moving them.

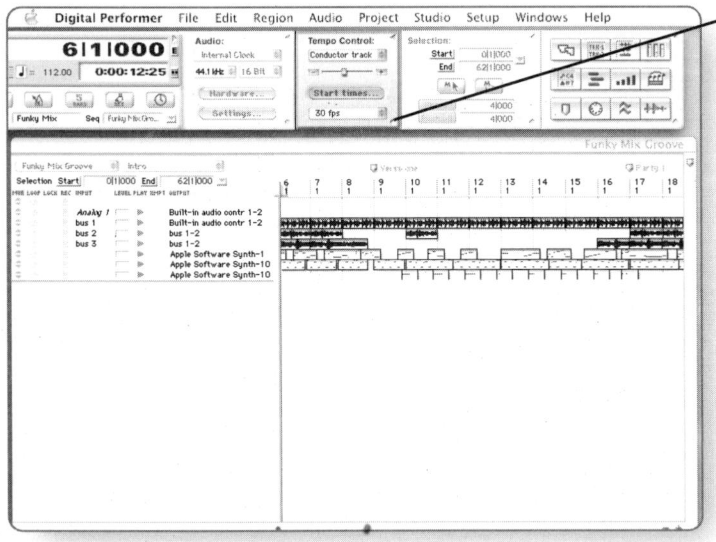

1. **Click** and **hold** the **circle** in the bottom-right corner of the drawer that you would like to move. A blue frame will surround the drawer.

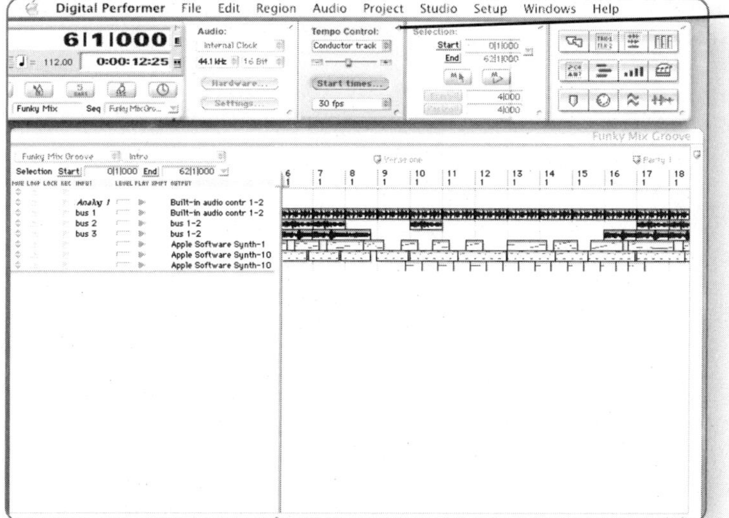

2. Drag the **drawer** to its new location. An outline will appear as you drag the drawer. A blue line will indicate the new position.

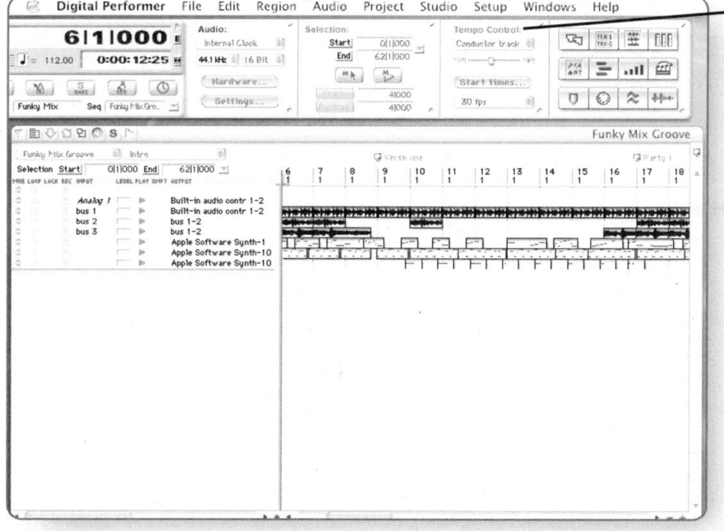

3. Release the **mouse button**. The drawer will be in its new location.

6 The Tracks Window

The Tracks window is the heart and soul of Digital Performer and it is where you will be spending most of your time. It contains much of the information about different tracks, including a visual representation of the music. With its many different icons, buttons, and labels, the Tracks window can seem confusing at first glance. In this chapter, you will learn how to:

- Identify the buttons and labels
- Navigate the Tracks window
- Access and use markers

Exploring the Tracks Window

The Tracks window can be very intimidating at first glance because of the sheer amount of data that it contains. Just like riding a bike, once you get going you'll never understand what you were afraid of in the first place.

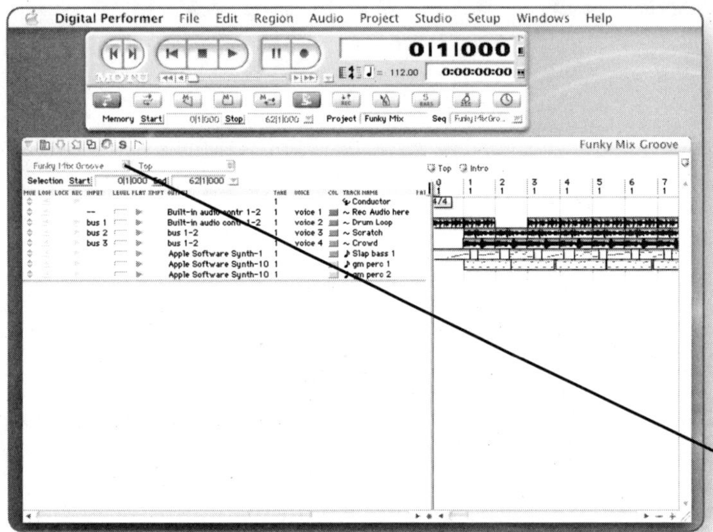

Selecting Sequences

Digital Performer allows you to include many different sequences within one file; however, they can only be accessed one at a time. Within the Tracks window, you can select the desired sequence to work with or you can create a new sequence.

1. Click on the **up-and-down arrows** beside the sequence name. A pop-up menu will appear.

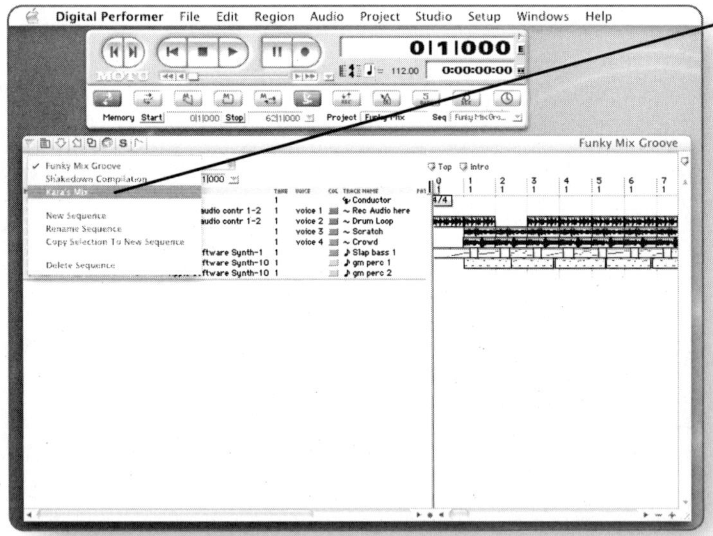

2. Click on the desired **sequence**. The sequence will open and all of its tracks will be visible.

Moving Tracks

To help keep your tracks organized, you might want to move them around. This is as simple as clicking and dragging the tracks to a new location.

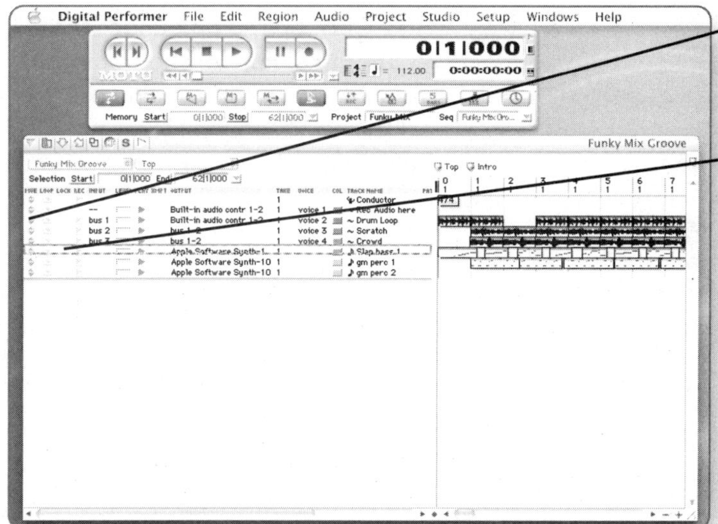

1. Position your **mouse pointer** over the up-and-down arrow in the column titled MVE.

2. Click and **drag** the **track** to a new location. As you drag, a dotted outline previewing the new location of the track will appear.

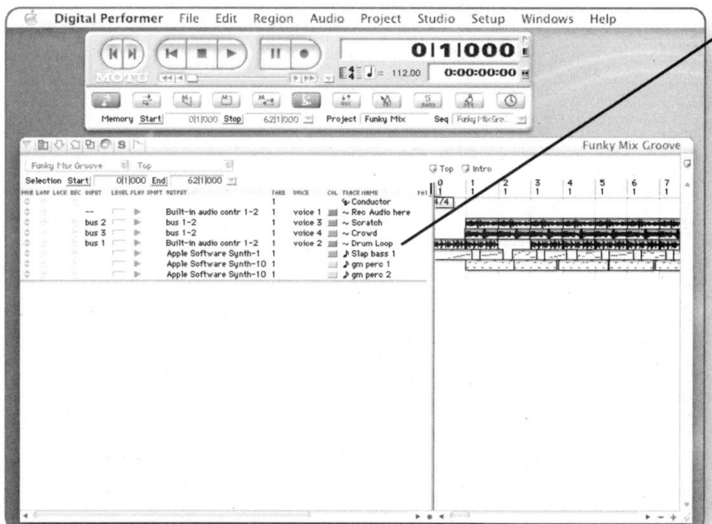

3. Release the **mouse button**. The track will be moved.

Output

Using the Tracks window, you can select a device to use to play your tracks. You can select from a variety of devices that you have attached to your computer or you can select internal devices.

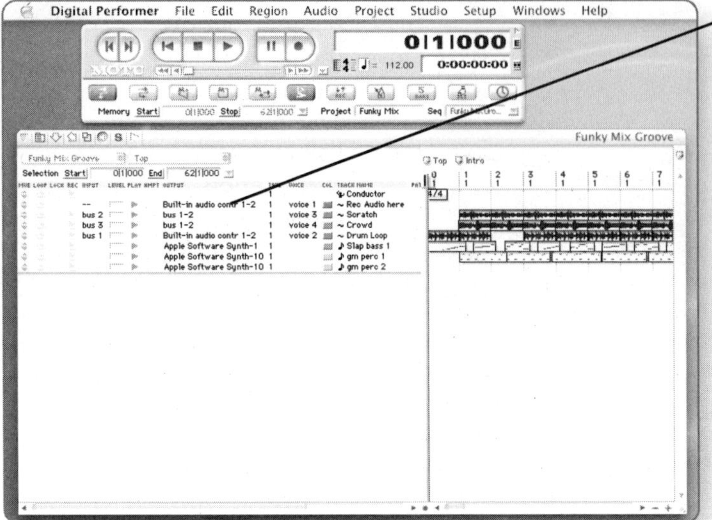

1. Click on the **box** under the Output column for the track you would like to set. A menu of different devices on your machine will appear.

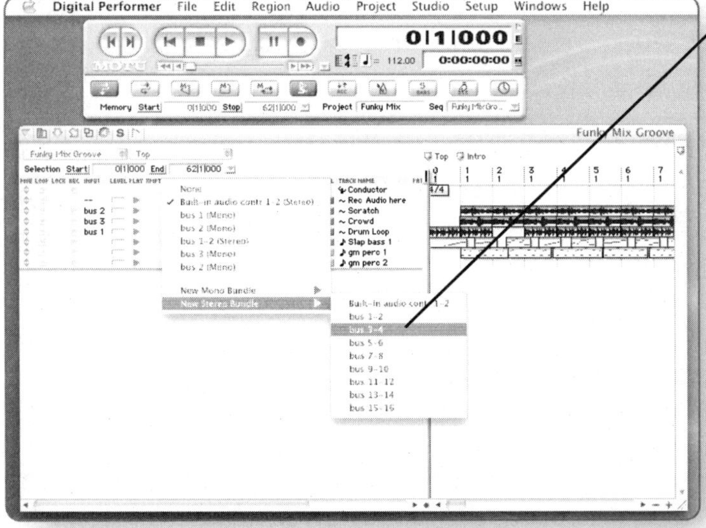

2. Click on the desired **device**. It will be set as the output for that track.

Track Name

The Track Name column in the Tracks window allows you to select track data, rename tracks, and even launch the Track Editing window. Beside each track name there is a little icon that indicates some additional information about the track.

- **MIDI.** An icon of a musical note indicates that it is a MIDI track.

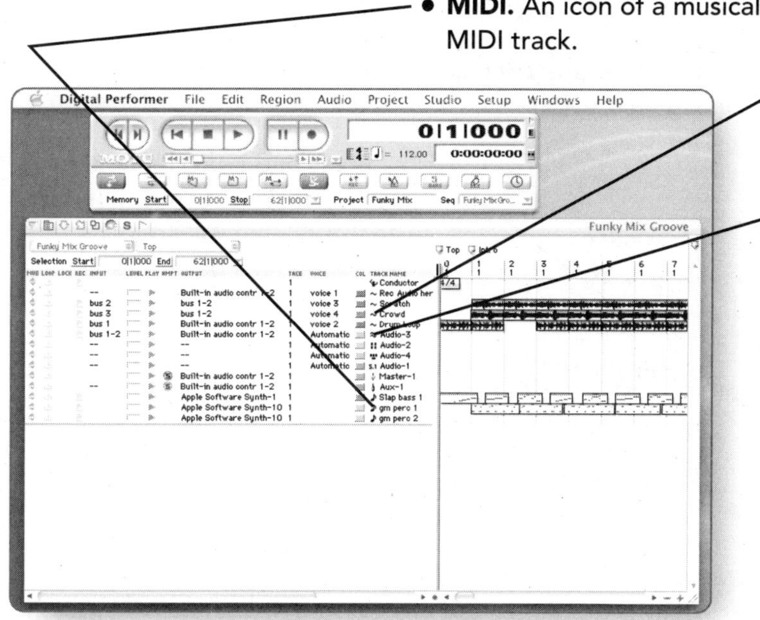

- **Mono.** A single tilde icon means that the track is an Audio Mono track.
- **Stereo.** A double tilde icon means the track is an Audio Stereo track.

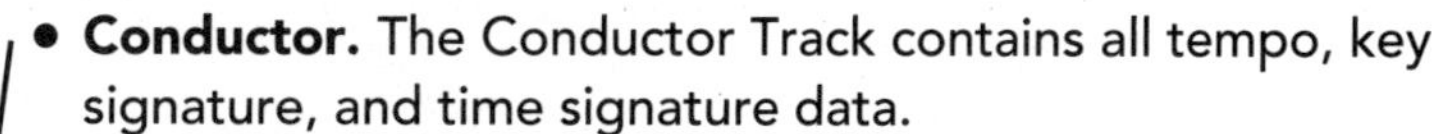

- **Conductor.** The Conductor Track contains all tempo, key signature, and time signature data.

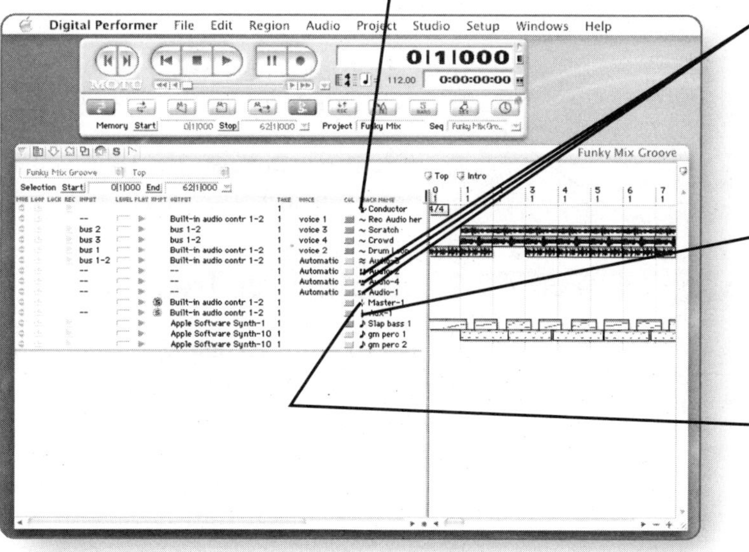

- **Surround Voice.** Depending on the type of Surround Voice track you create, there is a variety of icons to indicate a Surround Voice (Sound) track.
- **Aux.** An auxiliary track, represented by an icon that looks like a control slider, lets you add virtual instruments and plug-ins.
- **Master Fade.** An icon of a fade slider indicates a Master Fade track that can be used to control fade on the entire sequence.

Renaming Tracks

The following steps will take you through the process of renaming your tracks.

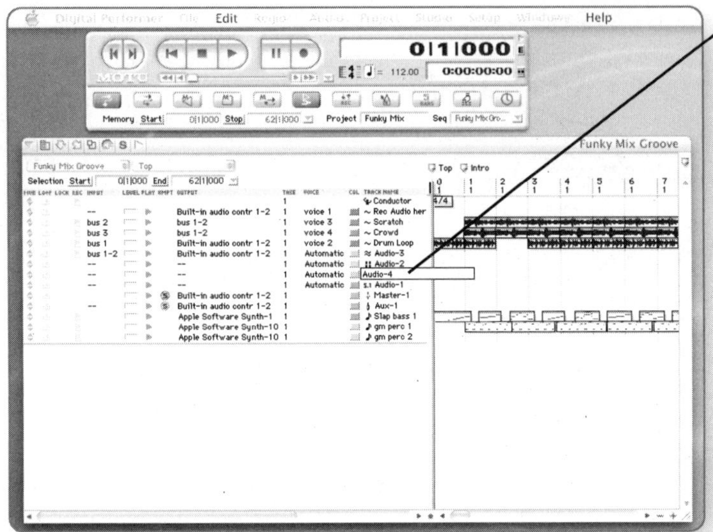

1. **Press** and **hold** the **Option key** and **click** on a **track name**. The track name will appear highlighted in a box.

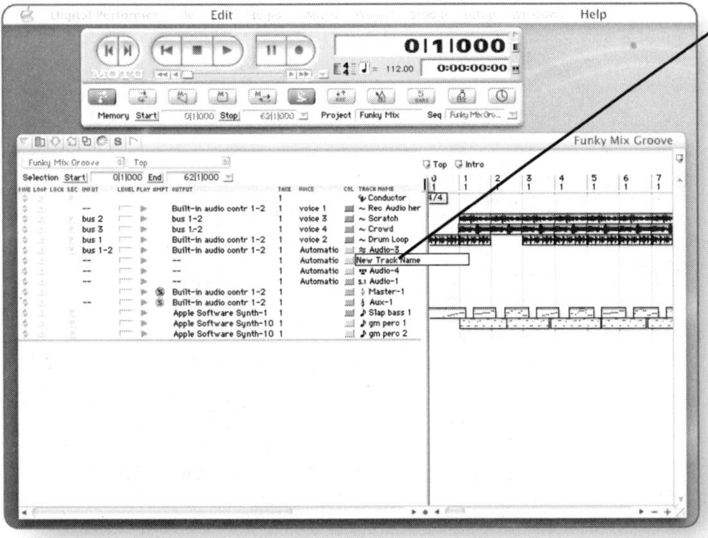

2. **Type** a new **name** for the track. It will appear as you type.

3. **Press Return**. The track will be renamed.

Coloring Tracks

In an effort to help you stay organized, you have the ability to assign a different color to each track.

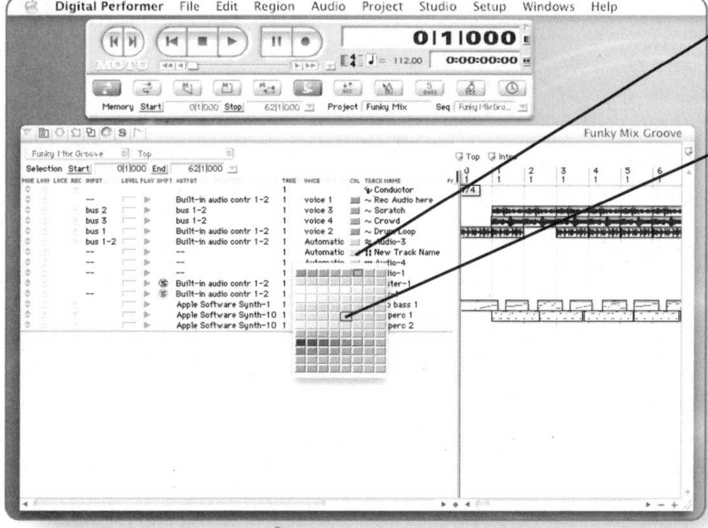

1. **Click** on the **color box** beside the desired track. A menu of different colors will appear.

2. **Click** on the desired **color**. That color will now appear in the Col column of the selected track.

Takes

It takes big movie stars five, six, or even more takes to get their performances right when shooting a movie, so why put yourself under the pressure of getting it right on the first take? Digital Performer allows you to assign multiple takes to any track. This means that you can record the same track multiple times and then select which take you would like to use.

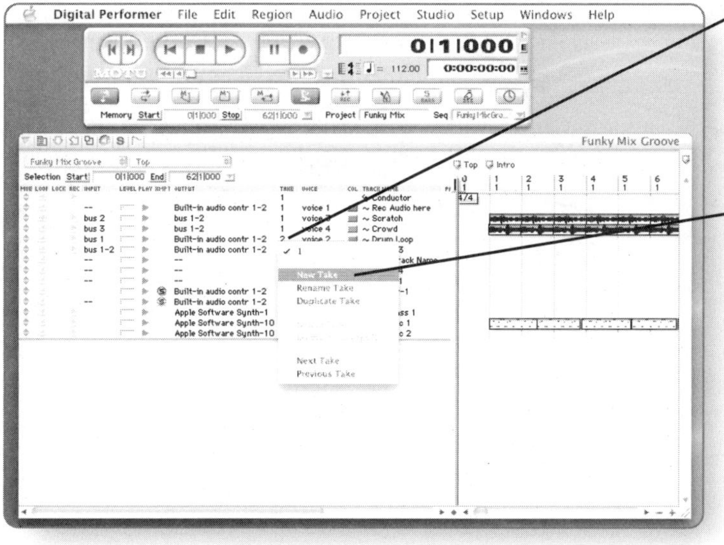

1. **Click** on the **number** in the Take column of the track in which you would like to add an additional take. A menu will appear.

2. **Click** on **New Take**. A new empty track will be created in place of the existing track. You can now record another take on this track.

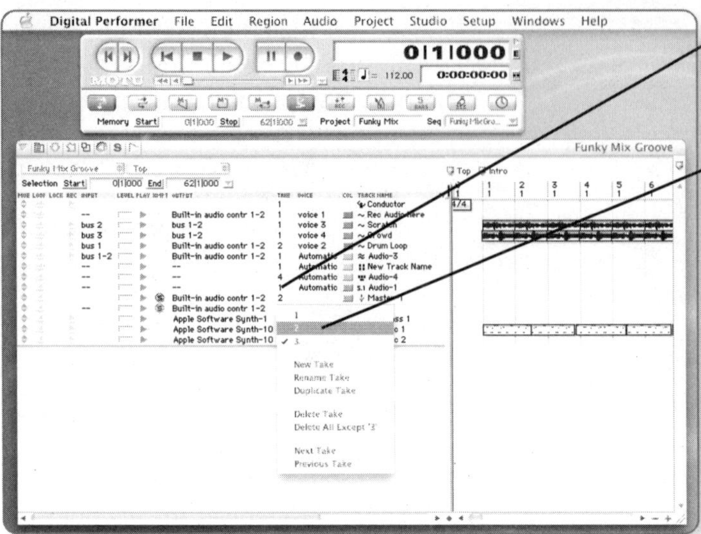

3. Click on a **number** in the Take column. A menu will appear.

4. Click on the desired **take**. The desired take of that track will appear.

Comments

Another great feature of the Tracks window is the Comments column. With the Comments column, you can add comments about specific tracks. Rather than having a notepad sitting around, you can add specific comments about certain tracks right in the Tracks window.

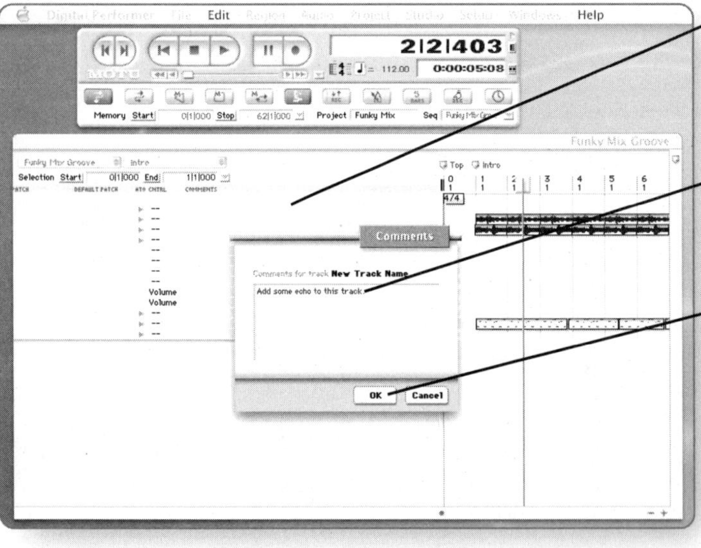

1. Click once on the **Comments box** of the desired track. A dialog box will appear in which you can add your comments.

2. Type the desired **comments** into the box. They will appear as you type.

3. Click on **OK**. The comments will be added to the track.

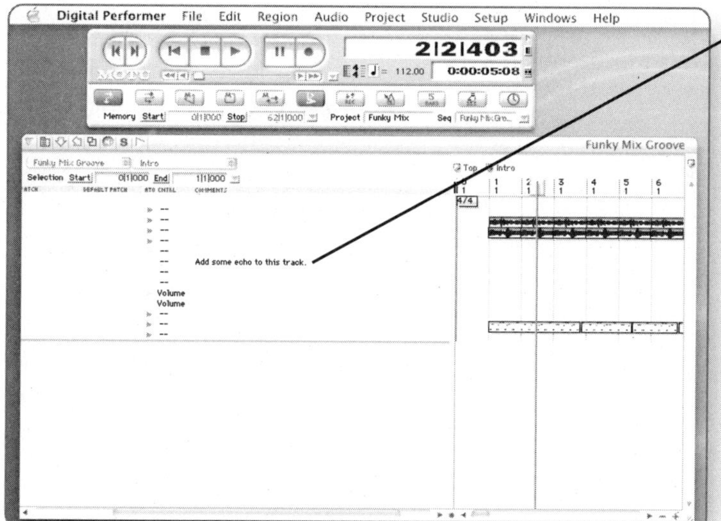

4. Click on the desired **comment** to edit it. The dialog box will reopen and you can edit the comment.

Other Tracks Window Elements

Many other elements are available in the Tracks window, some of which will be used infrequently, some for display purposes, and others that are central to the program.

- **Loop.** If the icon in the Loop column appears darker, it indicates that there is a loop in this track.

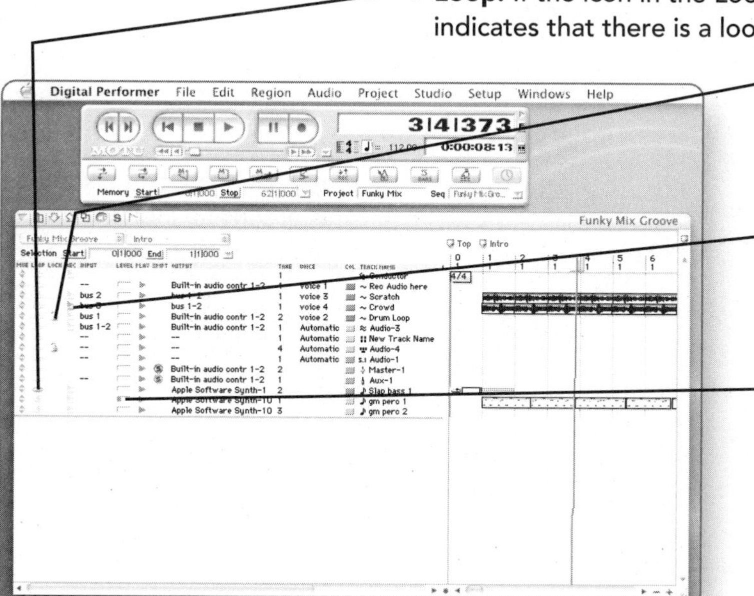

- **Lock.** Clicking on the Lock icon for a track will anchor all of the events in a track to their real locations.
- **Record.** Clicking on the Record icon in a track will allow that track to be recorded.
- **Levels Meter.** For display purposes, the Levels meter will bounce up and down to indicate when a track is being played.

- **Patch.** This column displays and allows you to select different patches for the track.
- **Default Patch.** This column displays the patch that the track always starts with. Using this column, you can also set the default patch.
- **Automation.** Clicking on this column allows you to control the playback and recording automation for a particular track.

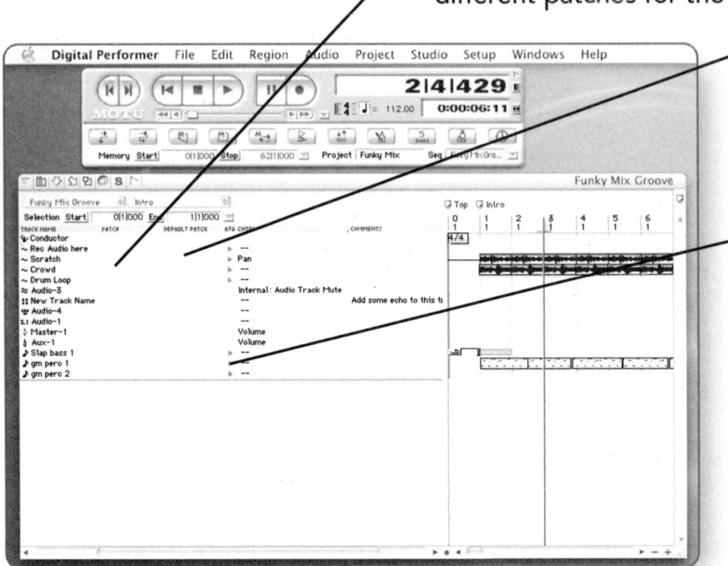

- **Controllers.** Clicking on this column will allow you to select different controllers for a track.
- **Playback and Scrub Wiper.** This green line indicates your position in the sequence.
- **MIDI data.** MIDI information is represented by boxes with small lines in them.

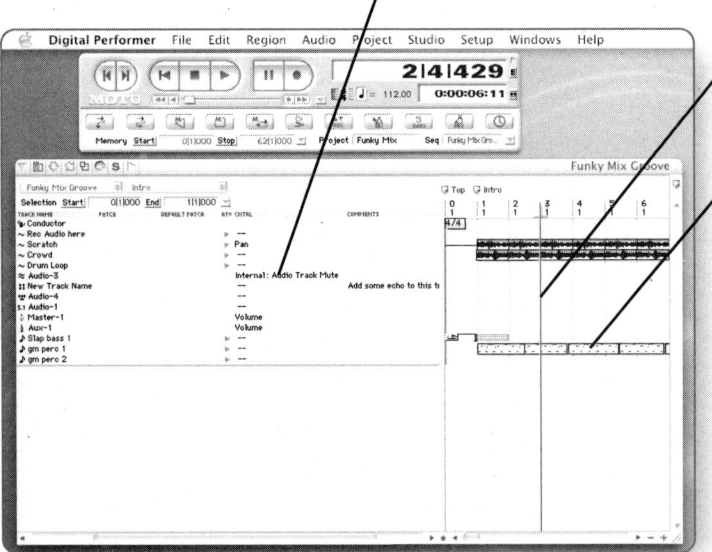

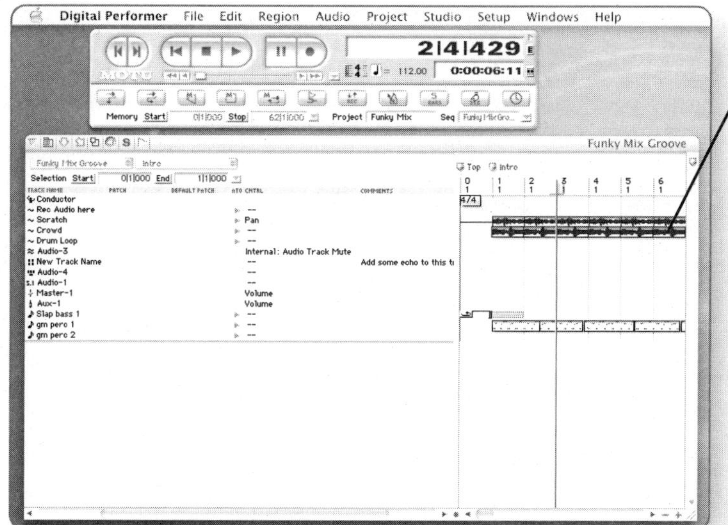

- **Audio data.** Audio data appears as a wavelength within a box.

Showing and Hiding Columns

As you can see, there is a long list of different columns in the Tracks window offering you a variety of information on your tracks. Depending on how you work, you might need some of this information all of the time and rarely use the rest. Digital Performer gives you the ability to hide those columns that you use infrequently.

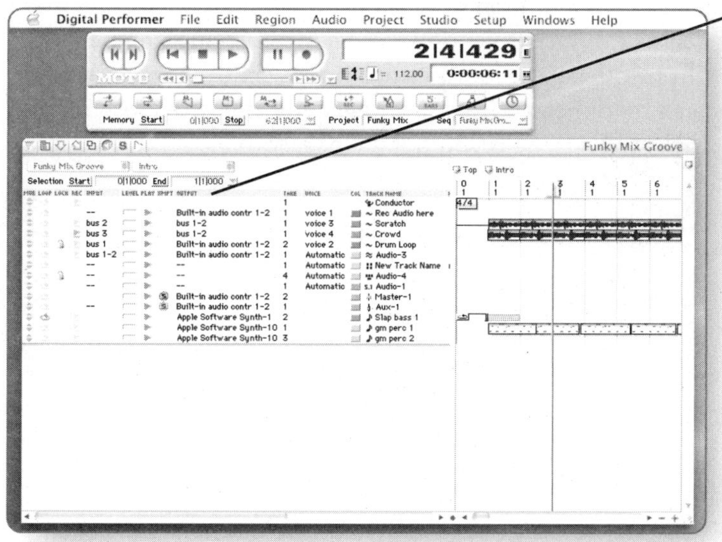

1. **Double-click** on any **column title**. A dialog box will open.

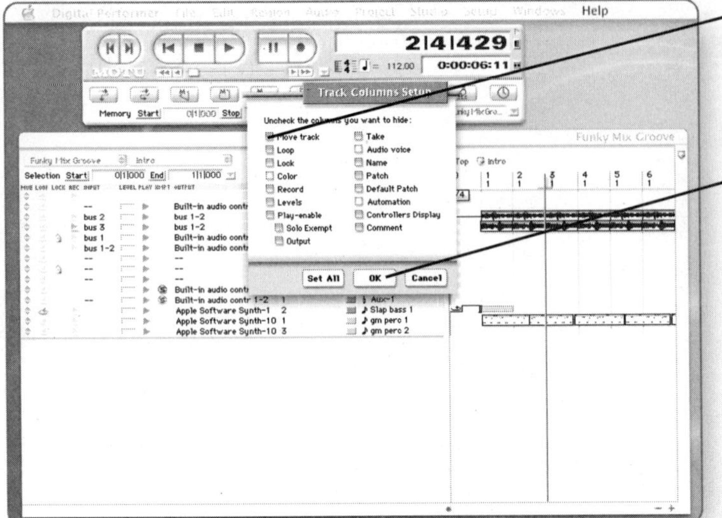

2. **Click** on a **box** to select or deselect a column to view. The boxes that are highlighted are selected.

3. **Click** on **OK**. The settings that you have applied will take effect.

Navigating the Tracks Window

Because of the amount of data that can be contained in the Tracks window, there are various tools provided in Digital Performer to help you navigate the window.

The Zoom Tools

The visual representation of different tracks can be seen in the right half of the Tracks window. Depending on the number of different tracks you have, the small boxes that represent your music can be difficult to see. Digital Performer provides you with Zoom tools to help you get a closer look.

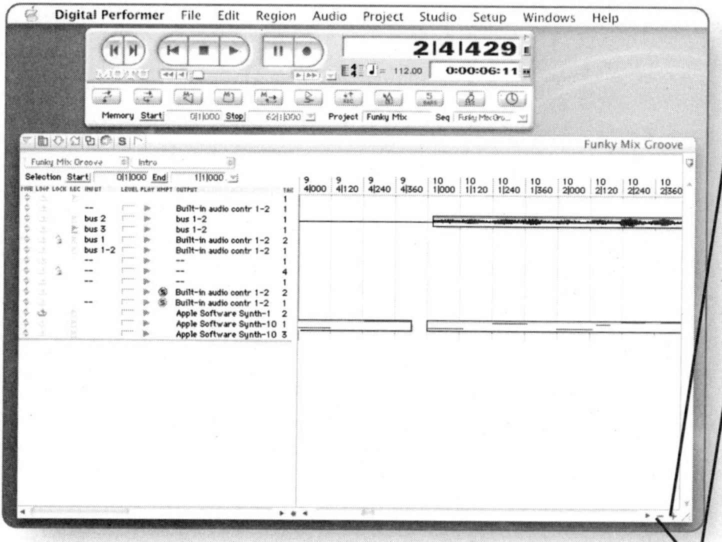

1. **Click** on the **Zoom In button**. A smaller range of time will be displayed in the Tracks window, allowing you a closer look.

2. **Repeat step 1** until the desired zoom level is achieved.

3. **Click** on the **Zoom Out button**. This will show a larger range of time in the Tracks window.

4. **Repeat step 3** until the desired zoom level is achieved.

Scrolling

Depending on the number of tracks and the length of your sequences, there is a good chance that you will not be able to see all of the data in the window. Scrolling allows you to pan to different areas.

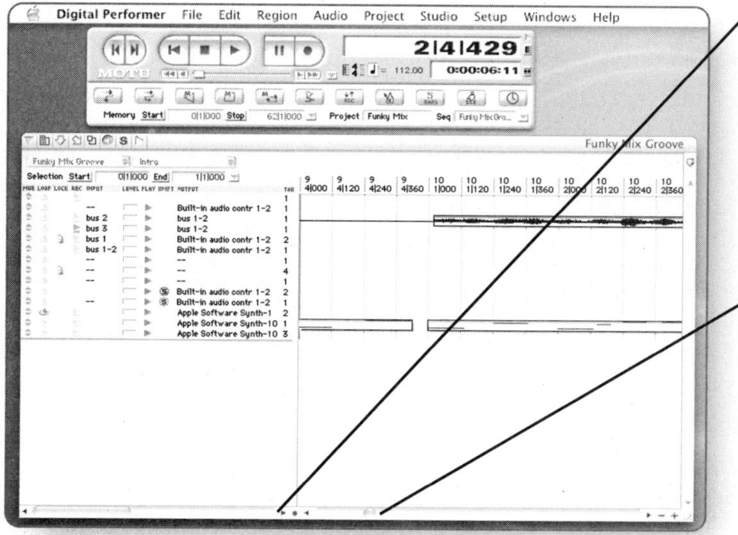

1a. **Click** on a **scroll arrow**. The window will scroll in that direction. If you click and hold the scroll arrow, the window will pan until you release the mouse button.

OR

1b. **Click** and **drag** along the **scroll bar** to pan the window until you've reached the desired location.

The Window Divider

You can see that the Tracks window is comprised of two distinct areas: the left half, which provides track information, and the right half, which shows a visual representation of the tracks. Depending on which half you are working with, you might want to make it larger or smaller to facilitate the task you are trying to complete. The Window Divider allows you to change the relative size of the sections.

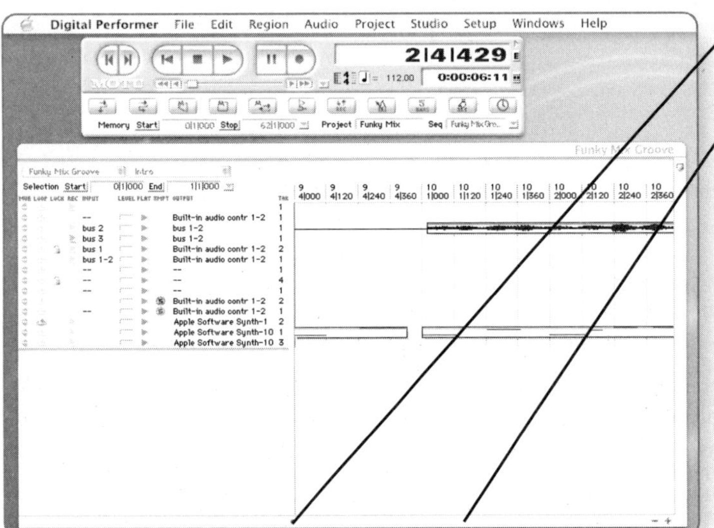

1. **Position** the **mouse pointer** over the Window Divider.
2. **Click** and **drag** to the **left** or **right**. Dragging to the left will shorten the information section and lengthen the visual representation window; dragging to the right will do the opposite. A dotted outline previewing where the split will be will appear as you drag.

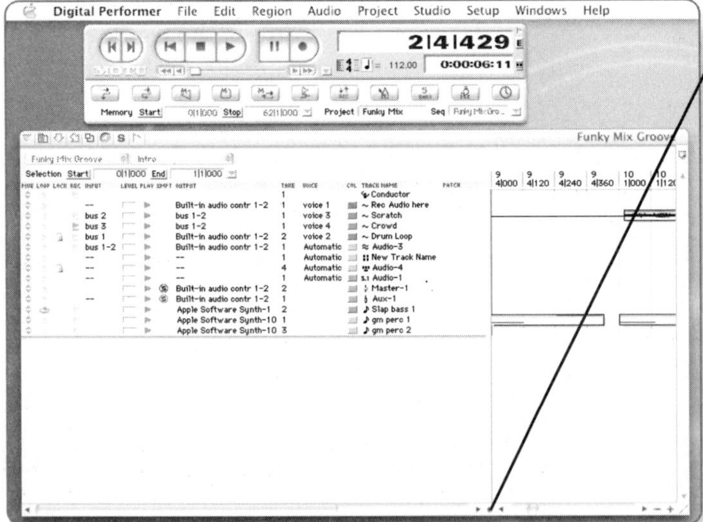

3. **Release** the **mouse button**. The sections will be resized.

Markers

If you are trying to get back to a specific spot in a sequence, it can be difficult if you have not written down its location. Rather than using trial and error by playing certain parts of the sequence, you can use markers. If you've ever bookmarked or created a Favorite for an Internet page, you'll understand how markers work. You specify a location in your sequence by placing a marker. You can then quickly get back to that location at any time.

Adding and Moving Markers

You can add a marker by clicking and dragging the marker to the desired location or you can specify an exact location using the Markers window. The Markers window will be discussed later in this chapter.

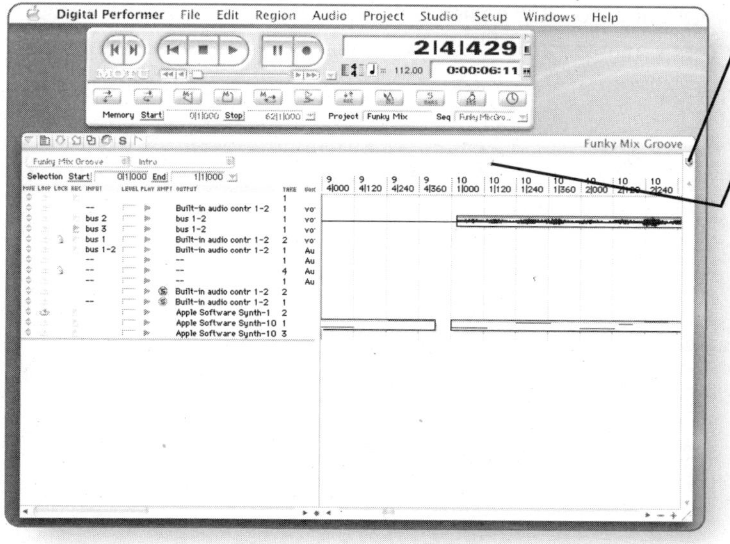

1. **Position** the **cursor** over the Marker icon in the Tracks window.

2. **Click** and **drag** a **marker** to the desired location. The marker has to be positioned above the Time Ruler.

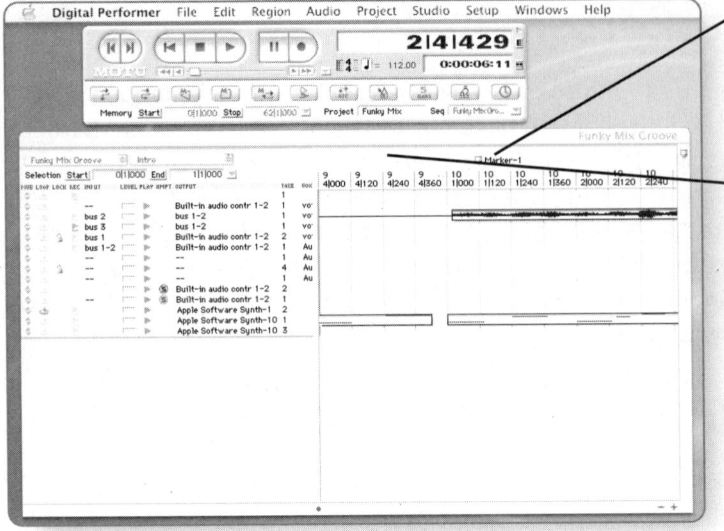

3. Release the **mouse button**. An icon representing the marker will appear, along with the name of the marker.

4. Click and **drag** the **marker** to a new location to move the marker.

Naming Markers

Markers become a lot easier to keep track of and access if you give them names rather than just accepting the default names they are given.

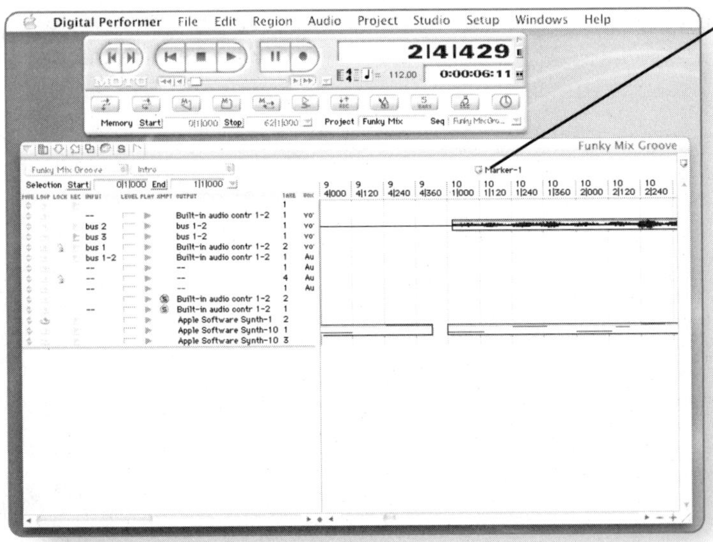

1. Press and **hold** the **Option key** and **click** on the **marker** that you would like to name. The existing name of the marker will appear highlighted in a box.

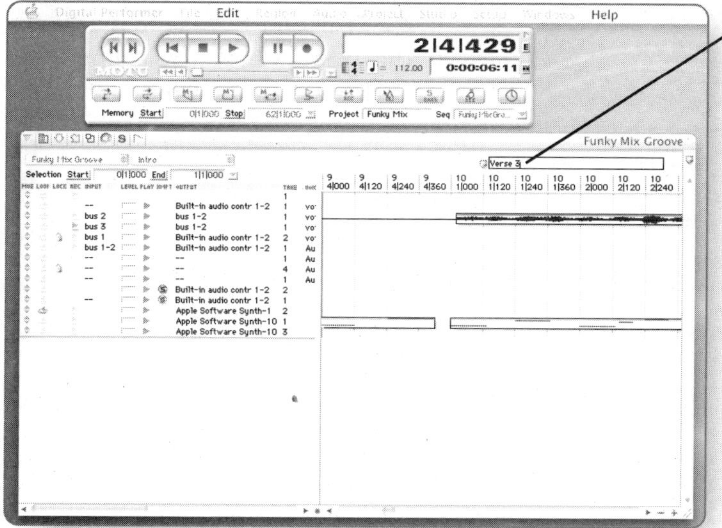

2. Type a **new name** for the marker. It's best to give it a descriptive name so that it is easy to access.

3. Press Return. The marker will now have a new name.

Accessing Markers

Within the Tracks window, there is a pop-up menu that will allow you to jump to the different locations of your markers.

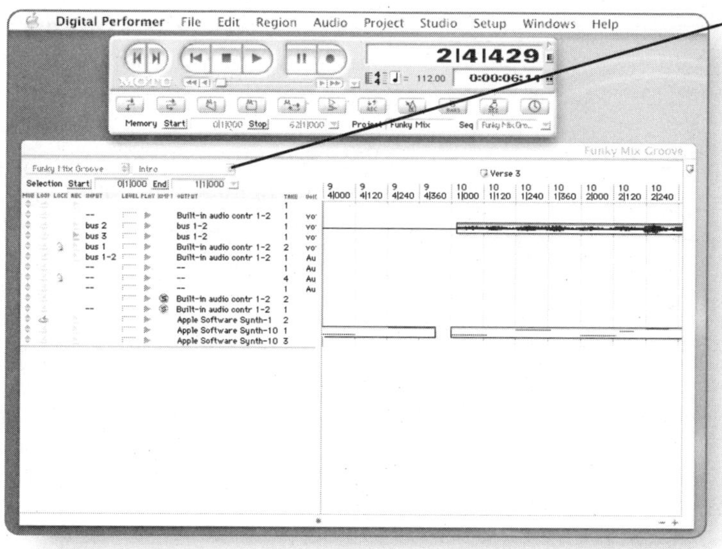

1. Click on the **up-and-down arrows** to display a list of your markers.

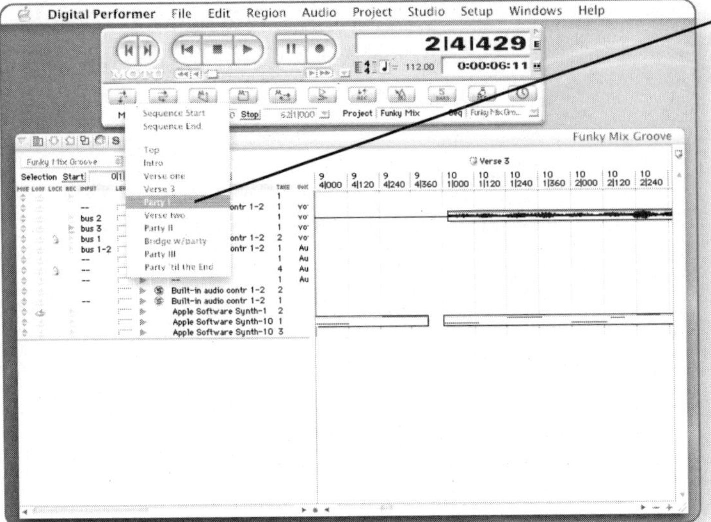

2. Click on the desired **marker**. The Tracks window will jump to the location of that marker.

The Markers Window

Everything that you've done so far visually can also be done manually by entering data into the Markers window.

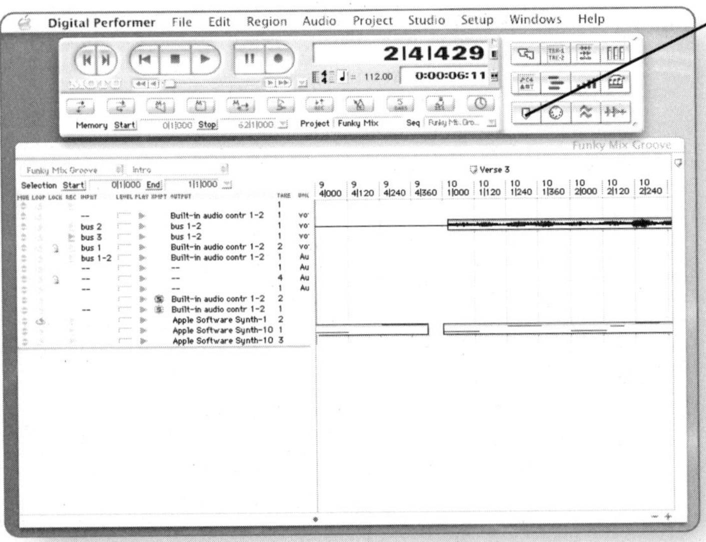

1. Click on the **Markers button** in the Control Panel. The Markers window will open.

At this point, you can do everything manually by entering the appropriate data.

7

Recording

Digital Performer is a fabulous tool for editing both your audio and MIDI tracks. Before you can apply all the wonderful effects it has to offer, you must first record something to edit. Digital Performer provides you with a complete recording environment to record all types of audio and MIDI tracks. In this chapter, you will learn how to:

- Record MIDI
- Record audio
- Create takes
- Use Overdub Recording
- Use Step Record

Recording Tracks

Once you have your hardware set up properly, recording audio into Digital Performer is a breeze. You can choose to record your audio onto an existing track or you can create a new track.

Recording onto an Existing Track

When you create a new file in Digital Performer, by default there are already a few different empty tracks set up. You can select any of these tracks to record on; just remember that audio needs to be recorded on an audio track, and MIDI needs to be recorded on a MIDI track.

Recording MIDI Tracks

When recording MIDI tracks, you simply have to enable the track and then begin recording.

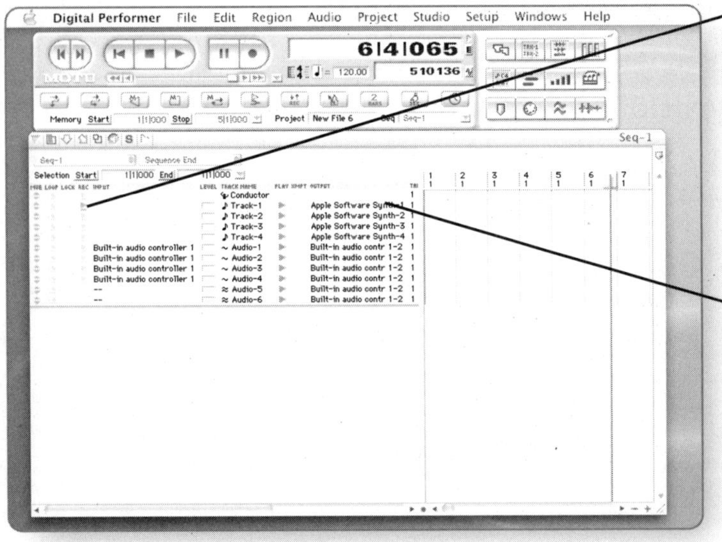

1. **Click** on the **Record button** in a MIDI track in the Tracks window. This will enable recording on that track. You'll know you are working with a MIDI track if you see a musical note icon in the track's Name column.

2. **Click** on the **output** for that track to select a MIDI channel. A list of available channels will appear.

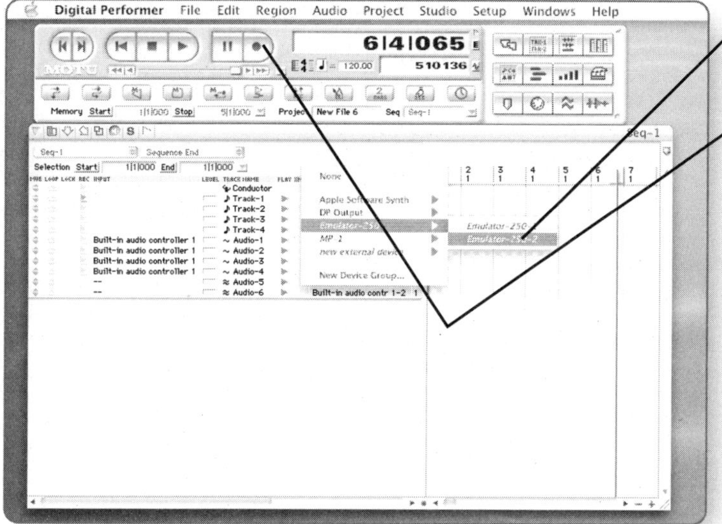

3. Click on the desired **channel**. It will be selected.

4. Click on the **Record button**. The Record and Play buttons will illuminate to indicate that you are recording. Begin playing your MIDI instrument. Chunks of data will appear in the Tracks window as you play.

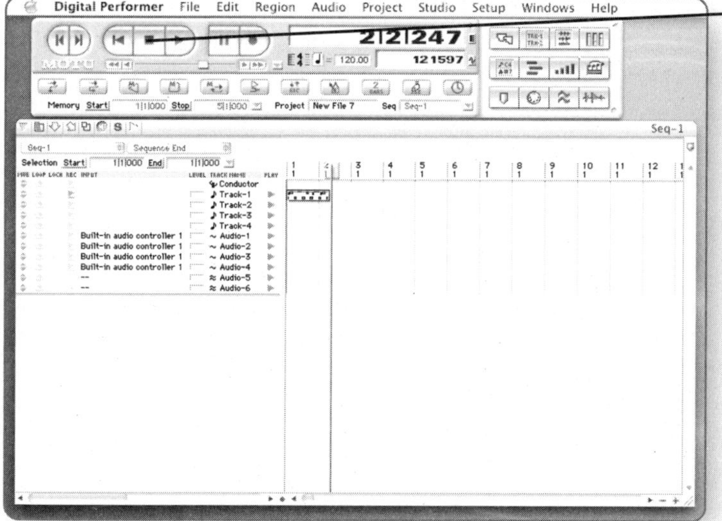

5. Click on the **Stop button**. The data from your MIDI source will be recorded.

Recording Audio Tracks

With audio you not only have to enable a track for recording, you must also choose a source for your audio input.

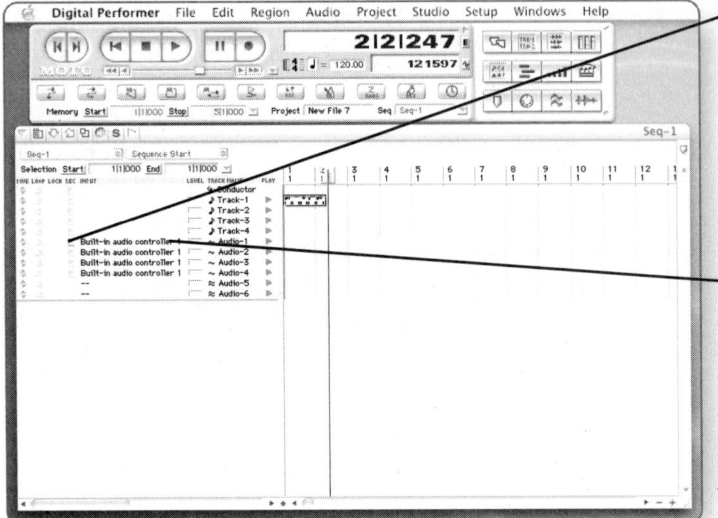

1. **Click** on the **Record button** on an audio track in the Tracks window. This will enable recording on that track. An audio track has a tilde before the name of the track in the Track Name column.

2. **Click** on the **Input box** for that track. A menu of different input options will appear.

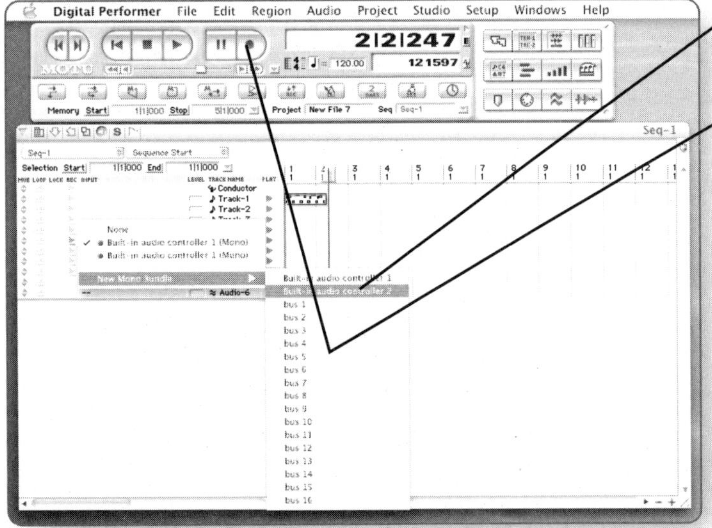

3. **Click** on the desired **input device**. It will be selected.

4. **Click** on the **Record button**. The Record and Play buttons will illuminate to indicate that you are recording.

5. **Begin playing** your **instrument** or **device**. Waveform data will appear in the Tracks window as you play.

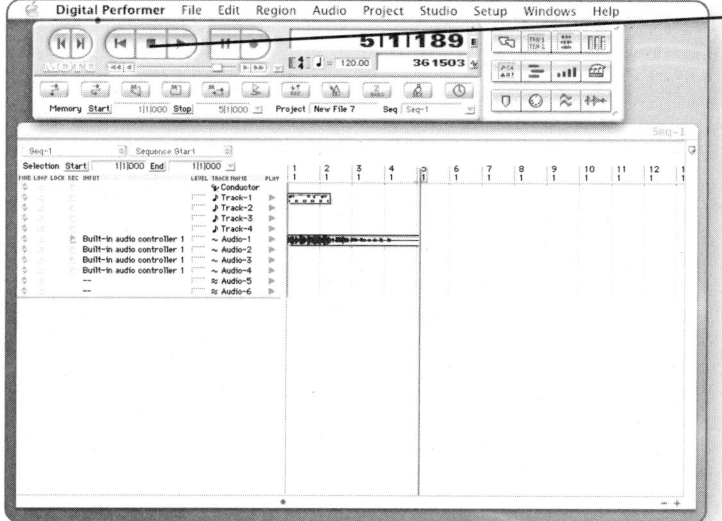

6. Click on the **Stop button**. The data from your MIDI source will be recorded.

> **NOTE**
>
> If you need to refresh your memory on how to set up automatic recording, see the "Auto Record" section in Chapter 5, "The Control Panel."

Creating New Tracks

Once you have used all of the existing tracks, you can create your own so that you can continue recording.

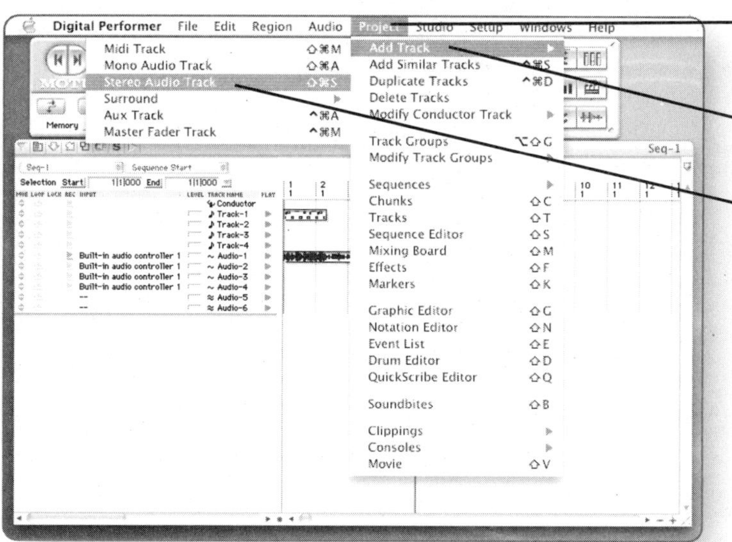

1. Click on **Project**. A menu of different commands will appear.

2. Click on **Add Track**. A submenu will appear.

3. Click the desired **track type**. The track will be added to the Tracks window and you can continue recording and editing.

Naming Tracks

It's a good idea to name your tracks so that you can easily keep "track" of them.

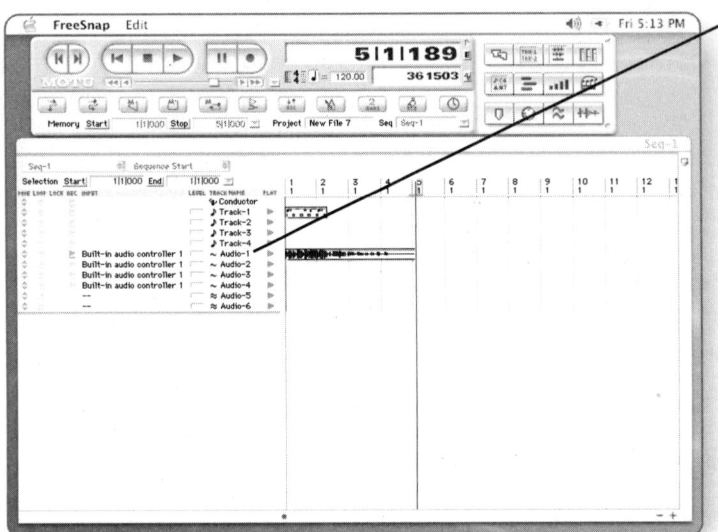

1. **Press** and **hold** the **Option key** and **click** on the **track name**. The name will appear highlighted in a box.

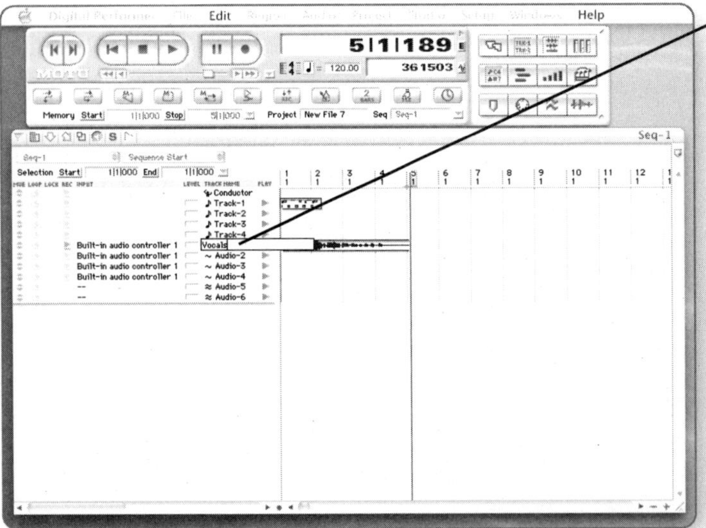

2. **Type** a **name** for the track. It will appear as you type.
3. **Press Enter**. The track will be renamed.

Recording Additional Takes

Nobody is perfect, and with Digital Performer, you don't have to be. Not only can you edit your tracks after they've been recorded, but you can also record multiple takes of the same track and then decide later which one you would like to use.

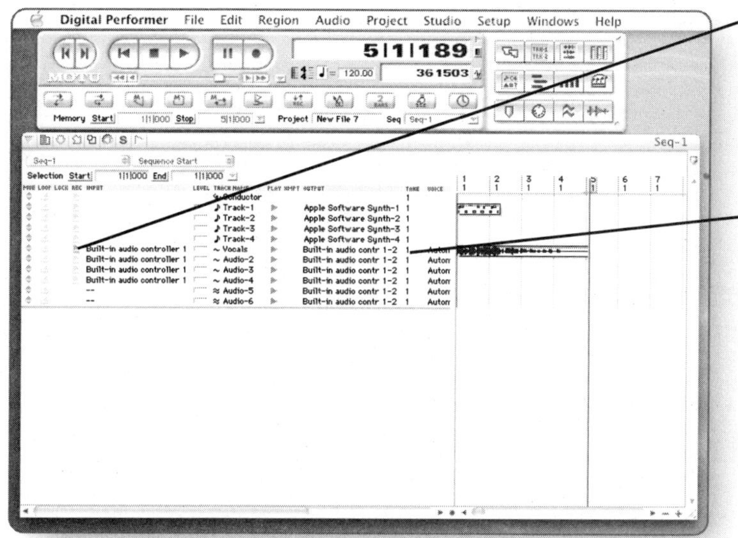

1. **Click** on the **Record button** in the Tracks window to enable recording on the desired track. The button will appear darker to indicate that it is selected.
2. **Click** on the **box** in the Take column. A menu will appear.

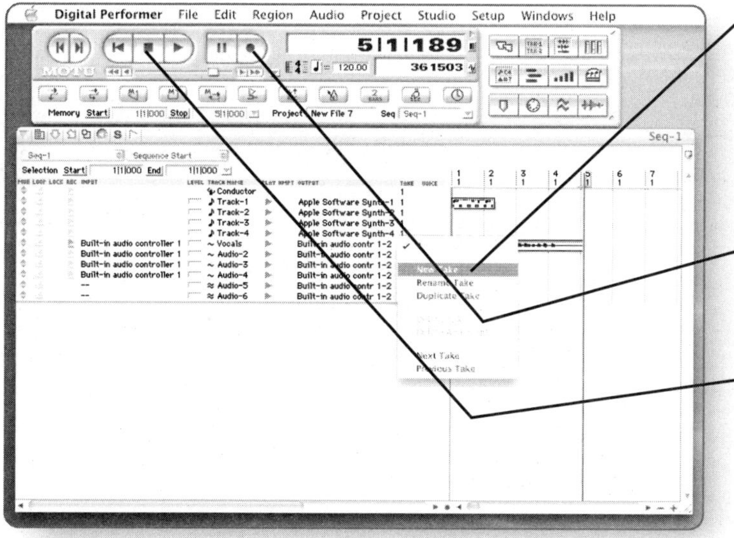

3. **Click** on **New Take**. The track will now appear empty. Even though it appears empty, the original information on the track is not gone; you will be able to access it as a different take.
4. **Click** on the **Record button** in the Control Panel to begin recording your take.
5. **Click** on the **Stop button** to end the recording.
6. **Repeat steps 2 to 5** to record additional takes.

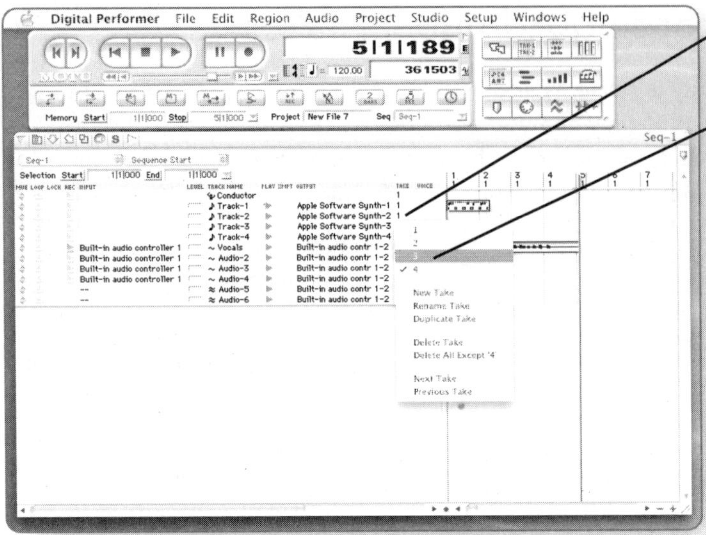

7. **Click** on the **box** in the Take column. A menu will appear.

8. **Click** the desired **take** for editing. The take you select will appear in the Tracks window.

Overdub Recording

You can add additional audio to your tracks by using the Overdub Record feature. Typically, when you record over a track, the existing audio or data on the track is deleted. With the Overdub Recording feature, you can add to a track and the incoming recording will merge with the existing data. You can overdub the same track as many times as you like; the information will just continue to build on that track. Overdub is great for building harmony on a track.

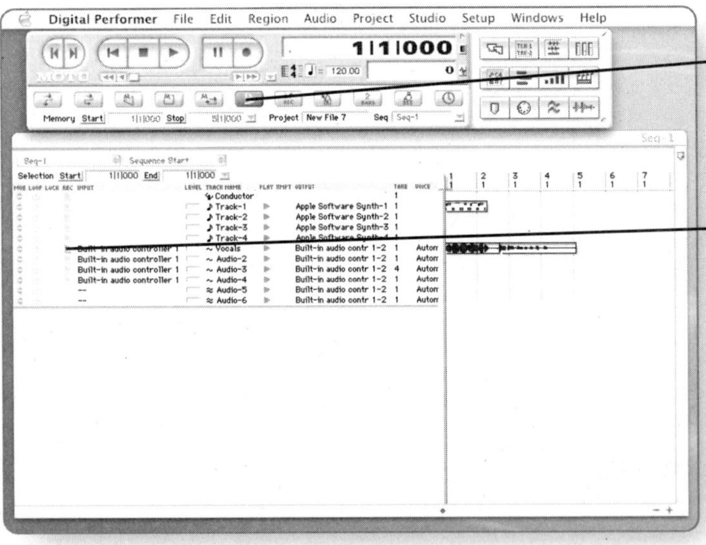

1. **Click** on the **Overdub Record button**. It will appear darker to indicate that it is turned on.

2. **Click** on the **Record button** in the Tracks window to enable recording on the desired track.

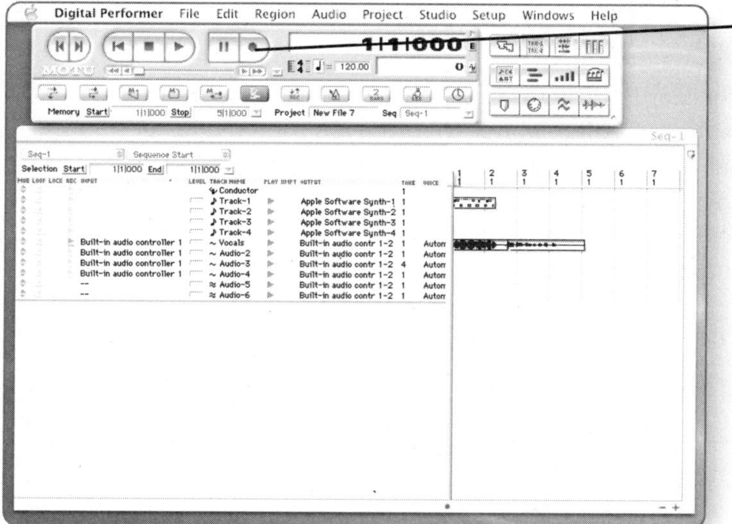

3. **Click** on the **Record button**. The new audio being recorded will merge with the existing track.

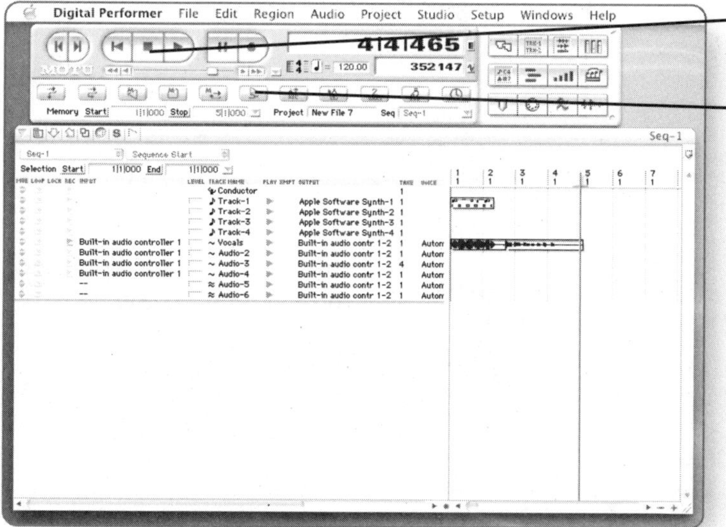

4. **Click** on the **Stop button** to end the recording.

5. **Click** on the **Overdub button** to turn off the feature.

Auto Recording

In Chapter 5, "The Control Panel," we examined one method for auto recording. In this chapter, you'll learn a faster, more visual way to auto record. Rather than having to press the Record button, you can use the Auto Record feature to set specific punch times to start and stop recording within a sequence.

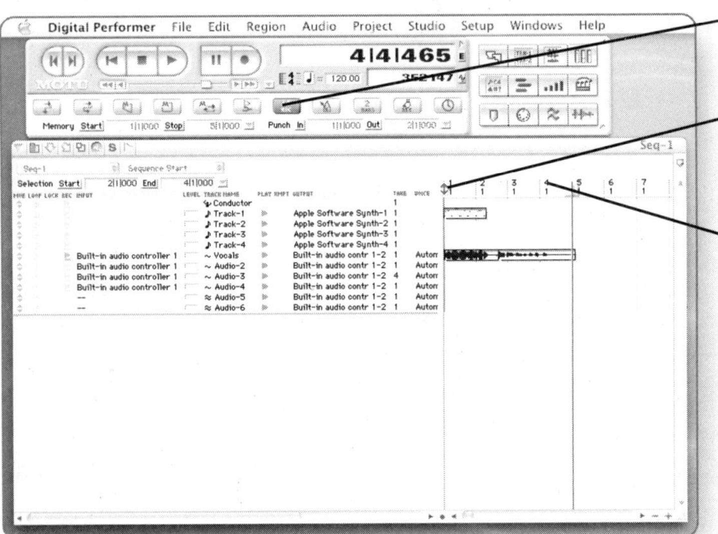

1. **Click** on the **Auto Record button** in the Control Panel.
2. **Position** your **mouse pointer** over the up part of the red arrow in the Tracks window.
3. **Click** and **drag** this **arrow** to a new location. This will represent your punch-out location.

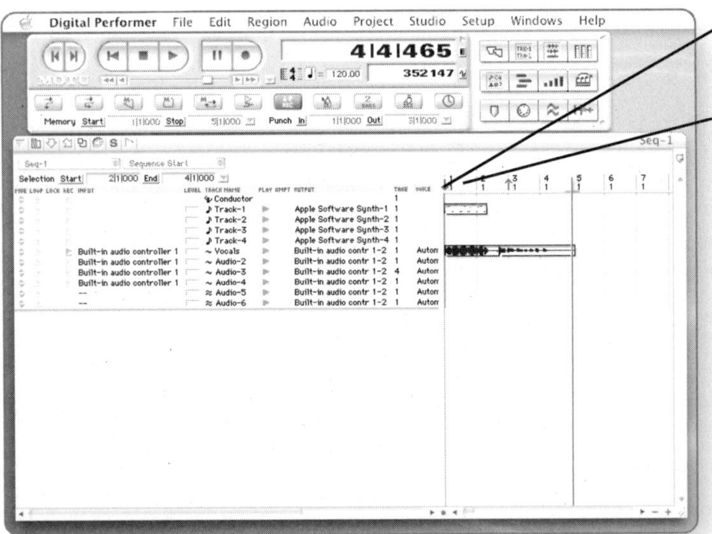

4. **Position** your **mouse pointer** over the red down arrow.
5. **Click** and **drag it** to a new location. This will represent the punch-in location.

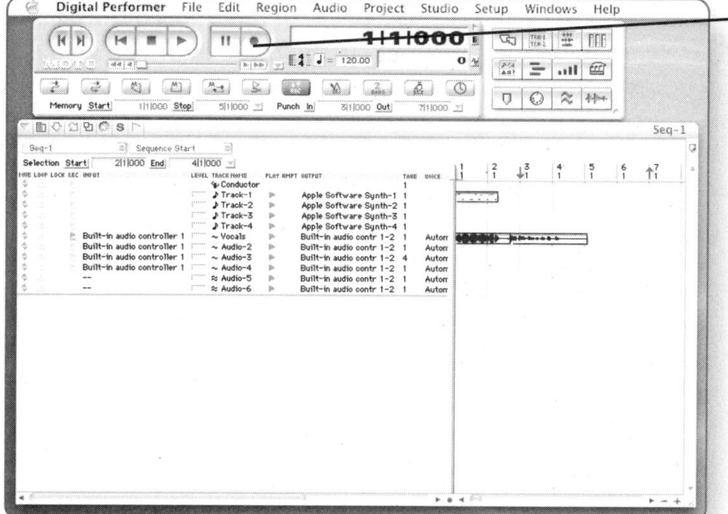

6. Click on the **Record button**. The recording will only take place between the punch-in and punch-out times.

MultiRecord

So, you manage to get the whole band together and you want to record some tracks. In Digital Performer's default state, each instrument would have to be recorded separately because you can only record one track at a time. Using MultiRecord, you can record multiple tracks at the same time.

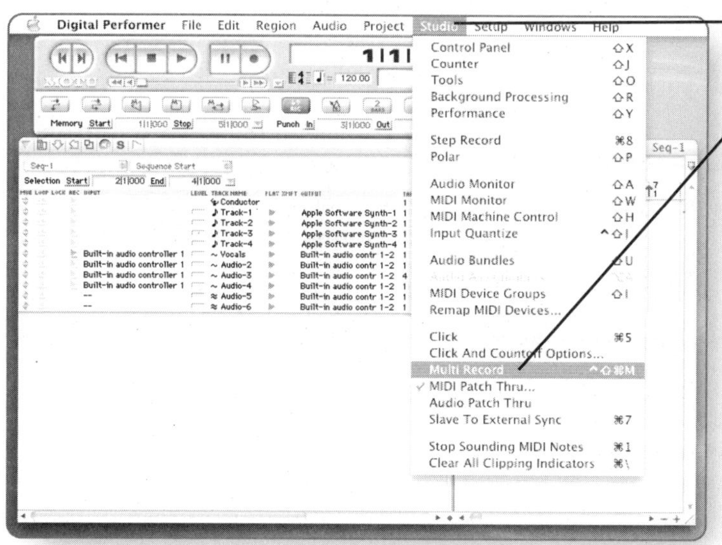

1. Click on **Studio**. The Studio menu will appear.

2. Click on **MultiRecord**. You will now be in MultiRecord mode, meaning that you can record more than one track at a time.

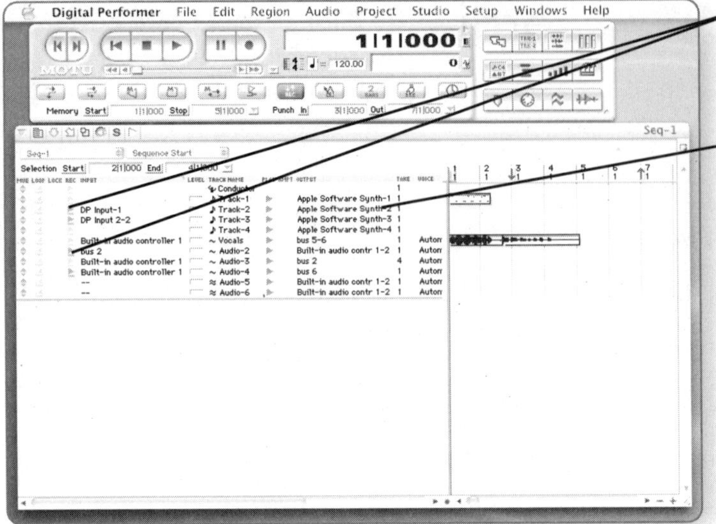

3. Click on the **Record buttons** beside the tracks that you would like to record.

4. Click on the **box** under Input for the desired track. A menu of different input sources will appear.

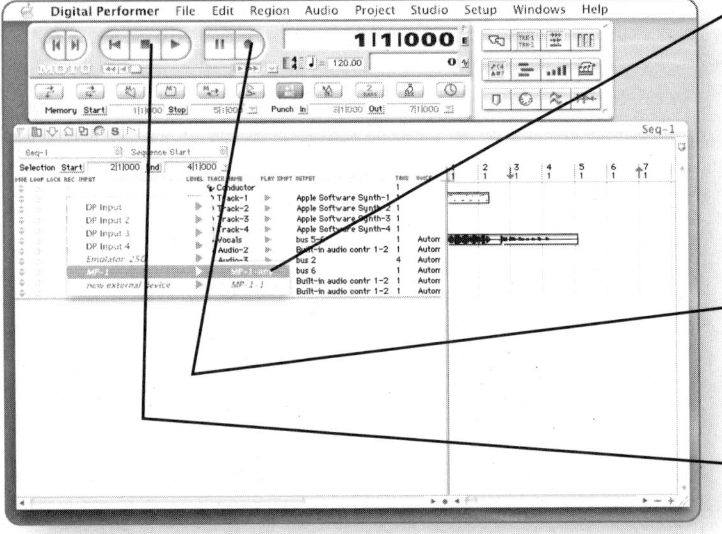

5. Click on the desired **input source**. This is the source of the instrument you want to record on that track.

6. Repeat steps 4 and 5 for all of the other tracks you are recording on.

7. Click on the **Record button**. The recording will start and you can begin playing the instruments on those tracks.

8. Click on the **Stop button** to end the recording. You will now have recorded multiple tracks at the same time.

Step Recording

By using the Step Record feature in Digital Performer, you can bypass having to record in real time. It allows you to record MIDI tracks note by note, and you can set the pitch and duration for each recorded note. This feature is particularly good for pieces that are just too fast or difficult to play.

1. **Click** on the **Record button** in the Tracks window for the track you would like to record on.

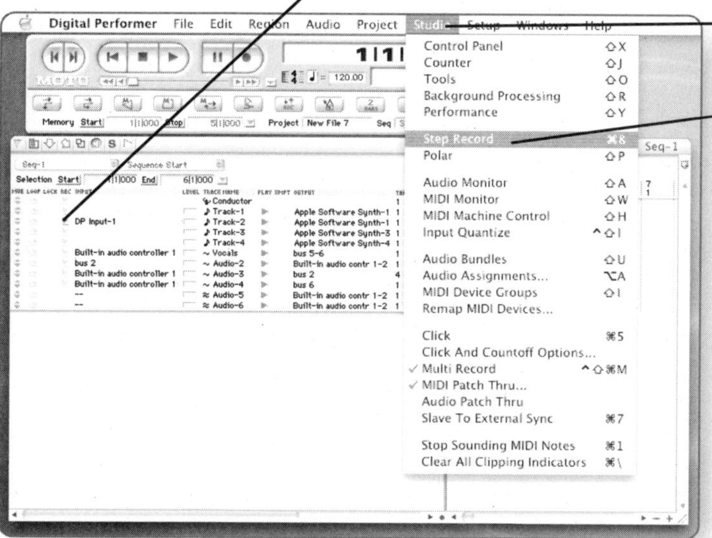

2. **Click** on **Studio**. The Studio menu will appear.

3. **Click** on **Step Record**. The Step Record dialog box will open.

> **TIP**
>
> The keyboard shortcut to open the Step Record dialog box is Command + 8.

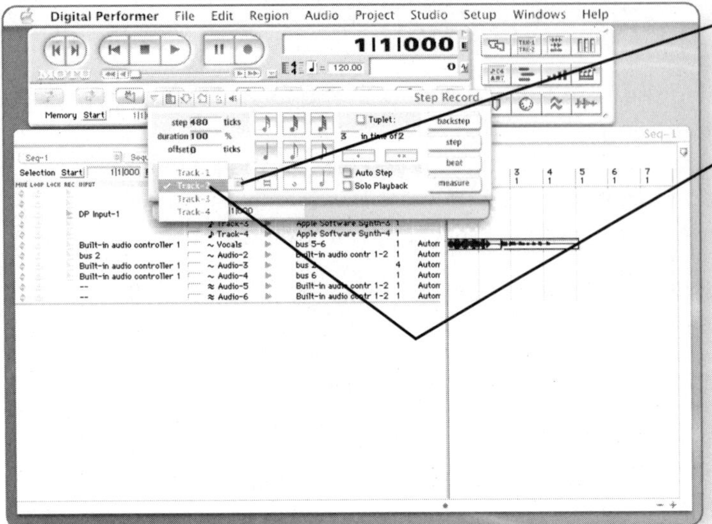

4. Click on the **double arrow** under Recording on. A menu of tracks will appear.

5. Click on the **track** that you would like to record on.

6. Click on the desired **note duration**. It will be highlighted once selected. The choices are as follows:

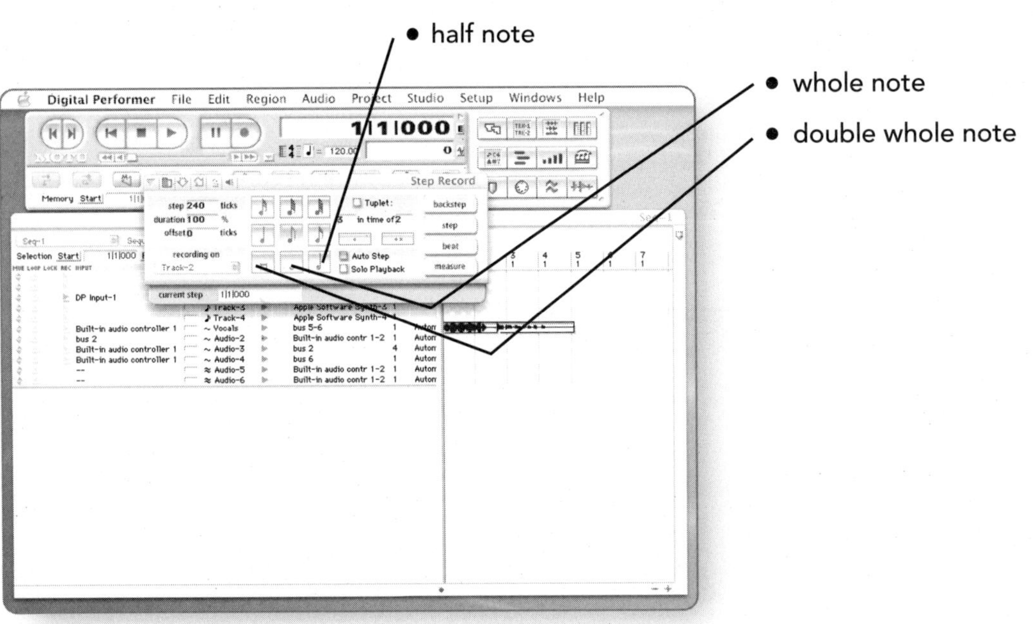

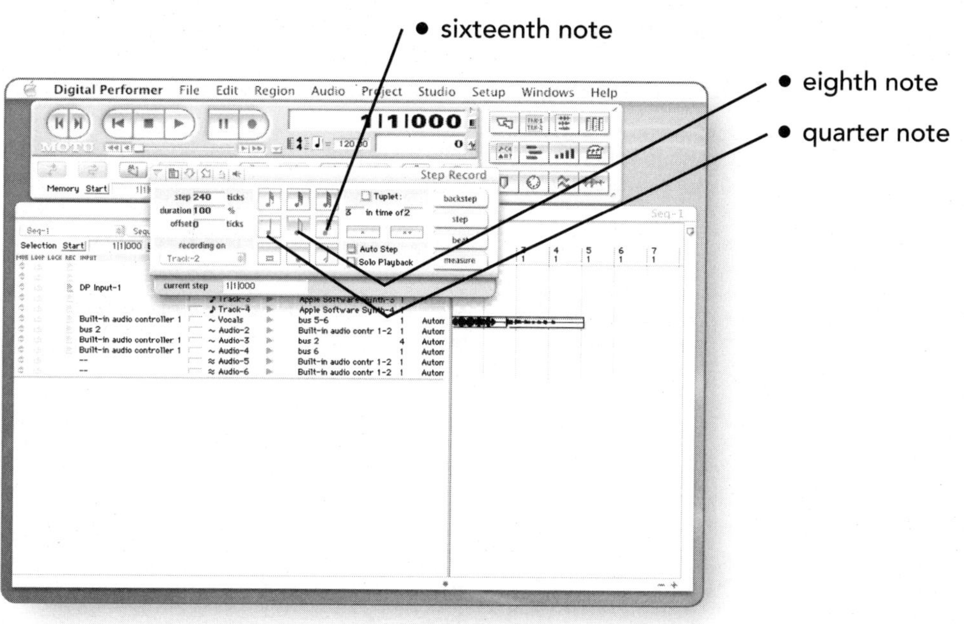

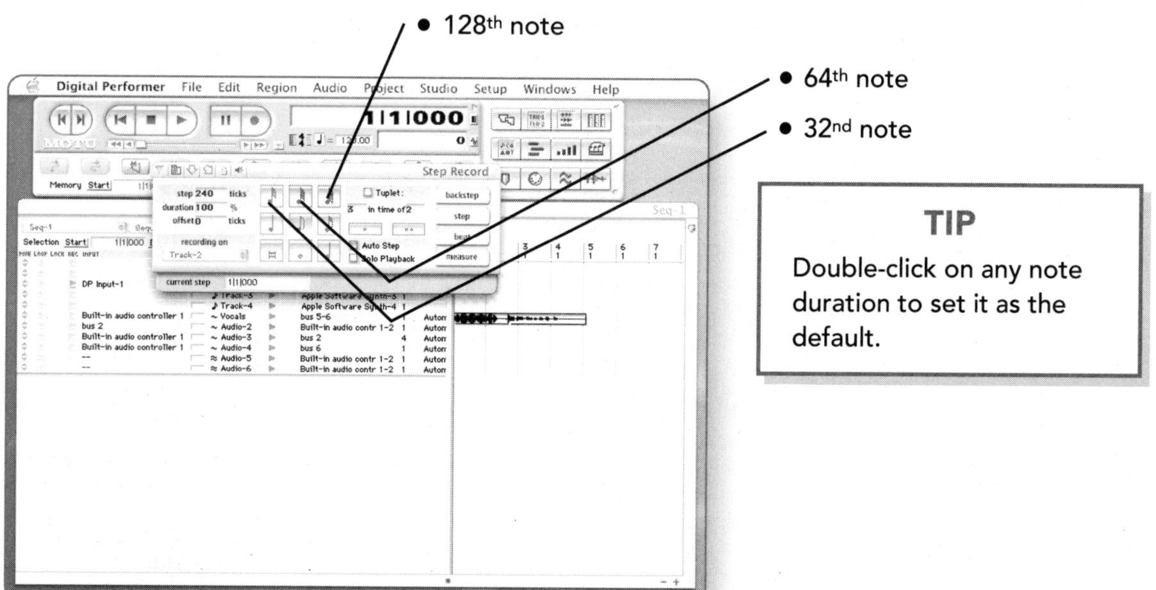

TIP

Double-click on any note duration to set it as the default.

7. **Play** a **note** on the instrument. It will be recorded.

8. **Repeat steps 5 and 6** until you have finished recording.

9. **Click** on the **Step button** to insert a rest the length of the note duration selected.

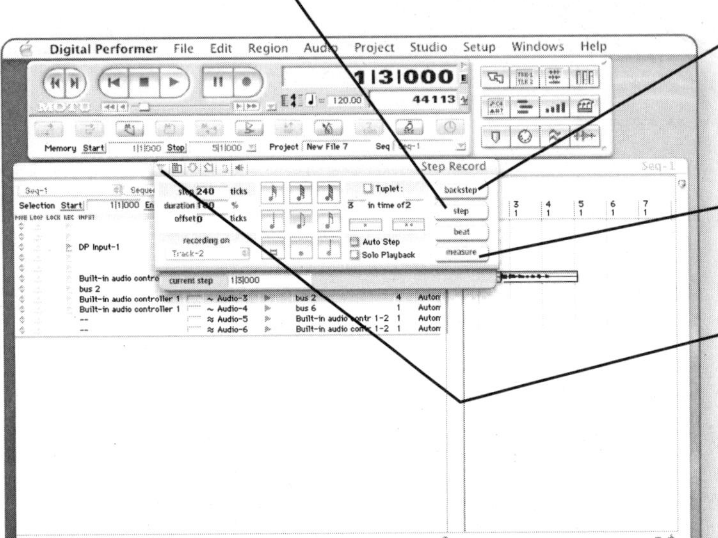

10. **Click** on the **Backstep button** to move back one duration. This will delete the previous data.

11. **Click** on the **Measure button** to jump to the beginning of the next measure.

12. **Click** on the **down arrow** to close the window once you have finished recording.

Advanced Step Record Settings

You can fully control note duration and offset for the Step Record feature by accessing several dialog boxes from its mini menu.

Note Duration

If you have a MIDI controller, you can take advantage of the advanced settings for note duration. Rather than having to use the note durations provided in the Step Record dialog box, you can configure them to any length using the Note Duration dialog box.

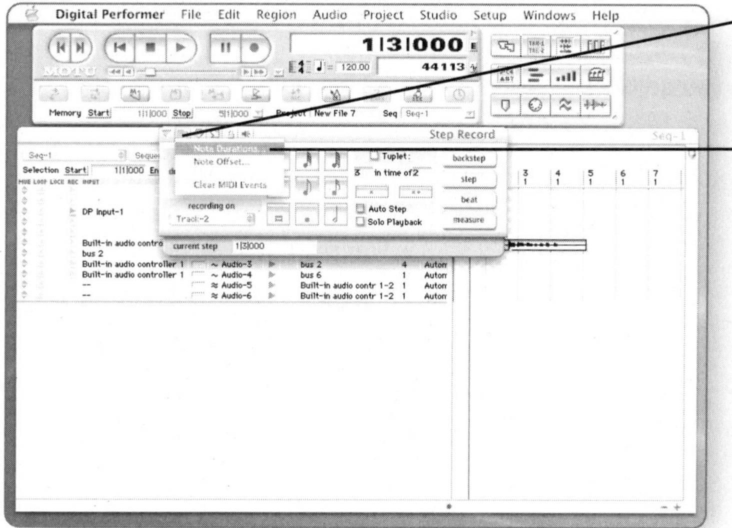

1. **Click** on the **Mini Menu button**. A menu of commands will appear.

2. **Click** on **Note Durations**. The Note Durations dialog box will appear.

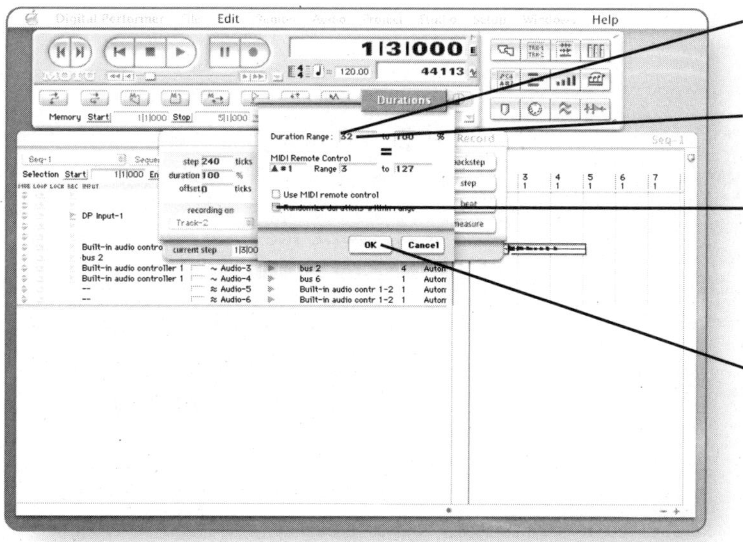

3. **Double-click** in the desired **box**. It will be highlighted.

4. **Type** the **new number**. It will appear as you type.

5. **Click** on the **box** beside a desired option to select it. The box will appear highlighted once selected.

6. **Click** on **OK** to accept the changes.

Note Offset

You can adjust the setting for the Note Offset feature using the Mini Menu feature.

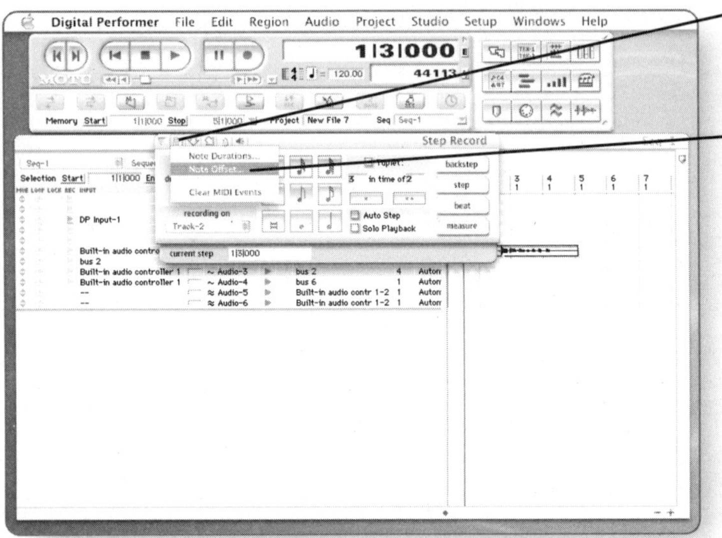

1. **Click** on the **Mini Menu button**. A menu of commands will appear.
2. **Click** on **Note Offset**. The Offset dialog box will appear.

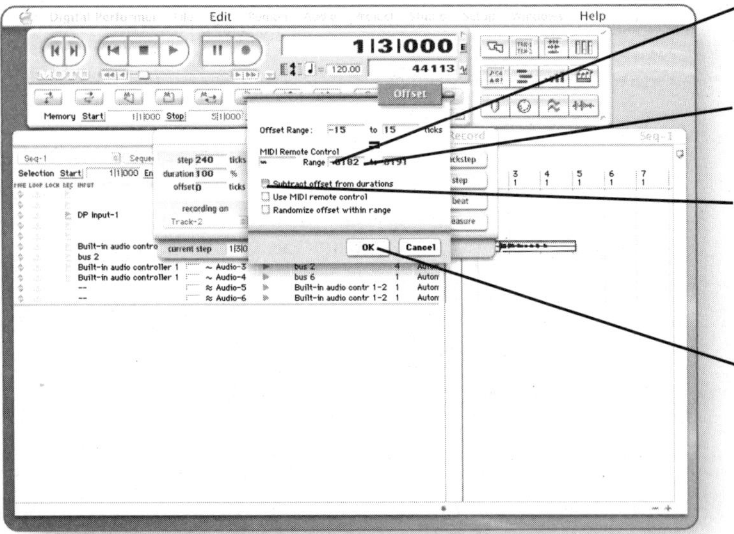

3. **Double-click** in the desired **box**. It will be highlighted.
4. **Type** the **new number**. It will appear as you type.
5. **Click** on the **box** beside a desired option to select it. The box will appear highlighted once selected.
6. **Click** on **OK** to accept the changes.

Phrases

Phrases are the small boxes in the Tracks window that represent the music you have recorded. The length of phrases and the way in which they appear can be altered using the Phrases window.

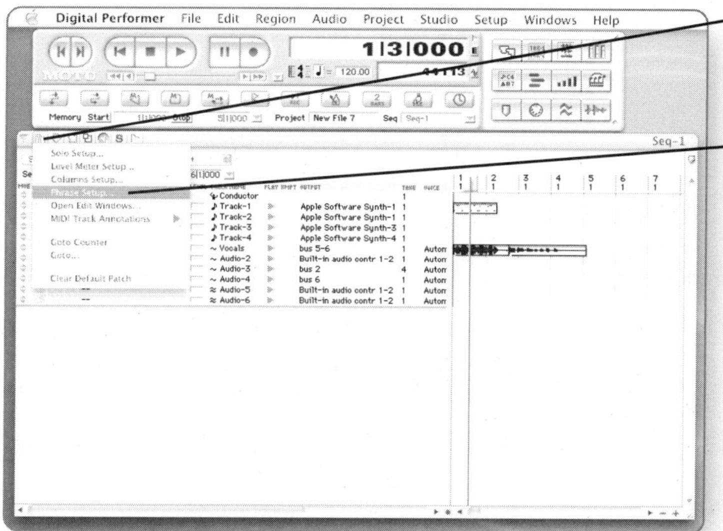

1. Click on the **Mini Menu button** in the Tracks window. A menu of commands will appear.

2. Click on **Phrase Setup**. A dialog box will appear which will allow you to change the settings for phrases.

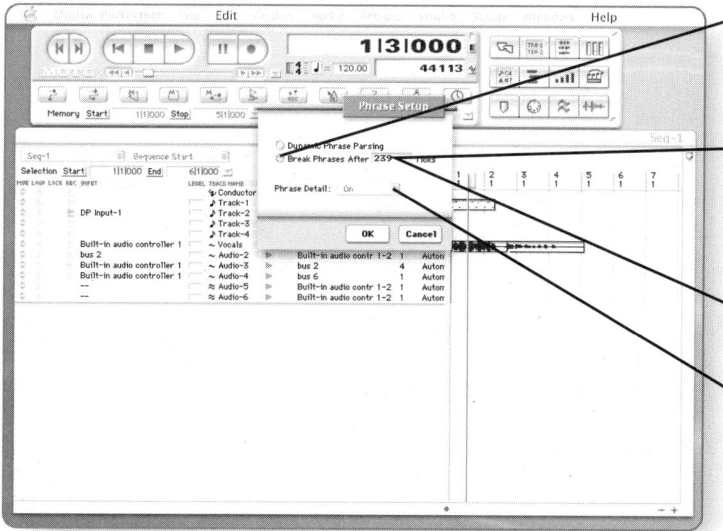

3. Click on the **circle** beside the desired option. The circle will appear highlighted.

4. Double-click in the **Break Phrases After [select] Ticks box** if you want to change the setting.

5. Type a new **number**. It will appear as you type.

6. Click on the **up-and-down arrows** beside Phrase detail to change the detail settings.

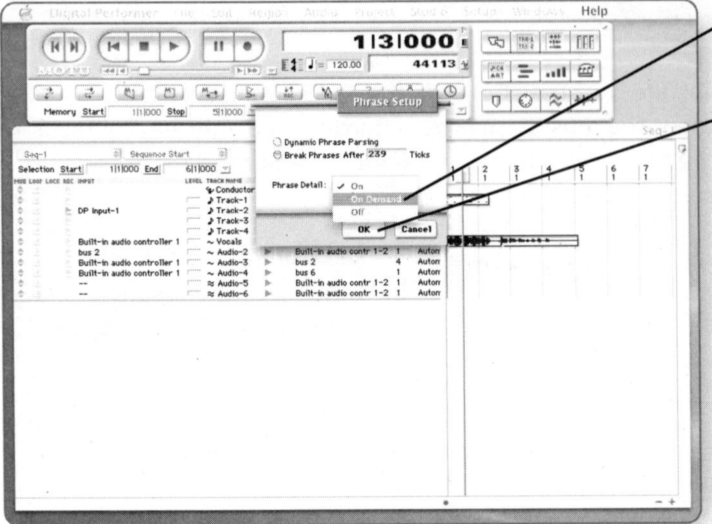

7. Click on the desired **setting**. The setting will be selected.

8. Click on **OK**. The settings you have altered will take effect.

8

Basic Editing

Digital Performer gives you total control over editing tracks. There is a vast range of adjustments, effects, and filters that you can apply to your audio. Before you get to the more advanced editing, it's a good idea to get a grip on the basics. In this chapter, you will learn how to:

- Create selections
- Move selections
- Create loops
- Manage sequences

Selections

When you begin editing, you must first select what part of the sequence you want to edit. Whether you want to edit part of a track, an entire track, multiple tracks, or an entire sequence, you must let Digital Performer know by making the appropriate selection. There are several methods for selecting tracks.

Selecting Phrases

Phrases are the small boxes of data that appear in the Tracks window. Individual phrases can be selected simply by clicking on them.

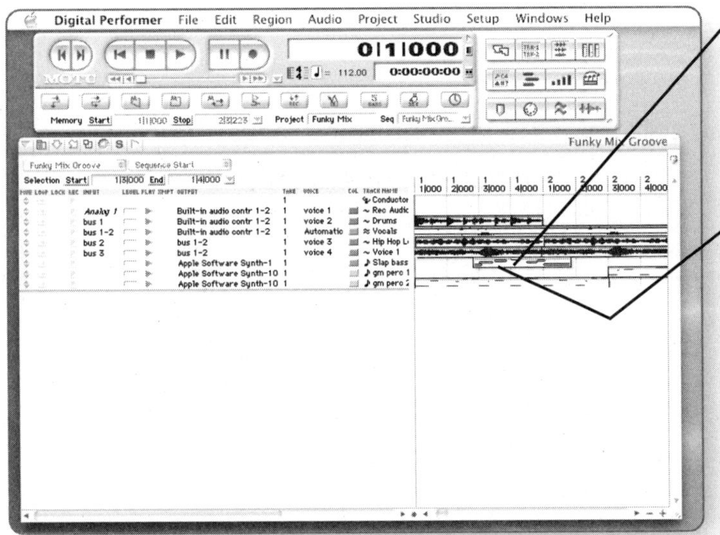

1. **Position** your **mouse pointer** over the blank area within a phrase. If the cursor turns into a crosshair, it means that you are not over a blank area.
2. **Click once**. The area will be highlighted with a yellow outline around the entire box to indicate that it is selected.

Creating Selection Bounds

When you want to select multiple phrases, you can create a selection bound. Once you have created selection bounds, every phrase in that bound will be selected whenever you click on a track. There are many ways to create selection bounds, including clicking and dragging in the Tracks window or specifying exact time coordinates.

Creating Selection Bounds Visually

You can create selection bounds visually by clicking and dragging across an area in the Tracks window. This way, you don't have to select an entire phrase; you can select all or parts of phrases on multiple tracks.

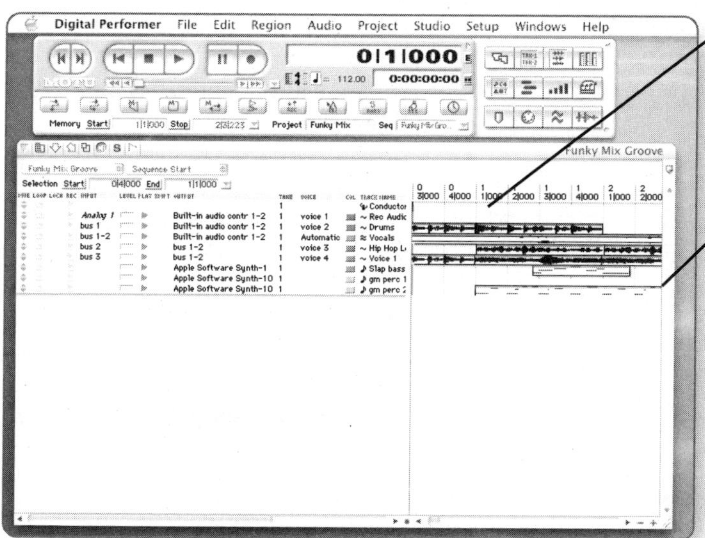

1. **Position** your **mouse pointer** at the upper-left point of where you would like your selection bound to begin. Your mouse pointer will become a crosshair.
2. **Click** and **drag diagonally to the right**. As you drag, a blue shadow defining your selection bounds will appear.

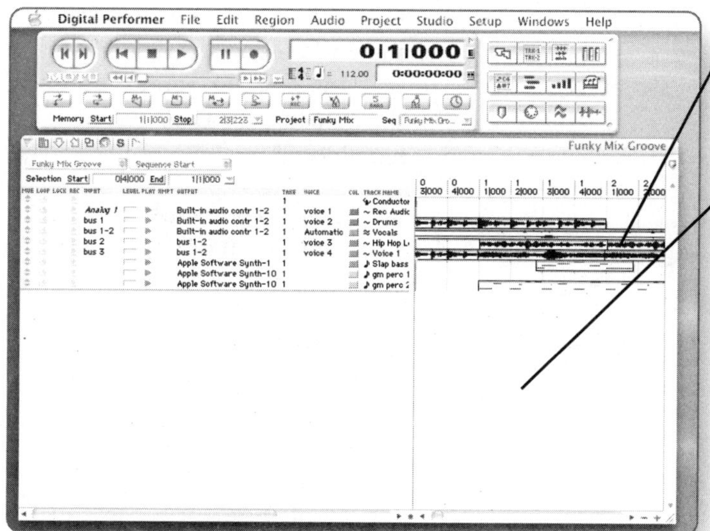

3. **Release** the **mouse button**. The selection bounds will be created and everything within the bounds will be selected.
4. **Click** in any **blank area** of the Tracks window to deselect the phrases.

> **NOTE**
>
> When you deselect phrases, it's important to note that the selection bounds remain in place until you create new selection bounds.

Creating Exact Selection Bounds

A more precise way of creating selection bounds is by specifying an exact start and stop location for the selection. This can be done from the Selection bar.

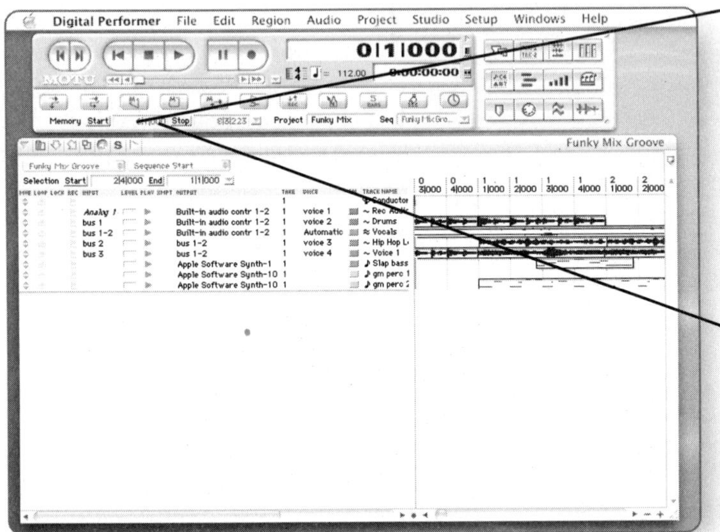

1. Click on the **first number** in the Start field of the Selection bar. The number, representing the measure location, will be highlighted.

2. Type a **new number** for the start measure. It will appear as you type.

3. Repeat steps 1 and 2 for the middle and far-right numbers in the Start field. The middle number represents beats and the far-right number represents ticks.

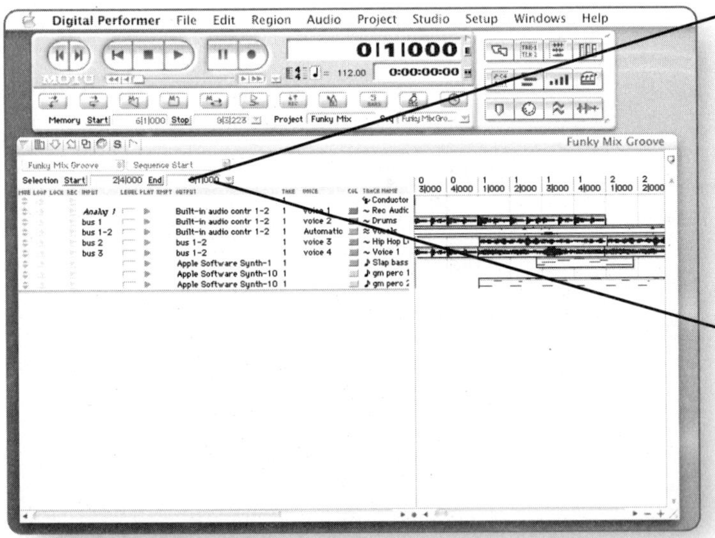

4. Click on the **first number** in the End field of the Selection bar. The number, representing the measure location, will be highlighted.

5. Type a **new number** for the End measure. It will appear as you type.

6. Repeat steps 1 and 2 for the middle and far-right numbers in the End field. The middle number represents beats and the far-right number represents ticks.

Selecting Parts of a Track

Once you have selection bounds in place, you can select the parts of a track that fall within the selection bounds simply by clicking the name of the track.

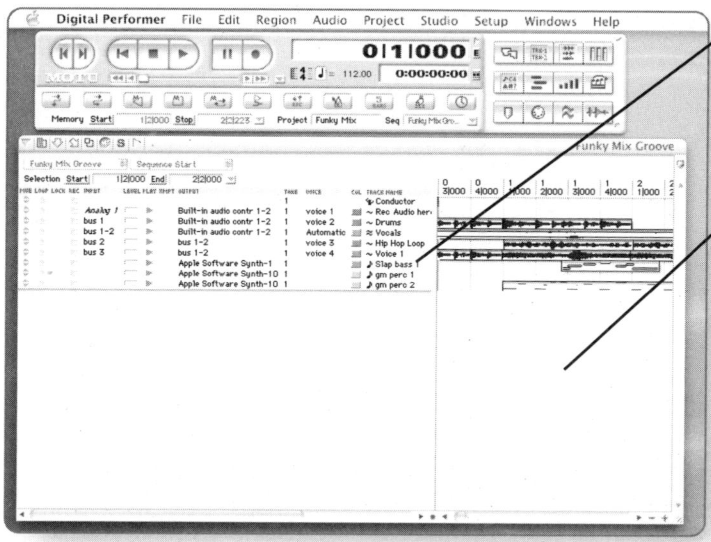

1. **Click** on the **name** of a track. All of the phrases on that track that are within the selection bounds will be highlighted to indicate that they are selected.
2. **Click** in any **blank area** of the Tracks window to deselect the phrases.

Selecting an Entire Track and All Tracks

There may be occasions where you will need to either select all of the tracks in your sequence or all of the phrases within an entire track. Rather than having to click and drag selection bounds that encompass all of the phrases, you can take advantage of the Select All feature.

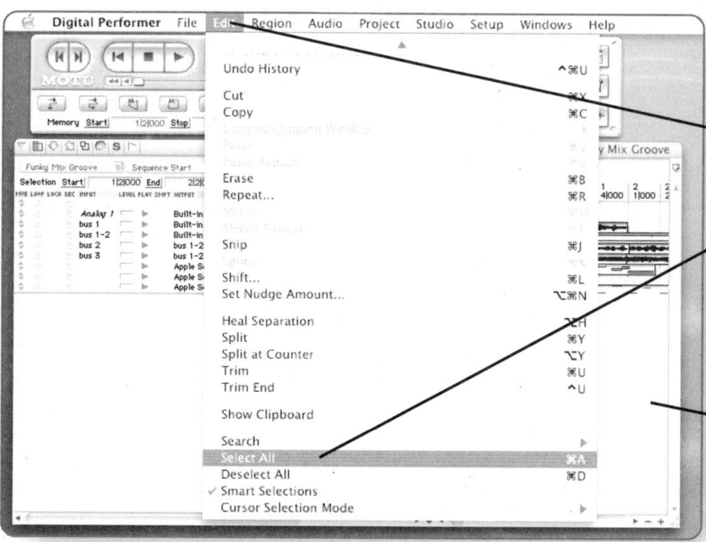

1. **Click** on **Edit**. The Edit menu will appear.
2. **Click** on **Select All**. A selection bound consisting of your entire sequence will be created and all phrases will be selected.
3. **Click** in any **blank area** of the Tracks window to deselect the phrases.

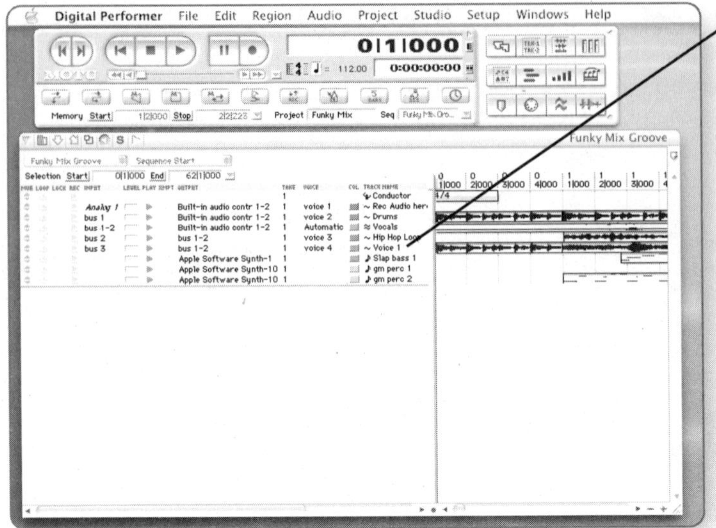

4. Click on the **name** of any track. All phrases in that track will be selected because the selection bounds are the entire sequence.

Smart Selections

By default, Digital Performer has the Smart Selections feature turned on. When you make a selection, Digital Performer will also select some of the data before or after the selection if it feels that it is part of the same region. This feature can be easily turned off or on.

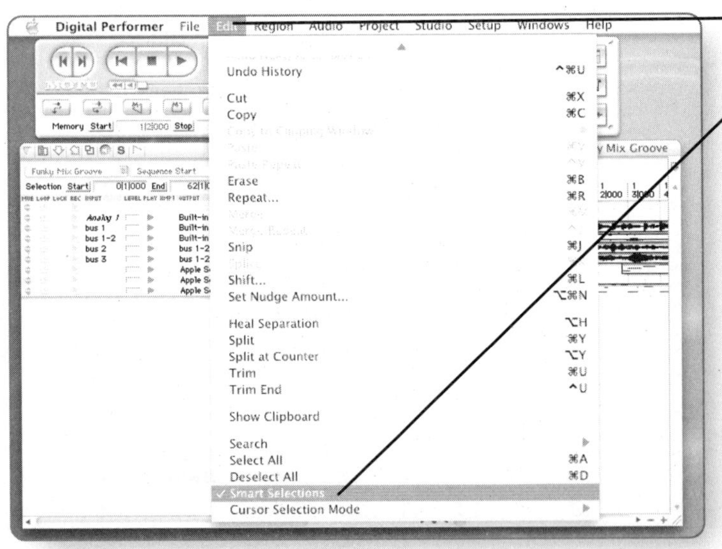

1. Click on **Edit**. The Edit menu will appear.

2. Click on **Smart Selections**. If a checkmark appears before Smart Selections, the feature is already on; otherwise, it is off.

Cutting, Copying, and Pasting

Like almost every other application, Digital Performer provides you with the Cut, Copy, and Paste functions to manipulate your data. These functions can be used to add or remove phrases in the Tracks window. When you cut or copy, the data is recorded in a virtual Clipboard. Data on this Clipboard can then be pasted in any location.

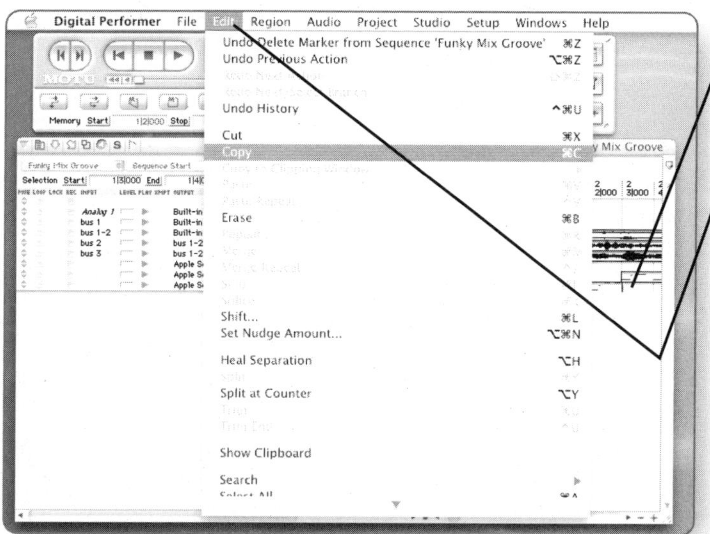

1. **Select** the desired **phrase** using one of the selection methods.

2. **Click** on **Edit**. The Edit menu will appear.

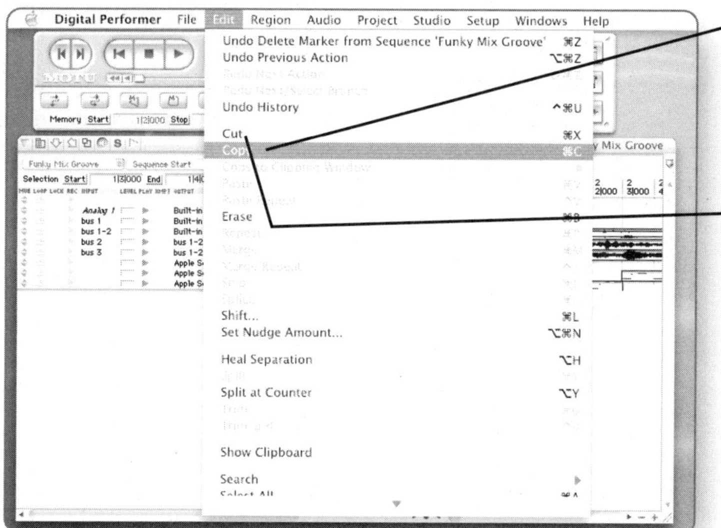

3a. **Click** on **Copy**. A copy of the item will be sent to the Clipboard.

OR

3b. **Click** on **Cut**. The selection will be removed to the Clipboard.

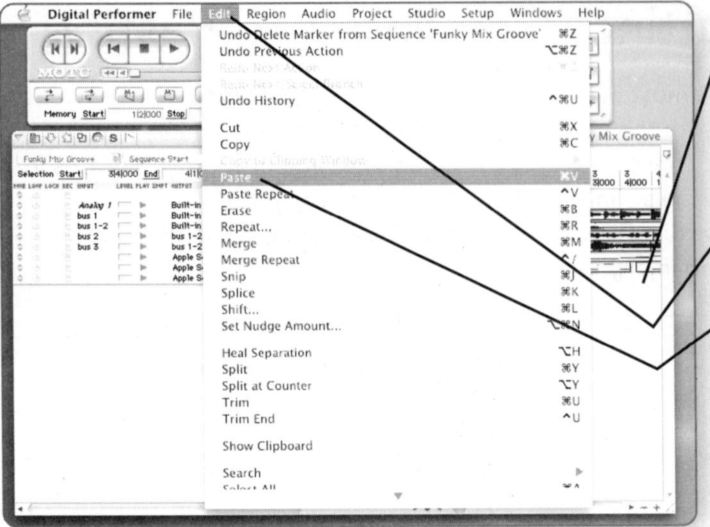

4. **Click** and **drag** a **selection** to where you want to place the item that has been cut or copied. If there is data in the selection, it will be replaced when you paste.

5. **Click** on **Edit**. The Edit menu will appear.

6. **Click** on **Paste**. The item will be pasted at the beginning of the selection.

> **NOTE**
>
> MIDI tracks can only be pasted to other MIDI tracks; Mono tracks can only be pasted to Mono tracks; and Stereo tracks can only be pasted to other Stereo tracks.

Paste Multiple

When you use the Paste function, you can only paste the item that is on the Clipboard to one location at a time. For instance, if I copied a selection and wanted to paste it to three different tracks, I would have to paste it three different times. Using the Paste Multiple feature, you can paste an item that is on the Clipboard to multiple tracks all at one time.

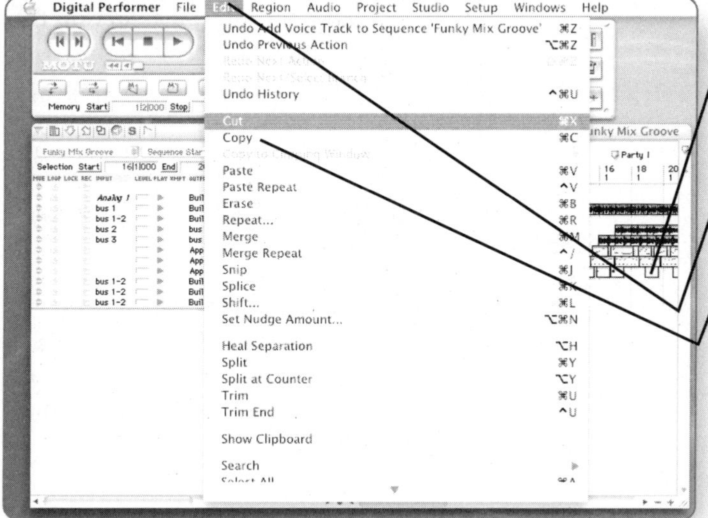

1. **Select** the desired **phrases** using one of the selection methods.

2. **Click** on **Edit**. The Edit menu will appear.

3a. **Click** on **Copy**. A copy of the selection will be sent to the Clipboard.

OR

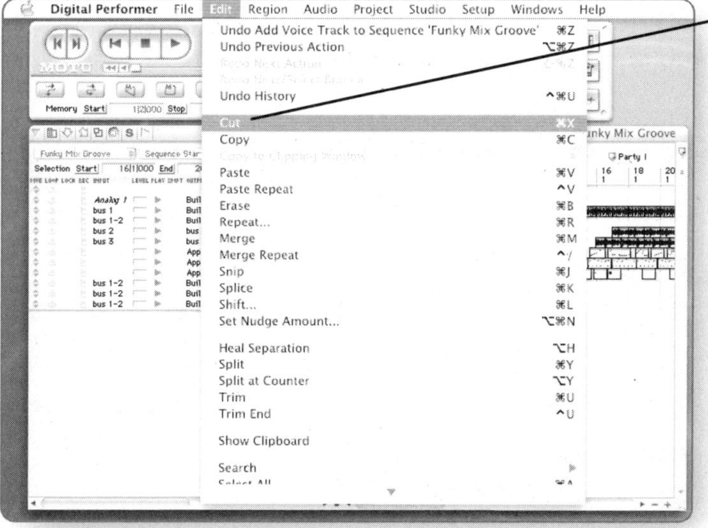

3b. **Click** on **Cut**. The selection will be removed to the Clipboard.

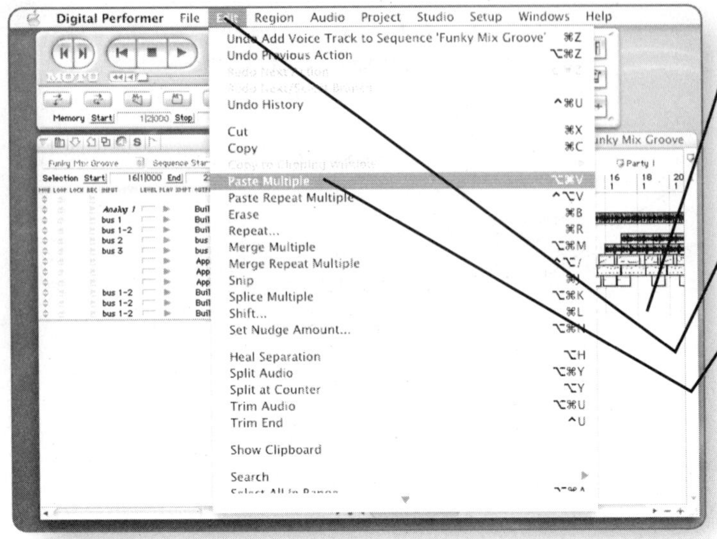

4. **Click** and **drag** a **selection** to where you want to place the item that has been cut or copied. You can select an area covering more than one track.
5. **Click** on **Edit**. The Edit menu will appear.
6. **Press** and **hold** the **Option key** and **click** on **Paste Multiple**. When you hold down the Option key, the Paste command will turn into Paste Multiple.

Moving Selections

Digital Performer provides you with a variety of different methods of moving selections throughout the Tracks window.

Clicking and Dragging

Whereas cutting and pasting is one way to move a phrase or a series of phrases, another faster way is to simply click and drag a selection to its new location.

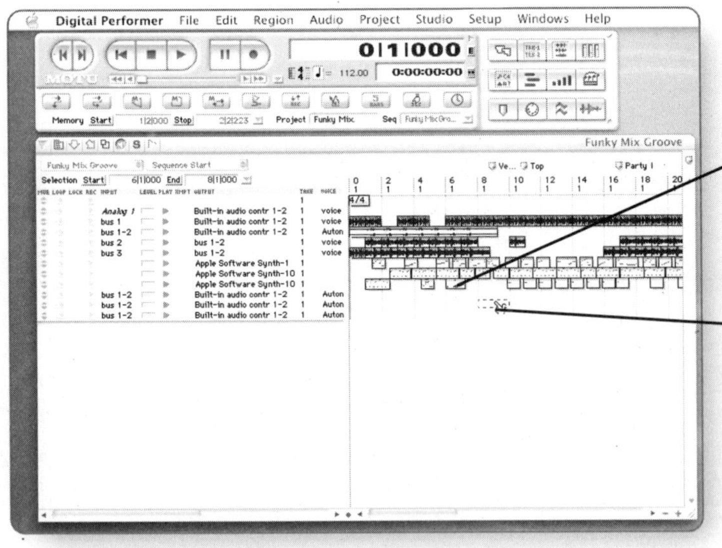

1. **Position** your **mouse pointer** over a selection. The mouse pointer will change to a small hand.
2. **Click** and **drag** the **selection** to its new location. As you drag, an outline of the selection will appear, indicating its new position.

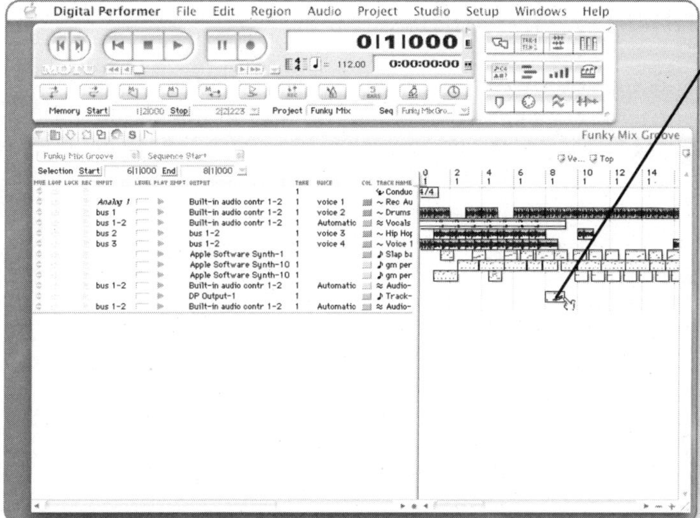

3. Release the **mouse button**. The selection will be in its new position.

> **TIP**
>
> When you move a selection, the selection snaps to a grid, which limits its mobility. Pressing and holding the Option key while moving a selection will override the Snap to Grid feature.

Shifting

For extremely accurate movement, you can take advantage of the Shift feature. The Shift dialog box allows you to specify where you want to move a selection. You can choose to move a selection by a certain amount of time or you can specify an exact location.

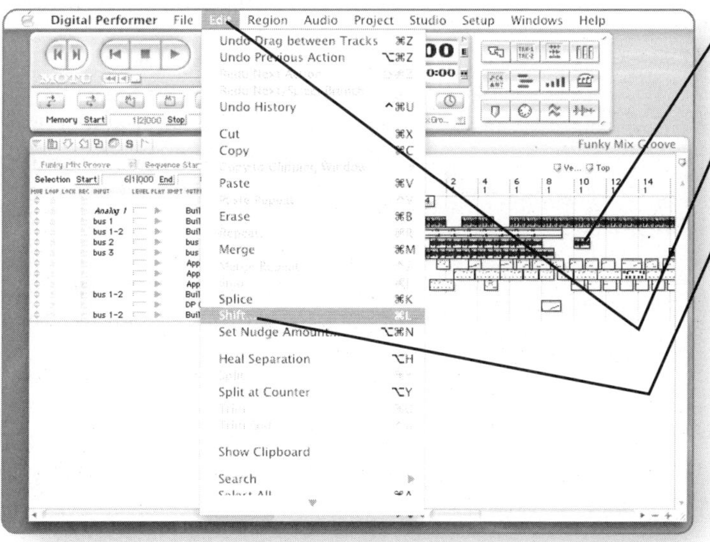

1. **Create** a **selection** using one of the selection methods.
2. **Click** on **Edit**. The Edit menu will appear.
3. **Click** on **Shift**. The Shift dialog box will appear.

Shifting by Amount

Using the Shifting by Amount option, you can specify whether you want to move a selection earlier or later in the sequence and by how much.

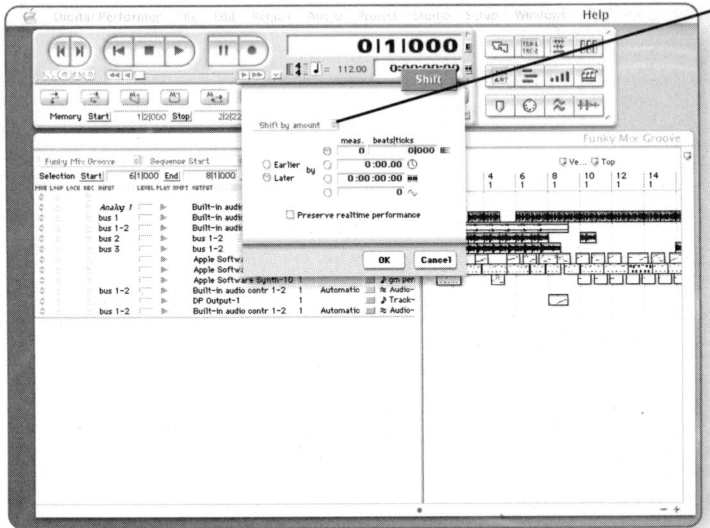

1. **Click** on the **up-and-down arrow**. A menu will appear.

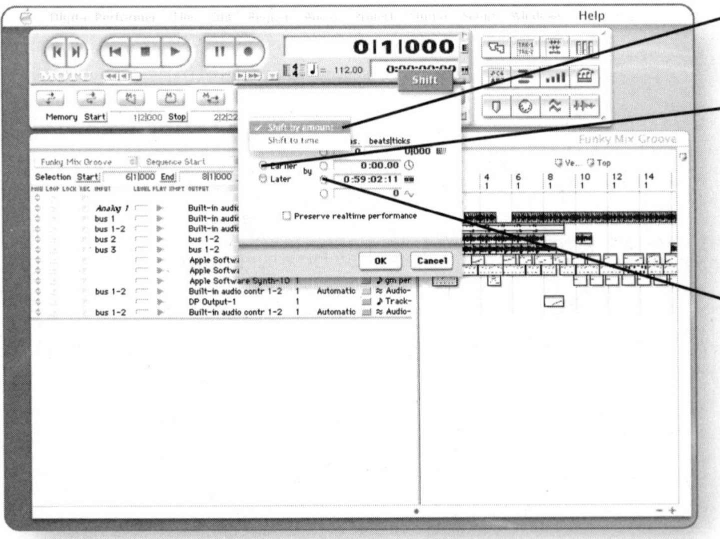

2. **Click** on **Shift by amount**. It will be selected.
3. **Click** on **Earlier** or **Later** to determine if the selection will move to earlier or later in the sequence. The circle will be highlighted once selected.
4. **Click** on the desired **option** to select the time increment used to move your selection.

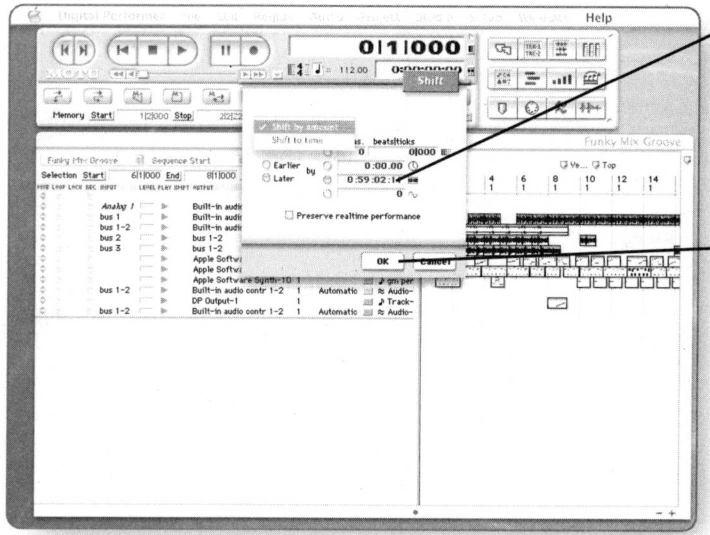

5. **Click once** in the corresponding **box**. The box will be highlighted.

6. **Type** the **increment**. It will appear as you type.

7. **Click** on **OK**. The selection you have made will move by the specified amount.

Shifting by Time

With the Shifting by Time option, you can specify an exact location to place your selection.

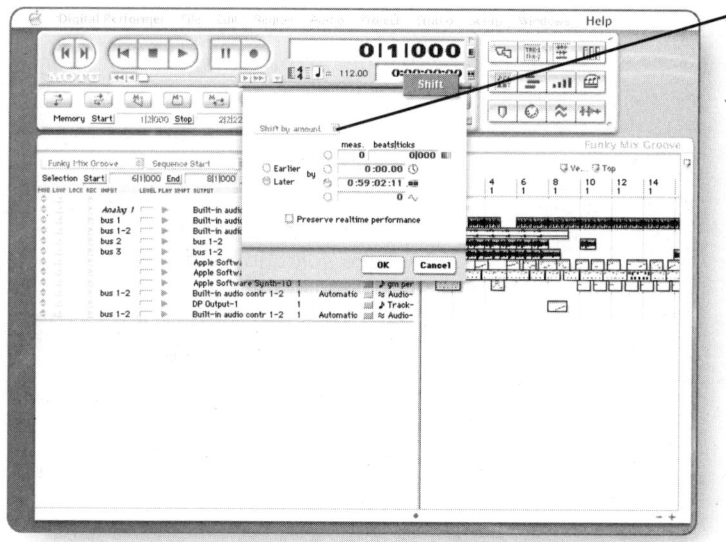

1. **Click** on the **up-and-down arrow**. A menu will appear.

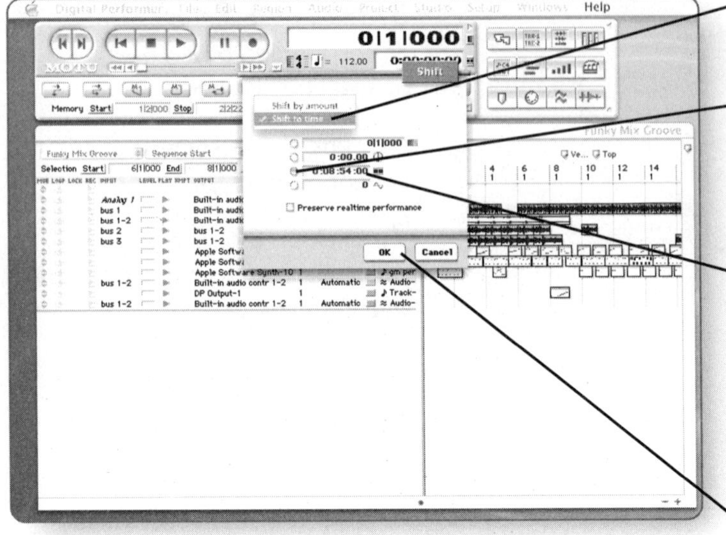

2. **Click** on **Shift by time**. It will be selected.

3. **Click** on the desired **option** to select the type of time measurement used to move your selection.

4. **Click once** in the corresponding **box**. The box will be highlighted.

5. **Type** the **time location** that you would like to move your sequence to.

6. **Click** on **OK**. The selection you have made will move by the amount specified.

Nudging

Another method for moving a selection is to use your arrow key. This method of movement is called *nudging*. Whenever you are moving a selection with your arrow keys, the selection will move in certain increments. Those increments can be easily changed to any level.

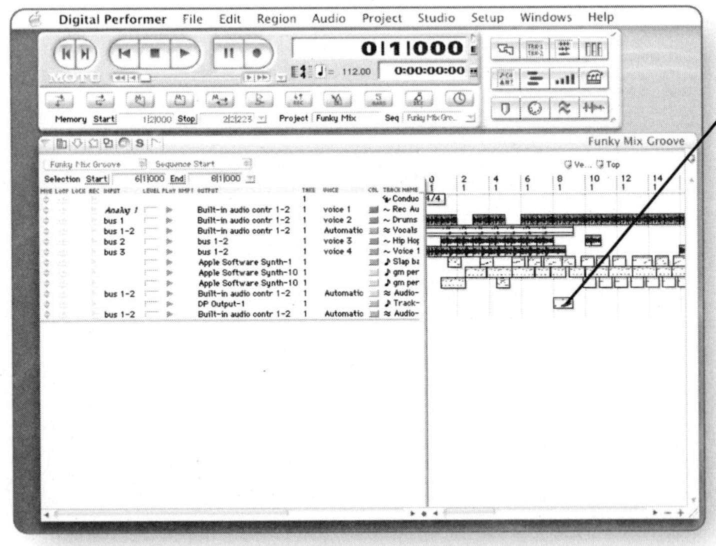

1. **Create** a **selection** using any of the selection methods.

2. **Press** the **right** or **left arrow key** to move the selection.

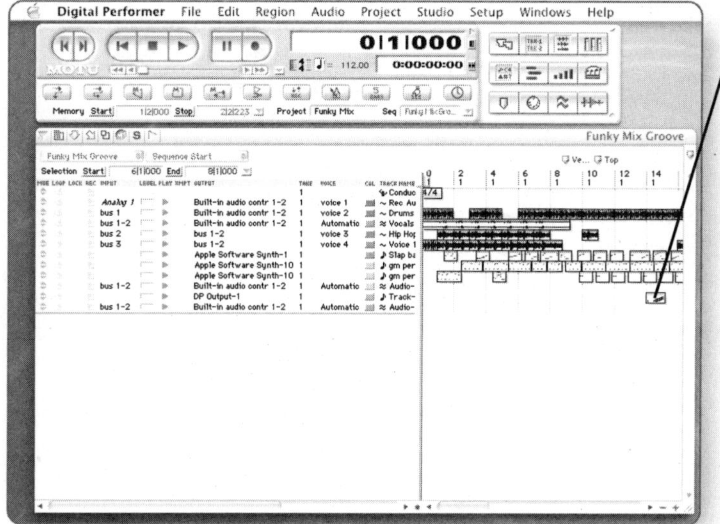

3. Repeat step 2 until the selection is in the desired location.

Adjusting the Nudge Amount

The increments that your selection moves when using nudge can be adjusted using the Edit menu.

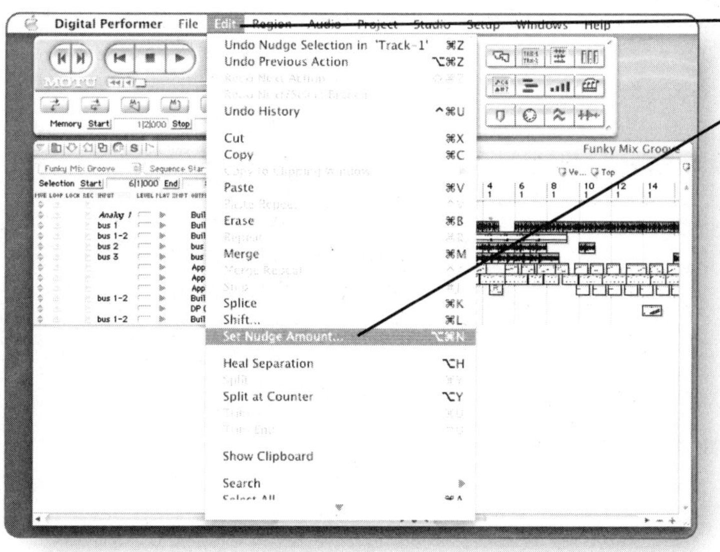

1. Click on **Edit**. The Edit menu will appear.

2. Click on **Set Nudge Amount**. A dialog box will appear, allowing you to set the increments for the nudge.

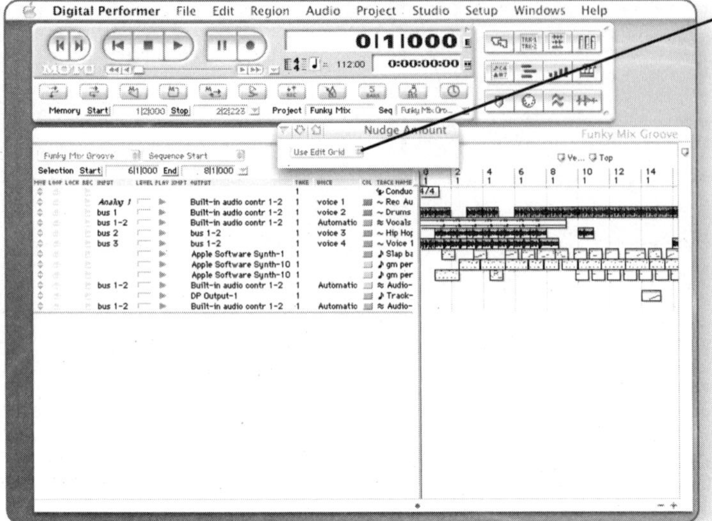

3. Click on the **up-and-down arrows** to bring up a menu of options.

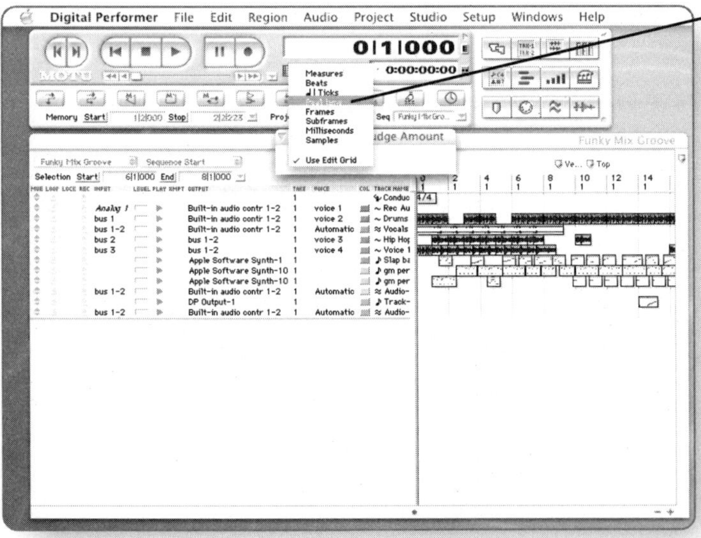

4. Click on the desired **nudge method**. Depending on the method you choose, a field box may appear in the dialog box for you to set an increment amount. For example, if you choose to nudge by beats, you would then have to enter the number of beats you would like your selection to move every time you press the arrow keys.

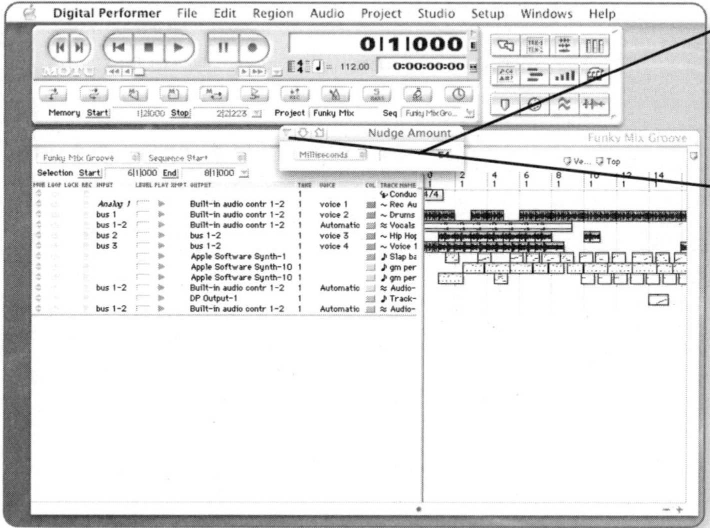

5. Type the **number** of increments for the selected nudge method.

6. Click on the **down arrow** in the top-left corner of the dialog box to close it. The nudge levels you have set will take effect.

Grid Snapping

When you move a selection with the mouse, you can only move it in certain increments. The current scale of the Time Ruler determines those increments. For example, if the Time Ruler is showing one measure per segment, you will only be able to move your segments by one-measure increments. By zooming in or out, you can change the scale of the Time Ruler, which in turn will allow you to move a selection in different increments.

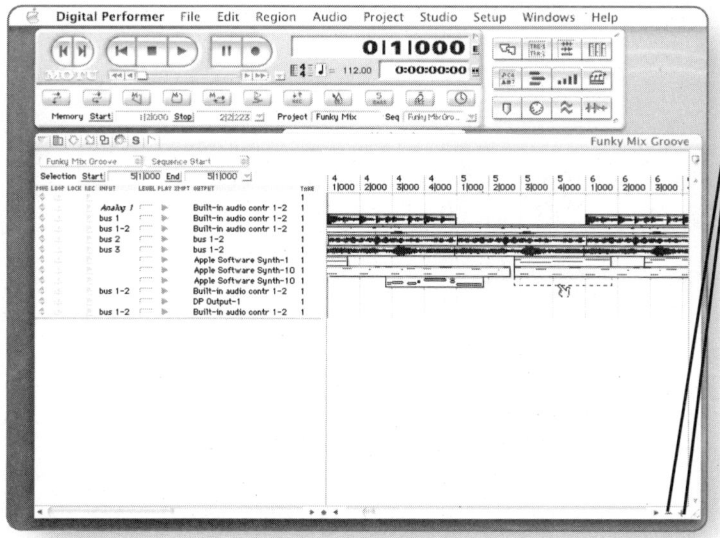

1. Click on the **+** or **–** **Zoom tools** to zoom in or out of the Tracks window.

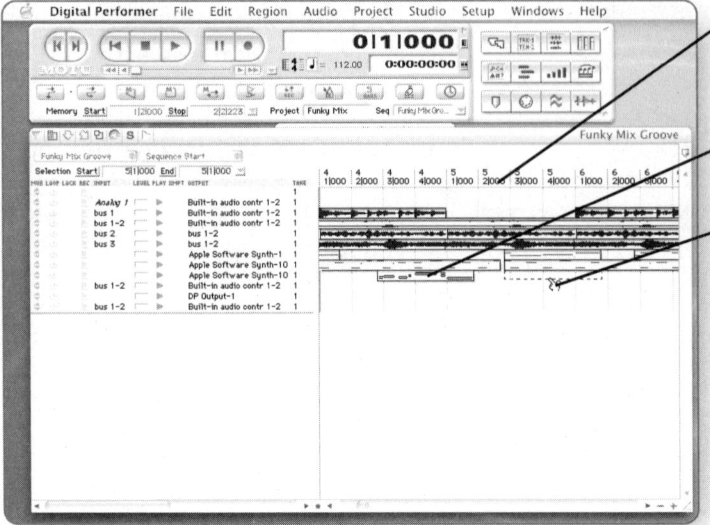

2. Repeat step 1 until the Time Ruler is at the increments you desire.

3. Position your **mouse pointer** over a selection.

4. Click and **drag** the **selection** to its new location. You will be able to move it in increments equal to those being displayed in the Time Ruler. An outline of the selection will appear as you drag.

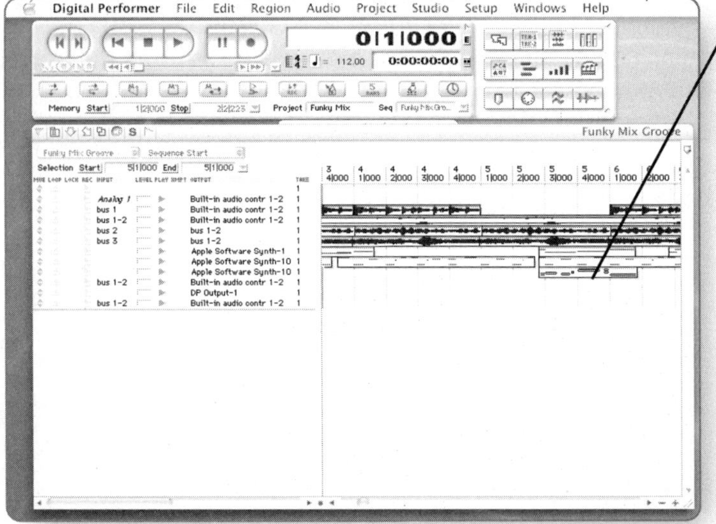

5. Release the **mouse button**. The selection will be moved.

Duplicating Phrases

One of the fastest ways to create a loop is to use your mouse. With the use of the keyboard and clicking and dragging, you can quickly duplicate selections. This method is perfect for creating loops.

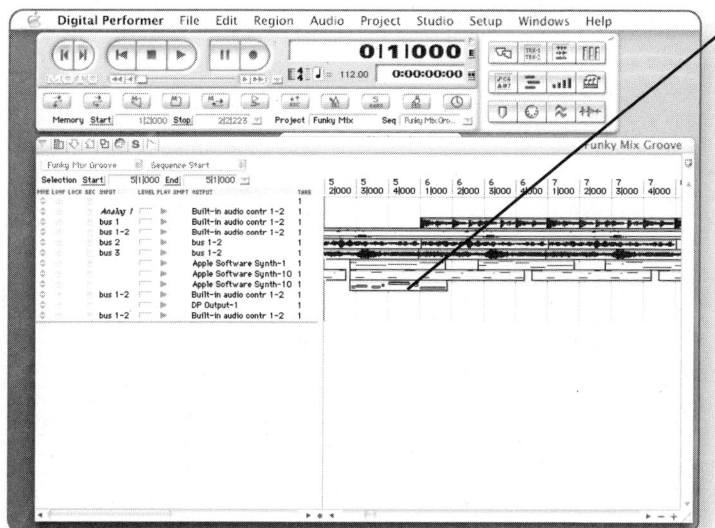

1. **Click once** on a **phrase** to select it. The phrase will appear highlighted to indicate that it has been selected.

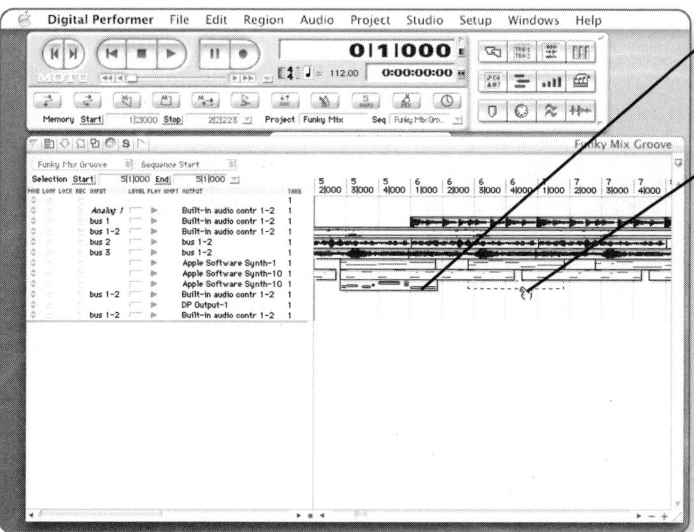

2. **Position** the **mouse pointer** over the selected phrase. The cursor will turn into a small hand.
3. **Press** and **hold** the **Option key** and **click** and **drag** the **phrase** to a location where you want the duplicate to appear.

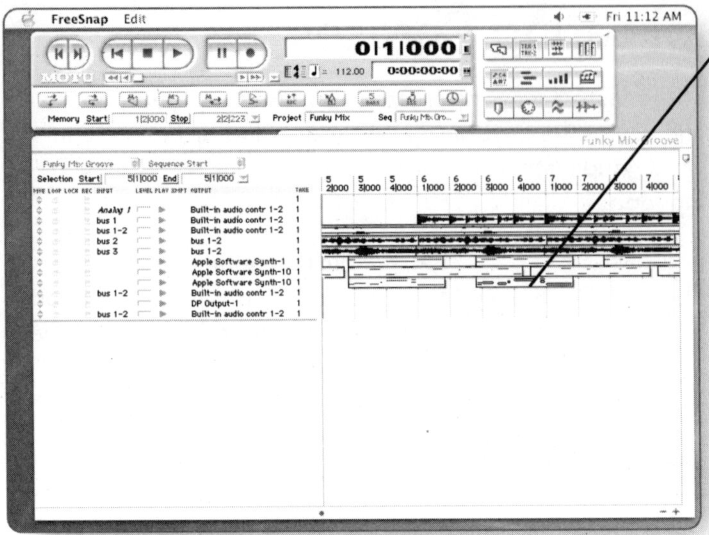

4. **Release** the **mouse button** and **Option key**. A duplicate of the phrase will appear.

Splicing

Splicing is similar to pasting, but rather than replacing existing data, splicing inserts the data from the Clipboard and pushes over the existing data.

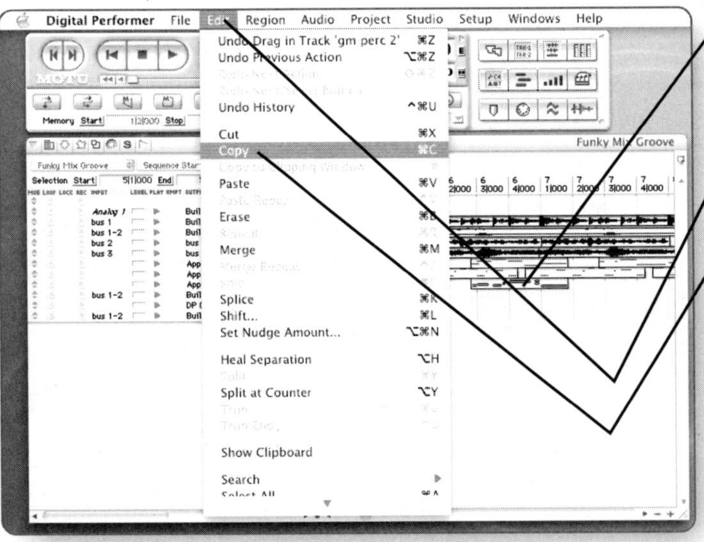

1. **Create** a **selection**. You can use any of the selection methods.

2. **Click** on **Edit**. The Edit menu will appear.

3. **Click** on **Copy**. The data in the selection will be copied. Alternatively, you can use the Cut command if you want to remove the data.

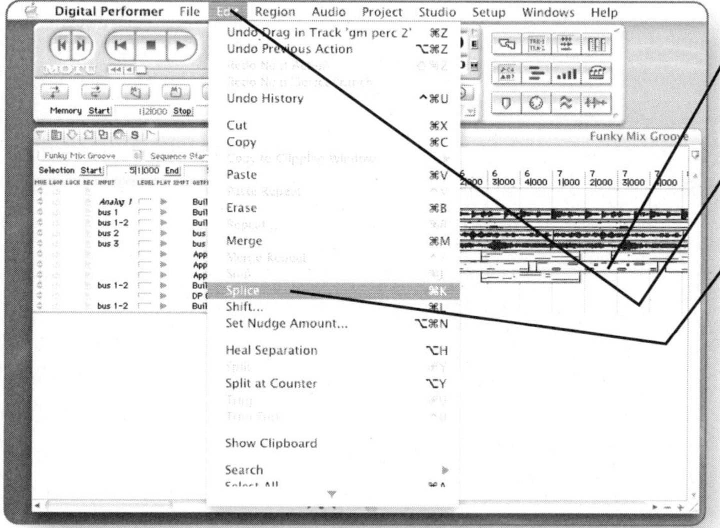

4. Make another **selection** where you would like to splice the data.

5. Click on **Edit**. The Edit menu will appear.

6. Click on **Splice**. The information that you copied onto the Clipboard will be inserted into the track, and will push existing data further on into the sequence.

Merging

While splicing will push existing data further into the sequence, merge, as its name would suggest, merges data from the Clipboard into a selected track. In other words, merging will combine what you have on the Clipboard with a selected track.

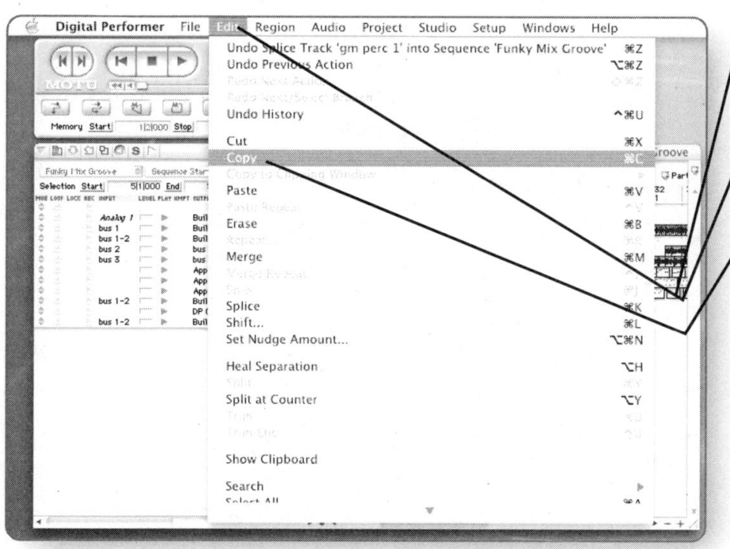

1. Create a **selection**. You can use any of the selection methods.

2. Click on **Edit**. The Edit menu will appear.

3. Click on **Copy**. The data in the selection will be copied. Alternatively, you can use the Cut command if you want to remove the data.

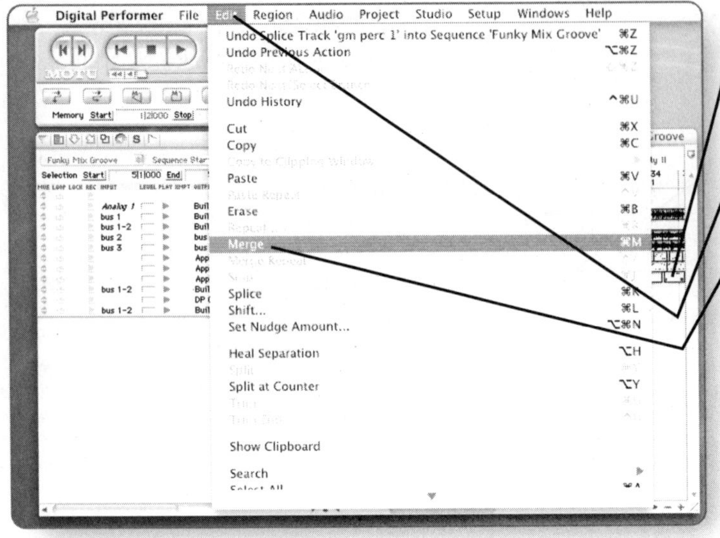

4. Click on a **Phrase** with which you want to merge. It will be highlighted.

5. Click on **Edit**. The Edit menu will appear.

6. Click on **Merge**. The information that you copied onto the Clipboard will be inserted into the track, and will merge into the sequence.

Snipping

Imagine you had a stack of dominos. If you took one domino away from the middle of the stack, you would not be left with an empty hole, because the rest of the dominos will move down one level to replace the empty area. That's similar to how Snip works in Digital Performer. The Snip feature allows you to delete both phrases and time regions at the same time. In essence, you will be deleting the selection and shifting all the rest of the data in the track to an earlier time to replace the snipped region.

1. Create a **selection** to be snipped using any of the selection methods.

2. Click on **Edit**. The Edit menu will appear.

3. Click on **Snip**. Both the data and the time region within the selection will be deleted.

Loops

If you are old enough to remember record players, then you should be familiar with the concept of a loop. When you had a record with a scratch on it, the same piece of music would play over and over. That's similar to the concept of a loop, which is any piece of music that plays repeatedly. Loops can be great for creating background tracks or experimenting with samples. Some of the editing features you have already seen in this chapter can be used to make loops, such as pasting and duplicating phrases. Digital Performer also offers several other ways to create loops.

Set Loop

Using the Set Loop function, you can choose how many times you want the selection to loop.

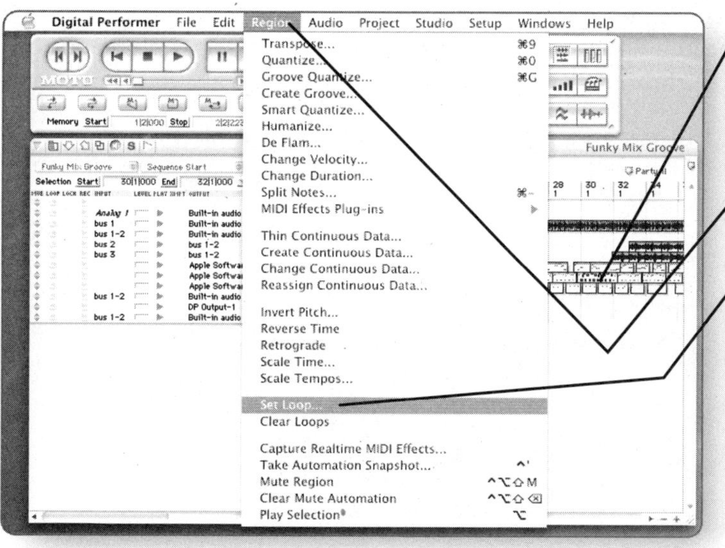

1. **Create** a **selection** from which you would like to create a loop. You can use any of the selection methods.
2. **Click** on **Region**. The Region menu will appear.
3. **Click** on **Set Loop**. A dialog box will open, allowing you to specify the length of the loop.

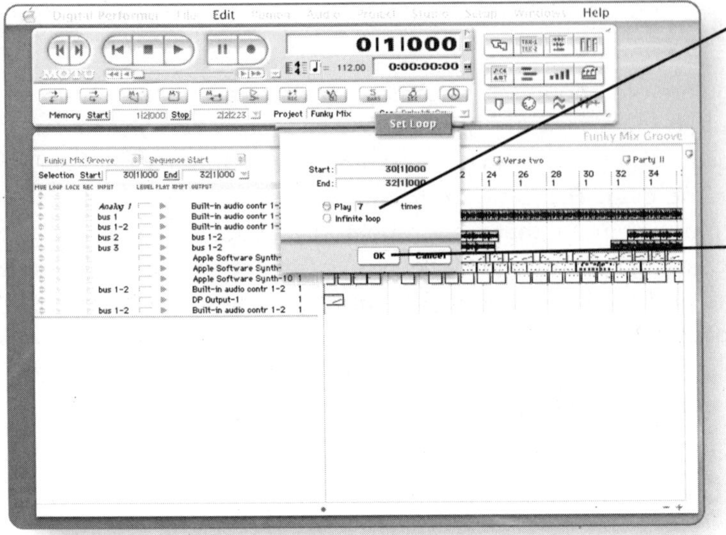

4. **Type** a **number** indicating how many times you want the selection to loop. Alternatively, if you would like it to loop infinitely, click on the circle beside Infinite loop.

5. **Click** on **OK**. The loop will be set.

Repeat

Using the Repeat function, you can repeat a selection by using one of three methods.

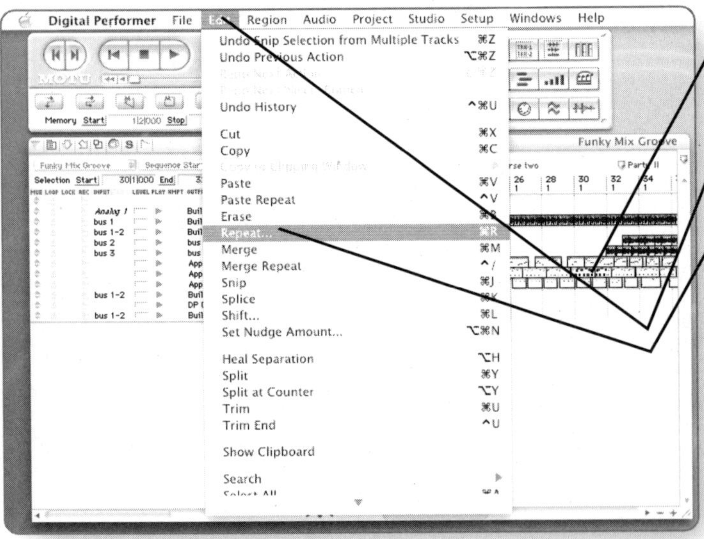

1. **Create** a **selection** using any of the selection methods.

2. **Click** on **Edit**. The Edit menu will appear.

3. **Click** on **Repeat**. The Repeat dialog box will open.

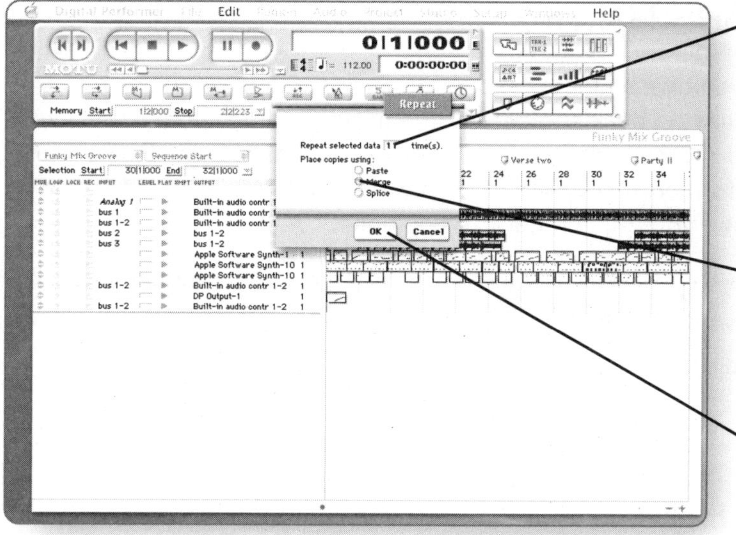

4. **Double-click** in the **Repeat selected data field box**. A cursor will appear.

5. **Type** a **number**. This number represents the number of times the sequence will repeat.

6. **Click** on the desired **repeat method**. The circle beside the option will be highlighted once selected.

7. **Click** on **OK**. The sequence will be repeated based on the settings you have created.

Undoing

Let's face it, we all make mistakes. You don't have to worry, though, because when you make a mistake in Digital Performer, you can quickly correct it by using the Undo command.

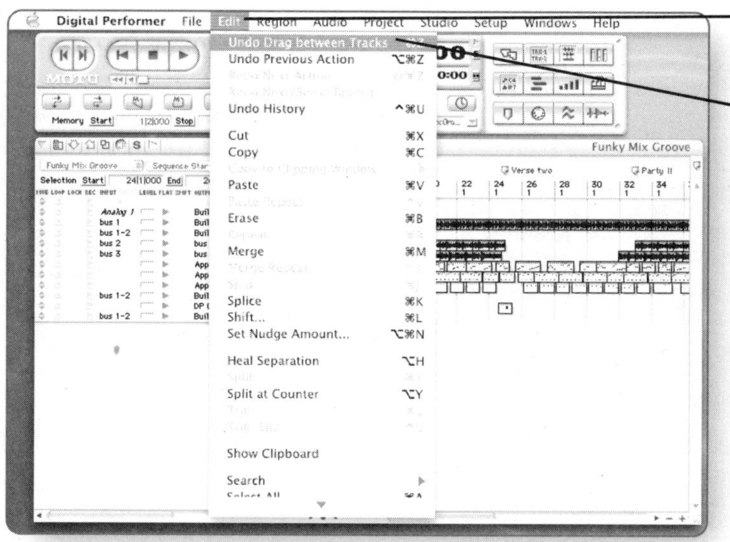

1. **Click** on **Edit**. The Edit menu will appear.

2. **Click** on **Undo**. The last action that you took will be undone.

Undo History

Haven't we all fantasized about having a time machine so that we can go back and correct the mistakes of the past? The Undo History feature is your virtual time machine in Digital Performer. It keeps track of the edits that you have made and allows you to jump back to any point.

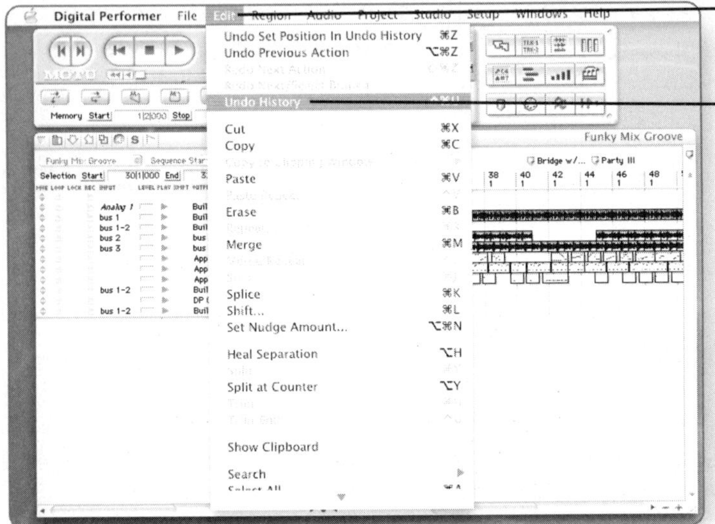

1. **Click** on **Edit**. The Edit menu will appear.
2. **Click** on **Undo History**. A dialog box will open.

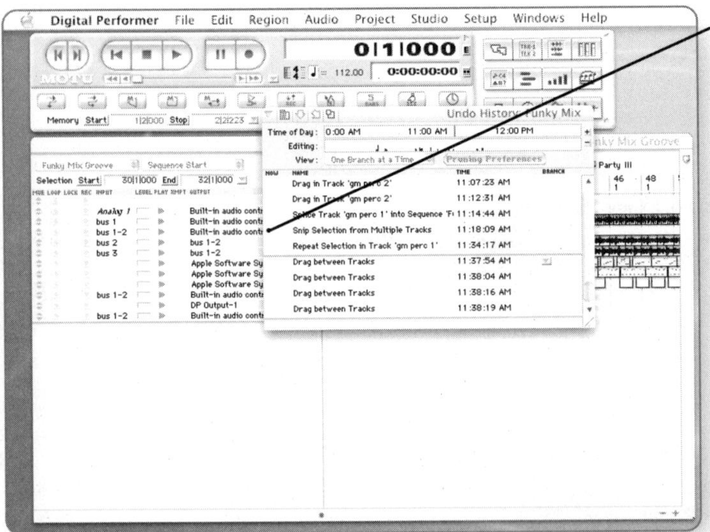

3. **Double-click** in the **NOW column** beside the action you would like to travel back to. A dot will appear in the column.

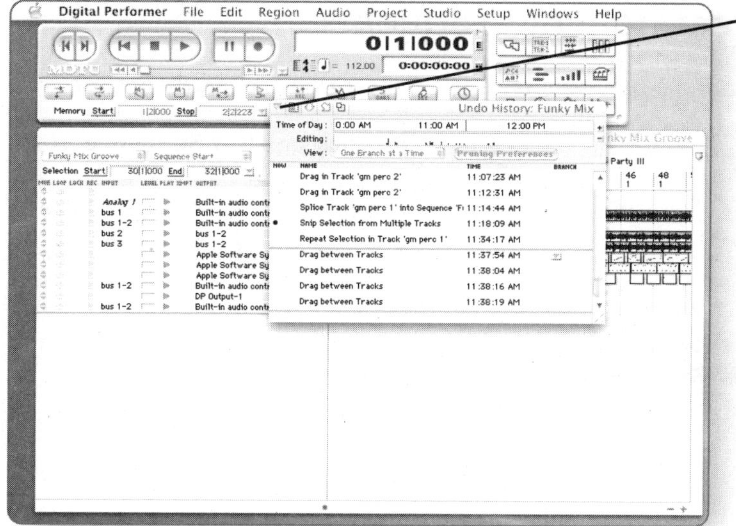

4. Click on the **down arrow** to close the window. You will now be at the point that you selected.

Sequences

The culmination of all of your tracks is called a sequence. Digital Performer allows you to have multiple sequences in one file. This is helpful when creating projects because you can include all the sequences for a particular project within one file. Digital Performer allows you to easily create sequences and access them. Most of the commands that have to do with sequences can be accessed from the Sequences pop-up menu.

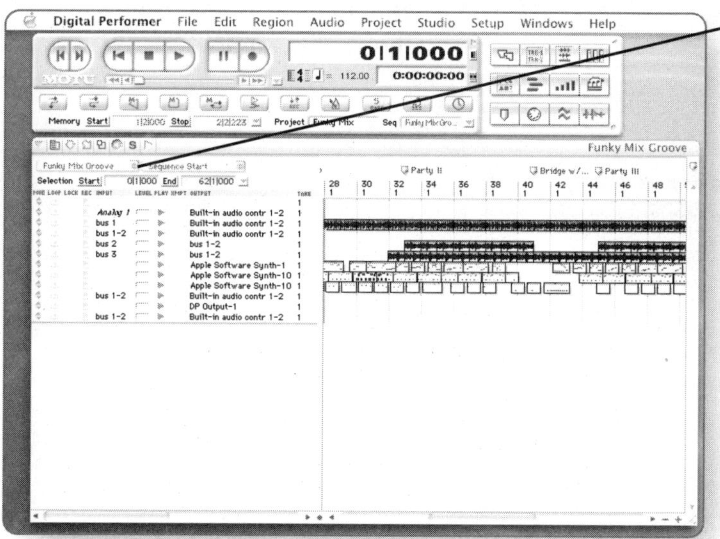

1. Click on the **up-and-down arrow** to access the Sequence pop-up menu. The menu will appear.

Creating New Sequences

Creating a new sequence is a matter of a click of the mouse.

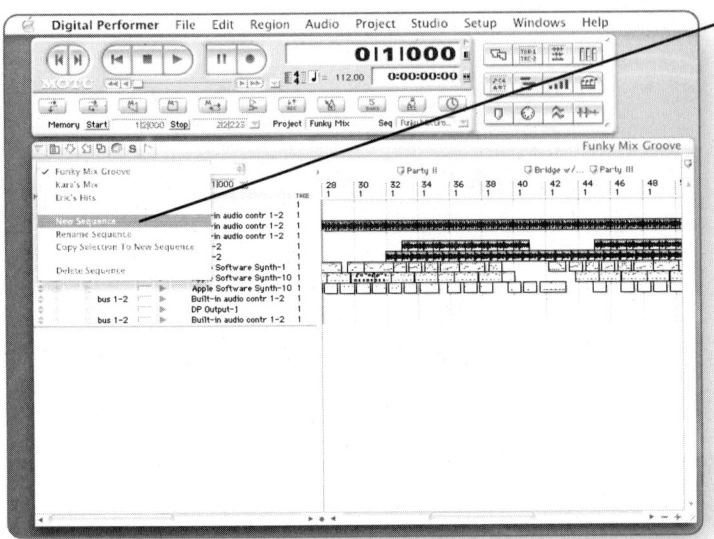

1. Click on **New Sequence**. A new sequence will be created with the same number of tracks as the original sequence.

Accessing Sequences

When you have multiple sequences in a file, you can quickly toggle between them using the Sequence pop-up menu.

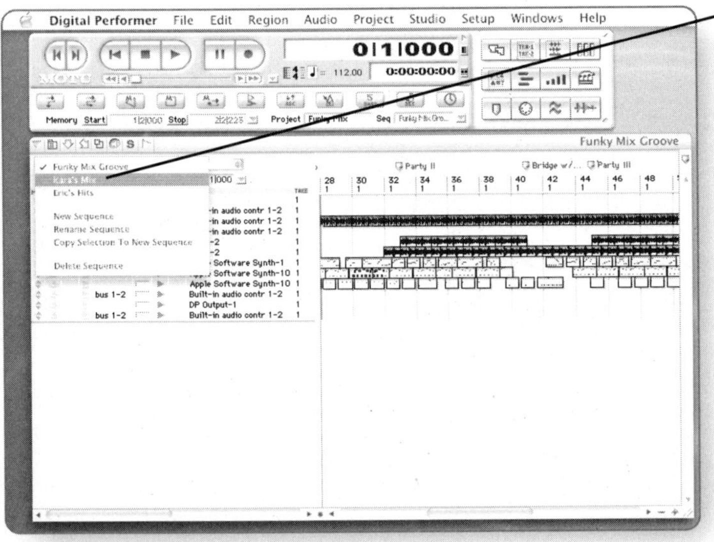

1. Click on the desired **sequence**. It will be displayed in the Tracks window.

Renaming Sequences

When you create a new sequence, it is given a generic name based on your initial sequence. It's a good idea to rename your sequence to make it easier to access.

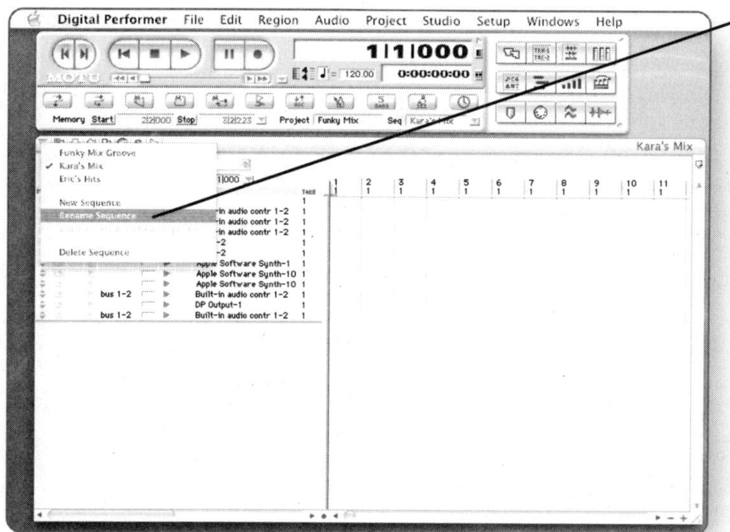

1. Click on **Rename Sequence**. A box will appear around the sequence name, allowing you to rename it.

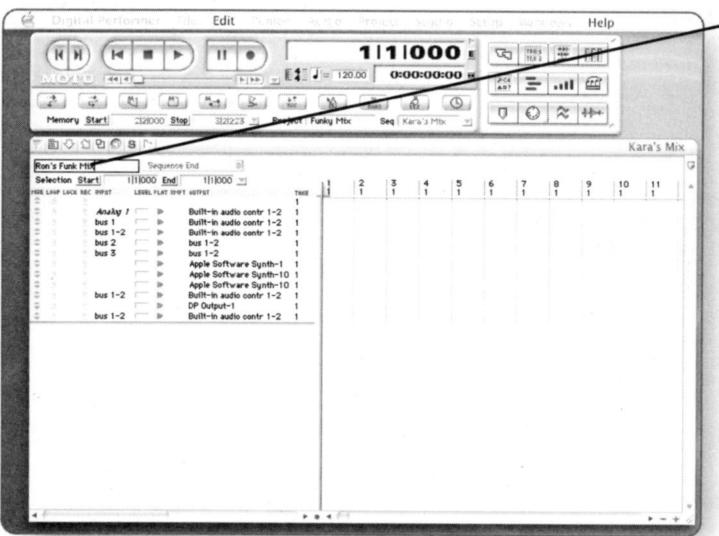

2. Type a **new name** for your sequence. It will appear as you type.

3. Press Return. The sequence will be renamed.

Transferring Data to a Sequence

When creating a new sequence, you may want to bring data from an existing sequence, rather than having to re-create it.

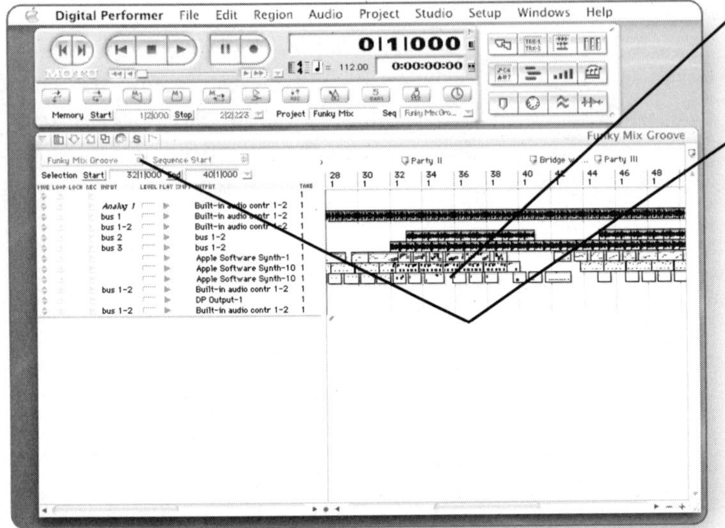

1. **Create** a **selection** in a sequence using one of the many selection methods.
2. **Click** on the **up-and-down arrow** to access the Sequence pop-up menu.

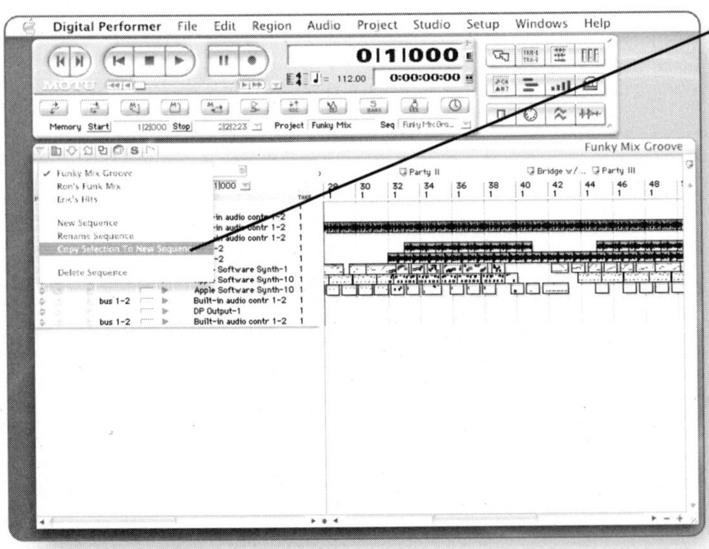

3. **Click** on **Copy Selection to New Sequence**. A dialog box will appear where you can adjust the settings for your new sequence.

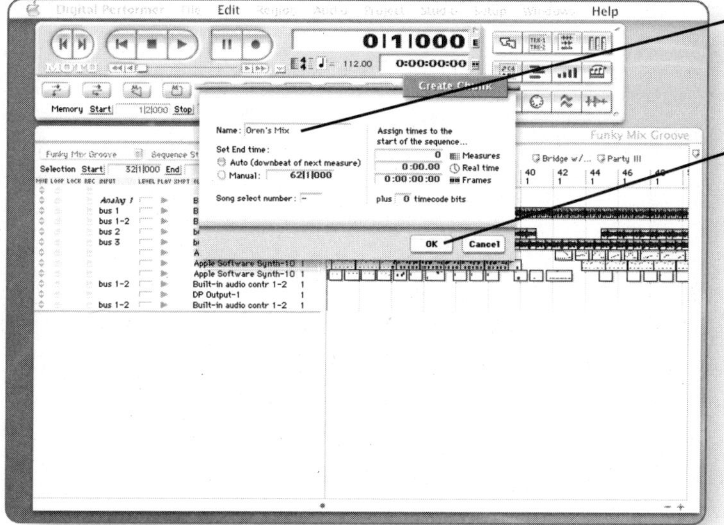

4. **Type** a **name** for the new sequence. It will appear as you type.

5. **Click** on **OK**. A new sequence will be made, which will include the selection you made in step 1.

9

General Editing

Digital Performer is one of the best tools for manipulating your tracks, offering a variety of different editing tools that can alter how and when different notes are heard. Some of these features are specific to audio tracks, others to MIDI, and some are available to both. In this chapter, you will learn how to:

- Transpose notes
- Change velocity and duration
- Create grooves
- Edit the Conductor Track

Transpose

In Digital Performer, you can transpose audio or MIDI notes using the same feature. In the Transpose window, you can transpose or harmonize notes by selecting a specific method.

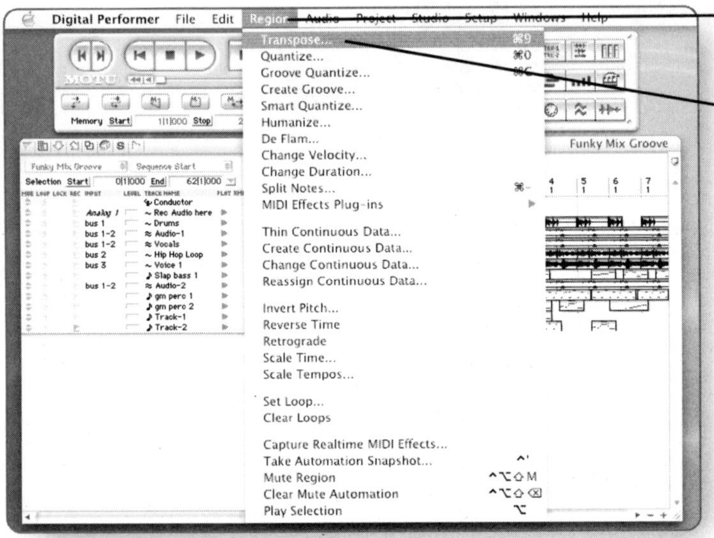

1. **Click** on **Region**. The Region menu will appear.

2. **Click** on **Transpose**. The Transpose window will open.

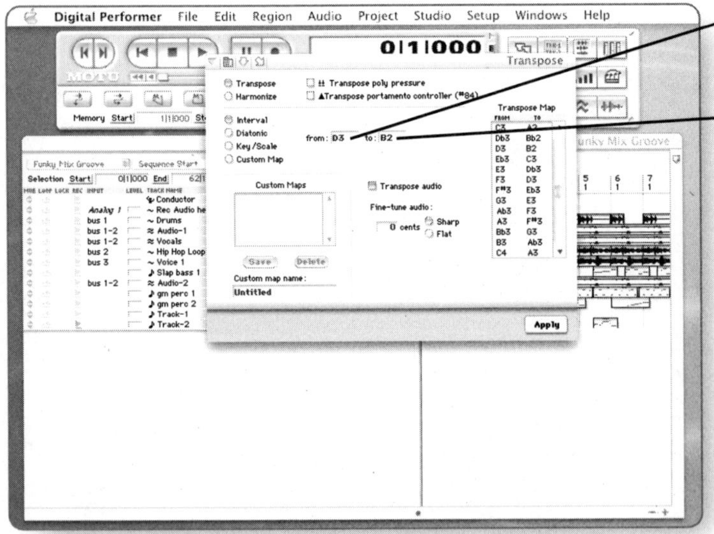

3. **Type** a **note** in the From field. It will appear as you type.

4. **Press** the **Tab key** to move to the To field.

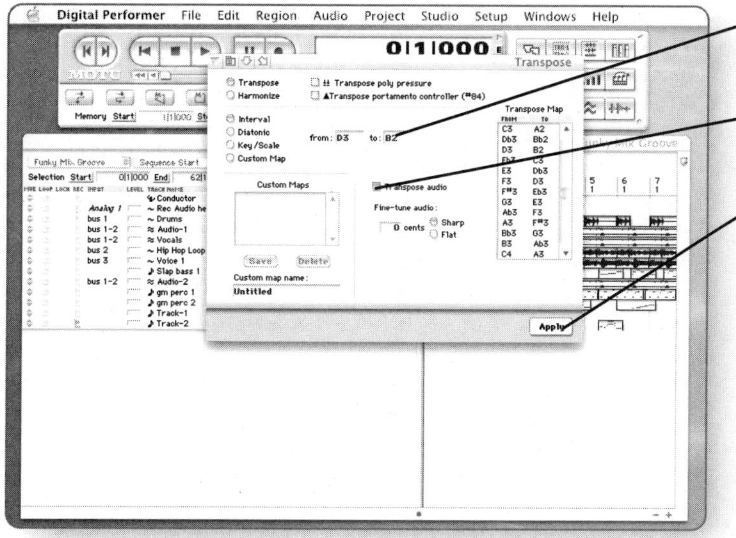

5. Type the **note** you would like to transpose to.

6. Click on any of the desired **options**.

7. Click on **Apply**. The transposition of the notes will be applied.

> **NOTE**
>
> Once you enter a note in the To field, the transpose map in the window will indicate how all of the other notes will be transposed.

Creating Grooves

If you really like the rhythmic feel of a certain MIDI track you've created, you can save it as a groove file and then apply it to other sequences.

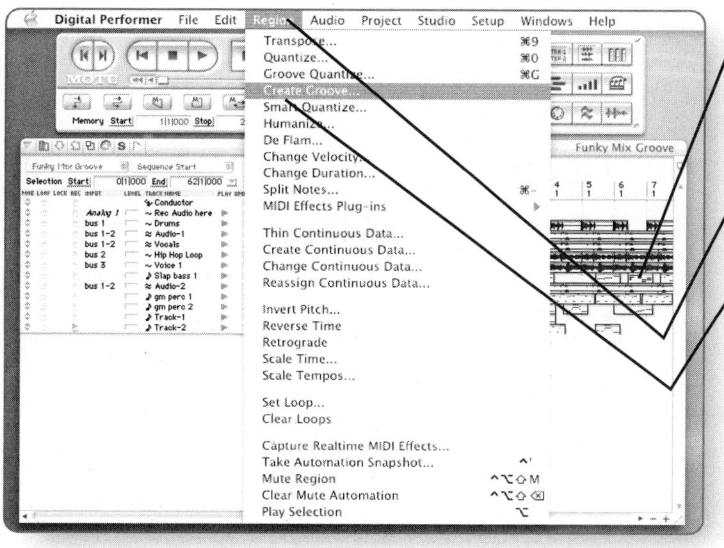

1. Select the **MIDI track** that you would like to make a groove from using one of the selection methods.

2. Click on **Region**. The Region menu will appear.

3. Click on **Create Groove**. A dialog box will open allowing you to select a location for the groove file.

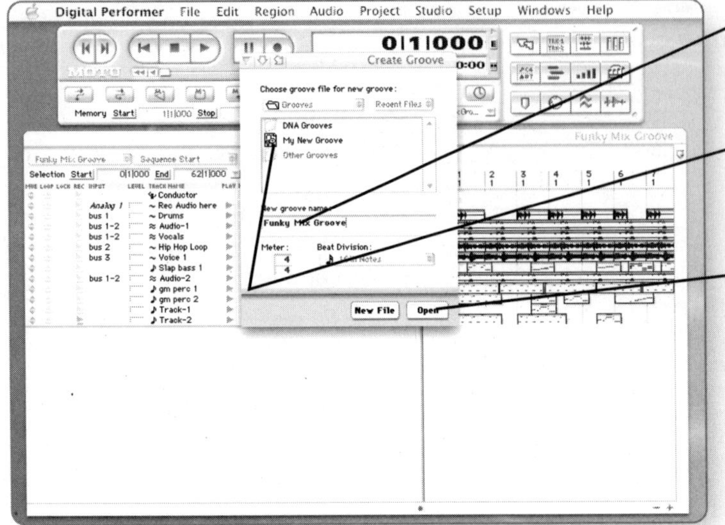

4. **Type** a **name** for your groove file. You can give it any name you choose.

5. **Click** on a **folder** in which you would like to save the groove file.

6. **Click** on **Open**. The selected folder will open.

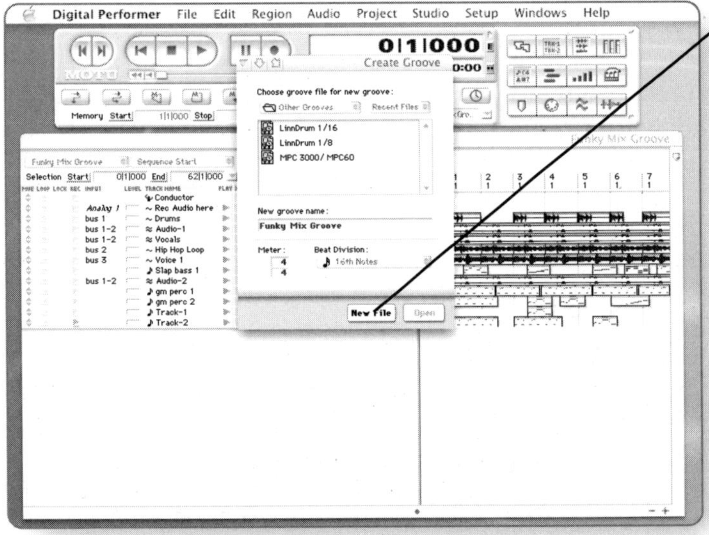

7. **Click** on **New File**. A dialog box will open.

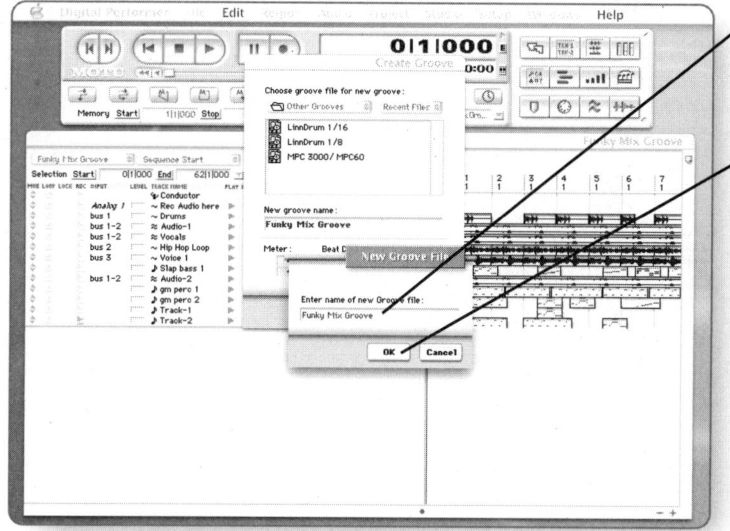

8. Type the **name** of your groove file. You can give it any name.

9. Click on **OK**. The dialog box will close. A new location will be created for your groove.

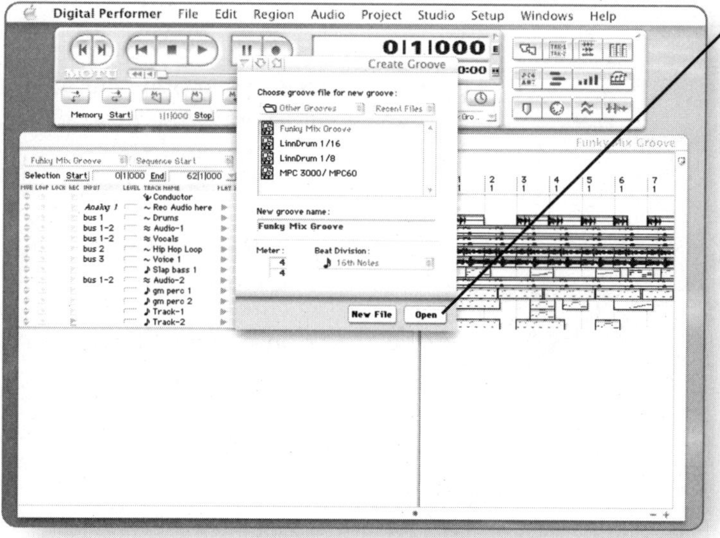

10. Click on **Open**. You will now be able to save your groove.

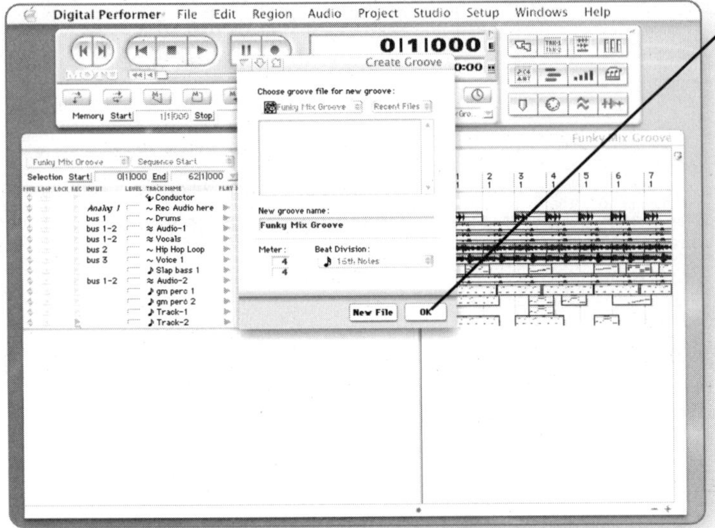

11. Click on **OK**. Your groove file will be saved to that folder.

Applying Grooves

Once you have saved a groove, you can then apply it to any selection.

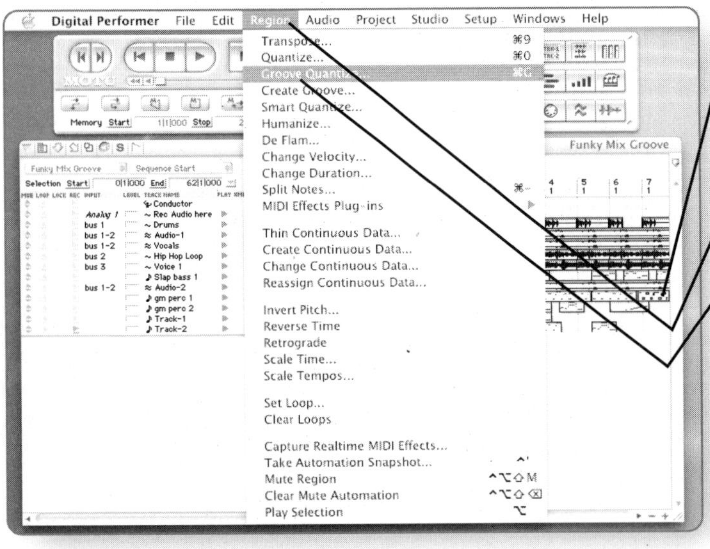

1. **Create** a **selection** where you want to apply the groove, using one of the selection methods.

2. **Click** on **Region**. The Region menu will appear.

3. **Click** on **Groove Quantize**. A dialog box will open.

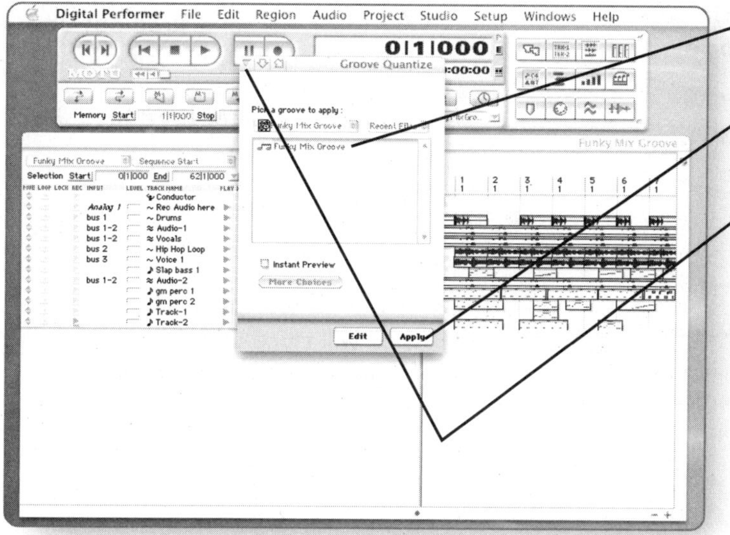

4. **Click** on the **groove** that you would like to apply.

5. **Click** on **Apply**. The groove will be applied.

6. **Click** on the **down arrow** to close the dialog box.

Humanize

I'm sure at some point in your life you've messed up and someone has said, "it's okay, you're only human." Tracks and mixes that are technically perfect don't sound realistic because when humans play instruments or sing vocals, they don't do it perfectly. Using the Humanize feature, you can randomize certain elements of your MIDI selections.

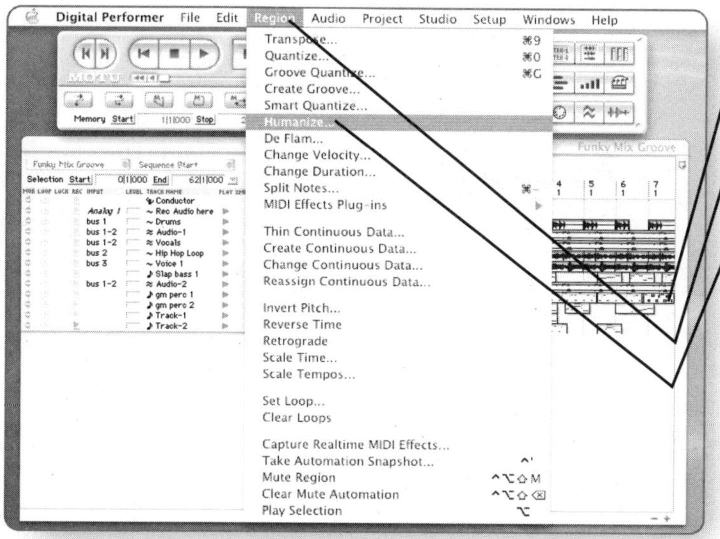

1. **Create** a **selection** using one of the selection methods.

2. **Click** on **Region**. The Region menu will appear.

3. **Click** on **Humanize**. The Humanize window will open.

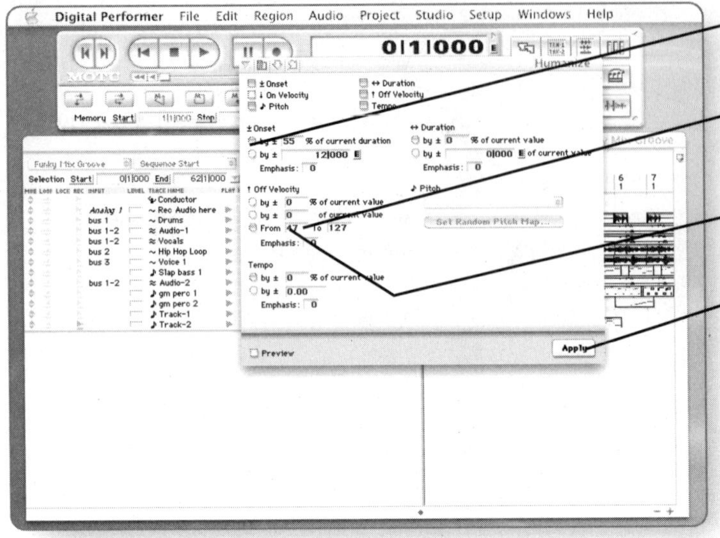

4. **Click** on the desired **options** for humanizing your selection.

5. **Click** in the desired **field**. It will be highlighted.

6. **Type** a new **number**. It will replace the existing number.

7. **Click** on **Apply**. The dialog box will close and the adjustments you made will be applied.

De Flam

The De Flam feature of Digital Performer will rearrange groups of MIDI notes that are close together, by calculating and then placing the notes at their average start time.

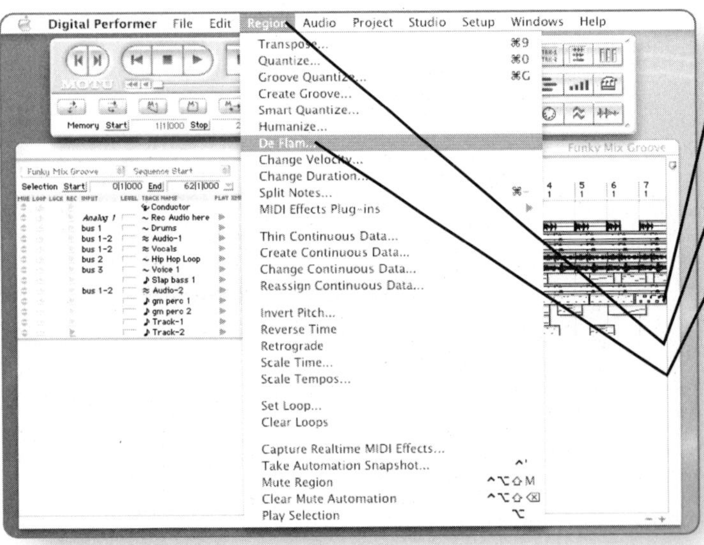

1. **Create** a **selection** of MIDI notes using one of the selection methods.

2. **Click** on **Region**. The Region menu will appear.

3. **Click** on **De Flam**. The De Flam dialog box will open.

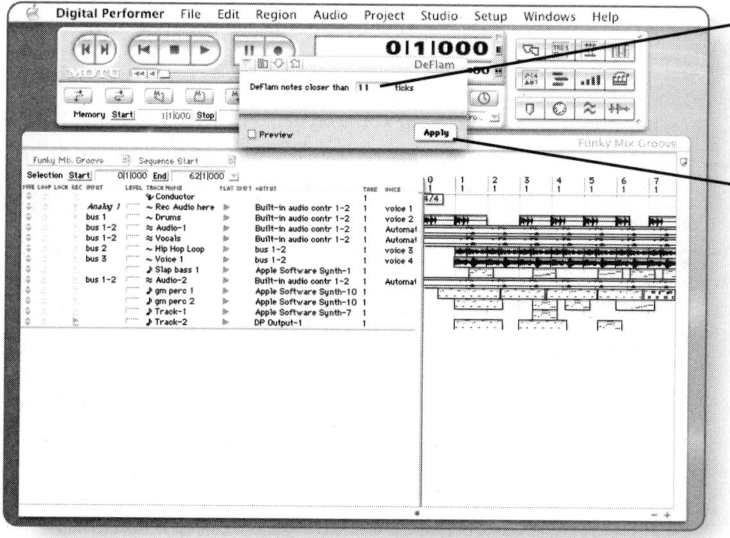

4. Type a **number** for the minimum number of ticks between notes that you would like to de flam.

5. Click on **Apply**. The notes within the selection that meet the criteria will be rearranged.

Changing Velocity

You can change the velocity of selections using the Change Velocity feature in Digital Performer. By adjusting Threshold and Gain dials, you can change the velocity of MIDI notes in your selections.

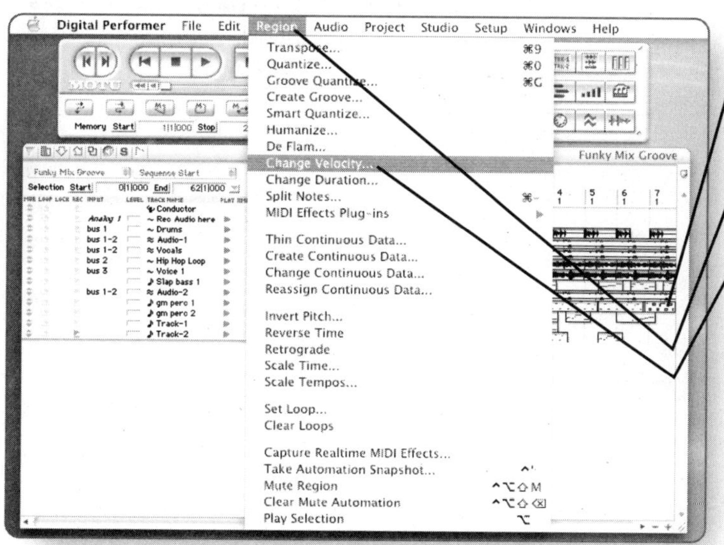

1. Create a **selection** of MIDI notes using one of the selection methods.

2. Click on **Region**. The Region menu will appear.

3. Click on **Change Velocity**. The Change Velocity window will open.

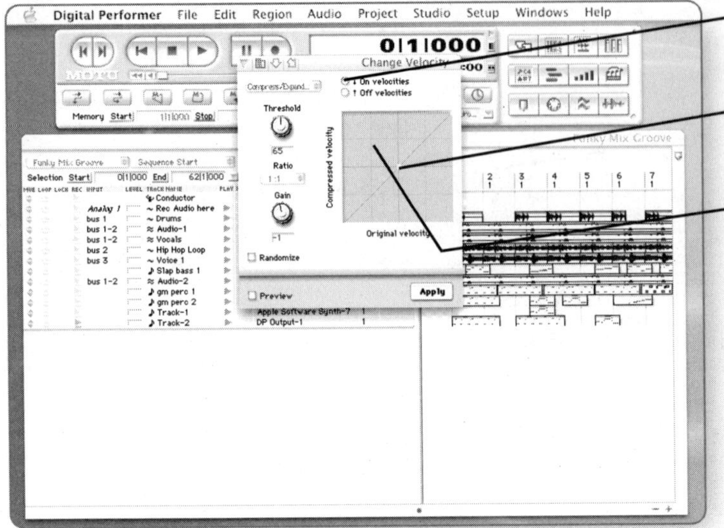

4. **Click** on the desired **On** or **Off** velocities.

5. **Position** your **mouse pointer** over the Threshold/Gain handle.

6. **Click** and **drag** the **handle** to a new location. The threshold and gain for the selection will change as you drag.

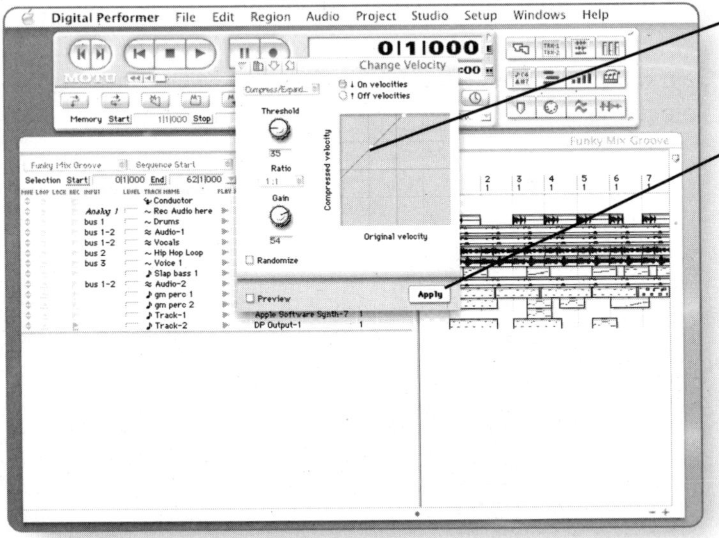

7. **Release** the **mouse button**. The threshold and gain will be adjusted.

8. **Click** on **Apply.** The changes will be applied.

Changing Duration

The duration of a note is defined as the length between its attack and its release. Rather than having to change the duration of MIDI notes one by one, using one of the editors, you can modify the duration of all of the notes within a particular sequence using the Change Duration function. This function will change the duration of the notes without changing the location of the attack times.

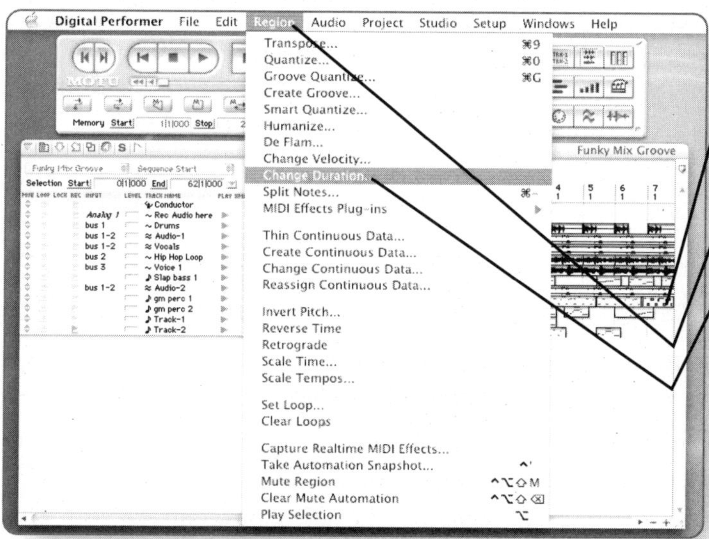

1. **Create** a **selection** of MIDI notes using one of the selection methods.
2. **Click** on **Region**. The Region menu will appear.
3. **Click** on **Change Duration**. The Change Duration window will open.

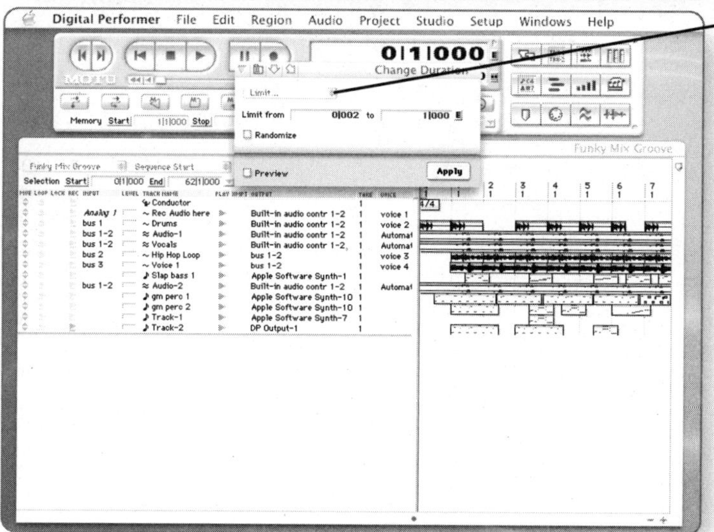

4. **Click** on the **up-and-down arrow**. A menu of duration options will appear.

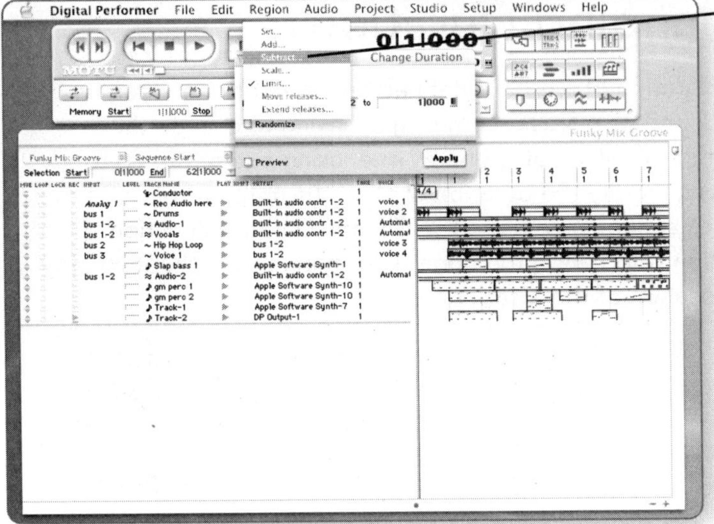

5. **Click** the desired **option**. It will be selected. The options include:

- **Set**. The value you enter will be used for all of the durations.
- **Add**. The value you enter will be added to the durations in the selection.
- **Subtract**. The value you enter will be subtracted from the durations in the selection.
- **Scale**. Enter a percentage value, and the durations in the selection will be increased by this amount.
- **Limit**. Set an upper and lower value, and all of the notes in the selection will get the longest or shortest value that you specify.
- **Move releases**. With this option, the release of each note in the selection will be moved to the closest attack.
- **Extent releases**. The notes will be extended until they reach the start of the next note.

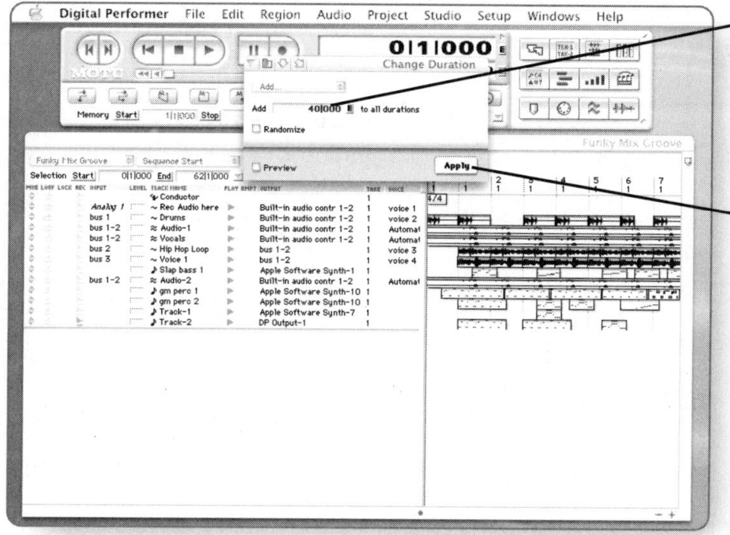

6. **Type** a **number**. Depending on the option that you have selected, you may have to enter a number to correspond with that option.

7. **Click** on **Apply**. The changes you have made will be applied and the dialog box will close.

The Conductor Track

The Conductor Track is different from all other types of tracks in Digital Performer. It contains special data, including information on the tempo, key, and meter of your sequences. When you make changes to tempo, key, or meter, they will be reflected in the Conductor Track.

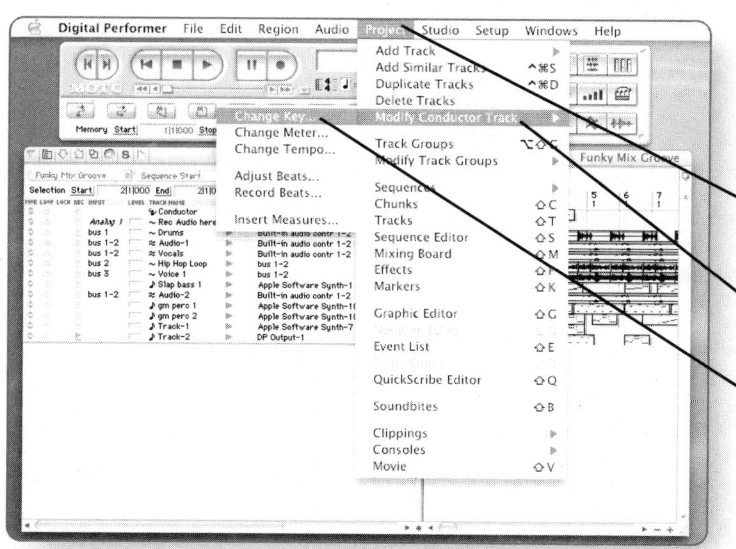

Changing Key

Using the Conductor Track, you can change the key of a particular MIDI selection.

1. **Click** on **Project**. The Project menu will appear.

2. **Click** on **Modify Conductor Track**. A submenu will appear.

3. **Click** on **Change Key**. The Change Key window will open.

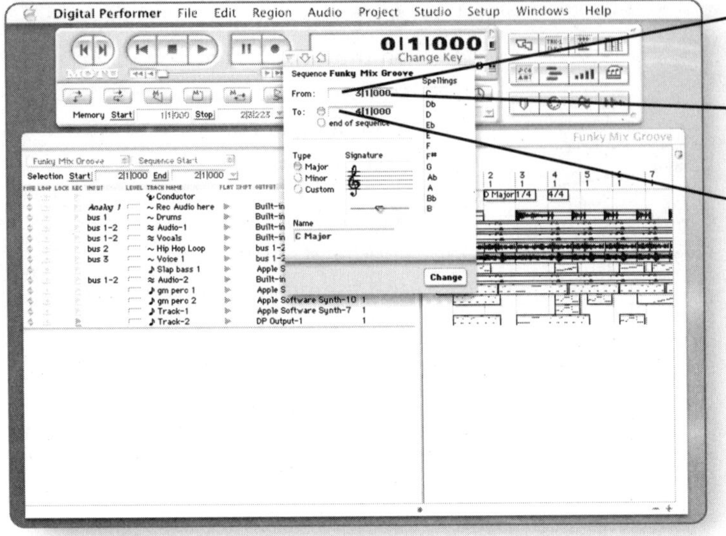

4. **Click** in the **From field**. It will be highlighted.

5. **Type** a **number** for the beginning of the key change.

6. **Click** in the **To field**. It will be highlighted.

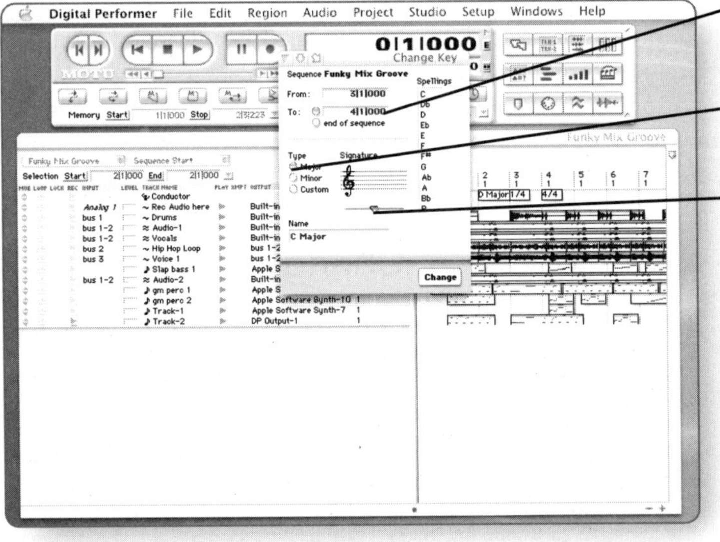

7. **Type** a **number** for the end of the key change.

8. **Click** on the **key type**. It will be selected.

9. **Position** the **mouse pointer** over the scroll bar.

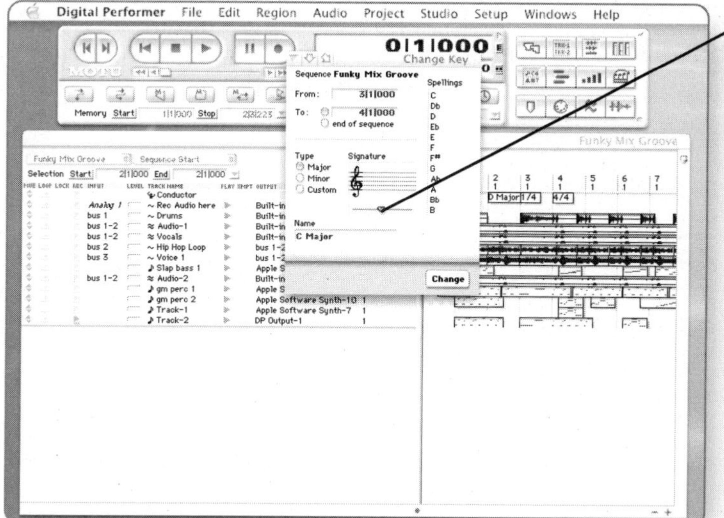

10. Click and **drag** the **scroll bar** left or right. As you drag, the key name and spelling will change.

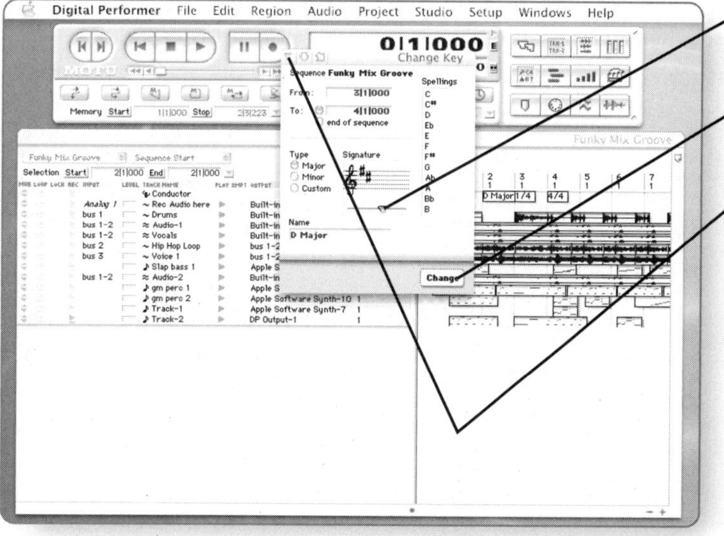

11. Release the **mouse button**. The key will be adjusted.

12. Click on **Change**. The key change will be applied.

13. Click on the **down arrow** to close the dialog box once you have completed all of your desired key changes.

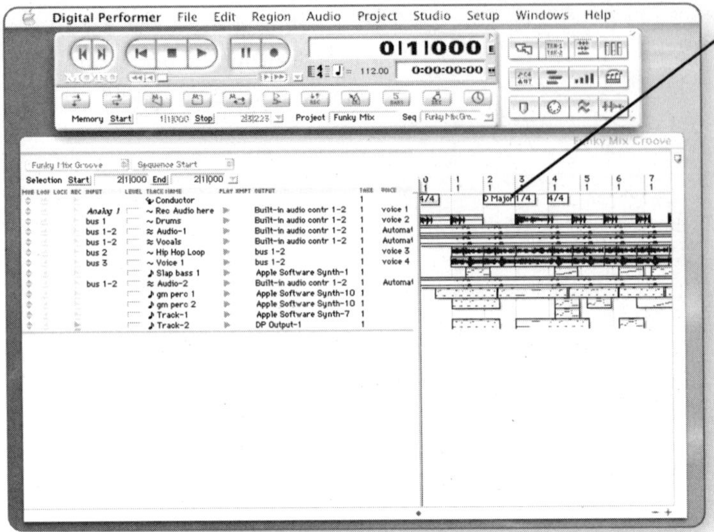

14. View the **Conductor Track**. Any changes you have made will be reflected there.

Changing Meter

You can change the meter for your entire track. You can change both the beat value and the number of beats per measure.

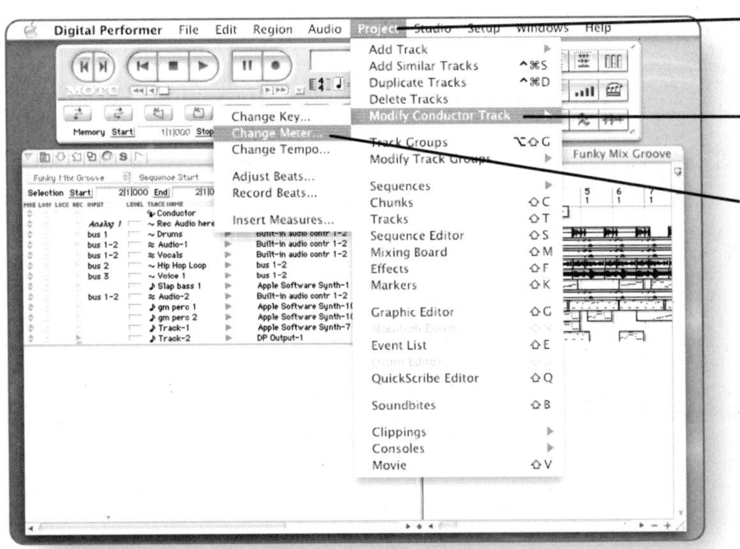

1. Click on **Project**. The Project menu will appear.

2. Click on **Modify Conductor Track**. A submenu will appear.

3. Click on **Change Meter**. The Change Meter window will open.

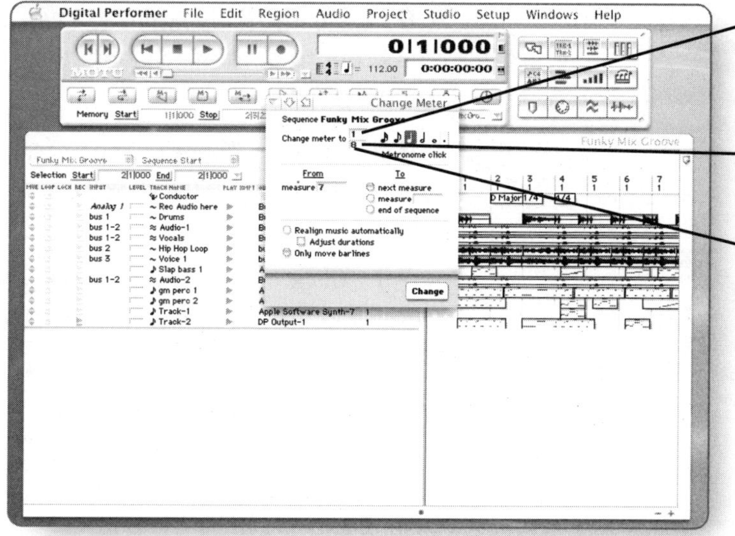

4. **Type** a **number** for the number of beats per measure. It will appear as you type.

5. **Press** the **Tab key**. You will move to the Beat Value field.

6. **Type** a **number** for the beat value. It will appear as you type.

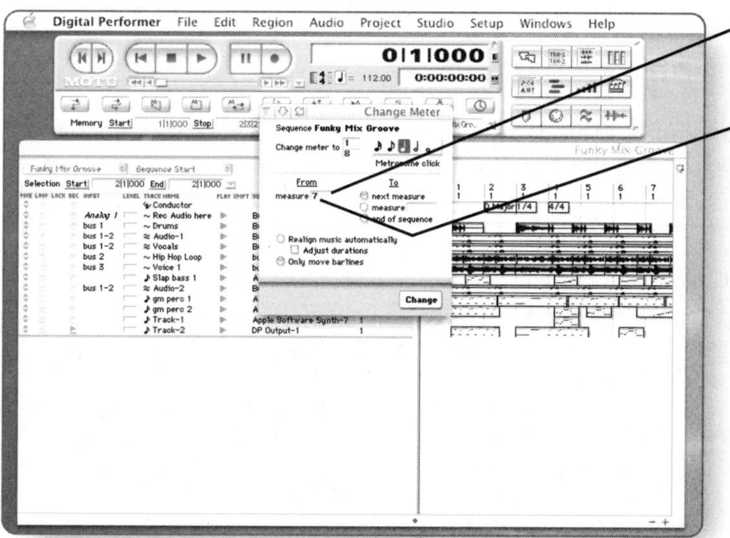

7. **Click** in the **From field**. It will be highlighted.

8. **Type** the **measure number** where you would like this meter change to start.

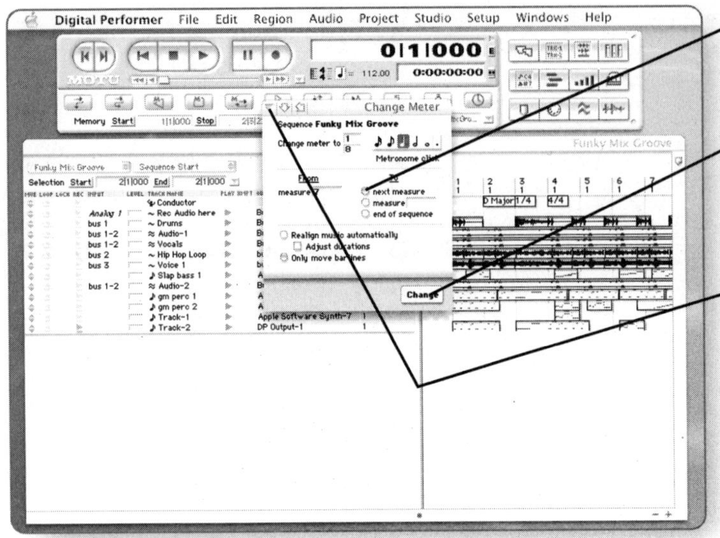

9. **Click** on an **option** under To in order to determine where this meter change will end.

10. **Click** on **Change**. The settings you have made will be applied.

11. **Click** on the **down arrow** to close the window.

> **NOTE**
>
> The number of beats per measure must be between 1 and 99, while the beat value must be 2, 4, 8, 16, 32, or 64.

Changing Tempo

Changing the tempo for a particular part of your sequence is a breeze using the Change Tempo window in Digital Performer.

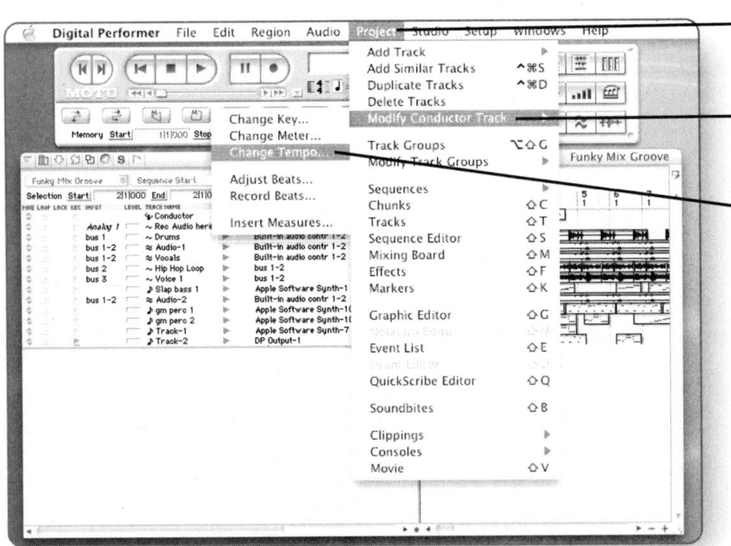

1. **Click** on **Project**. The Project menu will appear.

2. **Click** on **Modify Conductor Track**. A submenu will appear.

3. **Click** on **Change Tempo**. The Change Tempo window will open.

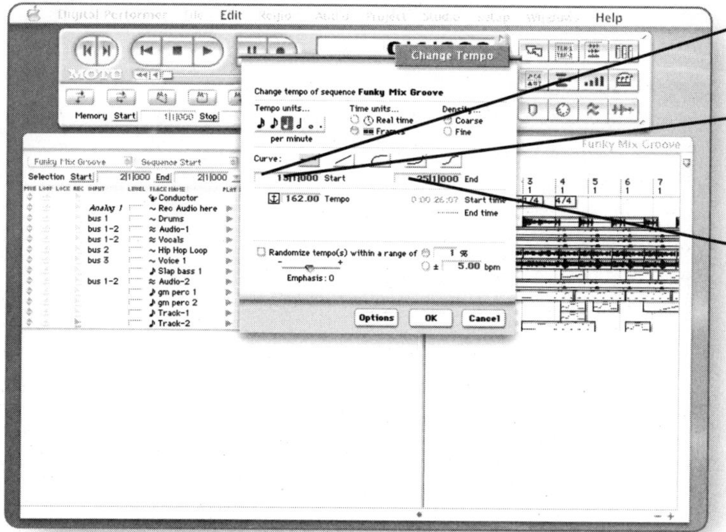

4. Click in the **Start field**. It will be highlighted.

5. Type a **number** indicating where you want the tempo change to begin.

6. Click in the **End field**. It will be highlighted.

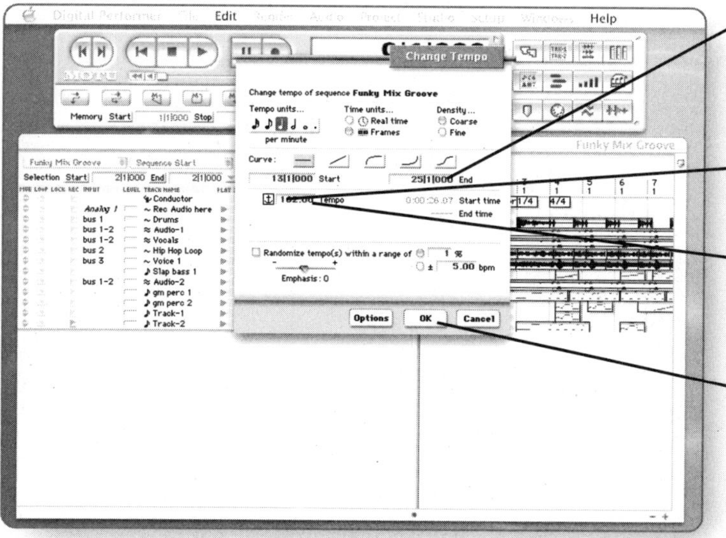

7. Type a **number** indicating where you want the tempo change to end.

8. Double-click in the **Tempo field**. It will be highlighted.

9. Type a **number** for the tempo. It will appear as you type.

10. Click on **OK**. The tempo change will take effect.

10

The List Editor

Digital Performer makes a distinction when it comes to editing audio files versus MIDI files. Basically, a MIDI file is just a bunch of data. The data is sent to a device such as a synthesizer, computer, or music keyboard, and that device assigns a sound to the data. Digital Performer provides you with a vast number of editing capabilities when it comes to MIDI files. This chapter examines one of those editing functions: the List Editor. In this chapter, you will learn how to:

- Edit MIDI data
- Create MIDI notes
- Insert MIDI events

Launching the List Editor

The List Editor is a dialog box that provides you with a wide variety of information on all of the data within a specific track. It shows all types of information, including MIDI data and corresponding events.

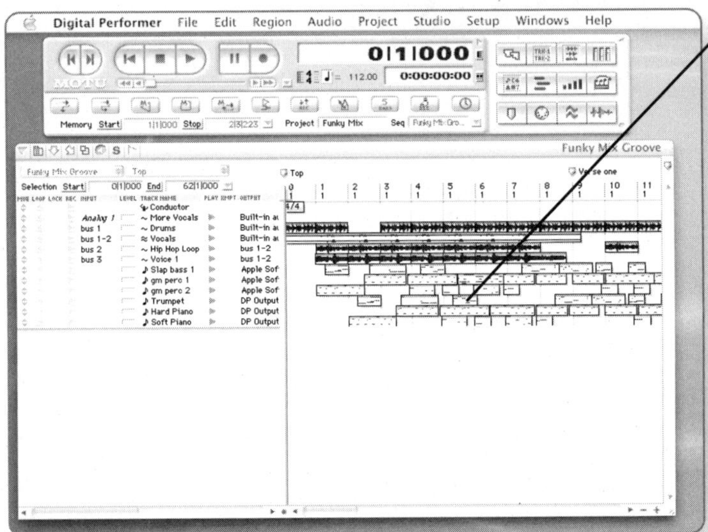

1. **Double-click** on any **MIDI phrase** in the Tracks window. A MIDI phrase appears as a box with a small note in it. The List Editor will launch.

Getting to Know the List Editor

When you first open the List Editor, the amount of data you see can be quite intimidating. Not all of the numbers and icons seem to make much sense at first glance. The List Editor contains information on each note within the track.

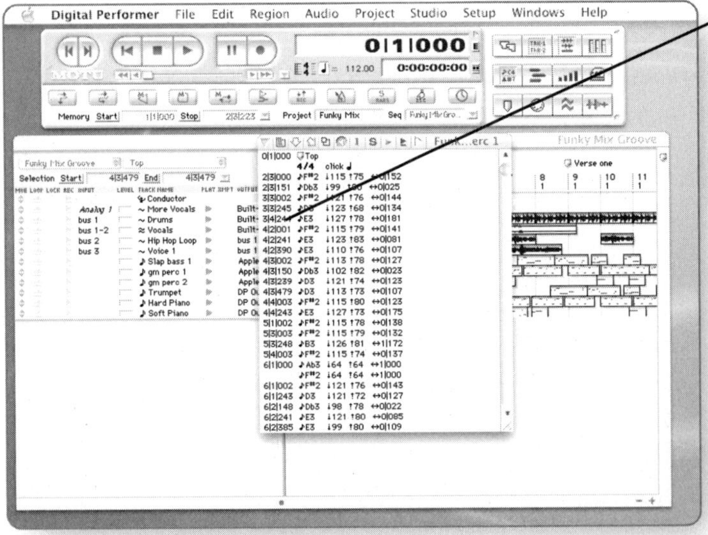

- **Location**. This number indicates the location of the note (in other words, the spot at which the note starts).

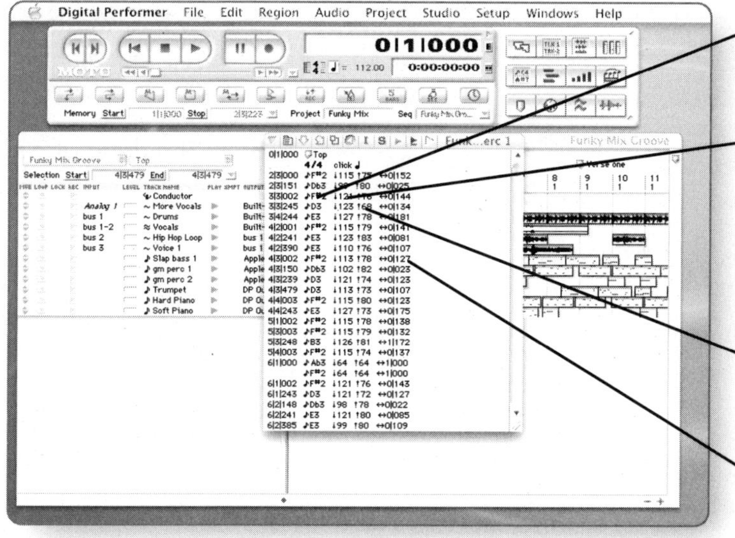

- **Note**. This shows you what note is being played at that location.
- **Velocity on Attack**. This represents the velocity when the note is started. This refers to how hard the key was pressed on your MIDI device.
- **Velocity on Release**. This represents the velocity as the note ends.
- **Note Duration**. This shows how long the note or event is played in beats and ticks.

Editing Data

You can change any of the data in the List Editor by simply double-clicking on an item and making the desired changes.

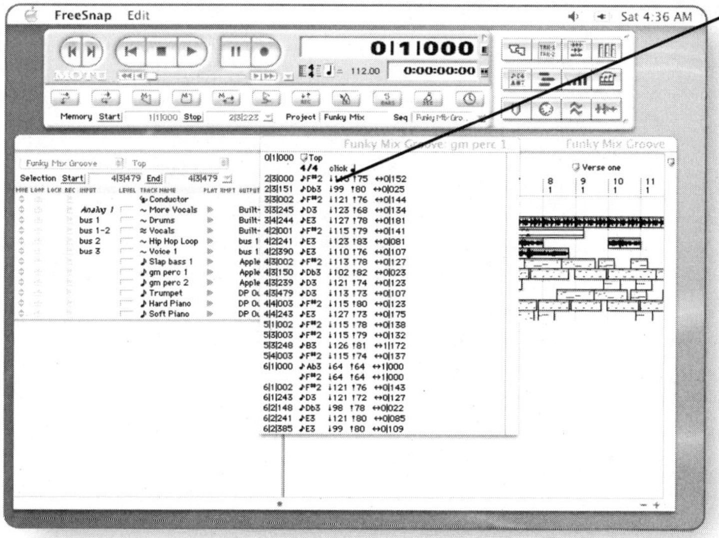

1. Double-click on any **item** in the List Editor. The item will appear highlighted in a box.

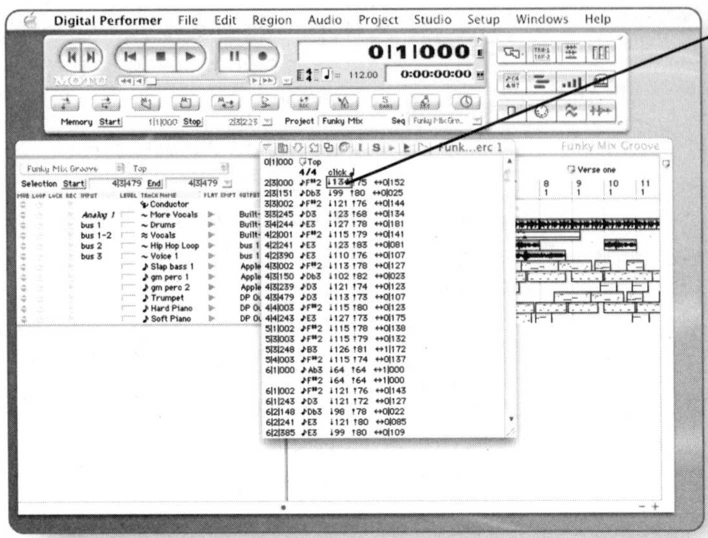

2. **Type** in the **new information** for the item. It will appear as you type.

3. **Press Return**. The data will be edited.

Deleting Notes

If you want to remove a note from your track, you simply have to select it and then delete it.

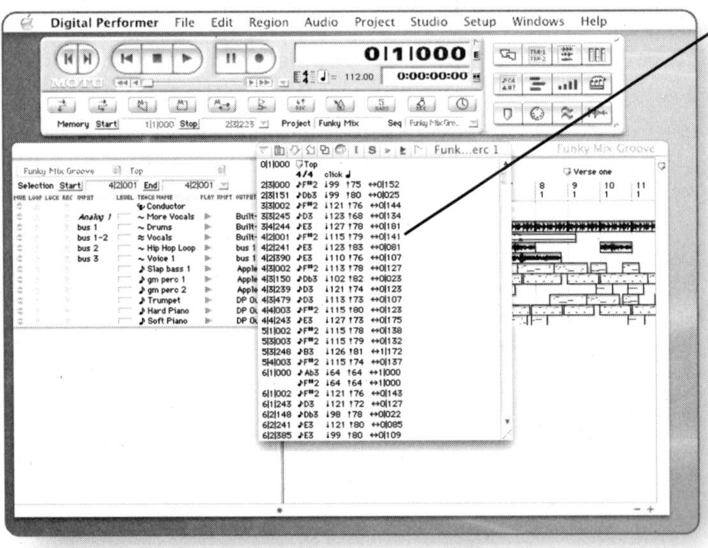

1. **Click once** on any **line** in the List Editor to select it. The line will be highlighted to indicate that it has been selected.

2. **Press** the **Delete key** on your keyboard. The line will be deleted, meaning the note that the line represented will be removed from the track.

Creating Data

The List Editor allows you to add a variety of data to your tracks, including new notes, pitch bends, patch changes, and other MIDI events.

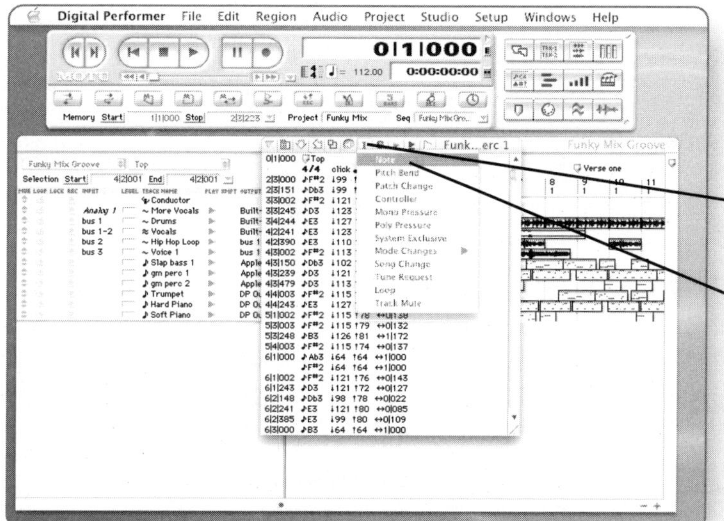

Adding Notes

Using the List Editor, you can add individual notes to your tracks.

1. **Click** on the **Insert button**. A menu will appear.
2. **Click** on **Note**. You will be prompted to enter information about the item that you would like to add.

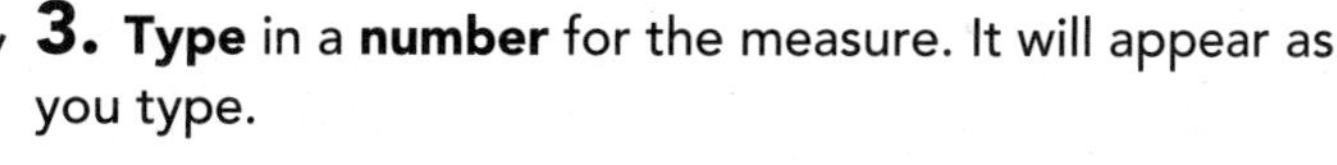

3. **Type** in a **number** for the measure. It will appear as you type.

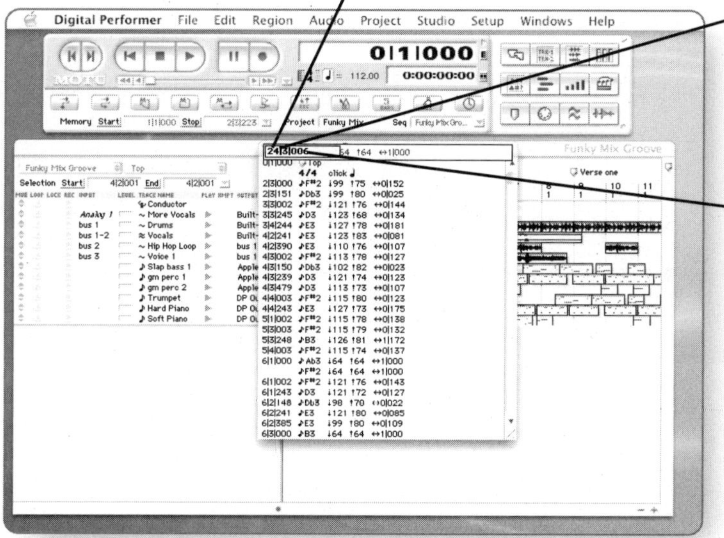

4. **Click** on the **beats number**. It will be highlighted.
5. **Type** in a new **number** for the beat.
6. **Repeat steps 4 and 5** for the ticks section.
7. **Press** the **right arrow** key on the keyboard to advance to the next field.

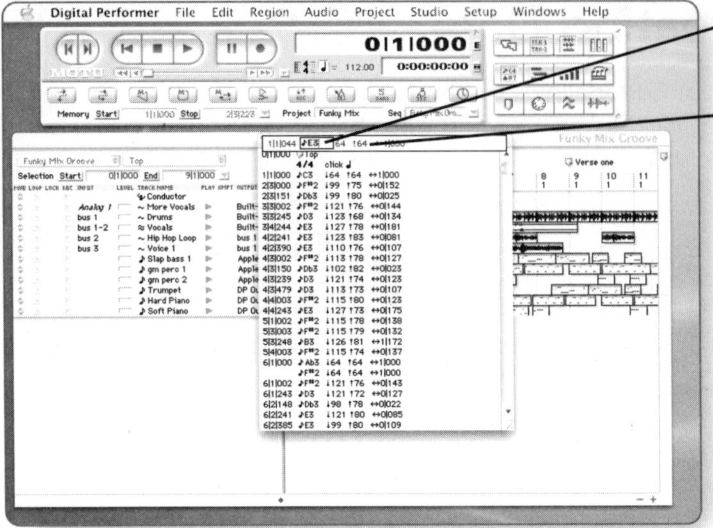

8. **Type** in a **new value** for the note in this field.

9. **Repeat steps 7 and 8** until the information for all the fields has been entered.

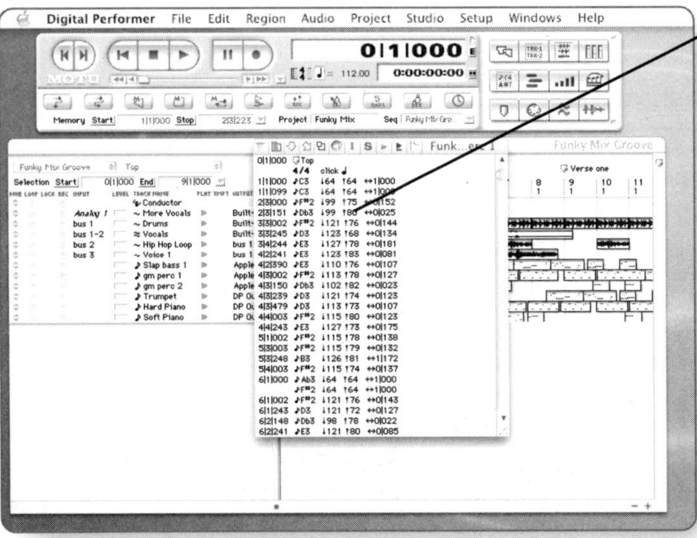

10. **Press Return**. The note will be added with the settings you have entered.

Pitch Bend

Many keyboards have a pitch bend wheel that allows you to change the pitch for a particular channel. In Digital Performer, you can create a pitch bend without having any extra equipment. You can insert a pitch bend at any location using the List Editor.

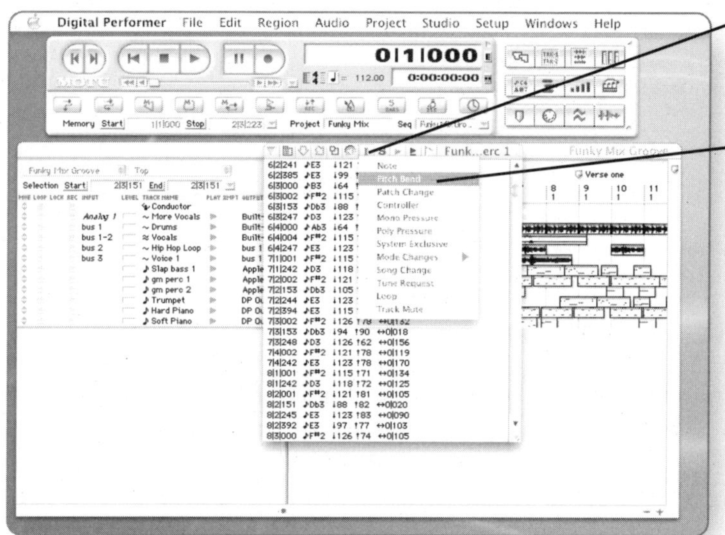

1. **Click** on the **Insert button**. A menu of different MIDI events will appear.

2. **Click** on **Pitch Bend**. A box will appear, prompting you to enter a time for the pitch bend to occur.

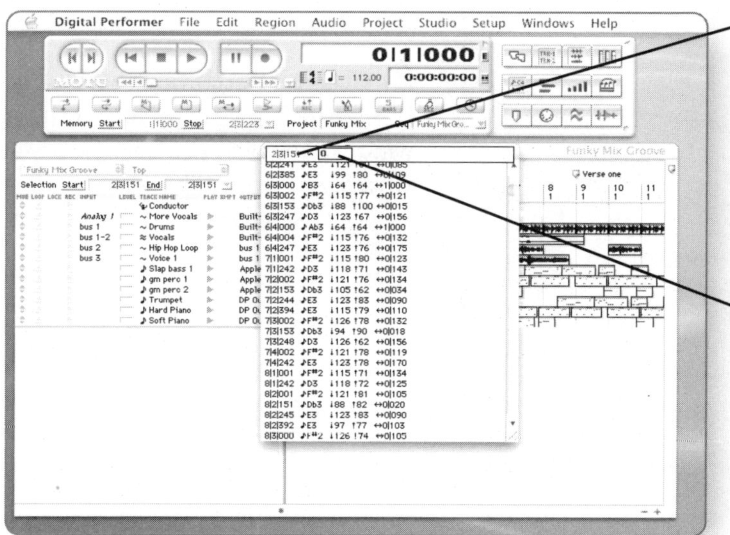

3. **Type** in a **location** for the pitch bend. Using the mouse, you can click on the different numbers to change the beat and tick information.

4. **Press** the **right arrow key** to advance to the next field.

5. **Type** a **number** for the pitch bend. You can enter any number between –8192 and 8191.

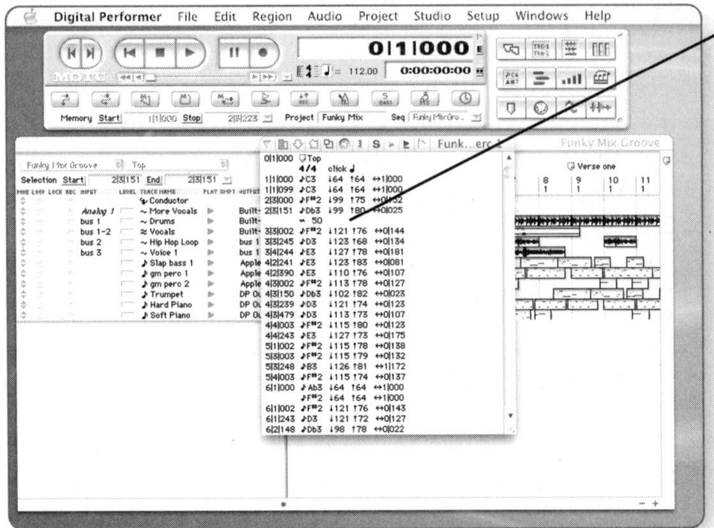

6. Press Return. The pitch bend will be added to the Events list. It can be edited like any other item in the window if you want to make changes.

Patch Change

Using the List Editor, you can assign a different patch to a MIDI track at any time. You simply have to determine where you want the patch change to occur and then select the appropriate patch.

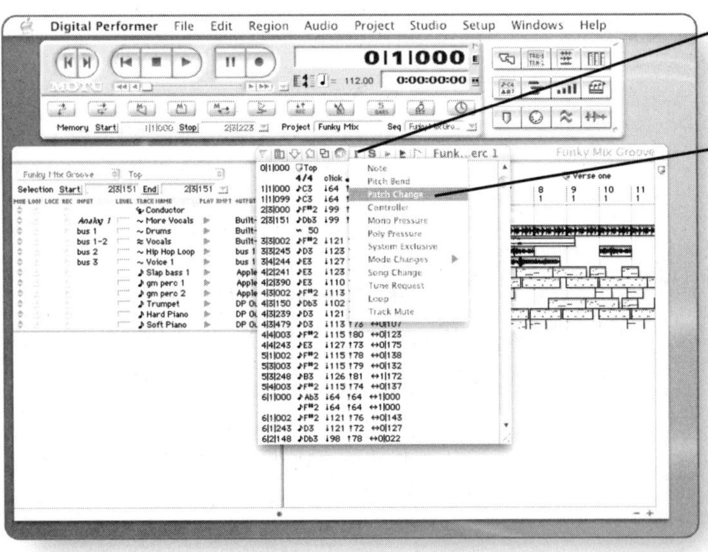

1. **Click** on the **Insert button**. A menu of different MIDI events will appear.
2. **Click** on **Patch Change**. A box will appear at the top of the window in which you can specify where you would like your patch change to occur.

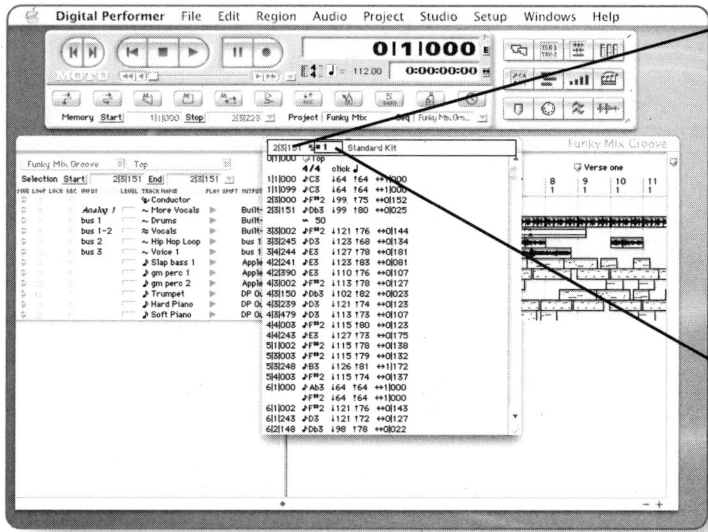

3. **Type** in a **location** for the patch change. Using the mouse, you can click on the different numbers to change the beat and tick information.

4. **Press** the **right arrow key** to advance to the next field. You will now be able to enter a number for the patch change.

5. **Type** the **number** of the patch you desire. If you don't know the number of the patch, don't worry; you can select it later from a list. Depending on your MIDI instrument, you can enter a range from 0 to 127.

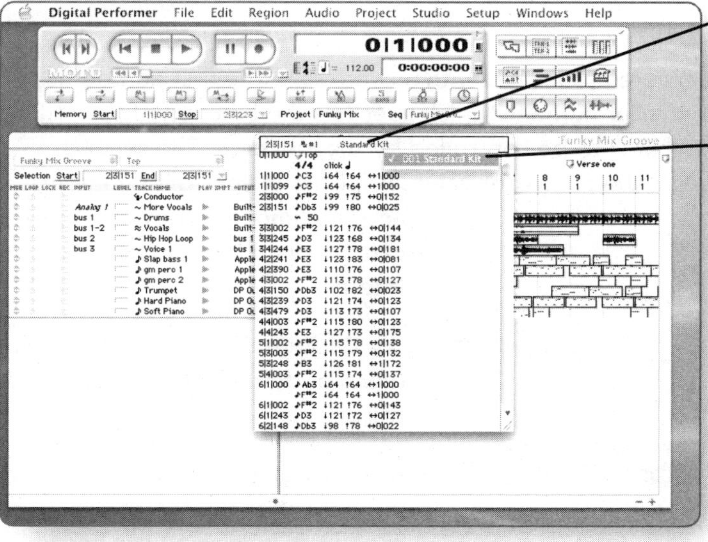

6. **Click** on the **patch name**. You can select the patch from a list.

7. **Click** on the desired **patch**. It will be selected.

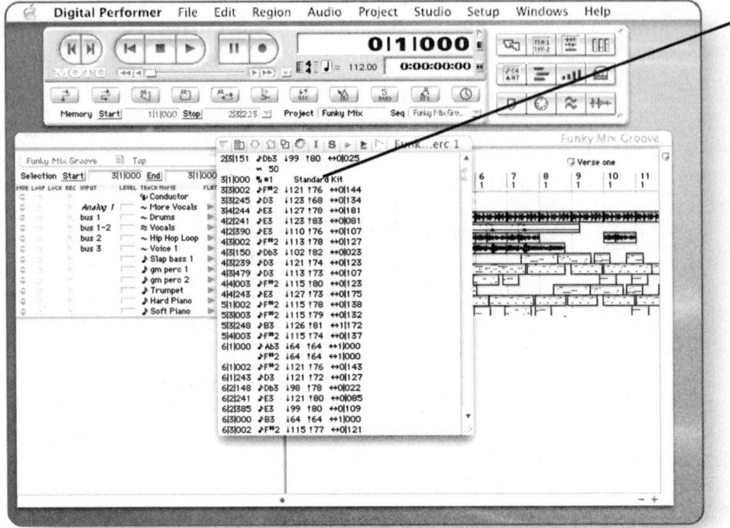

8. Press Return. The patch change will be inserted into the track.

Controller

A controller is used to send a message to a MIDI device. Two numbers are associated with a controller. The first number is the controller number, which specifies the function of the MIDI device that is to be controlled by the message. The second number is the controller value. A full list of controller numbers and the functions they provide can be found by searching the Internet.

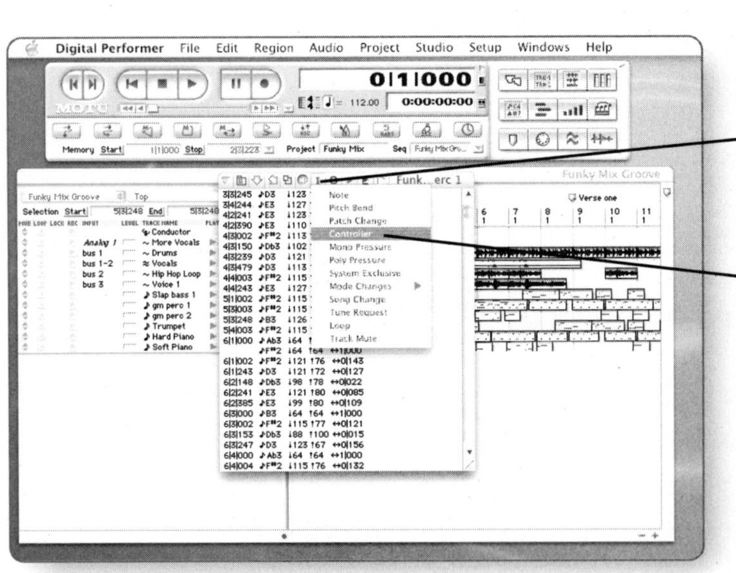

1. **Click** on the **Insert button**. A menu of different MIDI events will appear.

2. **Click** on **Controller**. A box will appear at the top of the window in which you can specify where you would like control message to occur.

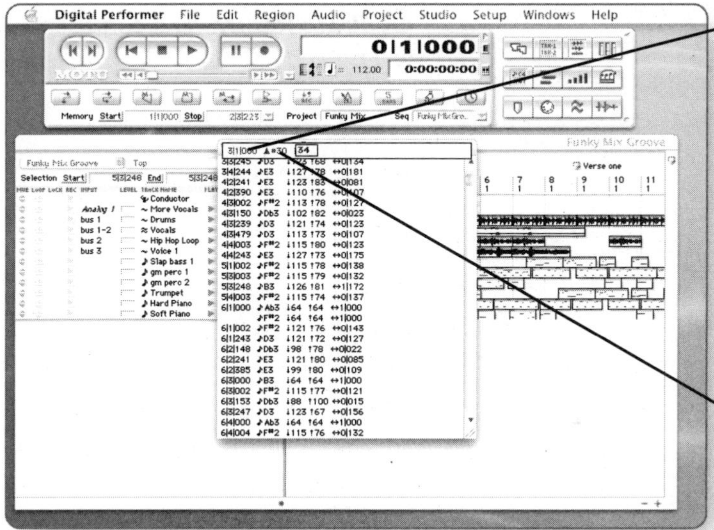

3. Type in a **location** for the control change. Using the mouse, you can click on the different numbers to change the beat and tick information.

4. Press the **right arrow key** to advance to the next field. You will now be able to enter a number for the controller number.

5. Type a **number** for the controller message. This can be any number between 0 and 120.

6. Press the **right arrow key** to advance to the next field.

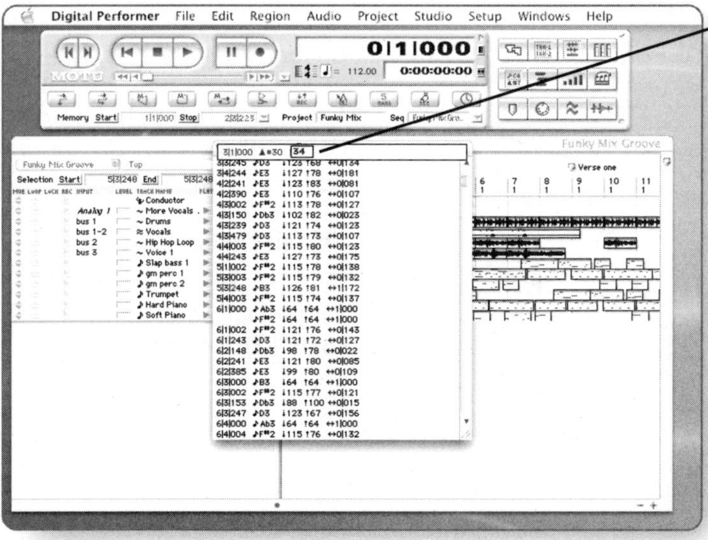

7. Type a **number** for the controller value. This can be any number between 0 and 127.

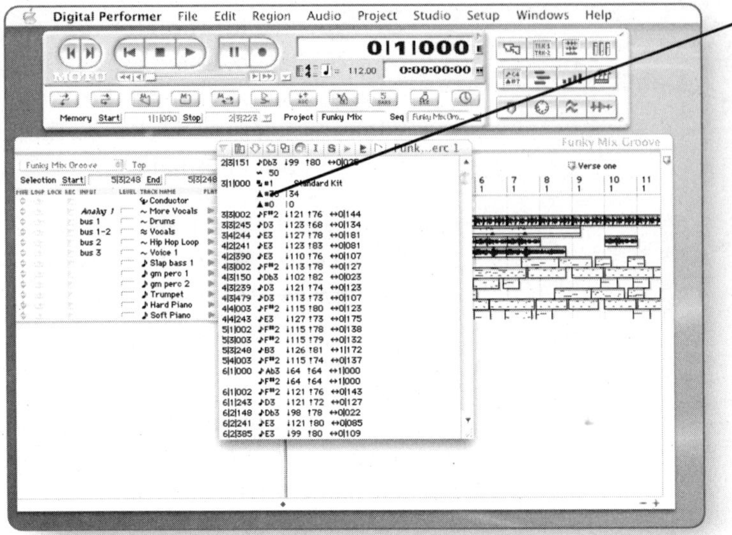

8. Press Return. The controller will be activated.

Loop

The List Editor offers a way to include loops in your tracks.

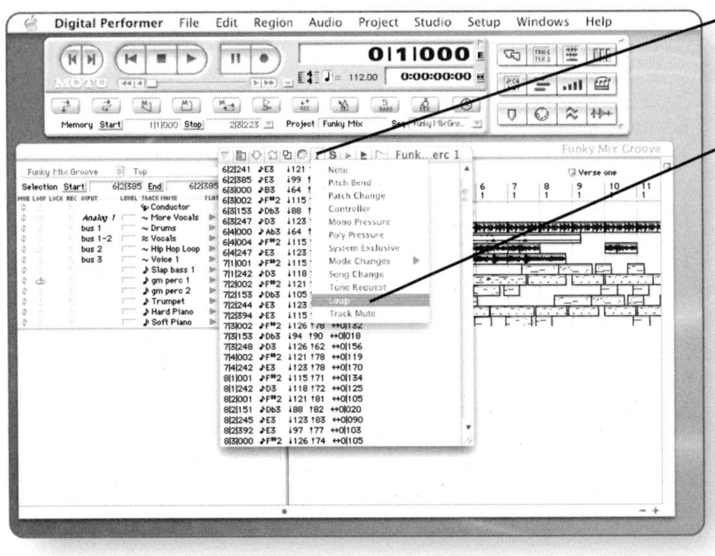

1. **Click** on the **Insert button**. A menu of different MIDI events will appear.
2. **Click** on **Loop**. A box will appear at the top of the window in which you can specify where you would like a loop to occur.

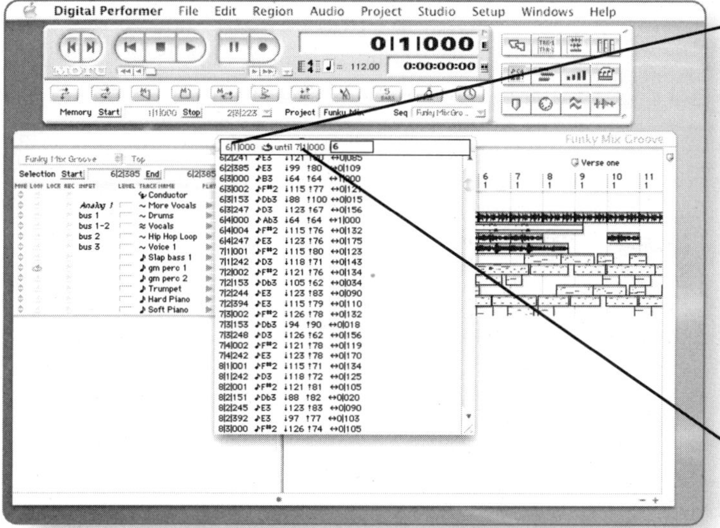

3. Type in a **location** where the loop should begin. Using the mouse, you can click on the different numbers to change the beat and tick information.

4. Press the **right arrow key** to advance to the next field. You will now be able to enter an end time for the loop. This corresponds to the song number on your drum machine.

5. Type in a **location** where the loop should end. Using the mouse, you can click on the different numbers to change the beat and tick information.

6. Press the **right arrow key** to advance to the next field.

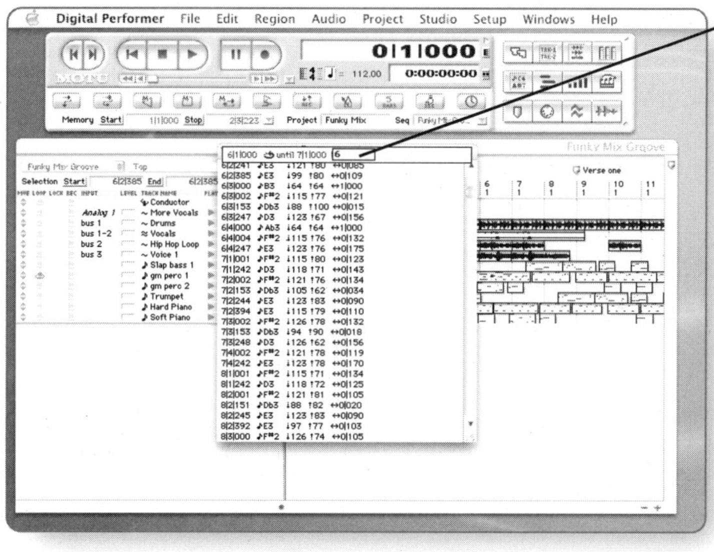

7. Type the **number** of times you would like the loop to occur.

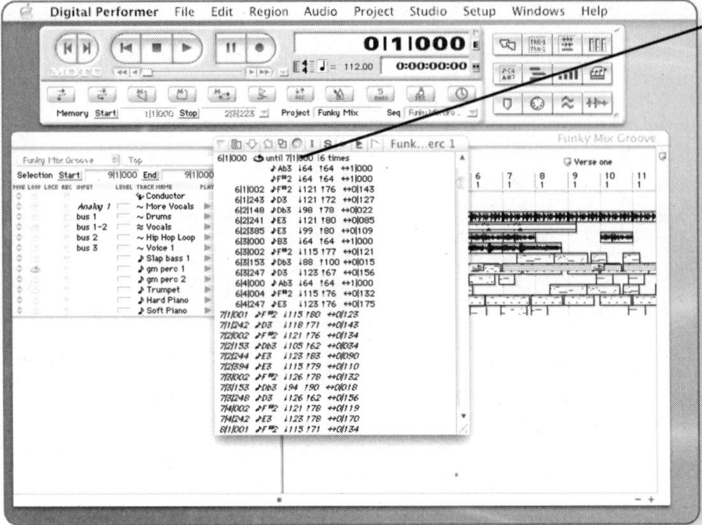

8. Press Return. The song change will be activated at the location you have specified.

11

The Graphic Editor

The Graphic Editor is another tool available for MIDI manipulation in Digital Performer. Unlike the List Editor, the Graphic Editor gives you a visual representation of your MIDI tracks, which means you can edit tracks live on-screen, without having to adjust data in a window. In this chapter, you'll learn how to:

- Use the Graphic Editor interface
- Edit MIDI tracks
- Add MIDI events

Launching the Graphic Editor

To launch the Graphic Editor, you simply have to select a track and then press the Graphic Editor button.

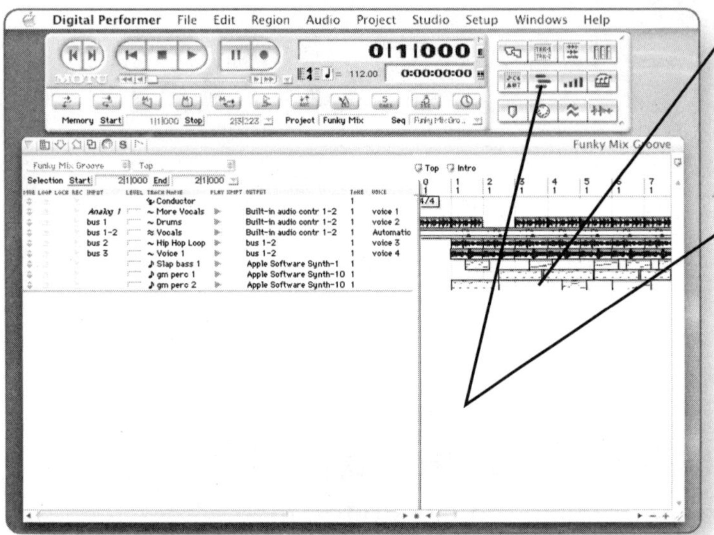

1. **Click** on the **MIDI track** that you would like to edit. You will be able to open other tracks once you are in the Graphic Editor.
2. **Click** on the **Graphic Editor button** in the Control Panel. The Graphic Editor will launch.

Getting to Know the Graphic Editor

The Graphic Editor is a powerful tool. The fact that it can do so much contributes to its complex appearance. Once you understand the environment of the Graphic Editor, the actual editing process will be a breeze.

- **MIDI Data window.** This window represents MIDI notes as small bars. These bars can be edited directly in this window.
- **Events window.** The Events window illustrates MIDI events as graphics. These events can be altered directly on the screen.

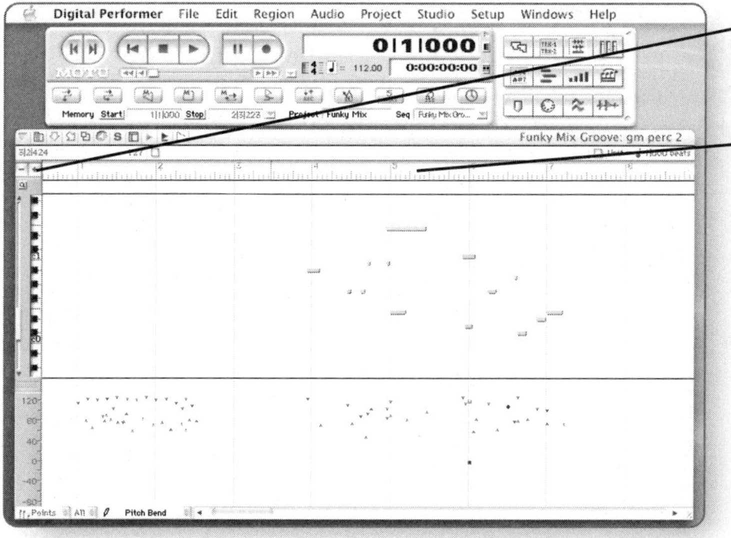

- **Zoom controls**. The Zoom controls allow you to zoom in and out of MIDI windows.
- **Continuous Data Ruler**. This ruler is used to measure MIDI events.

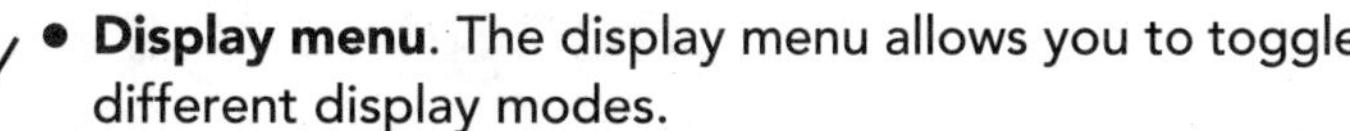

- **Display menu**. The display menu allows you to toggle different display modes.

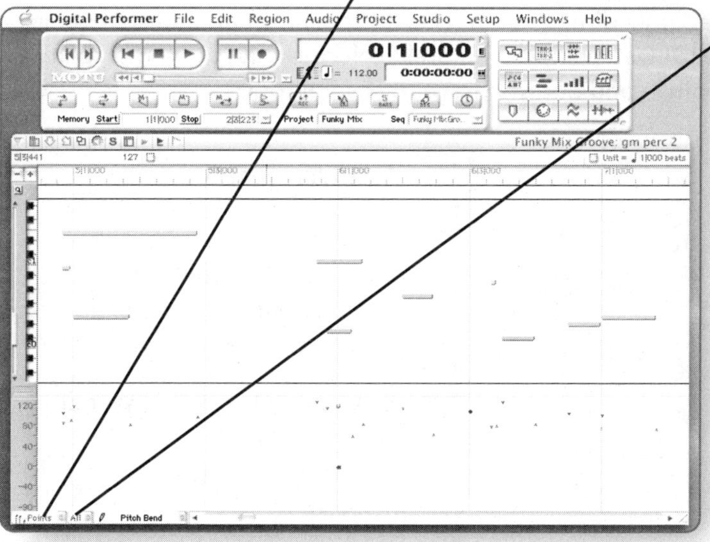

- **Grid View Filter menu**. This menu allows you to change what appears in the Events window.

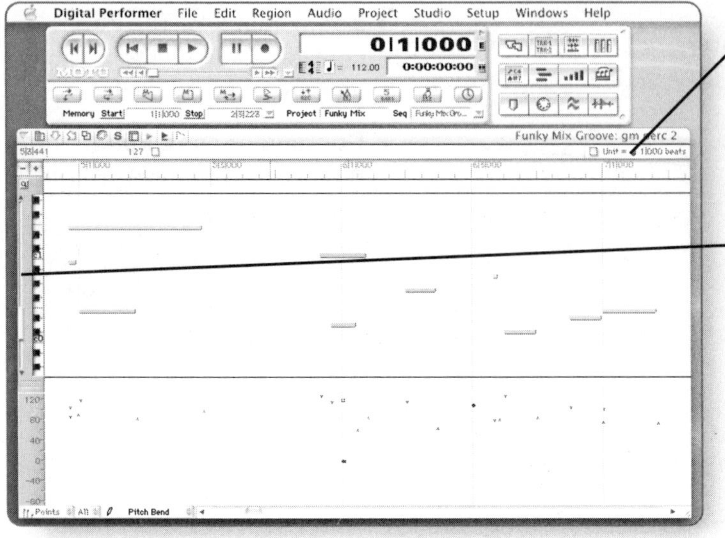

- **Resolution**. When positioning data, you can set it up so that the data snaps to the resolution grid. You can adjust the resolution of the grid in this area.
- **Mini scroll bar**. This can be used to scroll to different areas of the Pitch Ruler that are not within the current range.

Changing Views

Depending on the length and number of tracks, it can become exceedingly difficult to view all of the information displayed in the MIDI Data window. Digital Performer gives you the ability to zoom in and out of data with several tools.

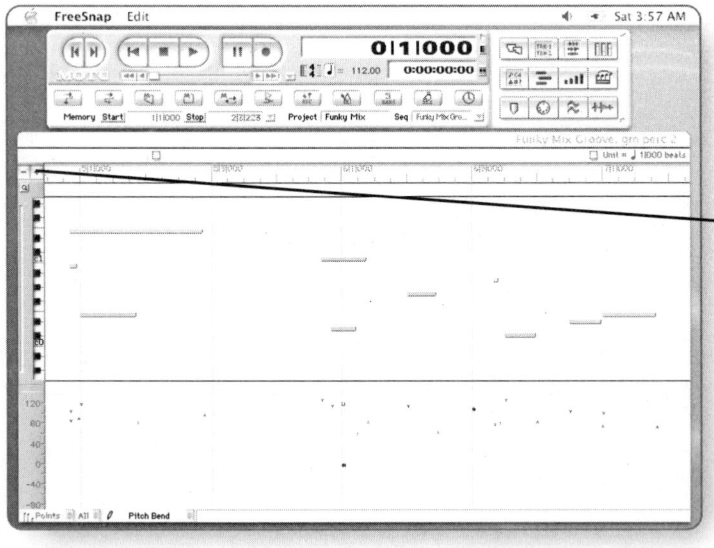

Zoom Tools

Using the Zoom tools, you can change the horizontal zoom of the MIDI Data window so you can get a better view of your data.

1. **Click** on the **+ Zoom tool** to zoom into the data. The horizontal zoom level will increase.
2. **Repeat step 1** until the desired zoom level is reached. Each time you click, the window will zoom in even further until the maximum zoom level has been reached.

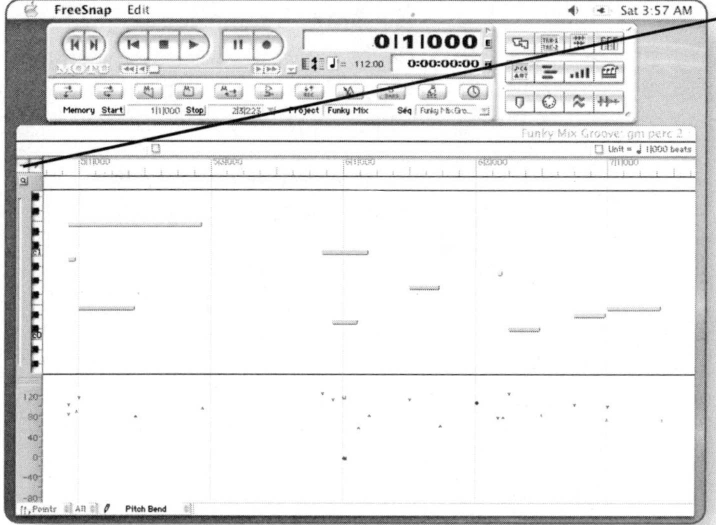

3. Click on the **– Zoom tool** to zoom out of the data. The horizontal zoom level will decrease.

4. Repeat step 3 until the desired zoom level is reached. Each time you click, the window will zoom out further until the maximum zoom level has been reached.

> **TIP**
>
> Pressing and holding the Option key while clicking the + or – Zoom tool will take you to the maximum zoom level.

Pitch Zoom

While the Zoom tools allow you to change the horizontal zoom, the Pitch zoom allows you to adjust the vertical zoom.

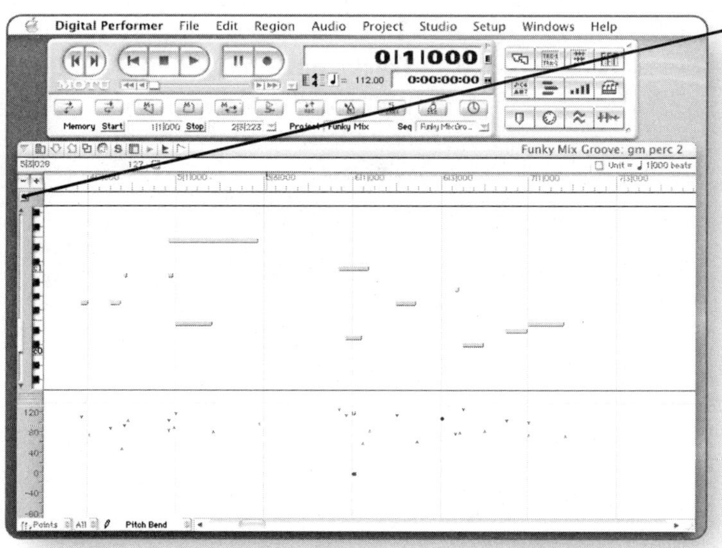

1. Click and **hold** the **Zoom button**. A small box with a zoom indicator will appear.

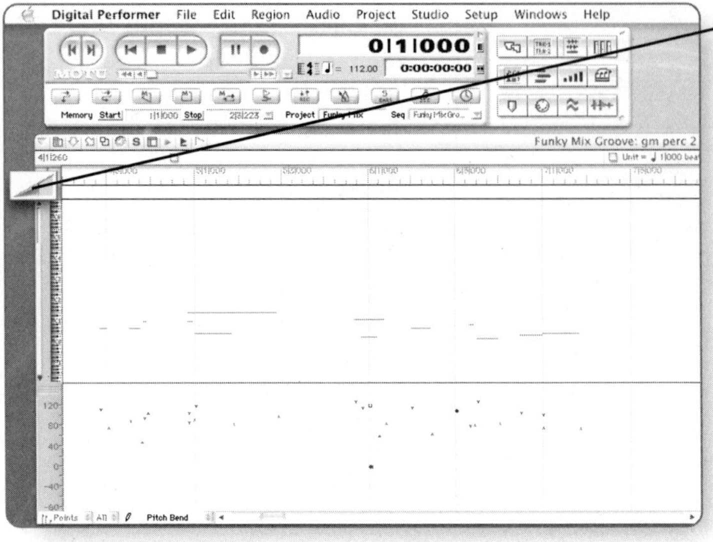

2. **Drag** to the **left** or **right** to decrease or increase the vertical zoom. The vertical zoom level will change as you drag.

3. **Release** the **mouse button**. The zoom level will be set.

Viewing Multiple Tracks

When you open the Graphic Viewer, you must first select a track that opens in the Viewer. Once you have the Graphic Viewer open, you can open all or some of the additional tracks in the same window.

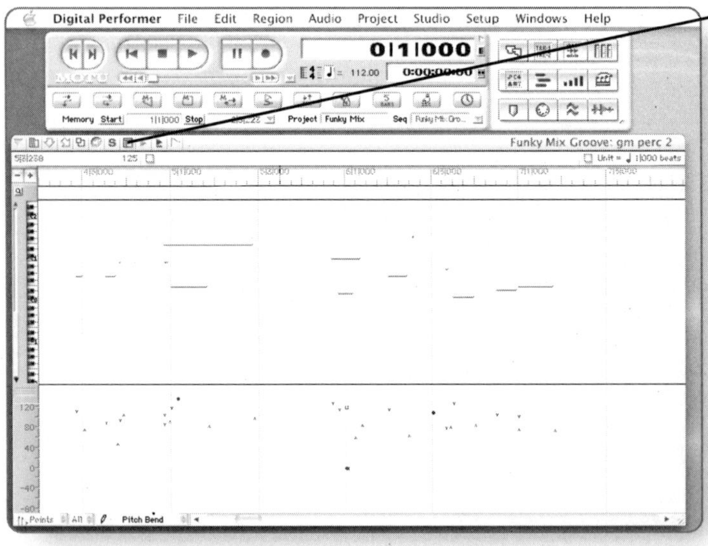

1. **Click** on the **Show/Hide Tracks button**. A list of all of the tracks in the sequence will appear on the left side of the window.

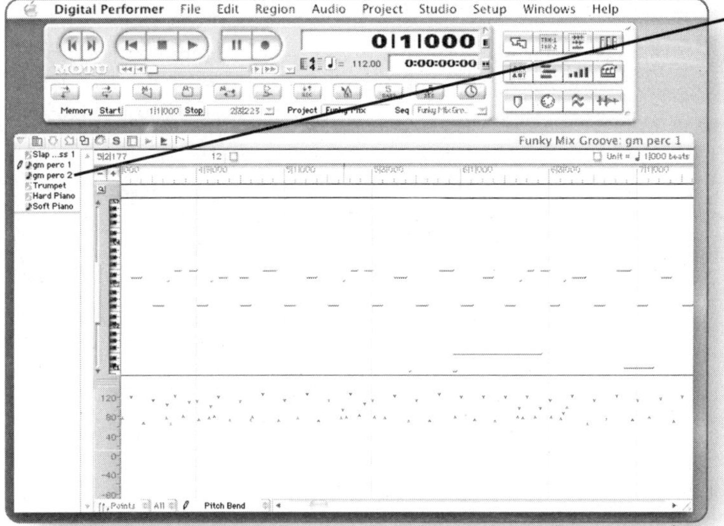

2. **Click** on the **tracks** that you would like to display. As you click, the track will be highlighted and the data will show up in the MIDI Data window.

3. **Click** on any **highlighted track** to deselect it.

Selecting Notes

In order to edit MIDI notes, you must first select them. Digital Performer provides you with a variety of different ways to select notes.

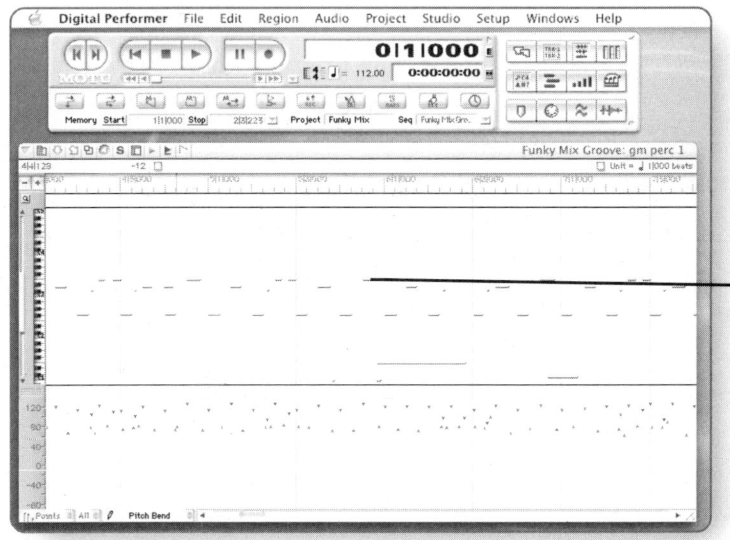

Selecting an Individual Note

To select individual notes, you simply have to click on the desired note and it will be selected.

1. **Position** your **mouse pointer** over the note that you would like to select. The mouse pointer will change from a crosshair to a pointer.

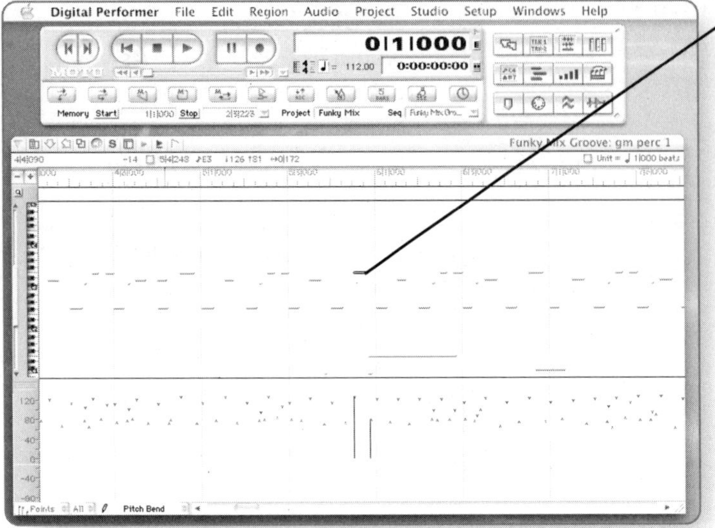

2. Click once on the **note**. The note will have a black outline to indicate that it is highlighted. If you position your mouse pointer over the selected note, the pointer will turn into a small hand.

> **TIP**
>
> You can click on any blank area of the window to deselect all notes.

Selecting Multiple Notes

Digital Performer provides you with two techniques to select multiple MIDI notes.

Shift Selecting

The Shift Select method is useful when you want to select a variety of individual notes that are non-contiguous.

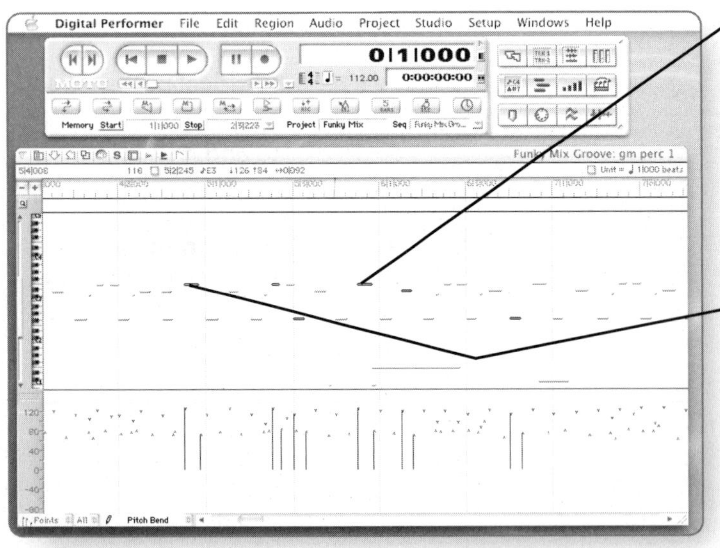

1. **Click** on a **note** to select it. The note will appear yellow with a black outline.
2. **Press** the **Shift key**. Continue holding the Shift key until you have completed all of your selections.
3. **Click** on **another note** to select it. Both the original note and this note will be selected.

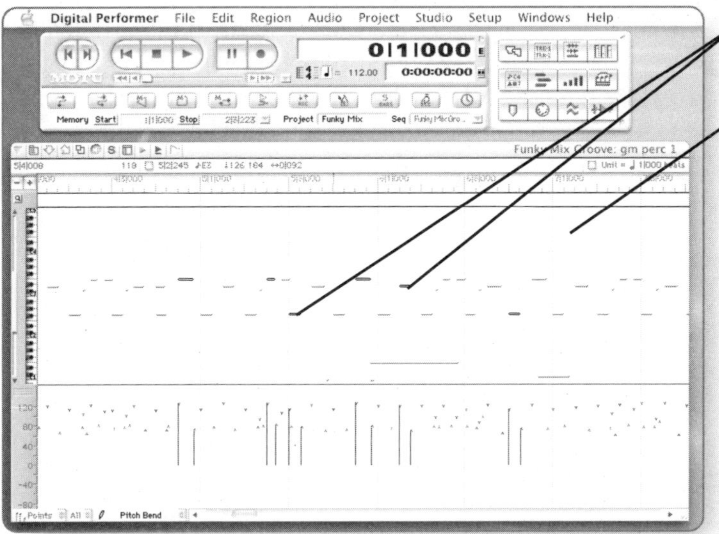

4. Repeat step 3 until you have completed selecting notes.

5. Click in any **blank area** of the window to deselect the notes.

Clicking and Dragging

Clicking and dragging is the fastest way to select multiple notes. You can combine the Shift Select method with clicking and dragging to select groups of notes that are non-contiguous.

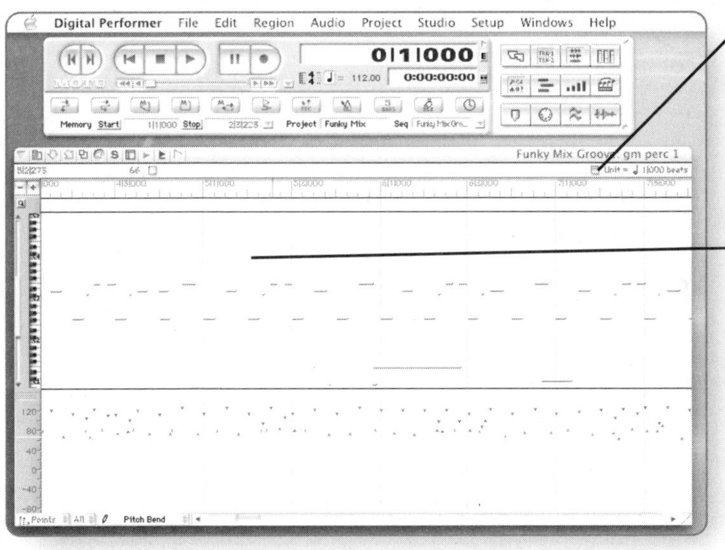

1. Click on the **square button** to the left of Unit to disable snapping to grid. This will allow you more freedom when making selections. The button will not be highlighted when disabled.

2. Position the **mouse pointer** up and to the left of the notes that you would like to select.

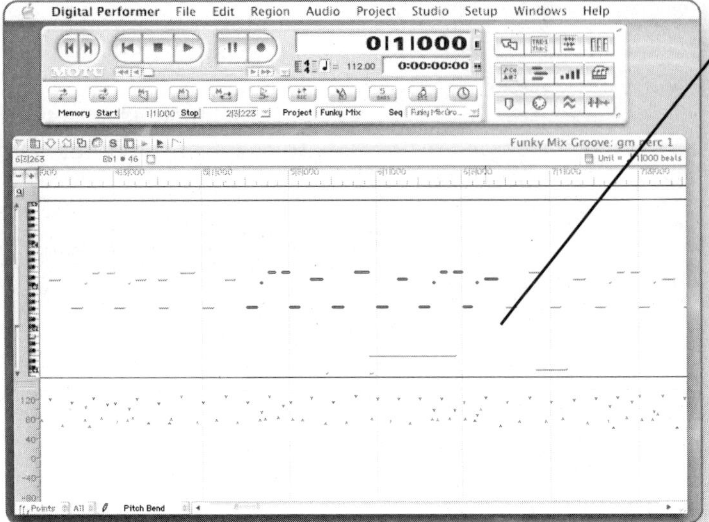

3. Click and **drag diagonally**. A light blue box will appear as you drag. Every note within that box will be selected when you release the mouse button.

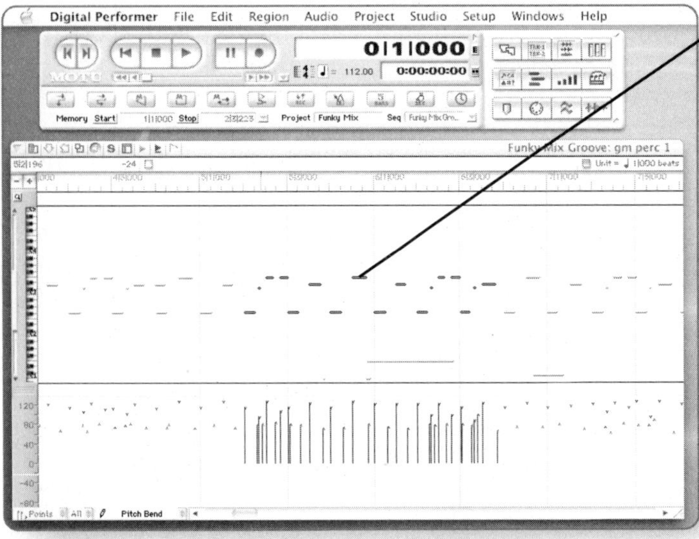

4. Release the **mouse**. Every note that was encompassed by the light blue box will be selected.

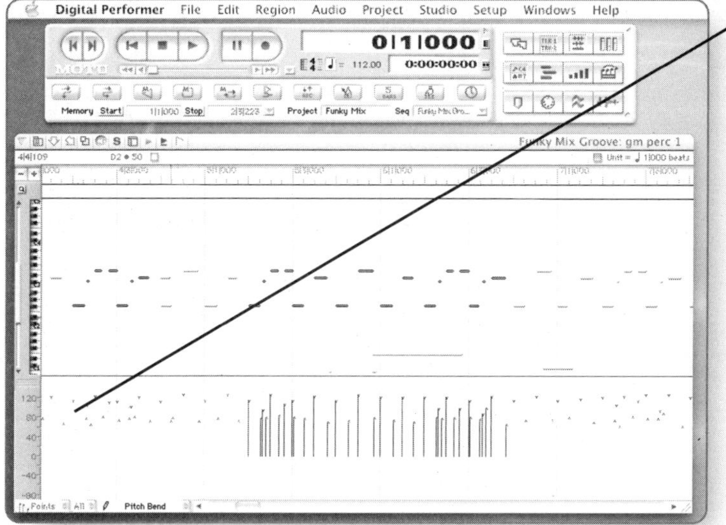

5. Hold down the **Shift key**. This will allow you to select a group or individual notes in another area and add them to your current selection. Keep holding down the Shift key until you release the mouse button in the next step.

6. Repeat steps 2 to 4 until you are finished selecting additional notes.

Selecting Time

Using the Graphic Editor, you can select chunks of time to edit. When you select a period of time, all of the notes that fall within that timeframe are selected.

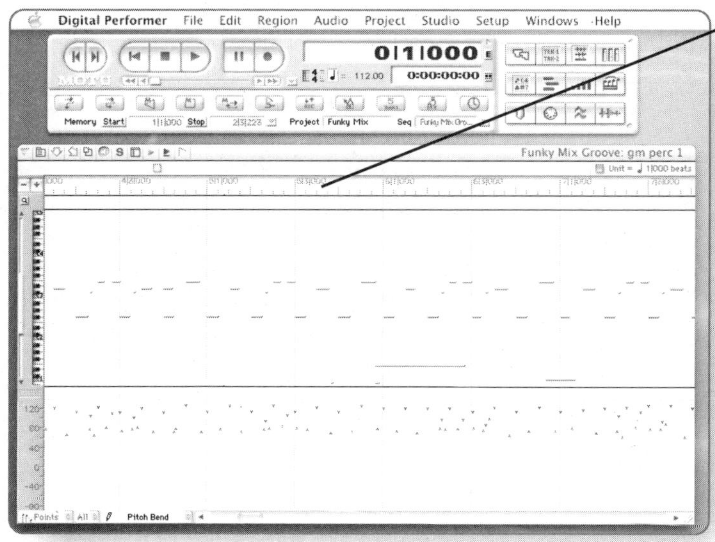

1. Position your **mouse pointer** at the point in the ruler where you want to begin your selection.

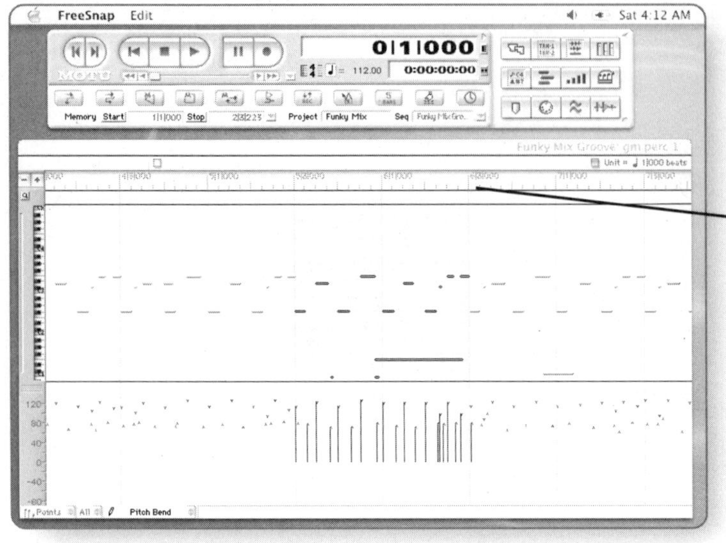

2. **Click** and **drag** to the **right** or **left** to create your selection. A blue highlight will appear as you drag, indicating your selection area.

3. **Release** the **mouse button**. The selection will be created.

Moving Notes and Adjusting Pitch

Using the Graphic Editor, you can quickly move notes to any location within the track. When you move a note up or down in the Editor, you are actually changing the pitch, while moving it left or right will change its location.

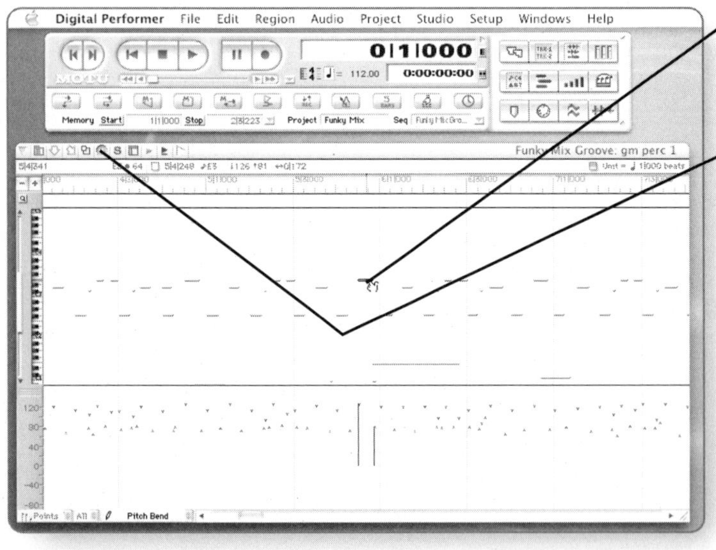

1. **Select** a **note** or various **notes** using one of the selection methods.

2. **Click** on the **Audible Mode button** if you would like to hear the change as you move a note. When the icon is yellow, Audible mode is turned on.

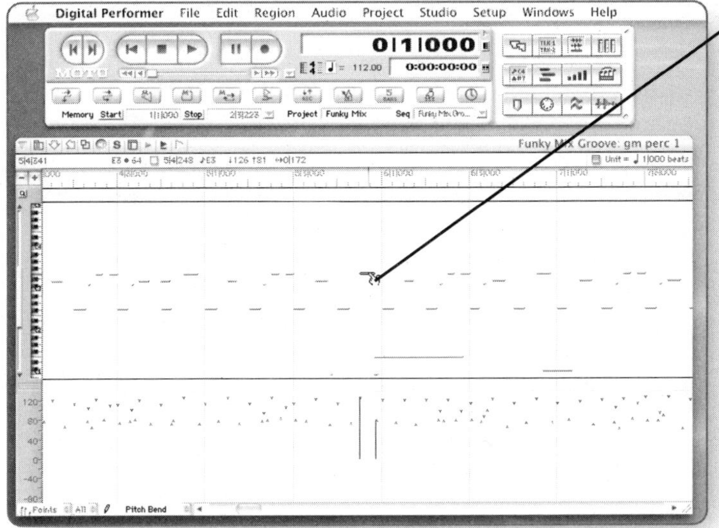

3. **Position** your **mouse pointer** over a selected note. It will change into a small hand.

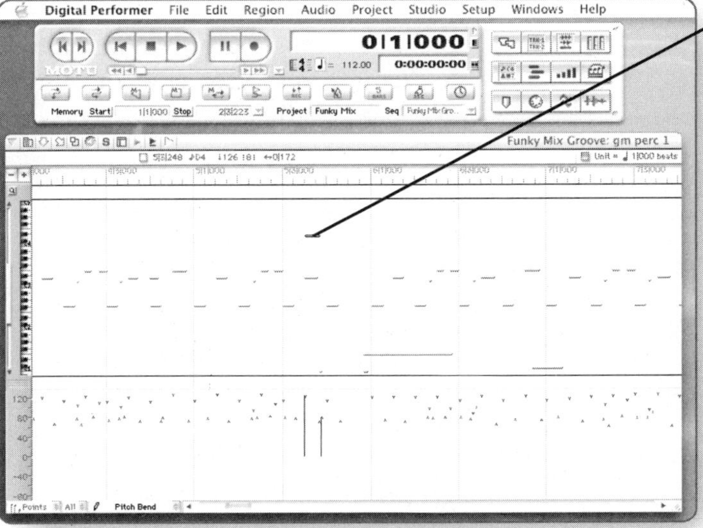

4. **Click** and **drag** the **note** to its new location. Moving a note up or down in the Editor will change its pitch, while moving it left or right will change its location.

5. **Release** the **mouse button**. The note will be moved.

> **TIP**
>
> Pressing and holding the Shift key while moving a note will constrain its motion to either up or down. This will prevent you from inadvertently moving a note when you are trying to create a pitch change.

> **NOTE**
>
> Basic editing of selections including cut, copy, paste, snip, and merge, is covered in Chapter 8, "Basic Editing."

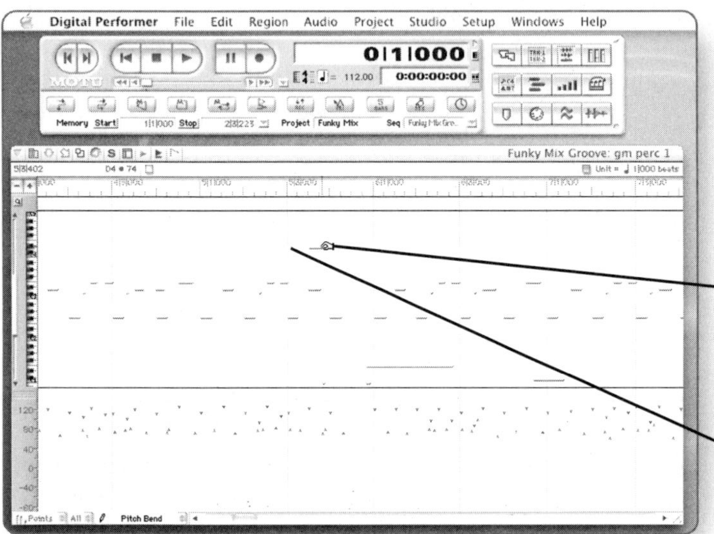

Adjusting Note Length

The duration that a note plays can be changed from within the Graphic Editor by clicking and dragging.

1. **Position** your **mouse pointer** over the right end of a note. The mouse pointer will change to a pinching hand.

2. **Click** and **drag** to the **right** or **left** to shorten or lengthen the duration that the note will play.

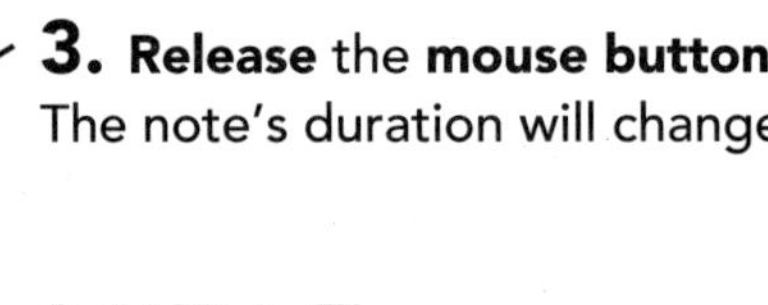

3. **Release** the **mouse button**. The note's duration will change

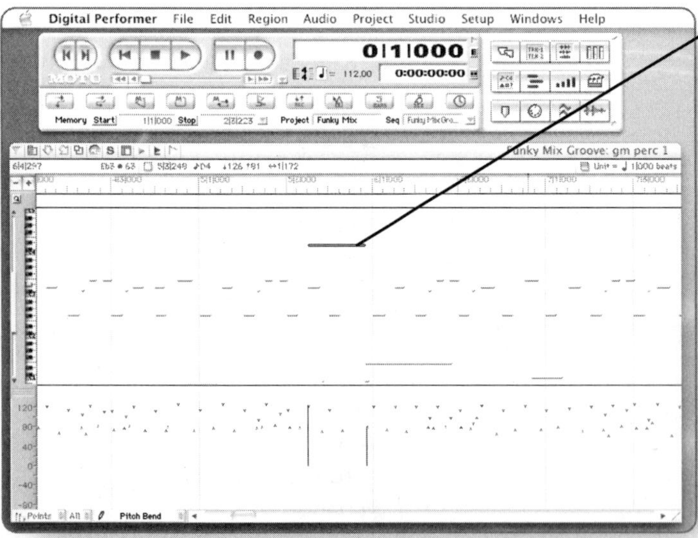

MIDI Events

Among the many things the Graphic Editor can do, it allows you to insert a variety of different MIDI events by drawing them in rather than having to manually enter them in a window. To graphically insert data you will need to open the Toolbar.

Opening the Toolbar

The Toolbar grants you access to a variety of different options for inserting data into your sequence graphically.

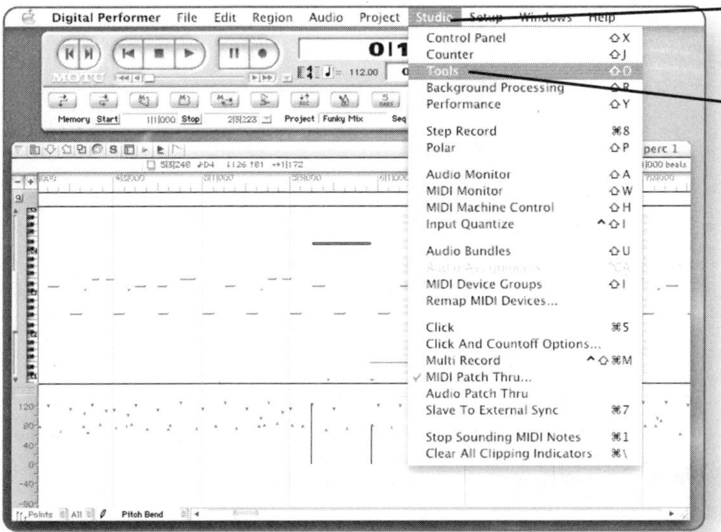

1. **Click** on **Studio**. The Studio menu will appear.

2. **Click** on **Tools**. The Toolbar will open.

Selecting Display Modes

Digital Performer offers you three different ways to view MIDI events within the Grid window. Data can be viewed as bars, points, or lines.

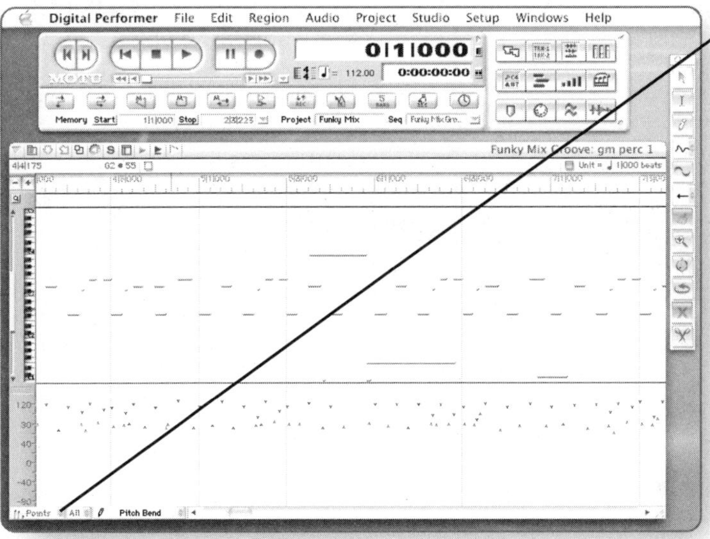

1. **Click** on the **up-and-down arrow** to open up the pop-up menu.

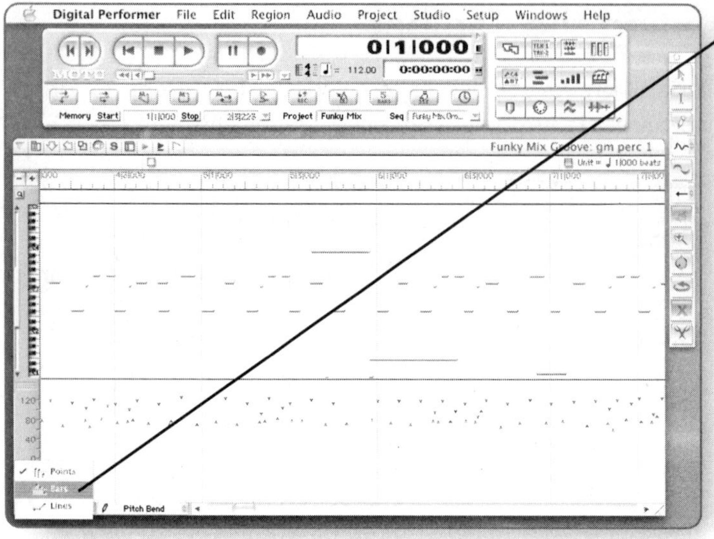

2. Click on the desired **display mode**. The grid display will change. There will be three modes to choose from, including:

- **Points**. This mode displays data as small unconnected icons.

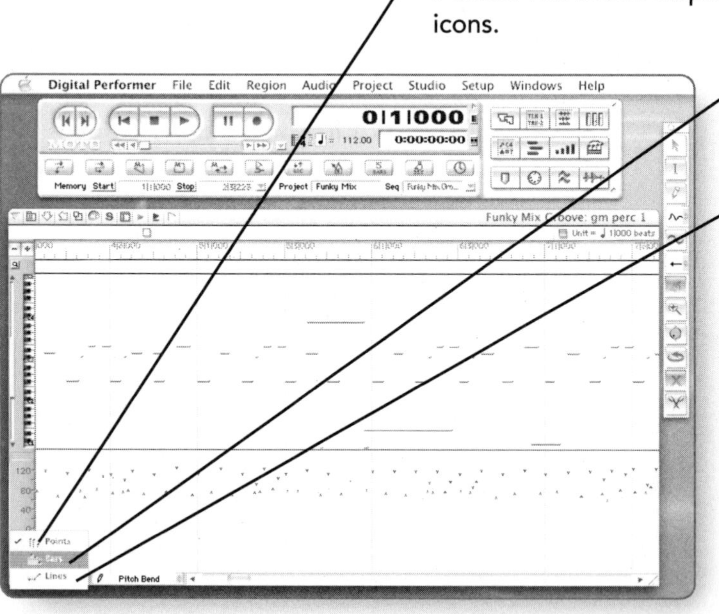

- **Bars**. This mode shows data as icons with colored bars that show their value.
- **Lines**. Data is displayed as dots connected by a continuous line.

Pencil Tool

Using the Pencil tool, you can create new notes and modify MIDI events by clicking and dragging directly on the screen.

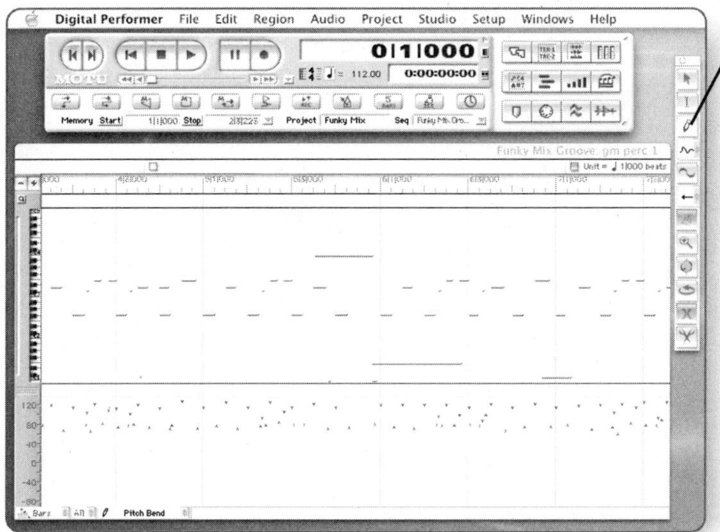

1. **Click** on the **Pencil tool** from the Tools window. Your mouse pointer will turn into a pencil.

Adding and Removing Notes

Adding additional notes to your sequence using the Pencil tool is simply a matter of a click of a button.

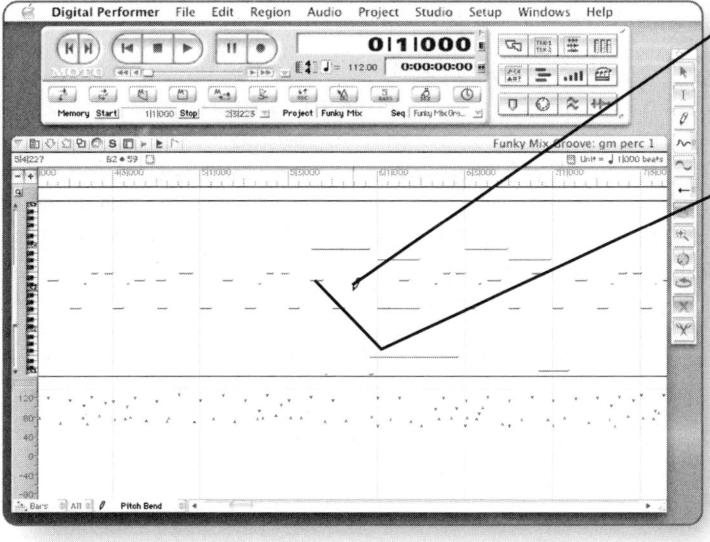

1. **Click** anywhere in the **Track window** with the Pencil tool. A note will appear at the location you clicked.
2. **Click** on any **note** with the Pencil tool to delete that note.

Modifying Events

Using the Pencil tool, you can graphically modify certain events like pitch change, pitch bend, track mute, and many others.

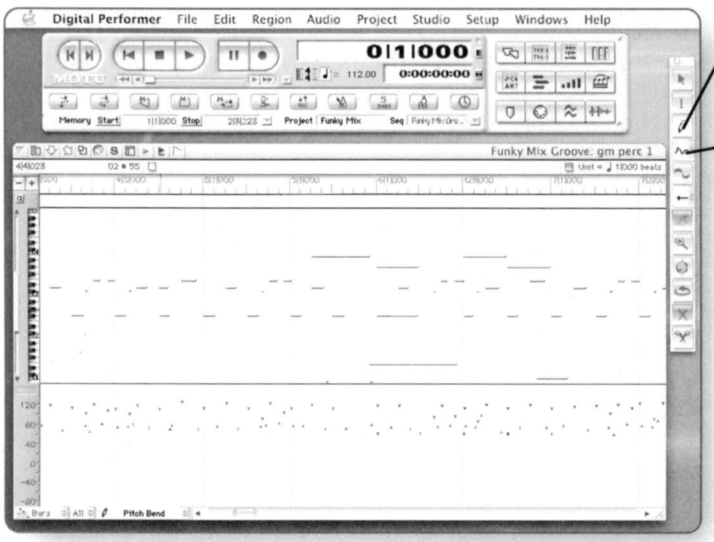

1. **Click** on the **Pencil tool**. The mouse pointer will change to a pencil.
2. **Click** on the **Line Shape button**. A menu of different line shapes will appear.

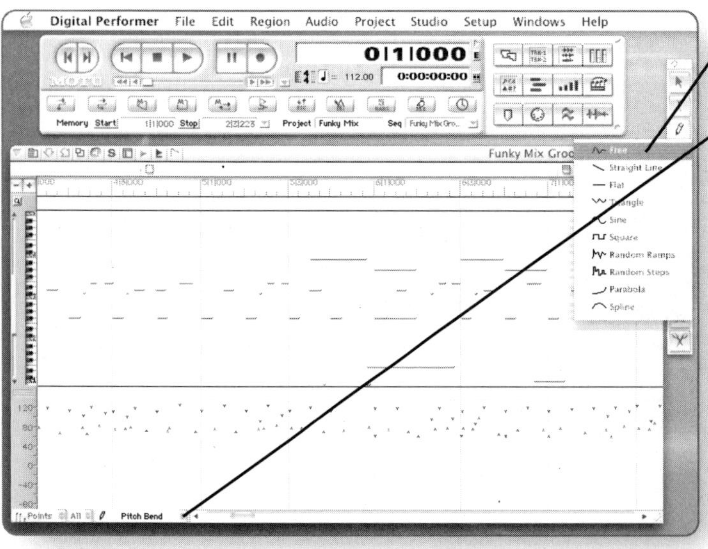

3. **Click** on the desired **line shape**. It will be selected.
4. **Click** on the **up-and-down arrow** to select the event type that you would like to modify. A list of different events will appear.

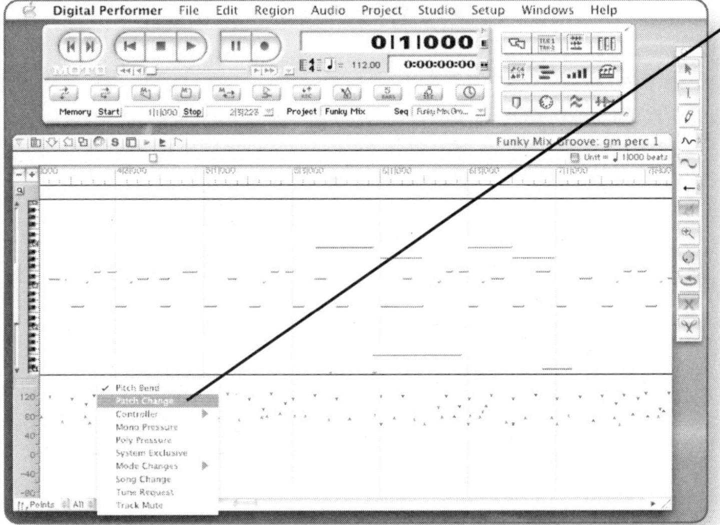

5. **Click** on the desired **event**. It will be selected.

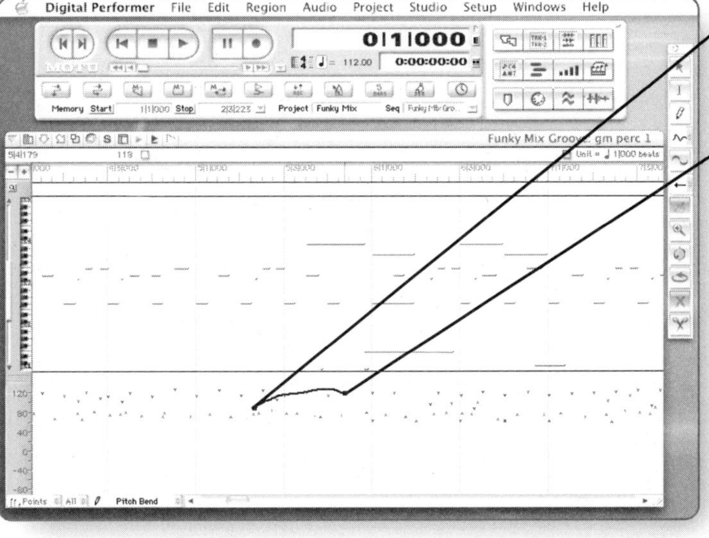

6. **Position** the **Pencil tool** over the line or point that you would like to modify.

7. **Click** and **drag** the **mouse**. As you drag, the point or line will be modified based on the type of line you selected.

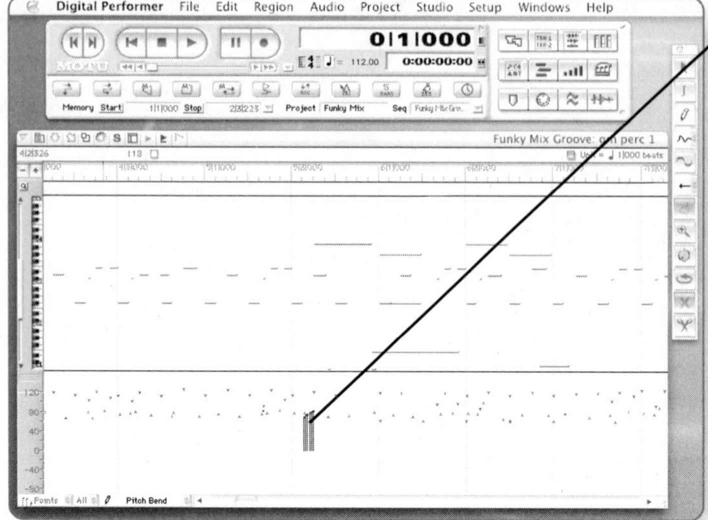

8. Release the **mouse button**. The event will be added or modified.

12

Audio Editing

Editing audio files is distinctly different from editing MIDI files. Unlike MIDI files, whose data is displayed as notes, audio files are presented in waves. Digital Performer provides you with a variety of tools to edit these waves, including the Waveform Editor, Sequence Editor, and Soundbites window. With these editors, you can cut, copy, and move information; add and manipulate soundbites; correct sound problems; and manage your audio information. In this chapter, you will learn how to:

- Navigate the Waveform Editor
- Manipulate audio tracks
- Work with soundbites
- Burn sequences to CD

The Waveform Editor

The Waveform Editor is a window that gives you a graphical representation of your audio tracks. Using the Waveform Editor, you can view audio segments, graphically manipulate audio, and create loops.

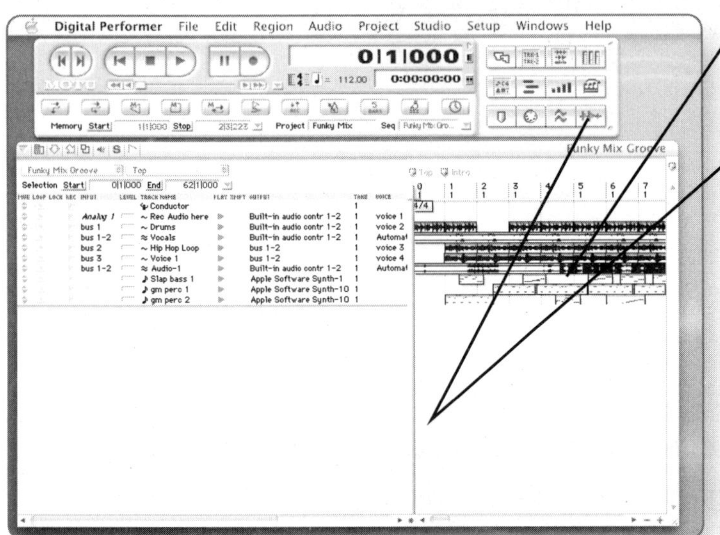

1. **Click** on the **phrase** that you would like to edit. It will be highlighted.
2. **Click** on the **Waveform Editor button** in the Control Panel. The Waveform Editor will open.

Navigating in the Waveform Editor

The waves created by an audio file can be quite long, and at first glance, provide little information as to what audio is contained in the wave. To help you manage your audio tracks, Digital Performer offers you a variety of ways to navigate around the Waveform Editor window.

Zooming

Being able to make a precise selection is essential when editing audio files. To help you get a closer look at the waves of an audio file, Digital Performer provides you with both vertical and horizontal zoom capabilities.

Vertical Zoom

By using the vertical Zoom tool, you can make the waveform appear taller.

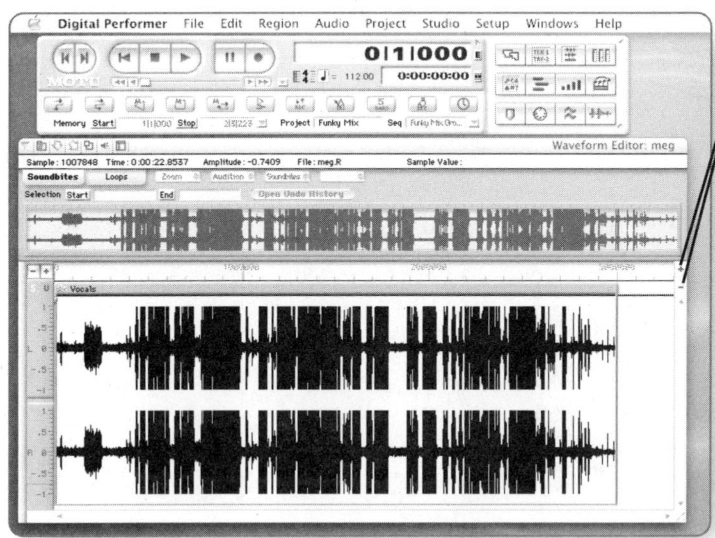

1. **Click** on the **+** or **– Zoom tool** on the right side of the window to vertically zoom in or out of the waveform.

> **TIP**
>
> Pressing and holding the Option key while clicking on one of the Zoom tools will lower the increments by which the program zooms in or out of the waveform.

Horizontal Zoom

The horizontal Zoom tool will stretch out your view of the waveform so you can do some detailed editing.

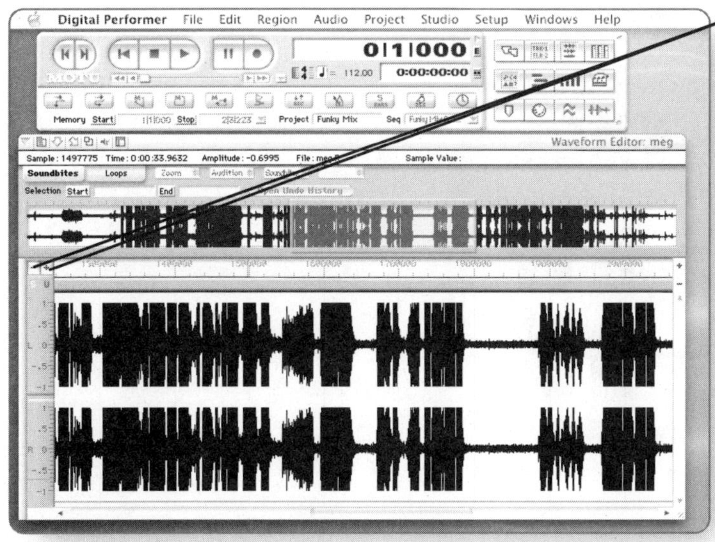

1. **Click** on the **+** or **– Zoom tool** on the left side of the window to horizontally zoom in or out of the waveform.

Zoom Pop-Up Menu

Another option for zooming is to take advantage of the Zoom pop-up menu.

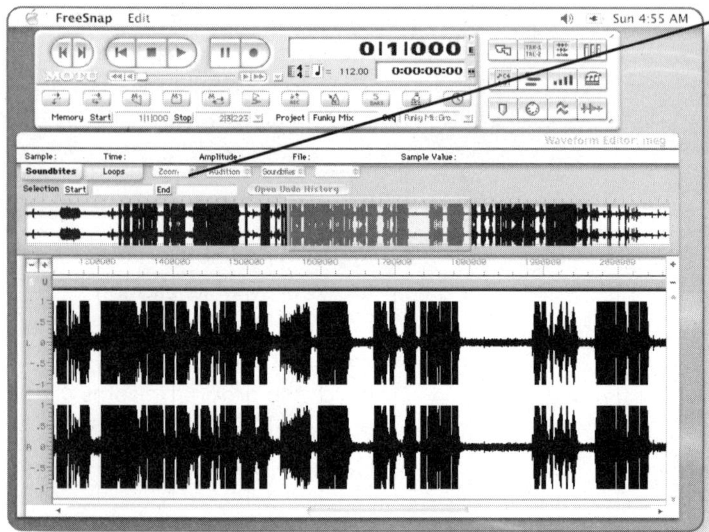

1. **Click** on the **Zoom pop-up menu** in the window. A list of zoom options will appear.

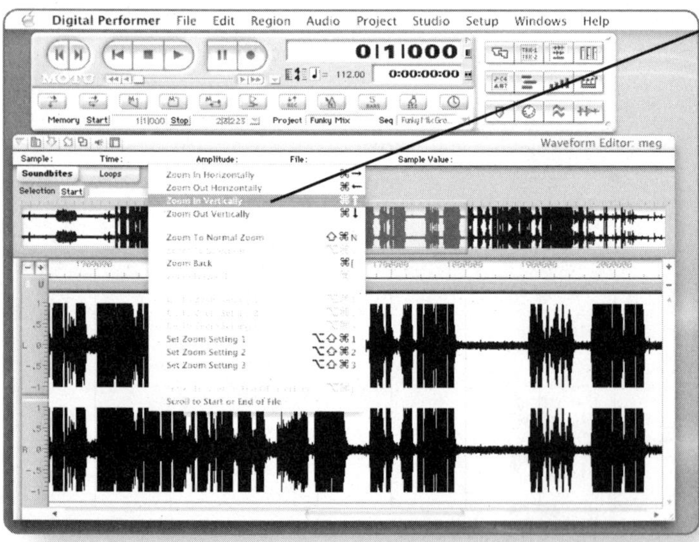

2. **Click** on the desired **option**. You will be taken to that zoom level.

Waveform Overview

The Waveform Overview is a graphical representation of your entire selection. Within the Overview window is a close-up lens that can be used to jump to different parts of your audio selection.

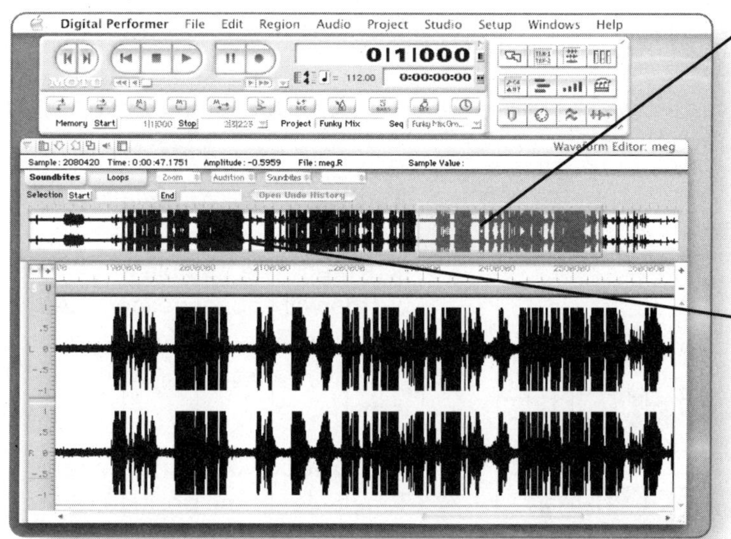

1. Position your **mouse pointer** over the close-up lens. The close-up lens shows the portion of your audio track that is being displayed in the Main window. The mouse pointer will turn into a small hand when you are over the lens.

2. Click and **drag** the close-up lens to a new location.

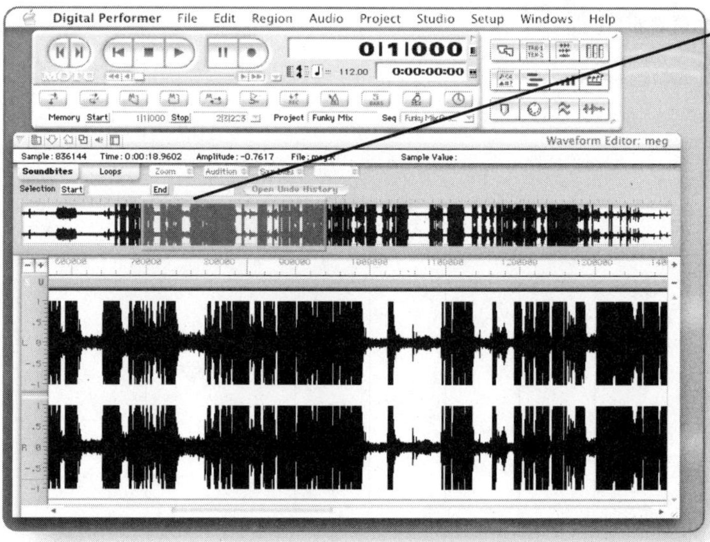

3. Release the **mouse button**. The display in the Main window will change to match the area indicated by the close-up lens.

Previewing and Selecting

In order to perform basic editing tasks on your audio, you must first create a selection. Whenever you create a selection, you can listen to its contents if the Audible mode is activated. Selections can be made graphically or through dialog boxes.

Selecting Graphically

The fastest way to make a selection is to click and drag within the Time Ruler.

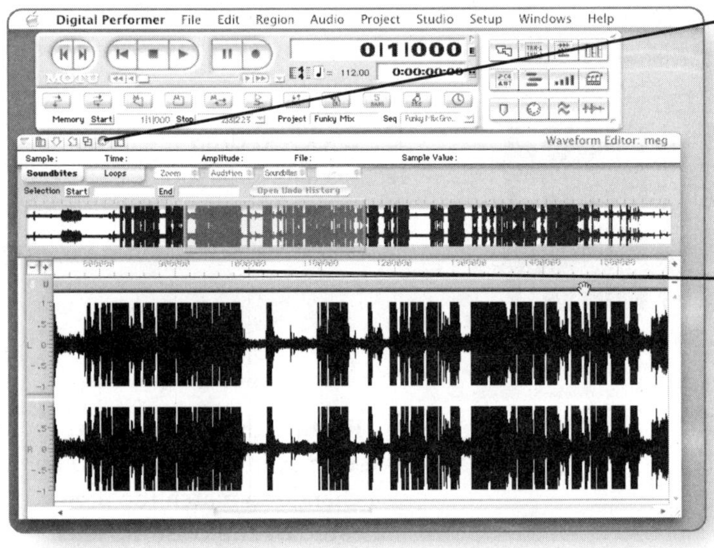

1. **Click** on the **Audible Mode button** if it is not already activated. The Audible Mode button will appear yellow when activated. This will enable you to hear your selection after it is made.

2. **Position** your **cursor** in the Time Ruler at the position where you would like your selection sto start.

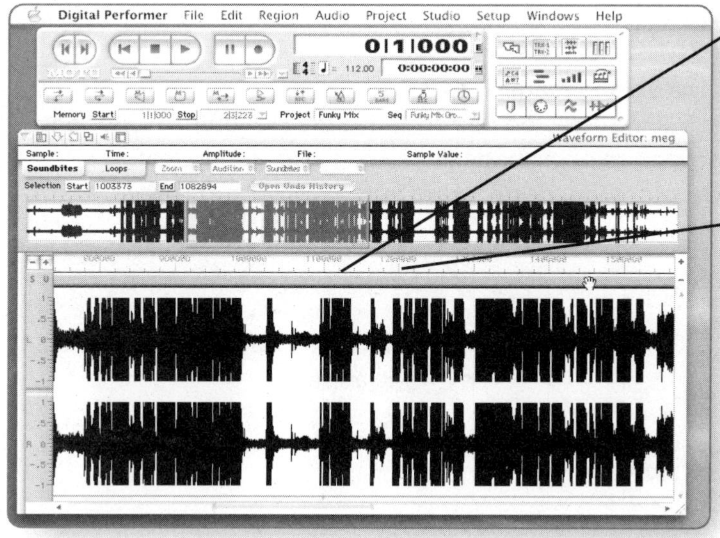

3. **Click** and **drag** to the **left** or **right** to create your selection. As you drag, the areas that will be part of the selection will be highlighted in blue.

4. **Release** the **mouse button**. Your selection will be created and a preview of the audio within the selection will play.

Selecting Manually

If you want to make exact selections, you can enter the specific locations where you would like to create a selection.

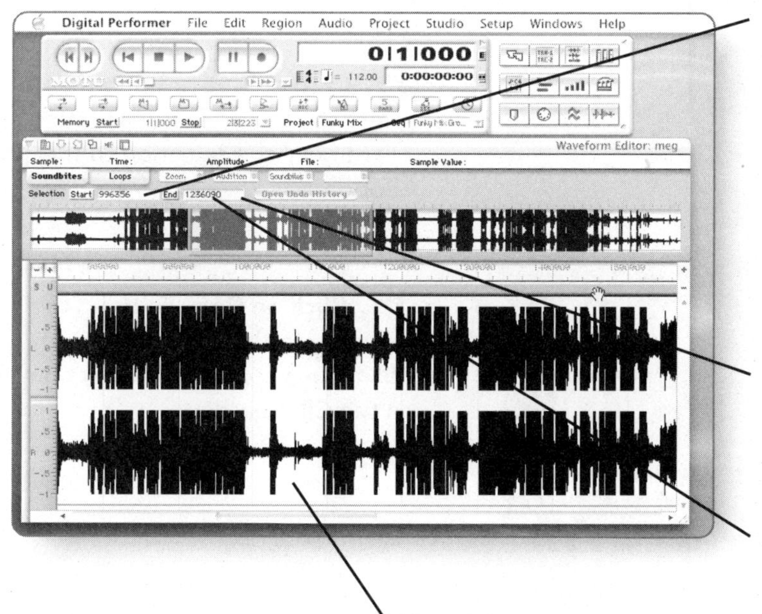

1. **Double-click** in the **Start box**. It will be highlighted. You can now specify where you would like your selection to begin.

2. **Type** a **number** for the start position. By default, time is measured in samples on the Time Ruler.

3. **Double-click** in the **End box**. It will be highlighted. You can now specify where you would like your selection to end.

4. **Type** a **number** for the end position of your selection.

5. **Press Return**. The selection will be created.

Basic Wave Editing

All of the editing features that were covered in Chapter 8, "Basic Editing," can be performed in the Waveform Editor once a selection has been made. Some of these editing features include, cut, copy, paste, erase, merge, snip, and splice.

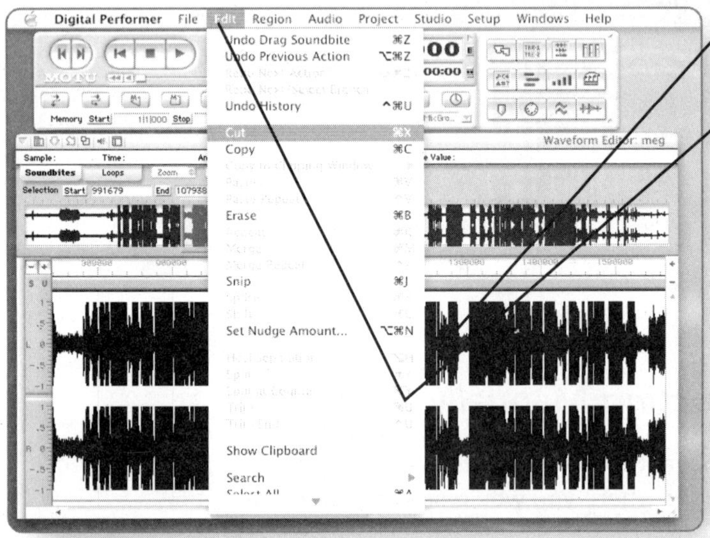

1. Create a **selection** using one of the selection methods.

2. Click on **Edit**. The Edit menu will appear.

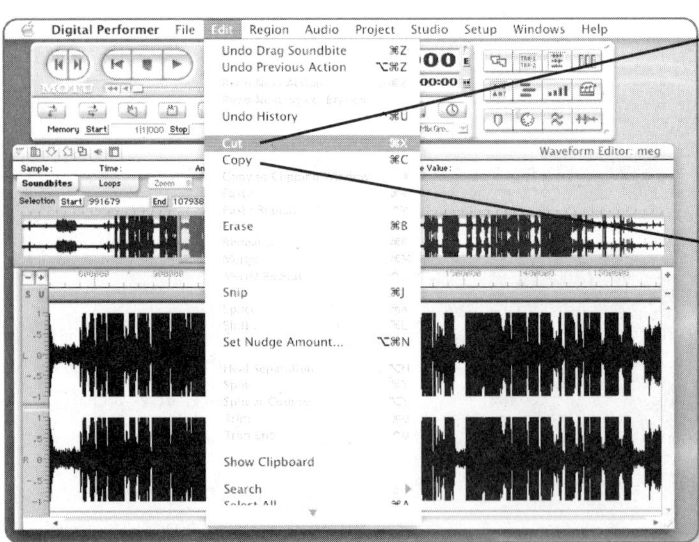

3a. Click on **Cut** to bring the selection to the Clipboard. Cut will remove the selection to the Clipboard.

OR

3b. Click on **Copy** to bring the selection to the Clipboard. Copy will make a copy of the selection on the Clipboard.

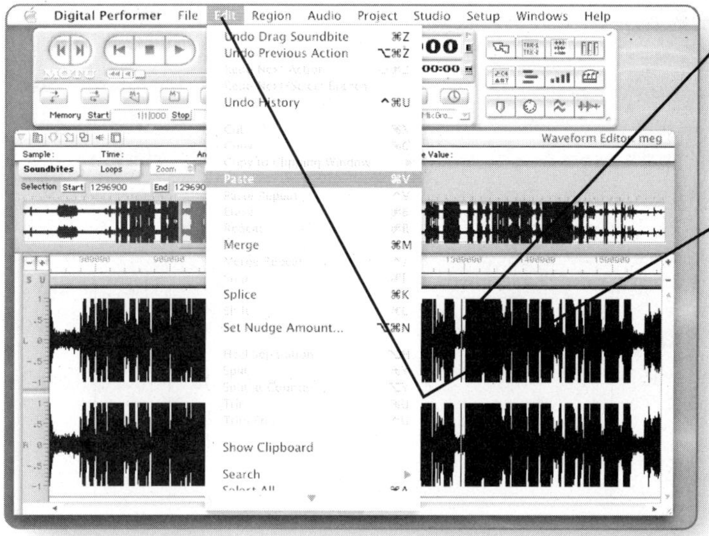

4. Click once in the **window** where you'd like the edit to take place. A flashing black line will indicate the area that you have selected.

5. Click on **Edit**. The Edit menu will appear.

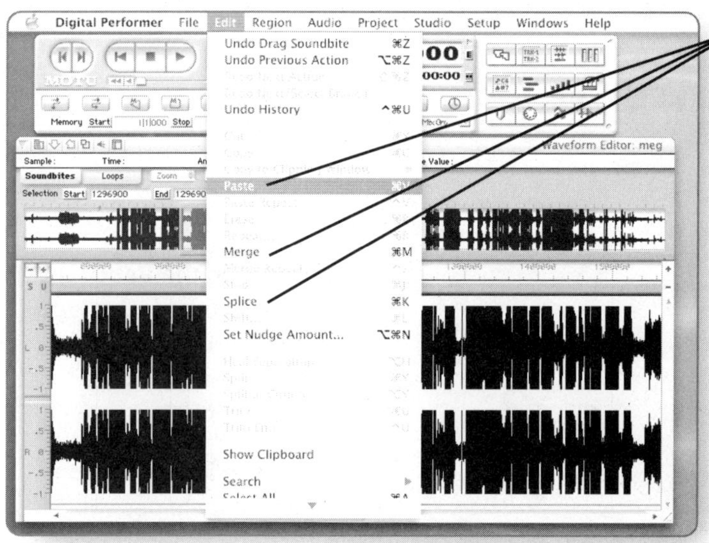

6. Click on the desired **Edit function** (Paste, Merge, or Splice). The edit will take place at the location you have specified.

Graphical Editing

Using the Pencil tool, you can alter the shape of the waveform graphically on-screen. The Pencil tool allows you to change the shape and sound of your audio selection. It's a good idea to use the maximum zoom level when editing with the Pencil tool to ensure you are making detailed edits.

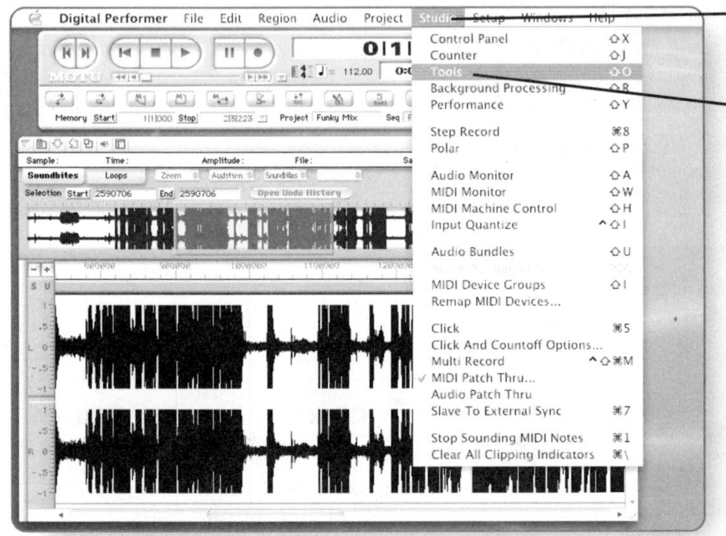

1. **Click** on **Studio**. The Studio menu will open.
2. **Click** on **Tools**. The Toolbar will appear, in which you can select the Pencil tool.

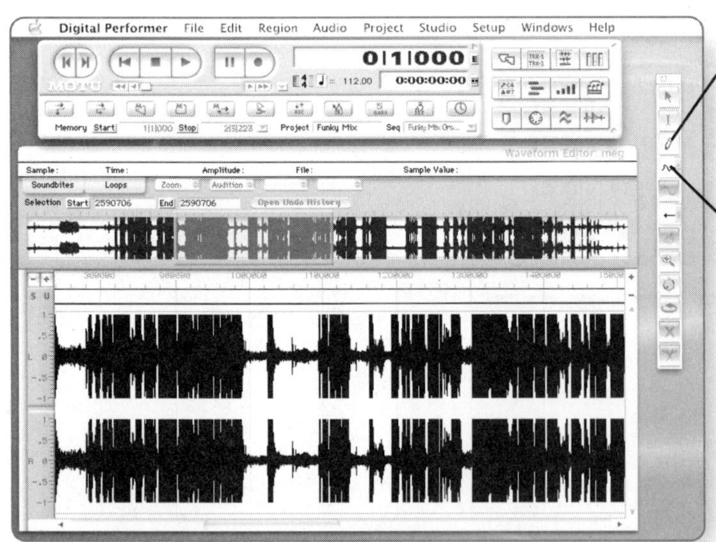

3. **Click** once on the **Pencil tool** to select it. You can now select what type of shape you would like the Pencil tool to create when you begin editing.
4. **Click** on the **Shape button**. A list of different shapes will appear.

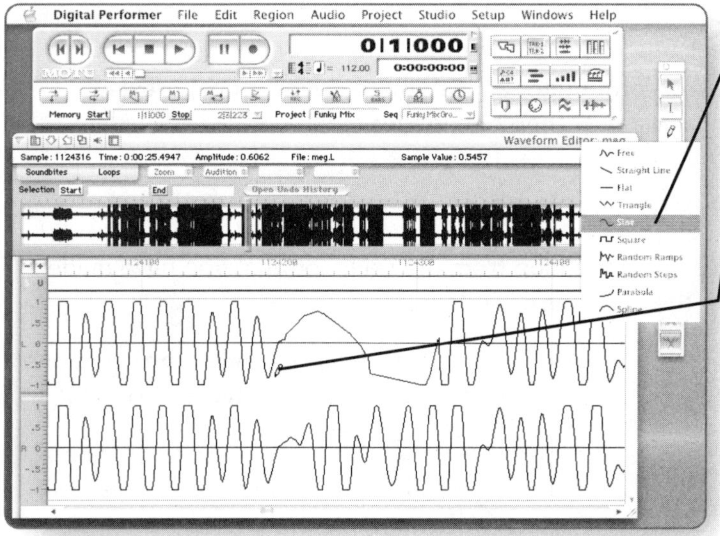

5. Click on the desired **shape**. It will be selected.

6. Position the **mouse pointer** (which now looks like a pencil) over the area that you would like to modify.

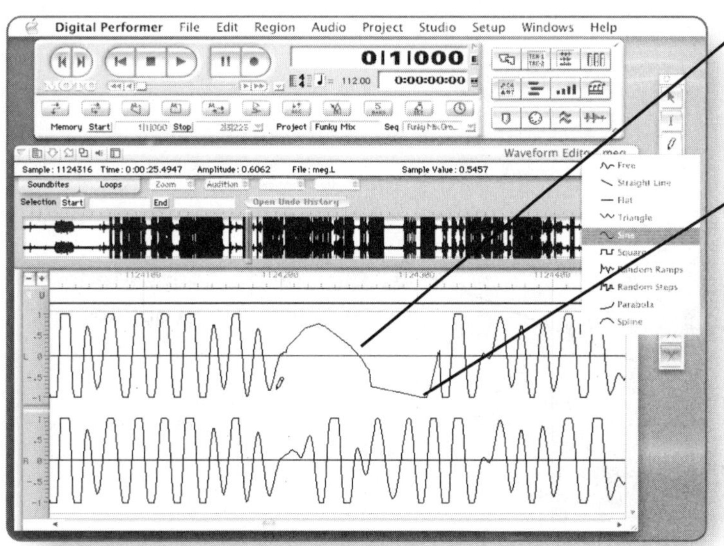

7. Click and **drag** the **mouse**. As you drag, the waveform will change based on the type of shape you have selected.

8. Release the **mouse button**. The waveform will now be edited.

> **TIP**
>
> To ensure detailed editing, make your graphical edits at a high zoom level.

Loops

The Waveform Editor allows you to define loops, preview them, and adjust their boundaries.

Creating Loops

You can create a loop from the selection that you have made within the Waveform window.

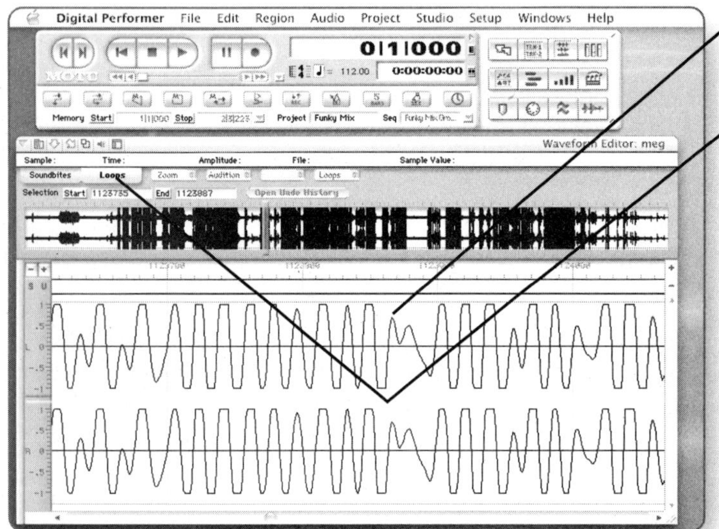

1. **Create** a **selection** using one of the selection methods.

2. **Click** on the **Loops Mode button**. The Loops options will now be activated.

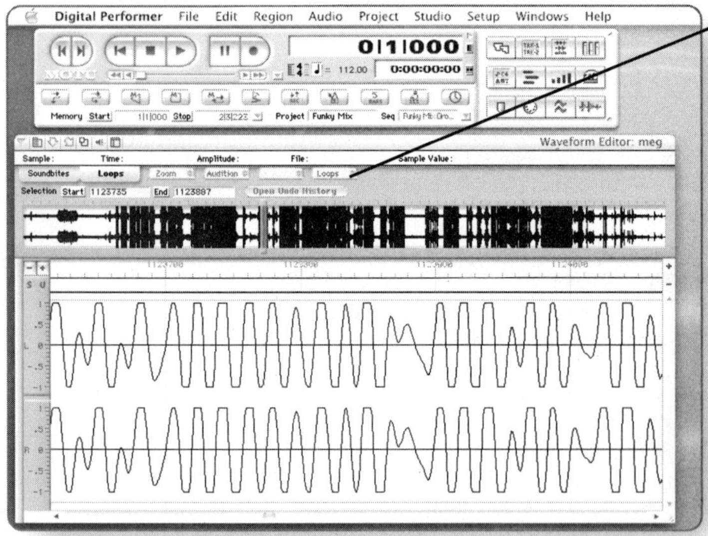

3. **Click** on the **Loops Mode menu**. A list of loop options will appear.

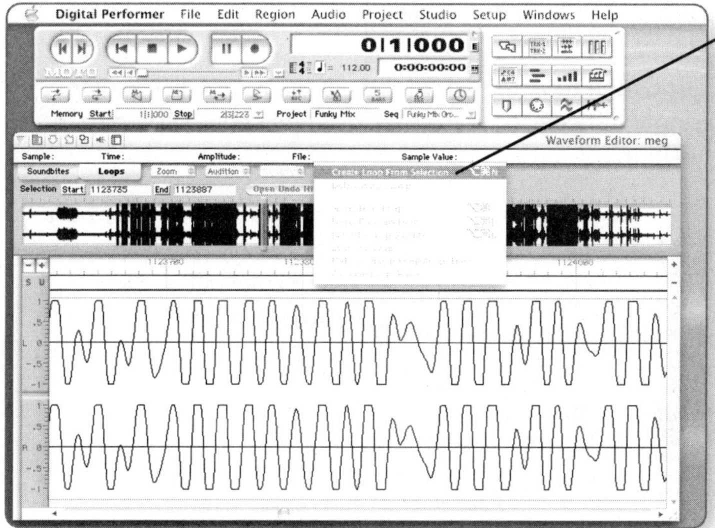

4. Click on **Create Loop From Selection**. A loop will be created from the selection that you made. A yellow box will define the loop.

Adjusting Loops

You can easily adjust the loops that you have created by clicking and dragging.

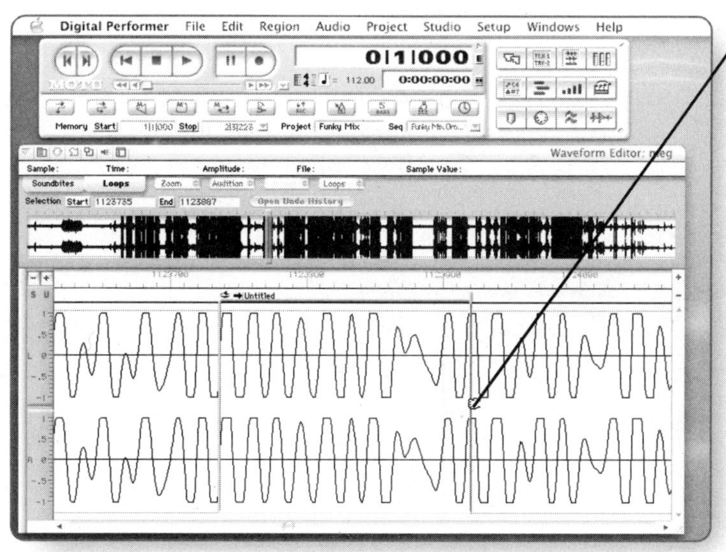

1. Position the **mouse pointer** at either edge of the loop. The mouse pointer will turn into a small hand.

2. Click and **drag** the **edge** of the loop to the desired location. As you drag, you will be able to preview the size of the loop.

3. Release the **mouse button**. The loop will be resized.

Naming Loops

It's a good idea to name your loops, because it will become increasingly difficult to keep track of them should you create multiple loops.

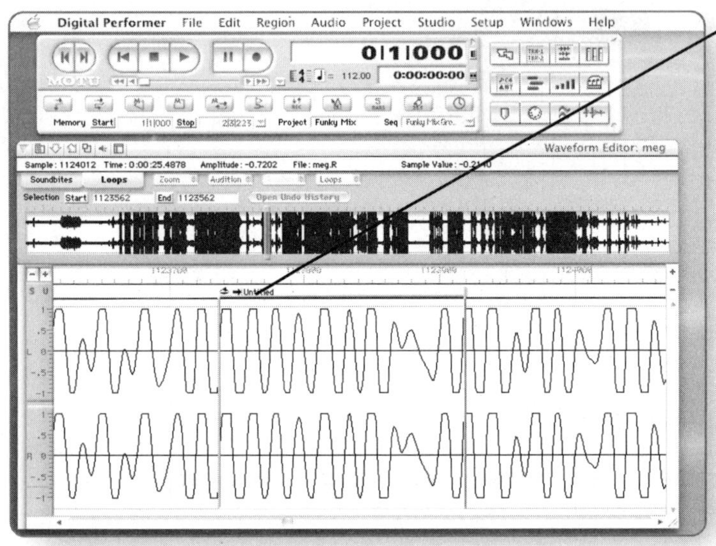

1. **Press** and **hold** the **Option key** and **click** on the **loop name**. The loop name will appear highlighted in a box.

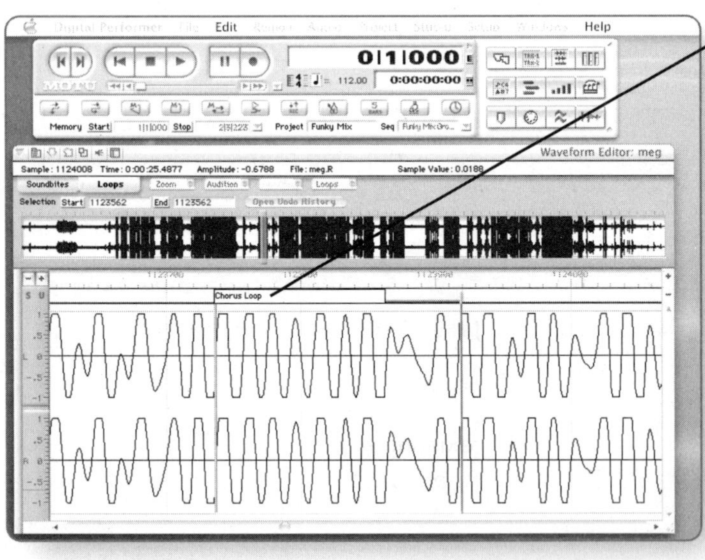

2. **Type** a new **name** for the loop. It's a good idea to give it a descriptive name.
3. **Press Return**. The loop will now have a new name.

Soundbites

The general definition of a soundbite is any piece of an audio track. In Digital Performer, a soundbite means something a little different. A soundbite in Digital Performer is a reference to a sound file somewhere on your computer. Basically, a soundbite points to a sound file on your hard drive that Digital Performer can then reference and play. The beauty of a soundbite is that it is located outside of the program so it doesn't take up as much disk space as regular audio tracks. Soundbites can be created within the Waveform Editor or through a variety of other means, but are best managed from the Soundbites window. Think of the Soundbites window as a library of all of your soundbites. You can deposit and withdraw different soundbites as needed.

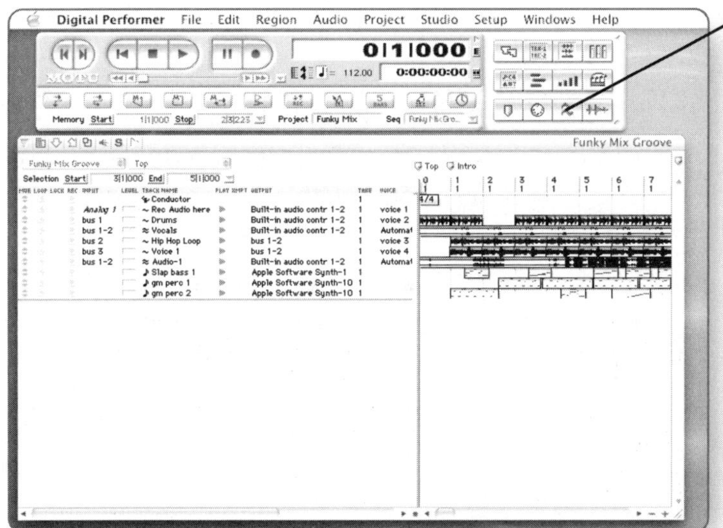

1. **Click** on the **Soundbites button** in the Control Panel. The Soundbites window will open.

Adding Soundbites

Any audio that you have recorded automatically becomes a soundbite. In addition, you can create soundbites from existing tracks or you can import them into Digital Performer.

Creating Soundbites in the Waveform Editor

You can take parts of an existing audio track and make a separate sound file from them using the Waveform Editor.

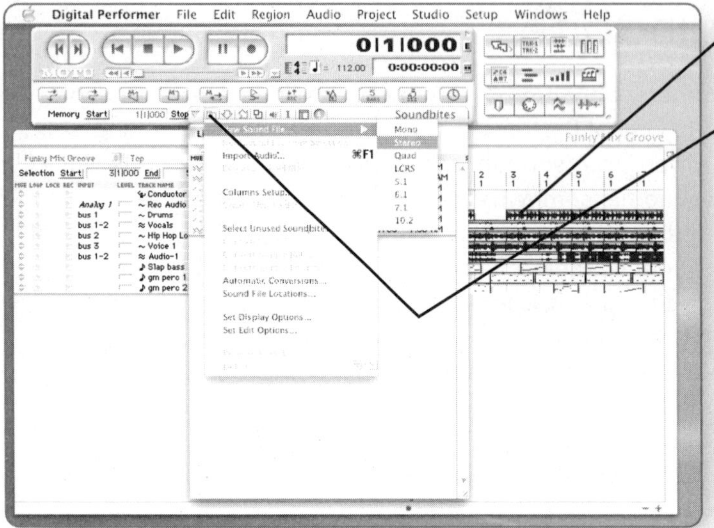

1. **Create** a **selection** using one of the selection methods.

2. **Click** on the **Mini Menu button**. A list of commands will appear.

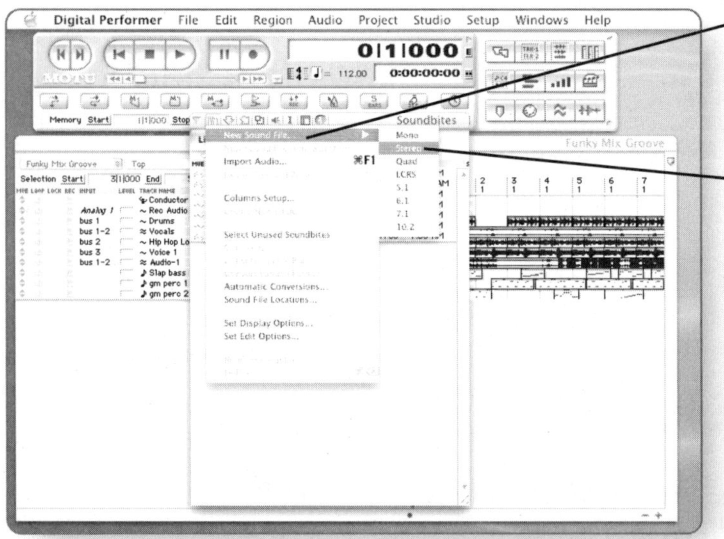

3. **Click** on **New Sound File**. The Soundbites window will open with a new soundbite created from the selection.

4. **Click** on the desired **type**. A new soundbite will be created based on your selection. You will now be prompted to name the soundbite.

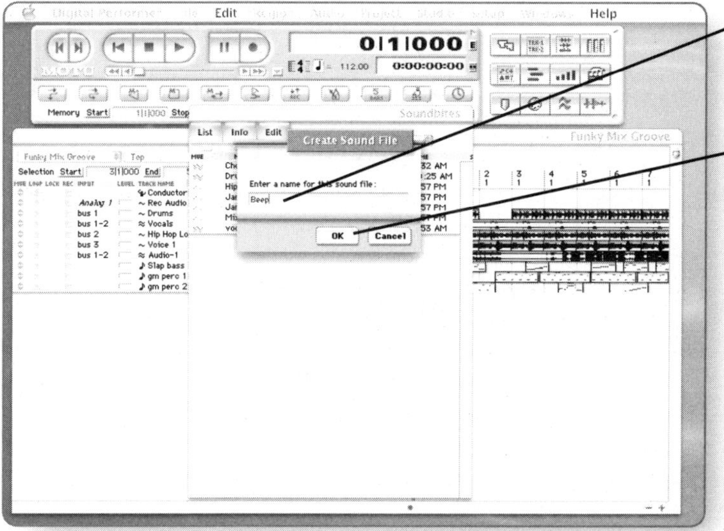

5. Type a **name** for the soundbite. It's a good idea to give it a descriptive name.

6. Click on **OK**. The new soundbite will appear in the window.

Importing Soundbites

Recording music isn't the only way to get audio into Digital Performer. Using the Soundbites window is the best way to import and manage audio clips. There are many ways to get your audio into the Soundbites window.

Mini Menu

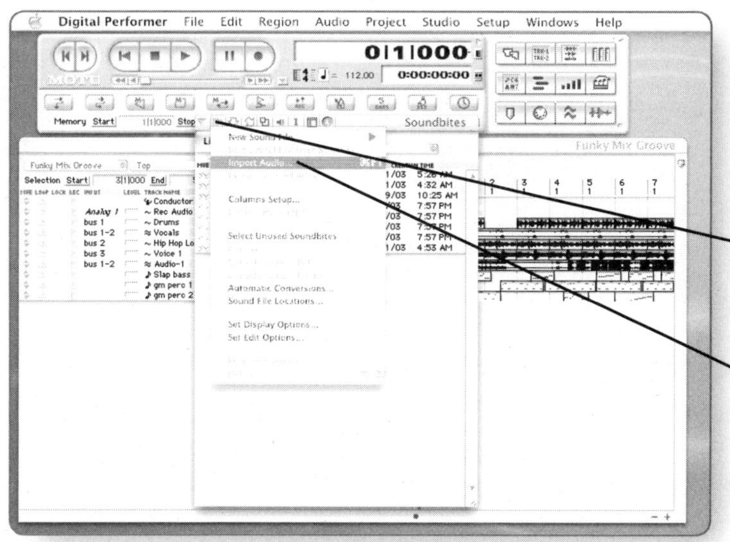

Using the mini menu within the Soundbites window, you can import soundbites from any location on your computer or network.

1. Click on the **Mini Menu button**. A list of commands will appear.

2. Click on **Import Audio**. A dialog box will open in which you can navigate your computer and select soundbites.

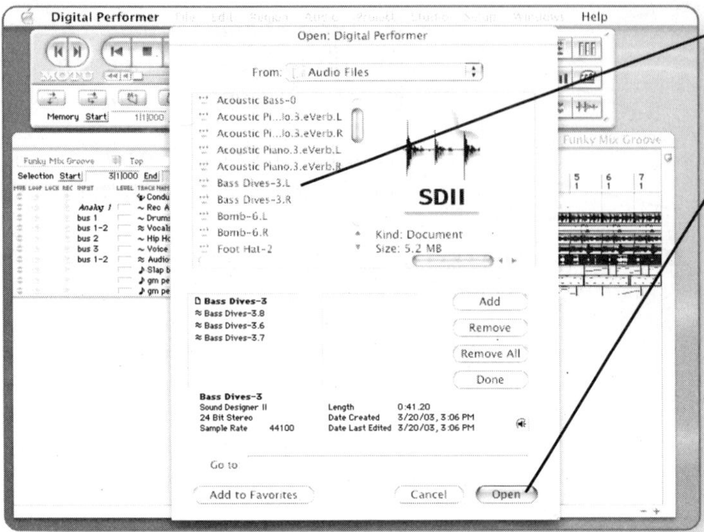

3. Click on the **file** that you would like to have as a soundbite.

4. Click on **Open**. The file will be added to the Soundbites window.

Click and Drag

Another method of bringing audio to the Soundbites window is clicking and dragging the audio clip from your desktop or File window into the Soundbites window.

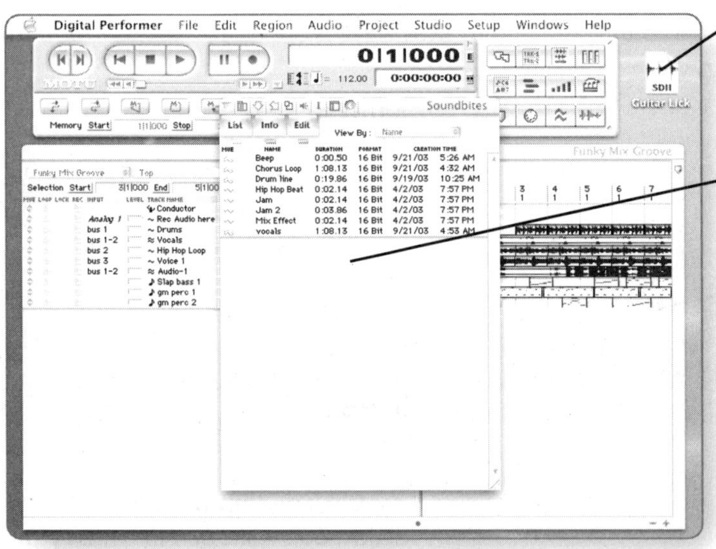

1. Position your **mouse pointer** over the file that you would like to bring to the Soundbites window.

2. Click and **drag** the **file** to the Soundbites window.

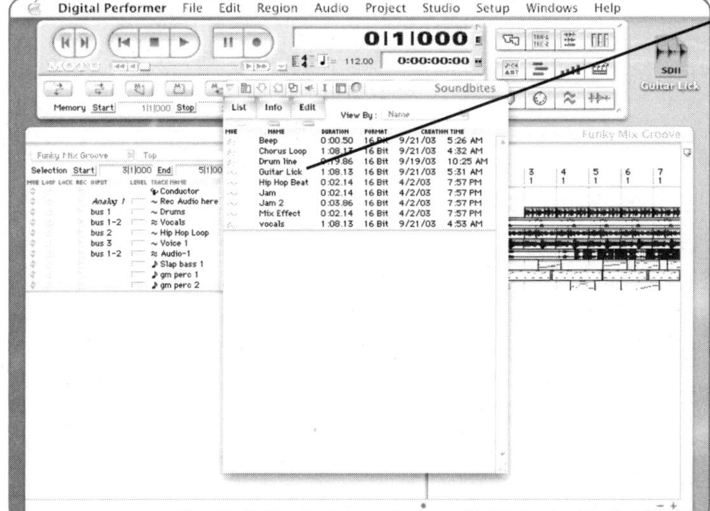

3. Release the **mouse button.** The file will be converted to a format that Digital Performer can understand, and it will be inserted into the Soundbites window.

Moving Soundbites to Your Tracks

Soundbites really don't serve a purpose unless you can bring them to your sequences.

> **NOTE**
>
> You can only move mono soundbites to mono tracks and stereo soundbites to stereo tracks.

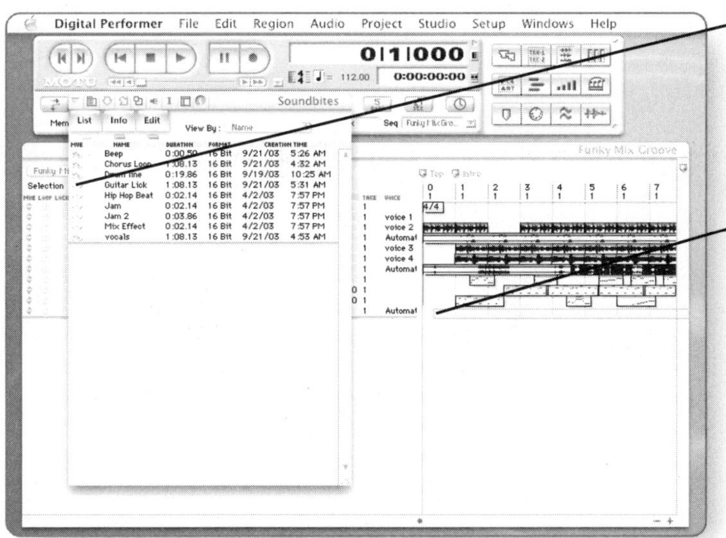

1. **Position** your **mouse pointer** over the symbol in the MVE column of the soundbite that you'd like to bring to the Tracks window.
2. **Click** and **drag** the **soundbite** from the Soundbites window to the Tracks window. An outline will appear, indicating its position.

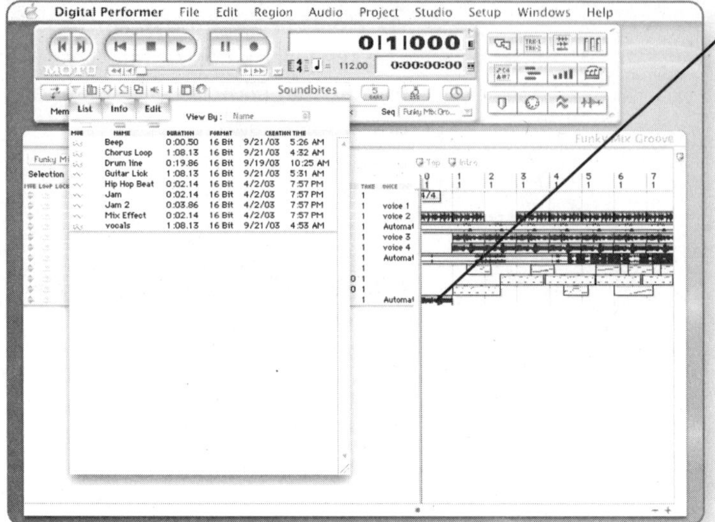

3. Release the **mouse button** when the soundbite is over the appropriate track. The soundbite will be inserted into the sequence.

> **TIP**
>
> When importing audio into Digital Performer, you can bypass the Soundbites window altogether. You can click and drag audio and MIDI files from the desktop or File window directly into the Tracks window of Digital Performer.

Managing Soundbites

Through the life of any particular project, it is quite possible to accumulate dozens of soundbites. The Soundbites window has several features available to help you manage your files.

Naming Soundbites

To help keep track of your soundbites, you can give them detailed names.

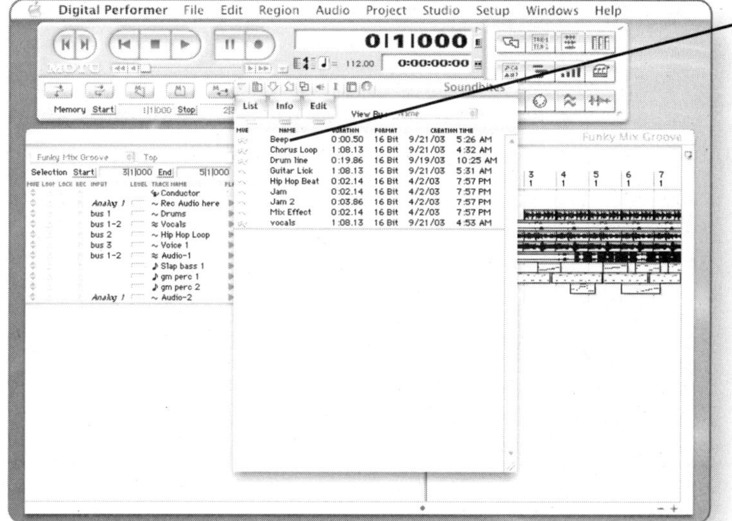

1. **Press** and **hold** the **Option key** and **click** on the **name** of a soundbite. The name will appear highlighted in a box.

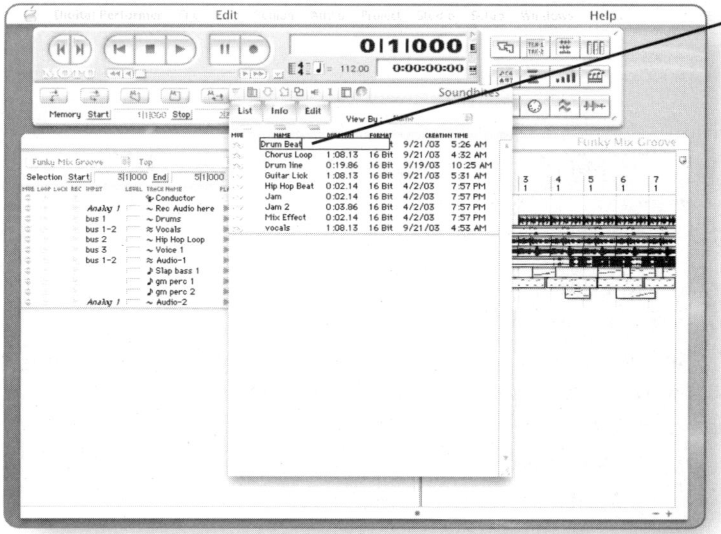

2. **Type** a new **name** for the soundbite. It's a good idea to give it a detailed name.

3. **Press Return**. The soundbite will be renamed.

Editing Soundbites

Rather than having to go to the Waveform Editor or any other audio editing window to make changes to your soundbites, the Soundbites window has an editor built right in.

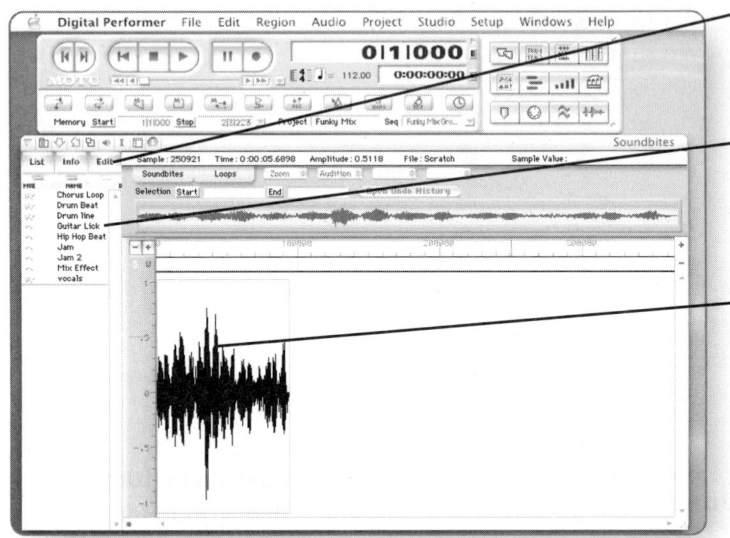

1. **Click** on the **Edit button**. A built-in Waveform Editor will appear.

2. **Click** on the desired **soundbite**. The waveform for that soundbite will appear in the window.

3. **Edit** the **waveform** as you desire, just as you would in the Waveform Editor.

Preparing Songs for Burning to CD

Once you've edited your audio and MIDI tracks and created the perfect mix, it's likely that you are going to want to share your music with others. In order to burn the tracks to a CD, you must first take some preparatory steps. The Bounce to Disk feature will create a single track from selected tracks that will be saved on your hard drive.

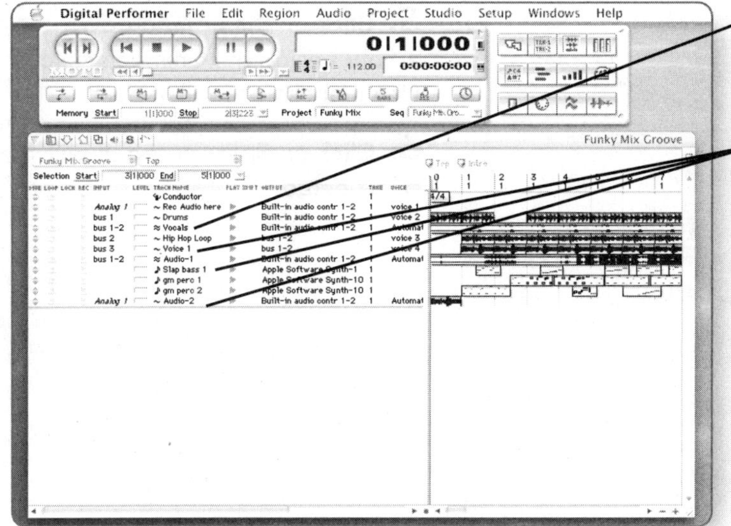

1. **Click** on the **name** of the first track that will be a part of the combination of tracks.

2. **Press** and **hold** the **Shift key** and **click** on the **names** of the other tracks to be combined.

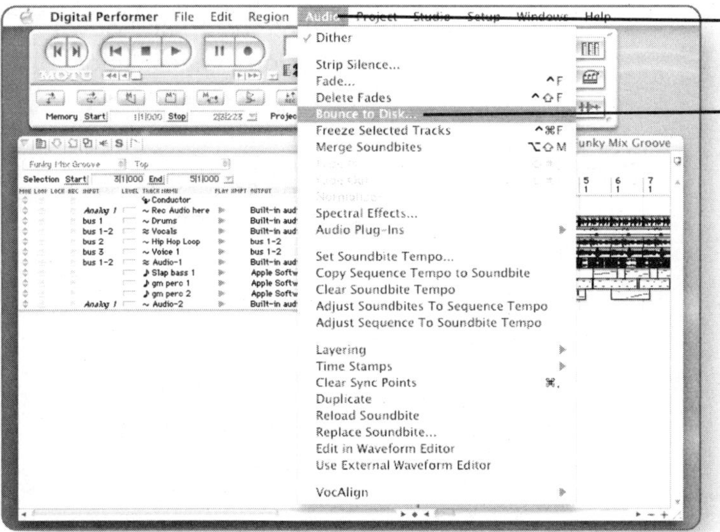

3. **Click** on **Audio**. The Audio menu will appear.

4. **Click** on **Bounce to Disk**. A dialog box will open.

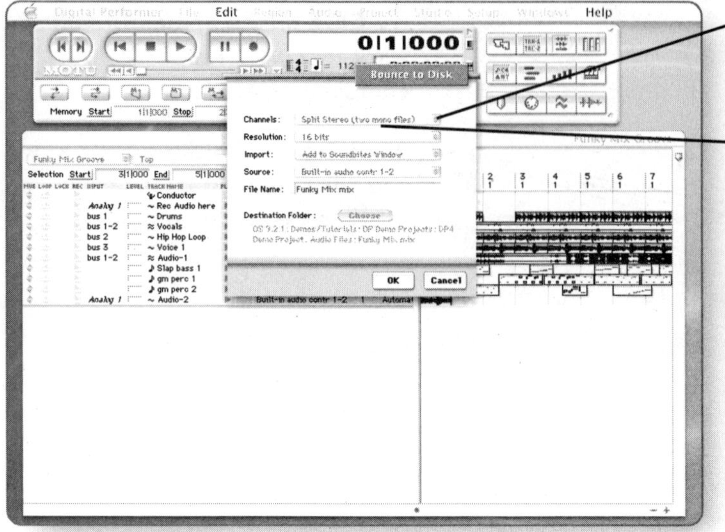

5. **Click** on the **up-and-down arrow** beside the Channels field. Channel options will appear.

6. **Click** on **Split Stereo**. It will be selected.

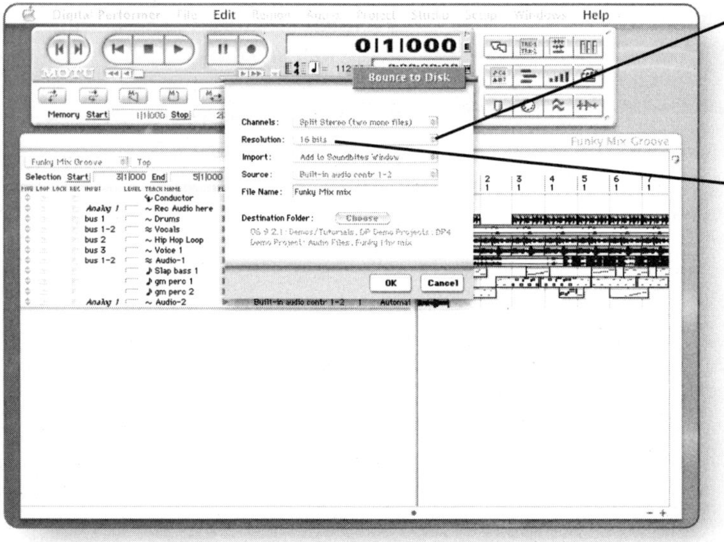

7. **Click** on the **up-and-down arrow** beside the Resolution field. Resolution options will appear.

8. **Click** on **16 bits**. 16 bits is the standard for CD audio.

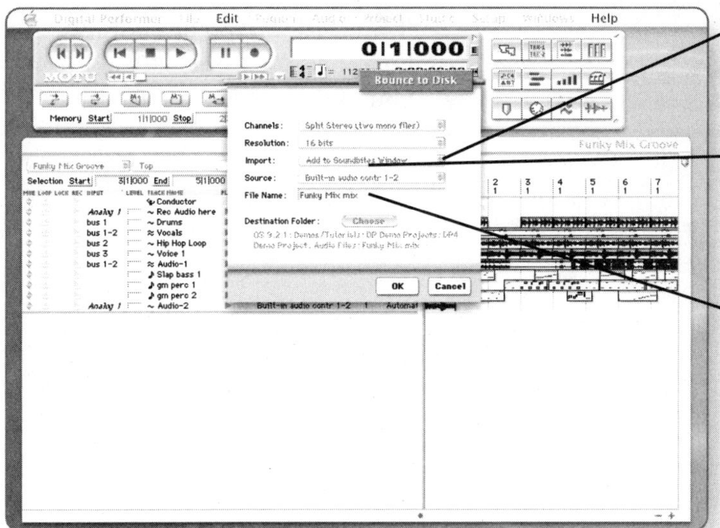

9. **Click** on the **up-and-down arrow** beside the Import field. Import options will appear.

10. **Click** on **Add to Soundbites Window**. This is the location where the new bounced tracks will be placed.

11. **Click** and **drag** across the **file name** to highlight it.

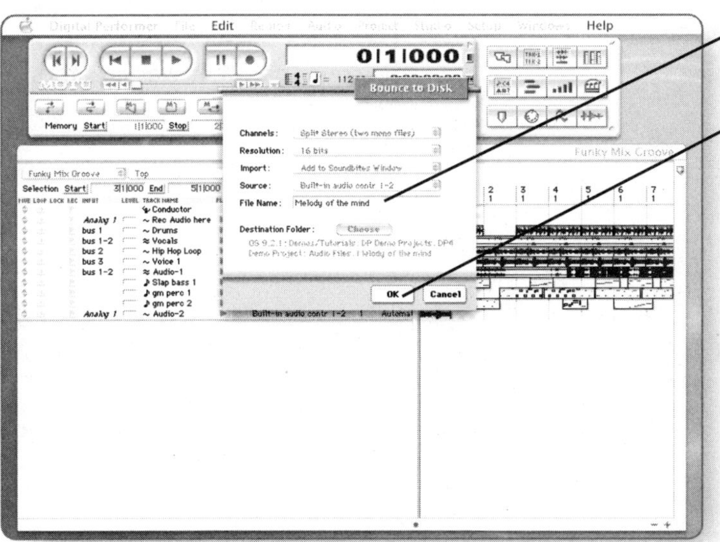

12. **Type** a **name** for the track that you are creating.

13. **Click** on **OK**. A new soundbite will be created.

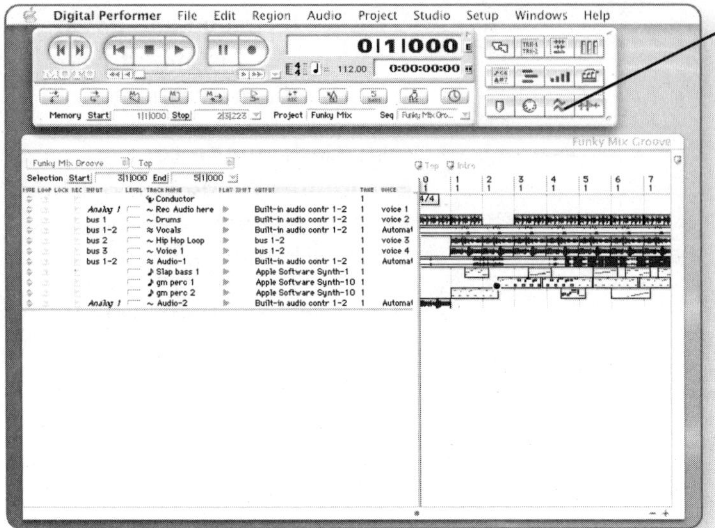

14. Click on the **Soundbites button** in the Control Panel. The Soundbites window will open.

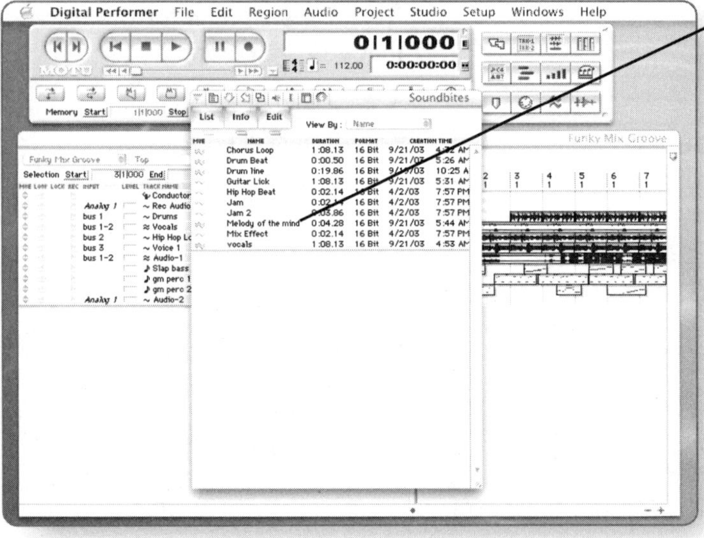

15. Click once on the **name** of the soundbite that was created during the Bounce to Disk session.

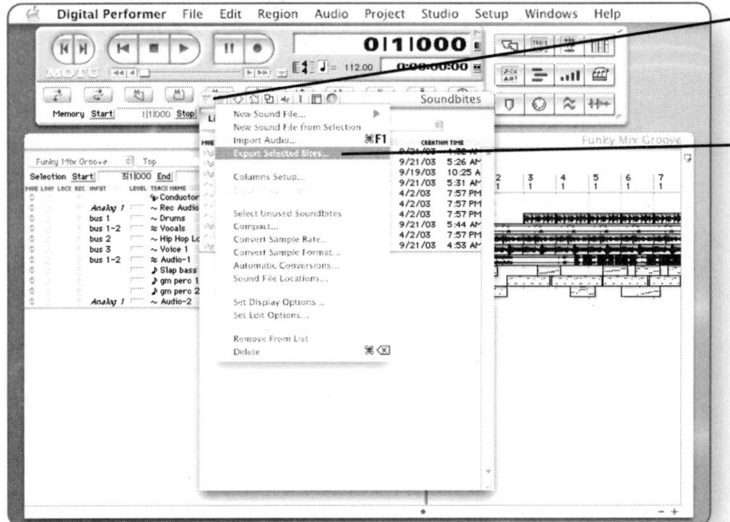

16. Click on the **Mini Menu button**. A list of options will appear.

17. Click on **Export Selected Bites**. A dialog box will open, allowing you to name and set options for the export.

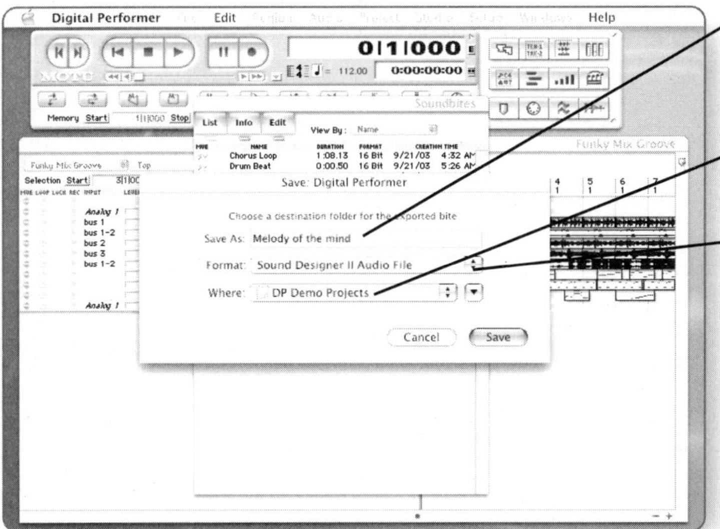

18. Type a **name** for the track that you are exporting. It will appear as you type.

19. Click on a **location** to save the file. It will be highlighted

20. Click on the **up-and-down arrow** to open the options for the file format. A list of formats will appear.

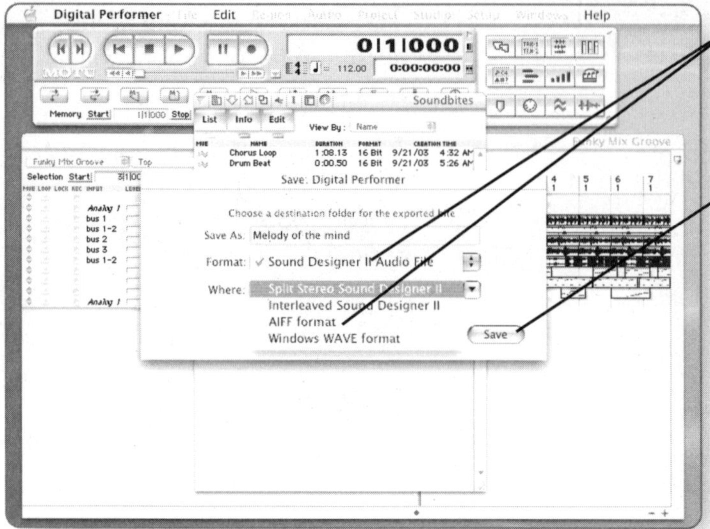

21. **Click** on **AIFF format** or **Sound Designer II Audio file**. Both are acceptable for CD audio.

22. **Click** on **Save**. The file will be saved to the location that you specified. You can now burn this file to CD using your favorite burning software.

13

Audio Effects and Plug-Ins

Digital Performer is like having thirty different programs in one. Not only does it have a variety of built-in effects, it also has a wide range of audio plug-ins. Think of a plug-in as a separate program that runs within Digital Performer that allows you to modify your audio tracks. You can punch up any of your audio tracks using one of the many audio plug-in filters. In this chapter, you'll learn how to:

- Remove silence
- Create a fade
- Add reverb to audio
- Assign delay

Strip Silence

The Strip Silence function of Digital Performer will break a soundbite into parts based on any silence in the selection. When you run this command, the program will look for areas of silence in your soundbite, remove them, and create separate soundbites at the point where the silence occurred.

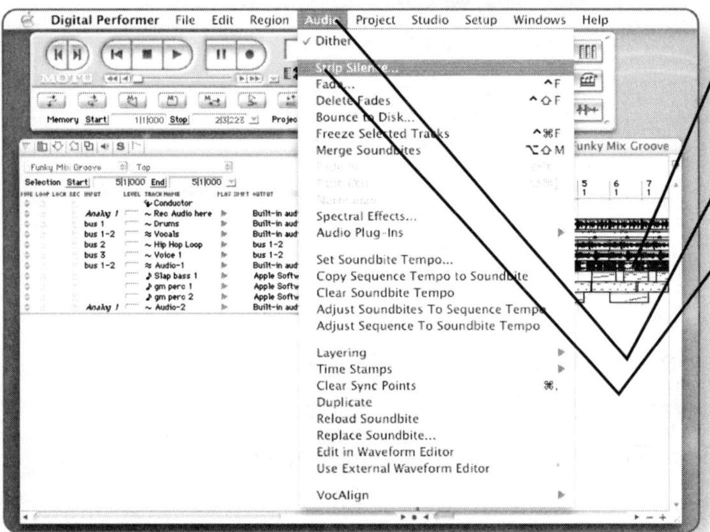

1. **Create** a **selection** in an audio track. You can use any of the selection methods.
2. **Click** on **Audio**. The Audio menu will appear.
3. **Click** on **Strip Silence**. A dialog box will appear in which you can adjust the settings.

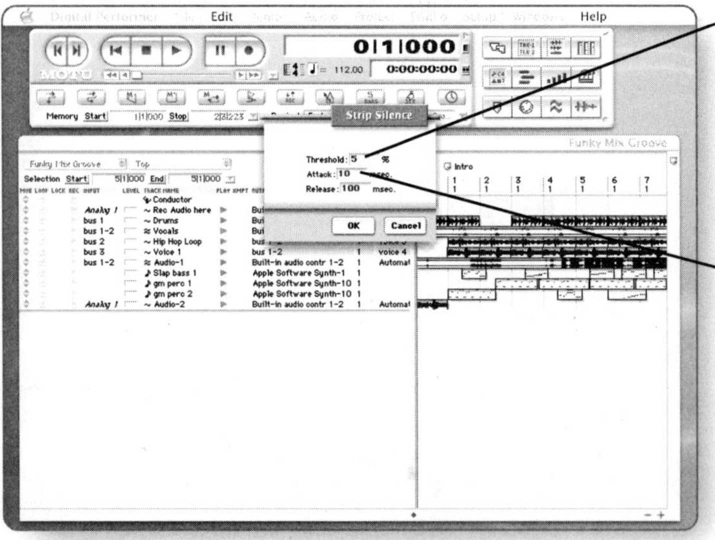

4. **Type** a **number** for the threshold. Any audio below this amplitude level will be considered silence.
5. **Press** the **Tab key** to move to the next field.
6. **Type** an **Attack number**. This is the minimum amount of time that audio will have to be above the threshold in order to not be removed.
7. **Press** the **Tab key** to move to the next field.

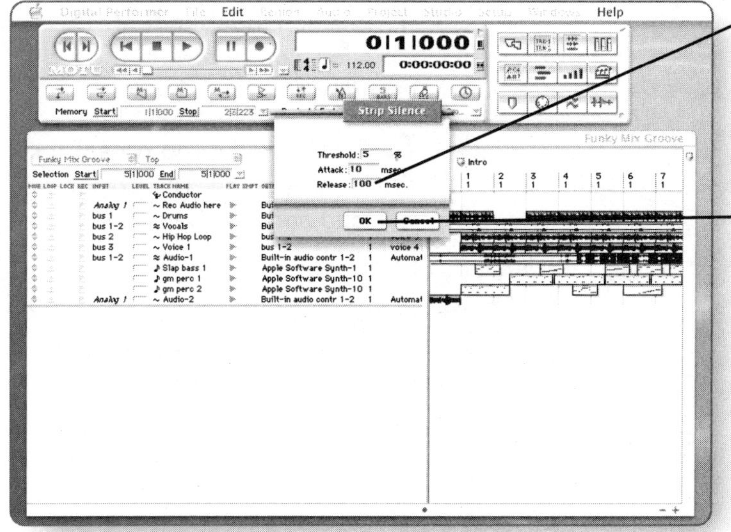

8. Type a **Release number**. This is the minimum amount of time that audio will have to be below the threshold in order to not be removed.

9. Click on **OK**. Strip Silence will search the selection and remove silence based on your specifications.

Fade

The Fade function allows you to create cross-fades between two or more soundbites that intersect one another. You are provided with a graphical representation of the fade, which can be manipulated by clicking and dragging.

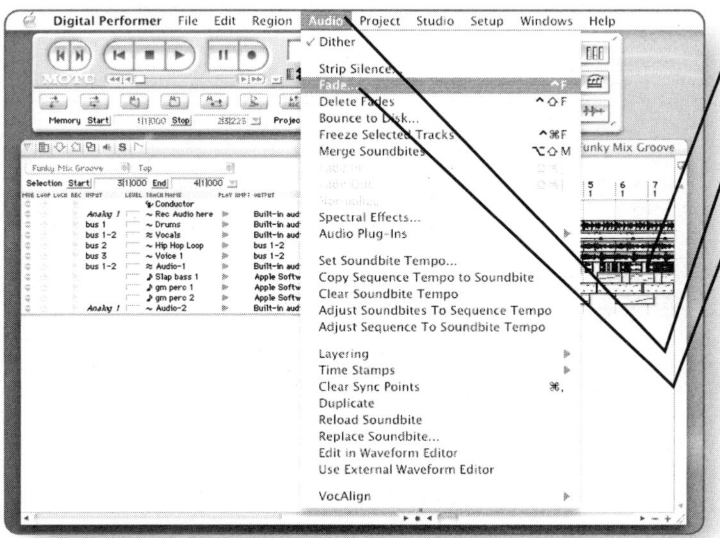

1. Create a **selection** using one of the selection methods.

2. Click on **Audio**. The Audio menu will appear.

3. Click on **Fade**. A dialog box will open, allowing you to graphically manipulate a fade.

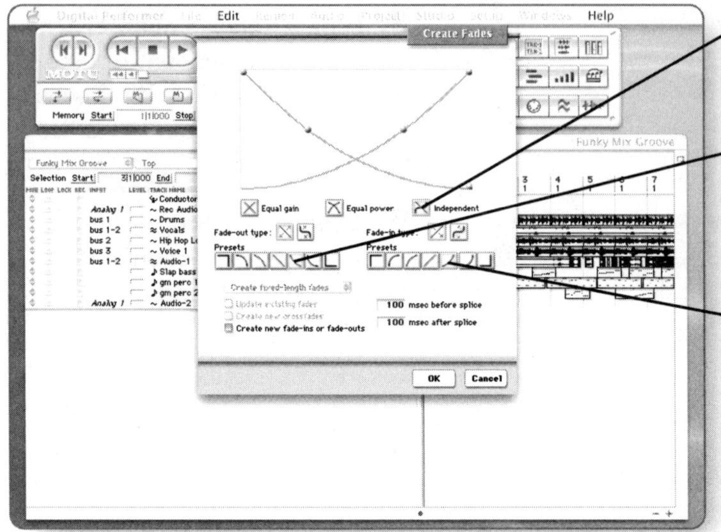

4. **Click** on **Independent**. This will allow you to control the fade in and out independently.

5. **Click** on a desired **preset** for the fade-out type. The preset will load and can then be further adjusted.

6. **Click** on a desired **preset** for the fade-in type. The preset will load and can then be further adjusted.

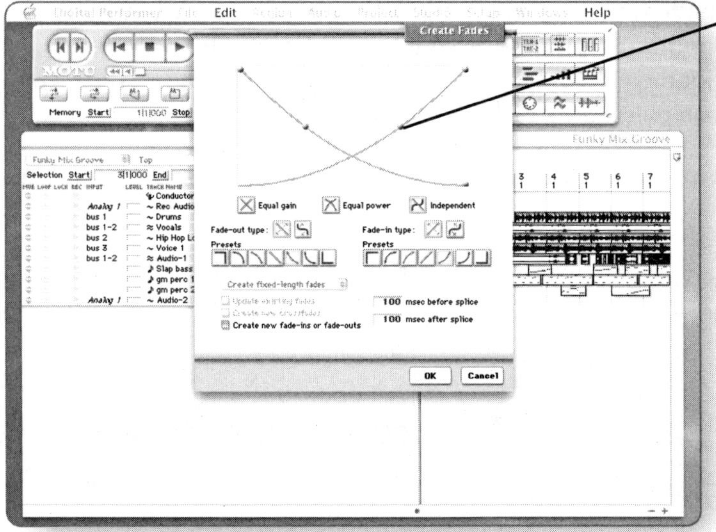

7. **Position** your **mouse pointer** over one of the red dots.

8. **Click** and **drag** the **dot** to the left or right to manipulate the fade.

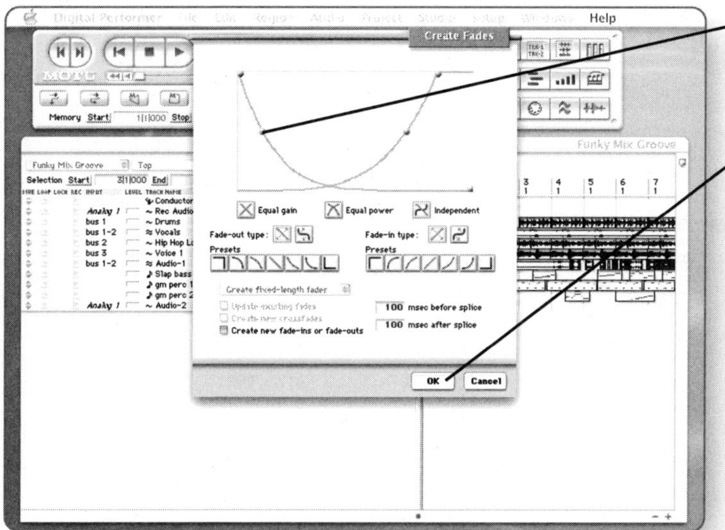

9. Release the **mouse button**. The fade will change based on where you moved the red dot.

10. Click on **OK**. The fade setting will take effect and the dialog box will close.

Merge Soundbites

Sometimes it's easier to manage and work with one soundbite than a series of small soundbites. Digital Performer allows you to combine two or more soundbites to create one.

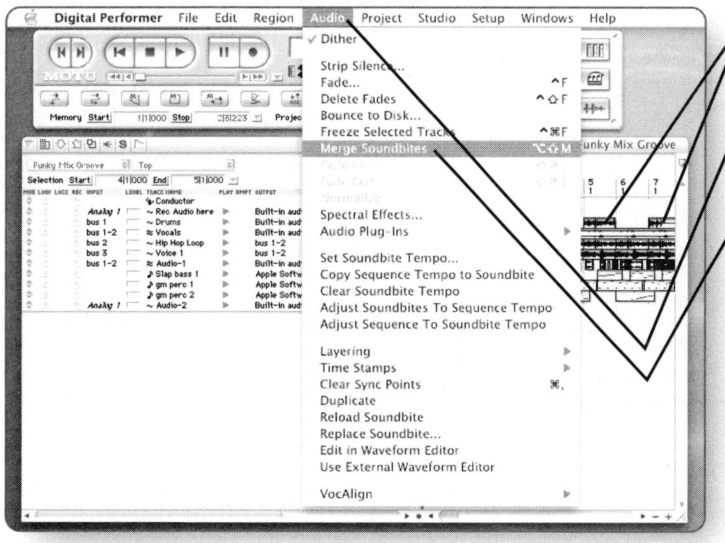

1. Create a **selection** that contains at least two soundbites.

2. Click on **Audio**. The Audio menu will appear.

3. Click on **Merge Soundbites**. The soundbites in the selection will be merged into a single soundbite.

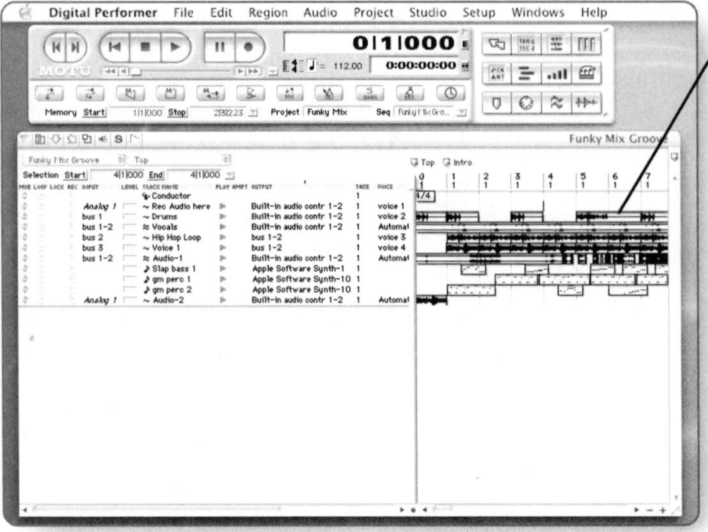

After you merge soundbites, they will appear as one phrase.

Spectral Effects

The Spectral Effects window allows you to graphically adjust different sound settings for your audio track. Some of these include time scaling, pitch shifting, and tempo. You are provided with a three-dimensional grid that can be adjusted to manipulate the settings. Digital Performer allows you to select from preset settings, or you can make your own manual adjustments.

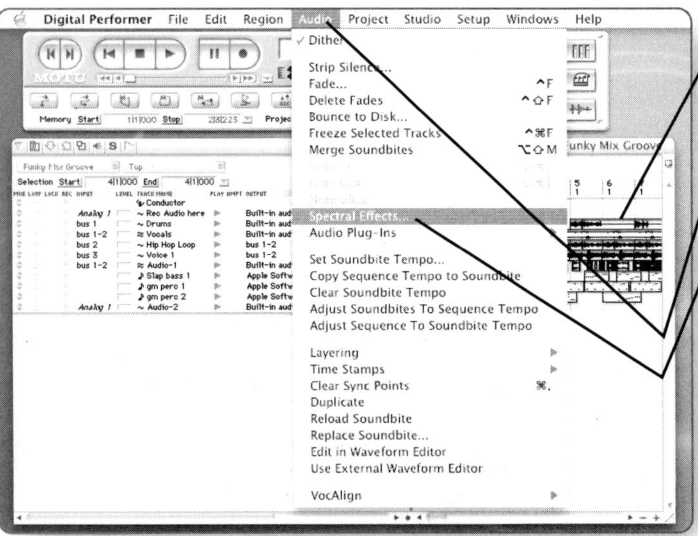

1. **Create** a **selection** using any of the selection methods.

2. **Click** on **Audio**. The Audio menu will appear.

3. **Click** on **Spectral Effects**. The Spectral Effects window will open.

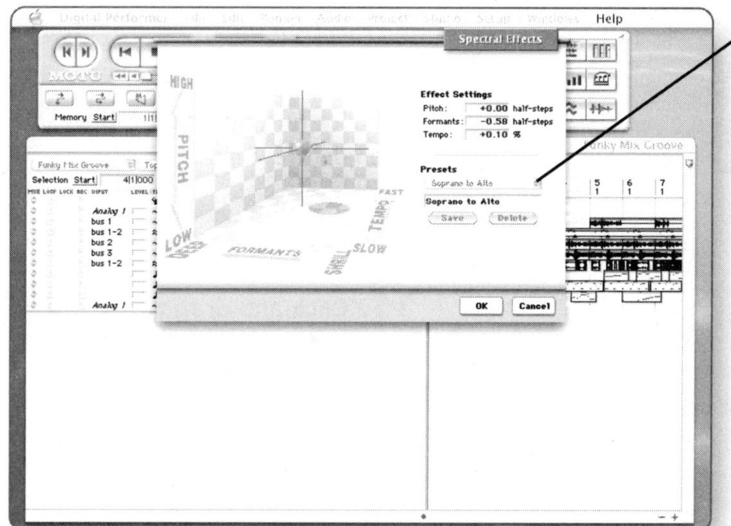

4. **Click** on the **up-and-down arrow** to open the Presets pop-up menu.

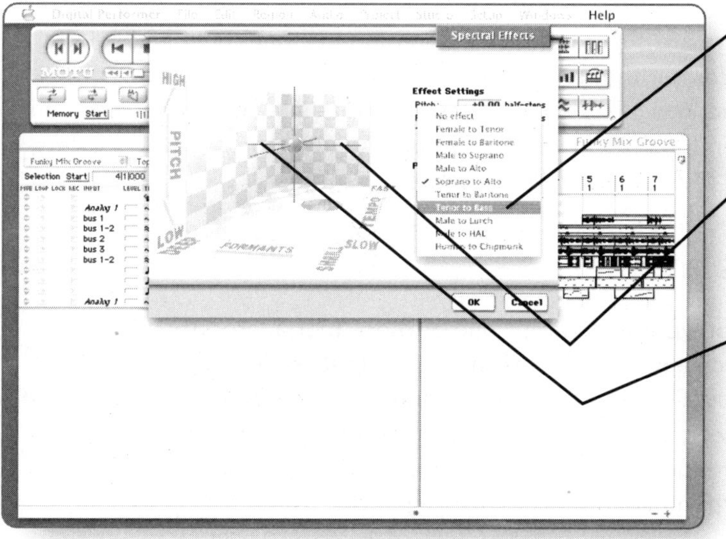

5. **Click** on the desired **preset**. It will be selected and the settings will change. The preset can now be further adjusted.

6. **Position** the **mouse pointer** over the x-axis. Your mouse pointer will change to a double-sided arrow.

7. **Click** and **drag** to the **left** or **right** to adjust the formants.

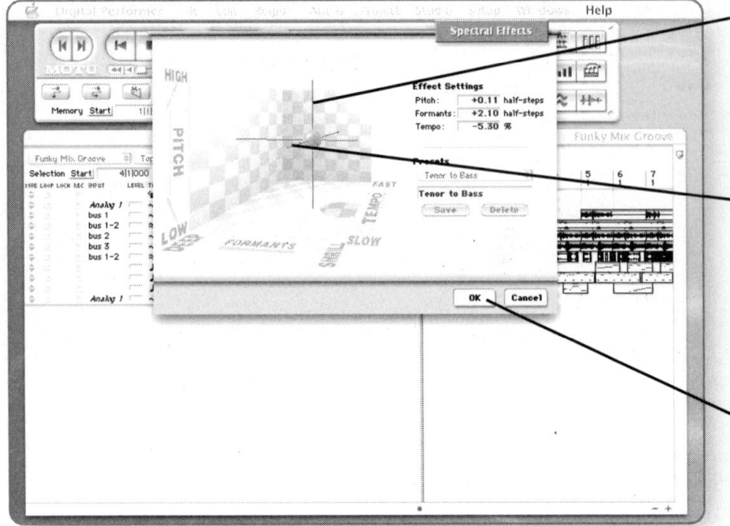

8. **Position** the **mouse pointer** over the y-axis.

9. **Click** and **drag up** or **down** to adjust the pitch.

10. **Position** your **mouse pointer** over the z-axis.

11. **Click** and **drag** to the **left** or **right** to increase or decrease the tempo.

12. **Click** on **OK**. The settings will take effect.

Audio Plug-Ins

There are several dozen audio plug-ins that come with Digital Performer that allow you to apply special effects to your audio selections. Almost all of them operate in a similar fashion. You open the Plug-in window, make the desired changes, preview, and then accept those changes.

Delay

If you've ever been to one of those mega-large theaters to watch a movie, there is no doubt that you've experienced delay. Delay refers to the amount of time between one speaker playing a particular sound and another speaker playing a corresponding sound. Delay is perfect for creating effects like surround sound, echoes, or even chorus.

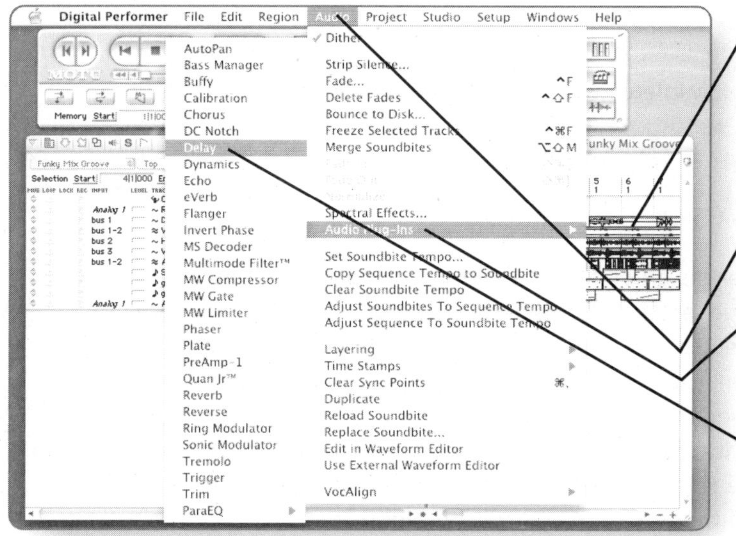

1. **Create** a **selection** that consists of the audio file you would like to add an effect to. You can use any of the selection methods.
2. **Click** on **Audio**. The Audio menu will appear.
3. **Click** on **Audio Plug-Ins**. A submenu of audio plug-ins will appear.
4. **Click** on **Delay**. The Delay window will open.

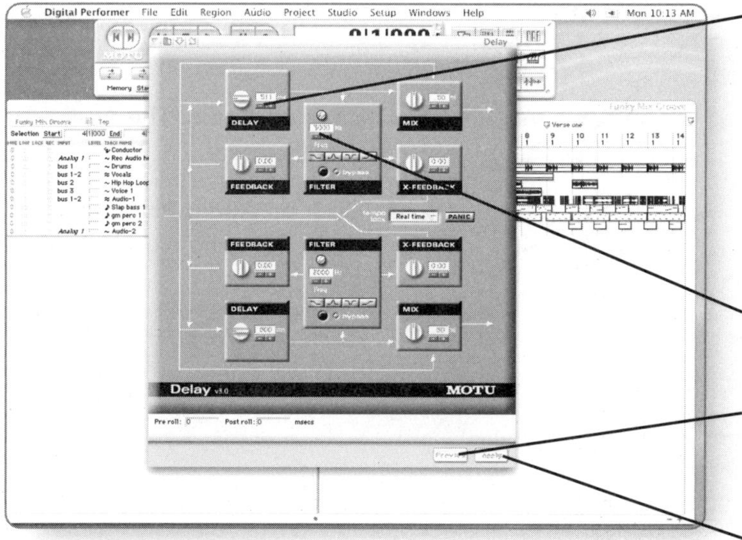

5. **Click** on the **+** or **– Zoom tool** in the Delay area to increase or decrease the amount of time it takes for sound to go from one speaker to the next. Alternatively, you can click and drag on the knob to adjust the settings.
6. **Adjust** any of the other **settings** as desired.
7. **Click** on **Preview** to listen to your selection with the changes you have made.
8. **Click** on **Apply** to apply these settings to the selection once you are satisfied with the results.

> **TIP**
>
> Double-clicking on any dial will return it to its default setting.

eVerb

eVerb is an effect that allows you to control the level of reverberation. Reverberation refers to the effect obtained when sound waves bounce off the walls of a room. Sound in a small room with glass walls will sound much different from sound in an auditorium with wood walls. The eVerb plug-in in Digital Performer allows you to mimic almost any kind of room. You can start by selecting a type of room for initial reflections and then modify it to suit your needs.

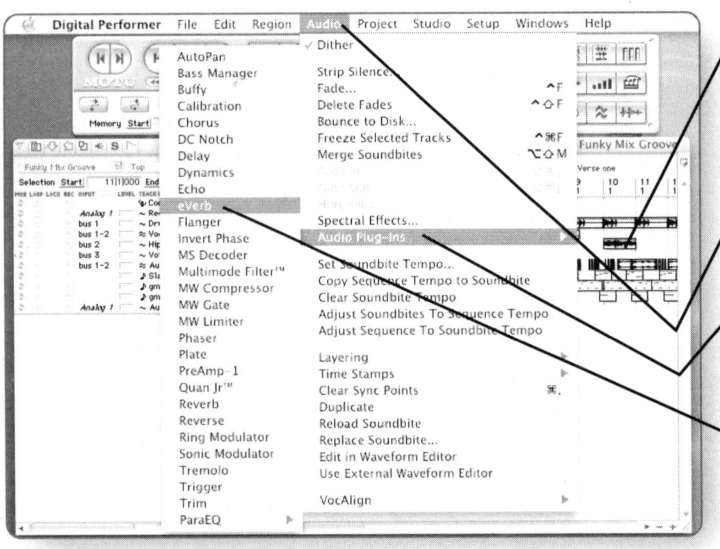

1. **Create** a **selection** that consists of the audio file you would like to add an effect to. You can use any of the selection methods.
2. **Click** on **Audio**. The Audio menu will appear.
3. **Click** on **Audio Plug-Ins**. A submenu of Audio plug-ins will appear.
4. **Click** on **eVerb**. The eVerb window will open.

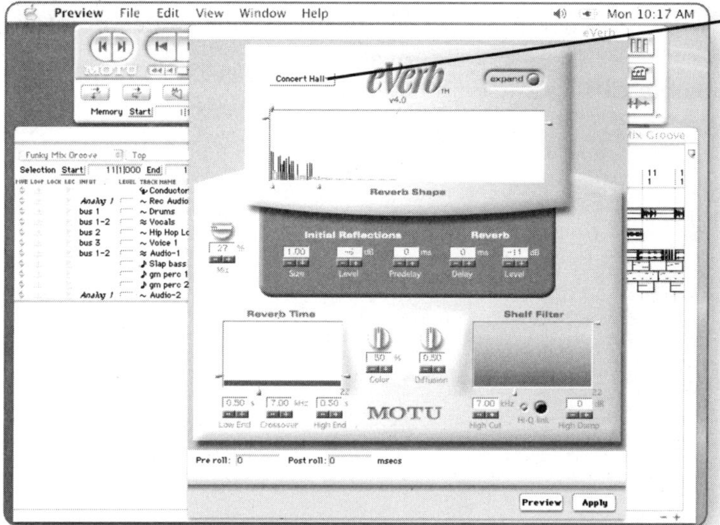

5. **Click** on the **Reflections List button**. A list of different room types will appear.

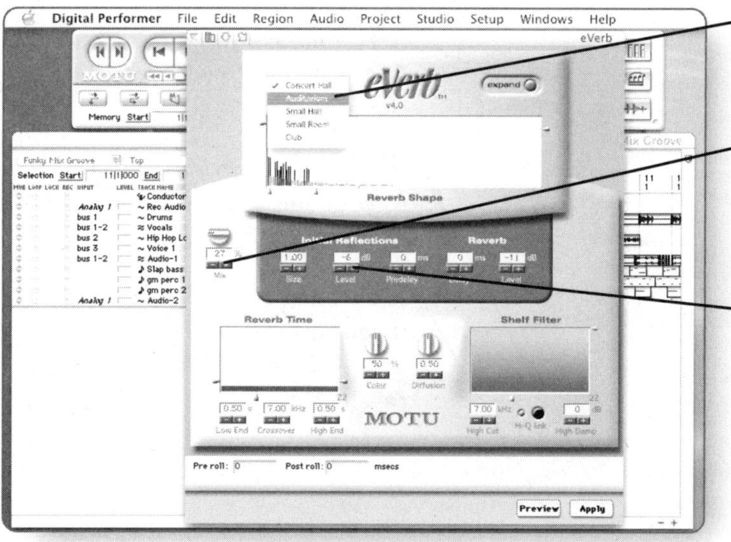

6. **Click** on the desired **room type**. The setting for that type of room will be loaded.
7. **Click** on the + or – **Zoom tool** to adjust the mix between the dry signal and the reverberation.
8. **Click** on the + or – **Zoom tool** to adjust any of the other settings.

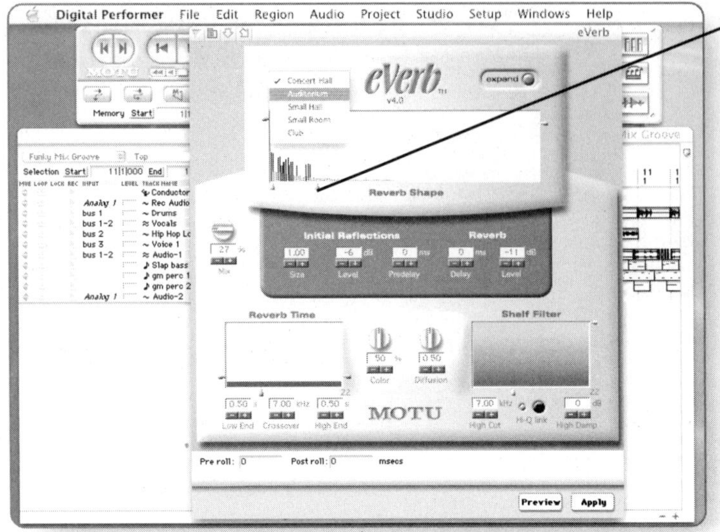

9. **Position** your **mouse pointer** over the Room Size Scaling Factor button.

10. **Click** and **drag** the **Room Size Scaling Factor button** to the right or left to adjust the scale factor for the room.

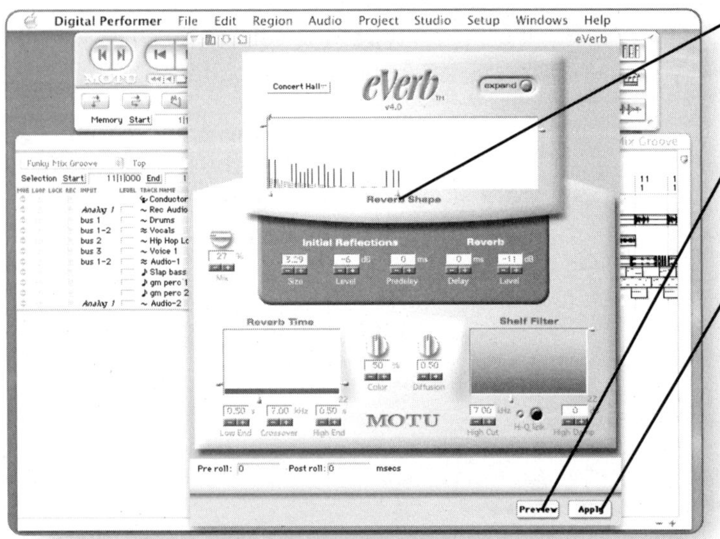

11. **Release** the **mouse button**. The scale factor will have changed.

12. **Click** on **Preview** to listen to your selection with the changes you have made.

13. **Click** on **Apply** to apply these settings to the selection once you are satisfied with the results.

Reverse

Are you old enough to remember LPs? Do you remember how people claimed some LPs played disturbed messages if played backwards? Here's your chance to find out. Just record any audio track and you can reverse it using Digital Performer's Reverse plug-in.

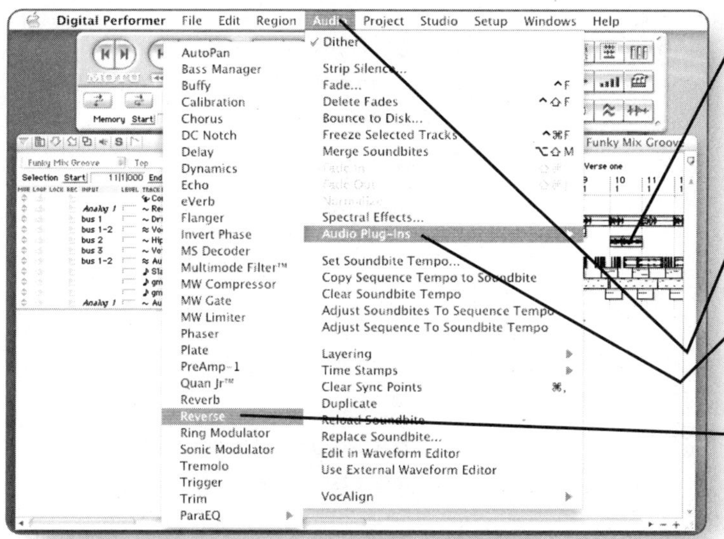

1. **Create** a **selection** that consists of the audio file you would like to add an effect to. You can use any of the selection methods.
2. **Click** on **Audio**. The Audio menu will appear.
3. **Click** on **Audio Plug-Ins**. A submenu of audio plug-ins will appear.
4. **Click** on **Reverse**. Your selection will be reversed and you can play it backwards.

Flanger

Flanger is a type of delay effect that creates a sound that seems like you're talking into a fan. It does this by creating a slightly distorted sound. Typically, Flanger effects are used on guitar tracks.

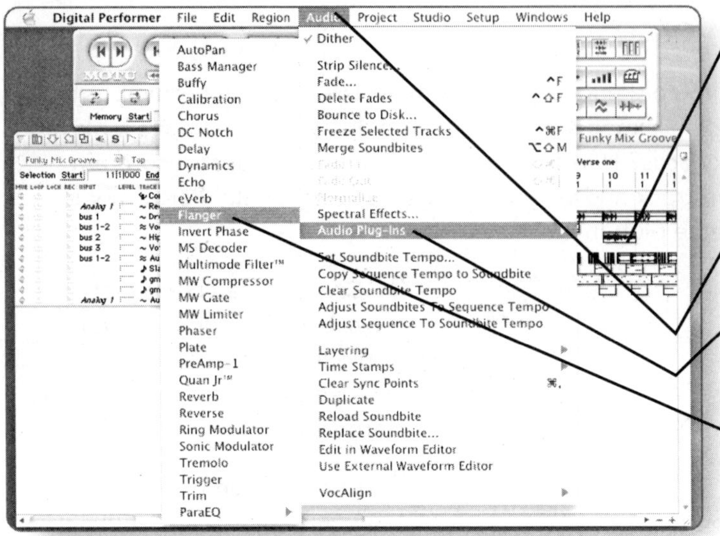

1. **Create** a **selection** that consists of the audio file you would like to add an effect to. You can use any of the selection methods.

2. **Click** on **Audio**. The Audio menu will appear.

3. **Click** on **Audio Plug-Ins**. A submenu of audio plug-ins will appear.

4. **Click** on **Flanger**. The Flanger window will open.

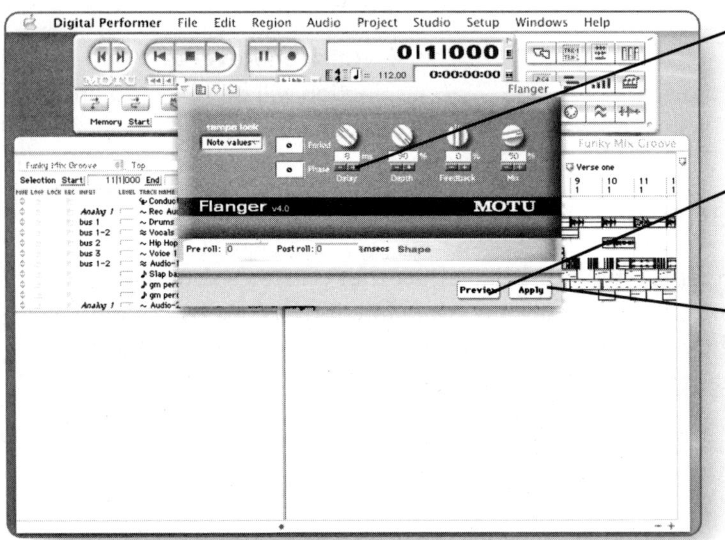

5. **Click** the – or + **Zoom tool** beside any of the dials to adjust its settings. Alternatively, you can click and drag the dial.

6. **Click** on **Preview** to listen to your selection with the changes you have made.

7. **Click** on **Apply** to apply these settings to the selection once you are satisfied with the results.

Chorus

The Chorus effect creates the illusion of several voices coming from your selection. You can adjust the delay, depth, wet and dry pan, as well as the mix.

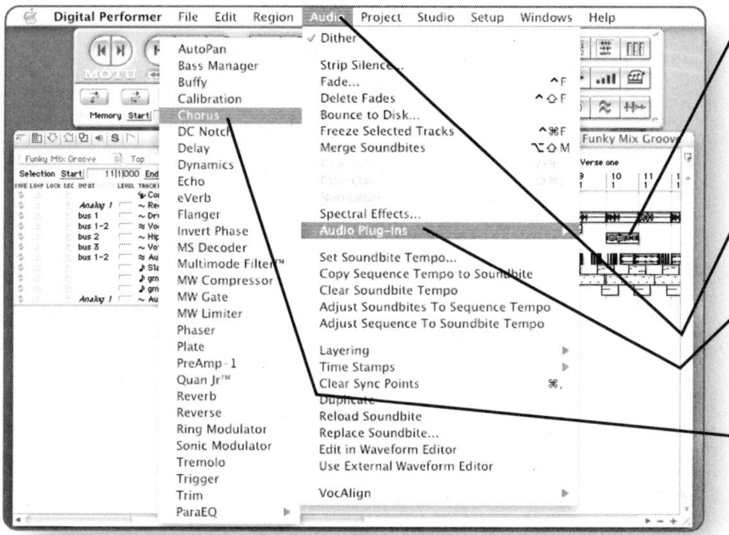

1. **Create** a **selection** that consists of the audio file you would like to add an effect to. You can use any of the selection methods.
2. **Click** on **Audio**. The Audio menu will appear.
3. **Click** on **Audio Plug-Ins**. A submenu of audio plug-ins will appear.
4. **Click** on **Chorus**. The Chorus window will open.

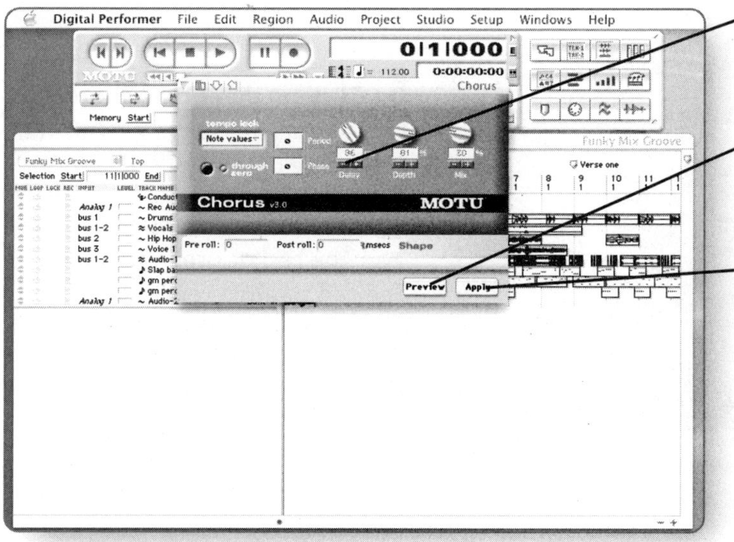

5. **Click** on the + or – **Zoom tool** under any of the dials to adjust its settings.
6. **Click** on **Preview** to listen to your selection with the changes you have made.
7. **Click** on **Apply** to apply these settings to the selection once you are satisfied with the results.

Trim

The Trim plug-in allows you to add up to 40db in gain to your audio selections and allows you to adjust the pan. In addition, you can control the maximum and minimum values displayed in your level meters.

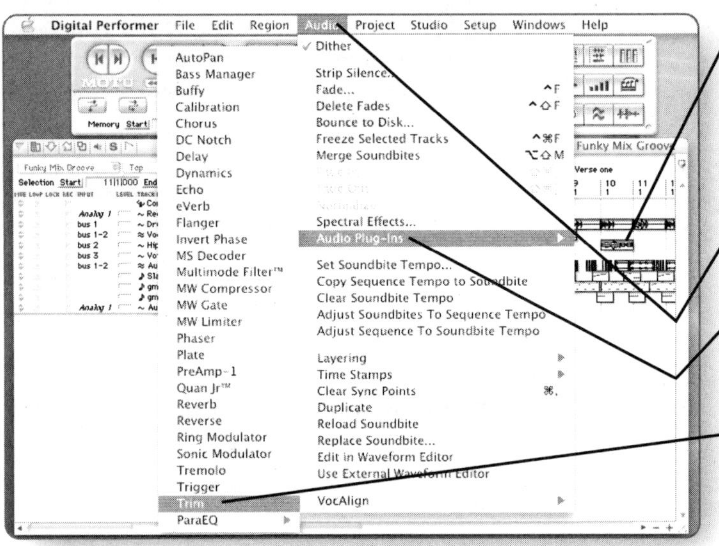

1. **Create** a **selection** that consists of the audio file you would like to add an effect to. You can use any of the selection methods.
2. **Click** on **Audio**. The Audio menu will appear.
3. **Click** on **Audio Plug-Ins**. A submenu of audio plug-ins will appear.
4. **Click** on **Trim**. The Trim window will open.

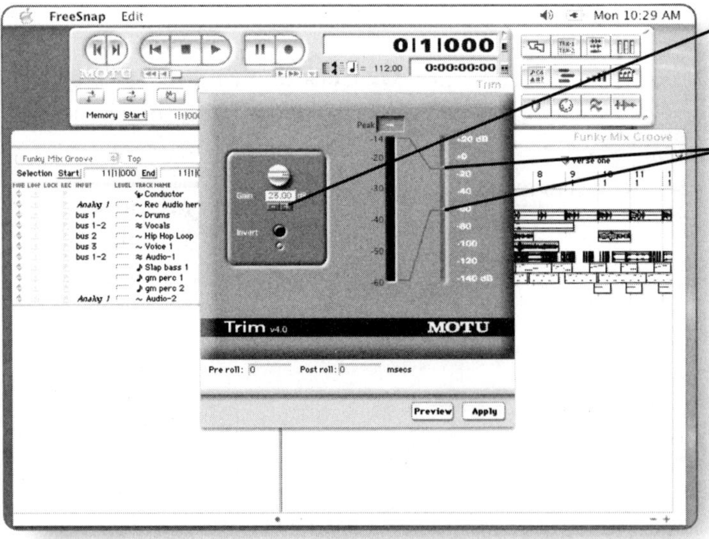

5. **Click** on the + or – **Zoom tool** under the Gain dial. This will adjust the gain.
6. **Position** your **mouse pointer** over the red or green triangles. The red triangle represents the maximum value that will be displayed in the levels meter and the green represents the minimum.
7. **Click** and **drag up** or **down** to adjust the minimum and maximum values that will be displayed in the levels meter.

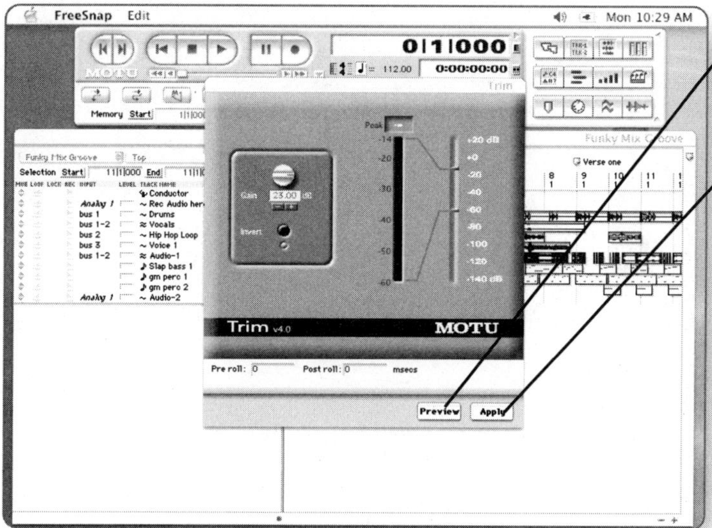

8. Click on **Preview** to listen to your selection with the changes you have made.

9. Click on **Apply** to apply these settings to the selection once you are satisfied with the results.

14

Mixing

If you have ever been to a rock concert, you've probably noticed a couple of roadies (well, technically they're called sound engineers) working a seemingly endless landscape of dials, buttons, and faders on a huge mixing board. Digital Performer has a built-in mixing board with full functionality. The mixing board allows you to adjust different settings, such as volume, pan, and effects for each track. In this chapter, you will learn how to:

- Adjust volume and pan
- Create mixes
- Create groups
- Use automation modes

Launching the Mixing Board

The mixing board can be accessed from the Control Panel.

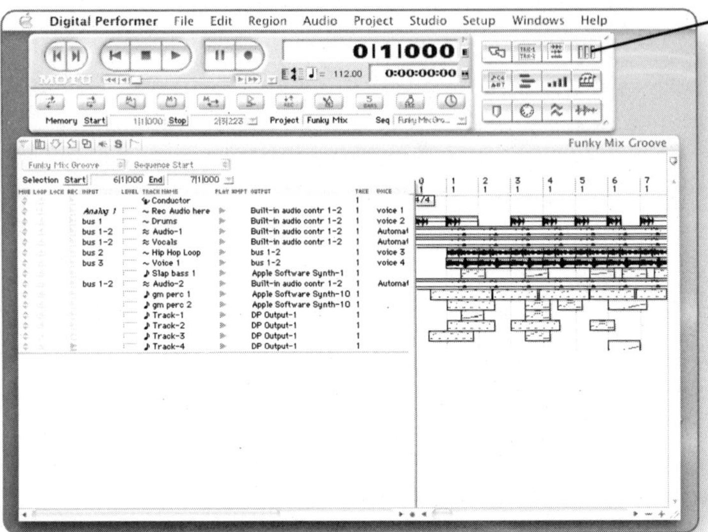

1. Click on the **Mixing Board button** in the Control Panel. The mixing board will launch.

Views

Because each track of a sequence can be represented in the mixing board, the more tracks you have, the larger the mixing board will become. Digital Performer offers many different ways to help you manage the views of your tracks. You can select different view modes, select specific tracks to view, or create customized layouts.

Narrow View

If you want to increase the number of tracks that can be seen on the screen, one option is to select Narrow view. Narrow view condenses channel strips so that they are 50 percent of their original size.

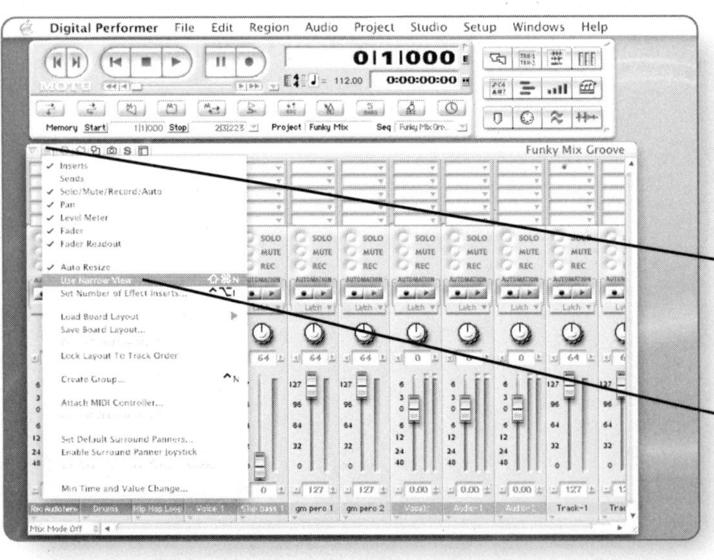

1. Click on the **Mini Menu button** in the Mixer Board window. A menu of commands will appear.

2. Click on **Use Narrow View.** Narrow view will be selected and all of the channel strips will be condensed.

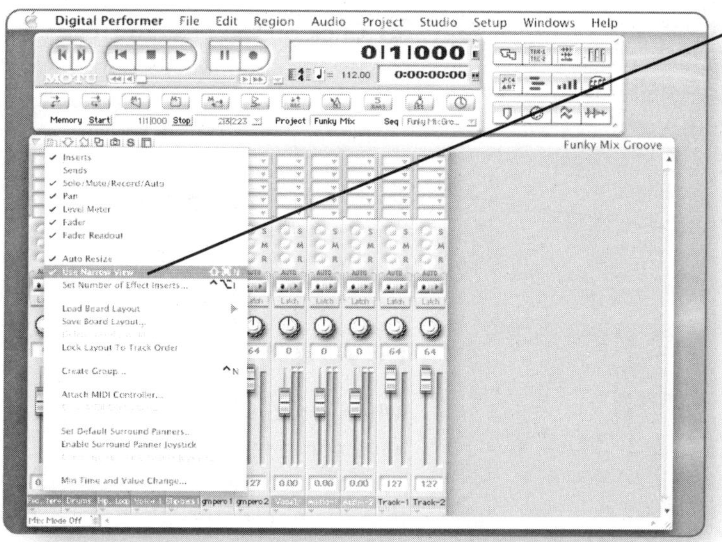

3. **Repeat steps 1 and 2** to return to Normal mode.

> **NOTE**
>
> When in Narrow view, all functions of the channel strip are available except for the Send Mute buttons.

Viewing Tracks

Digital Performer allows you to select the tracks that you would like to appear in the mixing board at any given time. By selecting or deselecting tracks, you can increase or decrease the size of the mixing board.

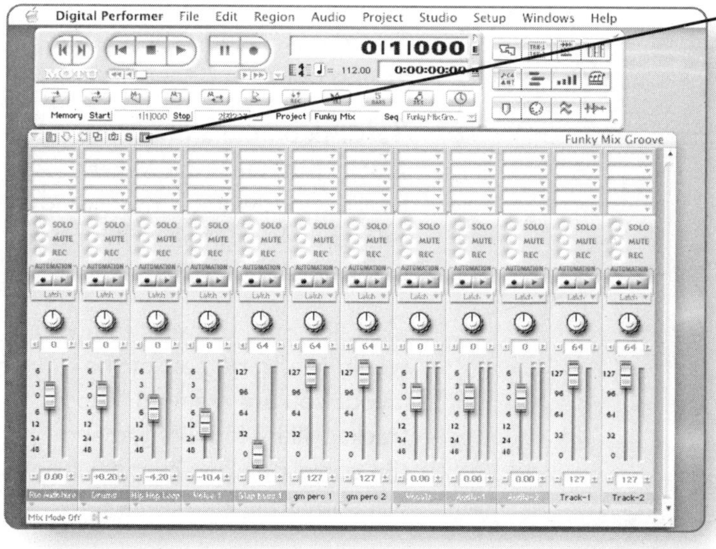

1. **Click** on the **Show/Hide Tracks button** in the Mixer Board window. A list of all of the tracks in the sequence will appear.

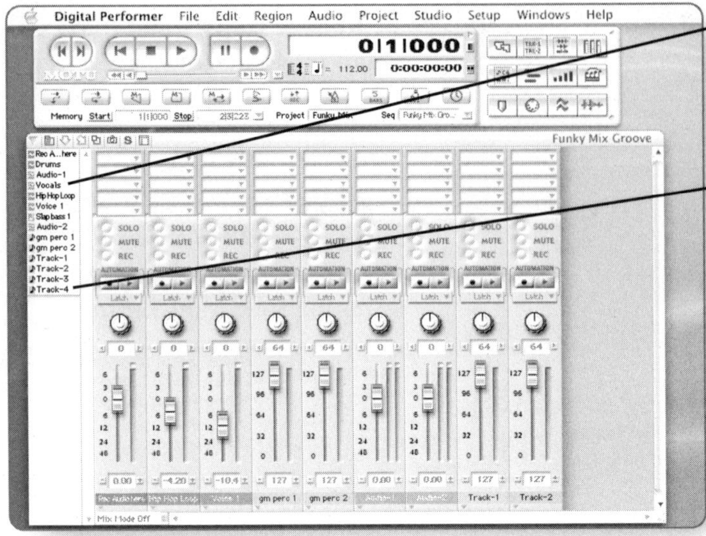

2. Click on the desired **tracks** to view as channel strips in the mixing board. Those tracks will be highlighted.

3. Click on any **highlighted track** to deselect it and remove its corresponding channel strip.

Layouts

When creating a mix, you will have some tracks that are pertinent to the mix and others that are not. Rather than spending time opening and closing certain channel strips, you can create specific layouts that contain only the tracks that are relevant to the mix you are working on.

Creating Layouts

To create a layout, set up the mixing board and then save it.

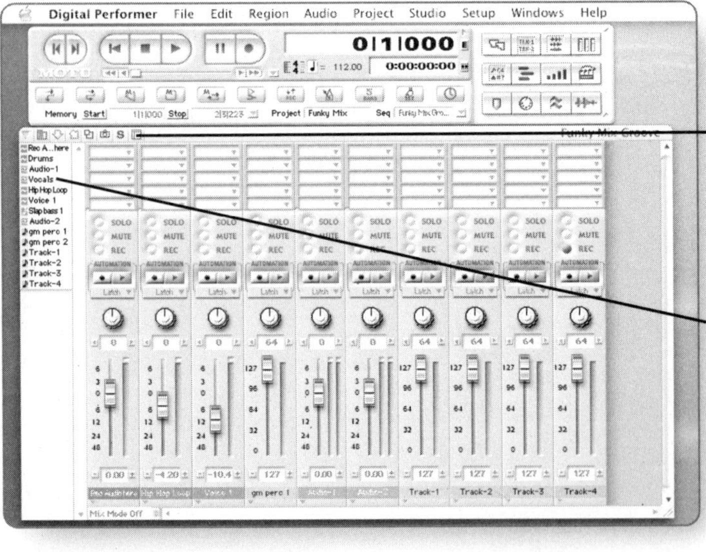

1. Click on the **Show/Hide Tracks button** in the Mixer Board window if it is not already selected. A list of all of the tracks in the sequence will appear.

2. Click on the **tracks** that you would like to be part of the layout you are creating. Those tracks will be highlighted and the corresponding channel strips will appear.

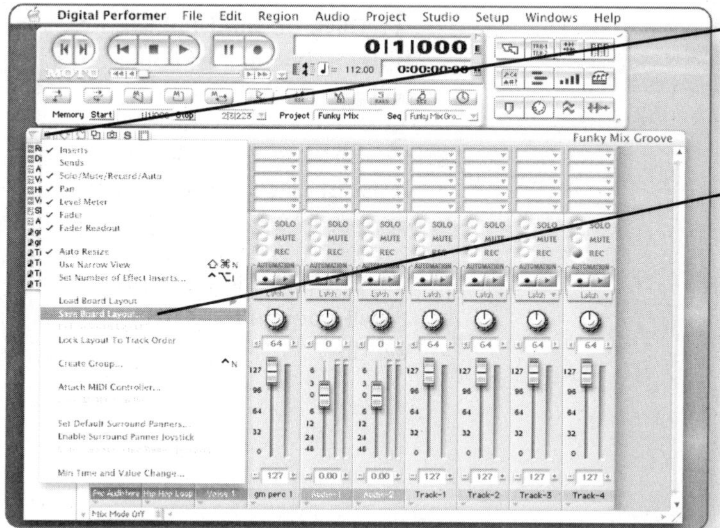

3. Click on the **Mini Menu button** in the Mixing Board window. A menu of commands will appear.

4. Click on **Save Board Layout**. A dialog box will appear in which you can name the layout.

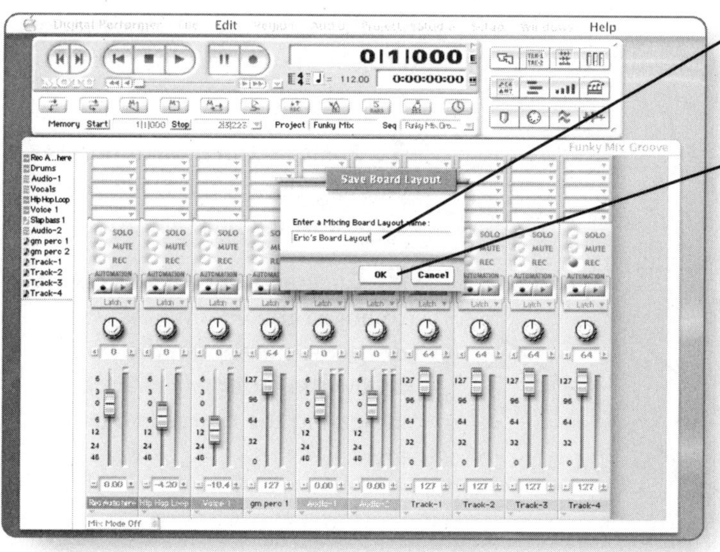

5. Type a **name** for the layout. It's best to give it a name that describes the layout.

6. Click on **OK**. The layout will be saved.

Accessing Layouts

Once you have saved a layout, you can access it at any time through the mini menu.

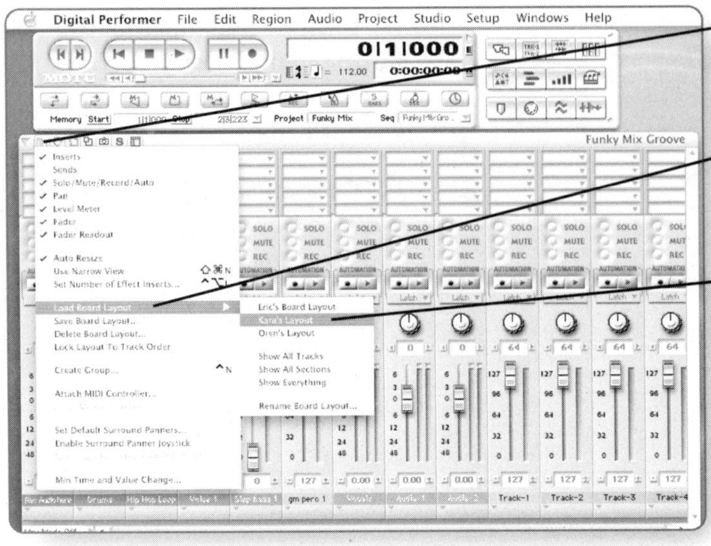

1. **Click** on the **Mini Menu button**. A menu of commands will appear.
2. **Click** on **Load Board Layout**. A list of all saved layouts will appear in a submenu.
3. **Click** on the desired **layout**. It will open in the Mixing Board window.

Volume Adjustment

Digital Performer provides you with a graphical representation of a fader that can be adjusted to set the volume for particular tracks.

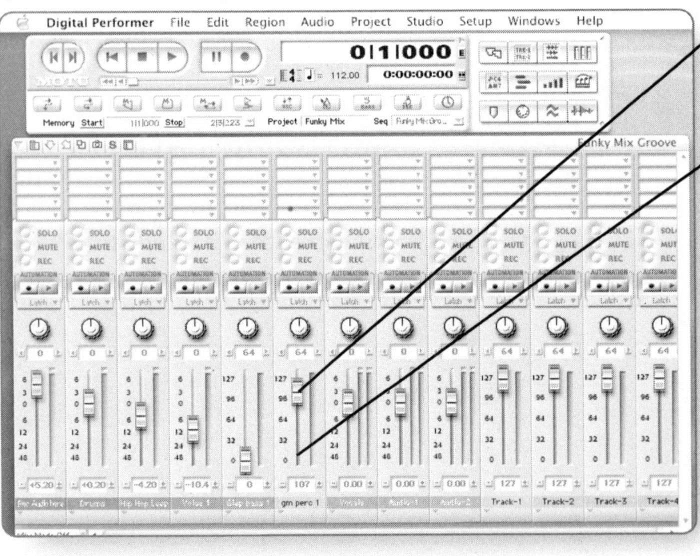

1. **Position** the **mouse pointer** over a fader on the track whose volume you would like to adjust.
2. **Click** and **drag up** or **down** to adjust the volume. As you drag, the number in the box below the fader will change, indicating the current volume level.

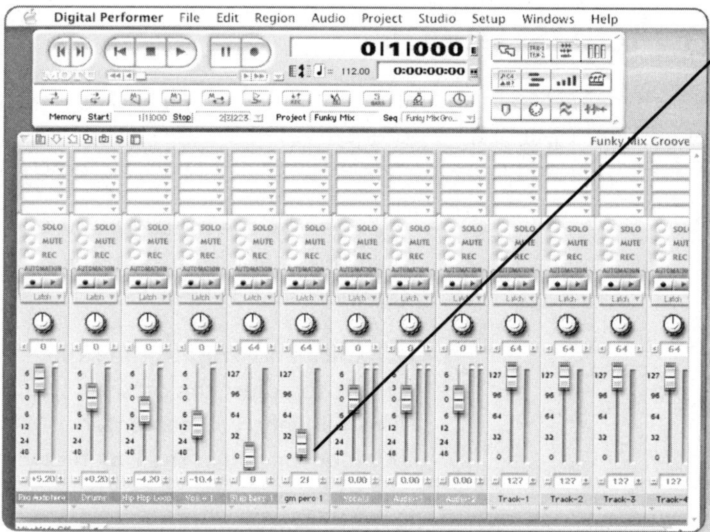

3. Release the **mouse button**. The volume for that track will be set.

Setting Precise Volume Levels

Rather than using the faders, if you know the exact volume levels that you would like to set, you can enter them in the boxes below the volume faders.

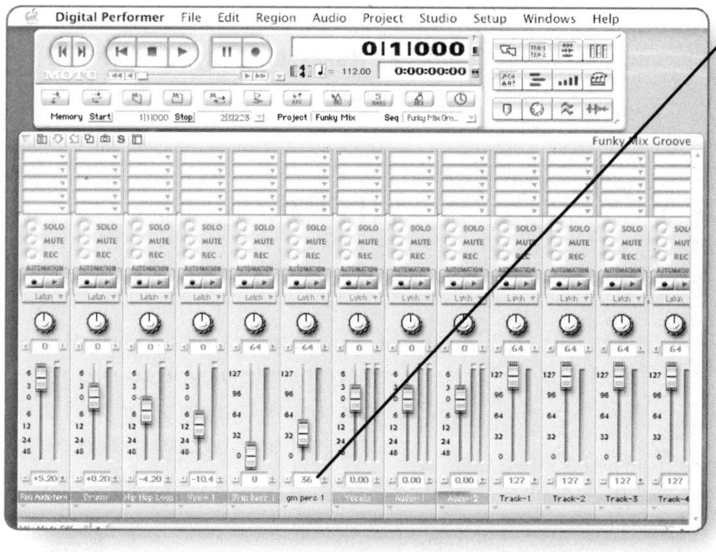

1. **Click once** in the **box** under the volume fader for the track whose volume you would like to adjust. The box will be highlighted.
2. **Type** a **number** for the volume level. You can enter a level of 0 to 127 for MIDI tracks and -∞ to 6.00 for audio tracks.
3. **Press Return**. The new volume level will be set.

Pan Adjustment

On each channel strip of the mixing board, you will find a panpot (short for panoramic potentiometer) that will allow you to control how sound is proportioned between left and right.

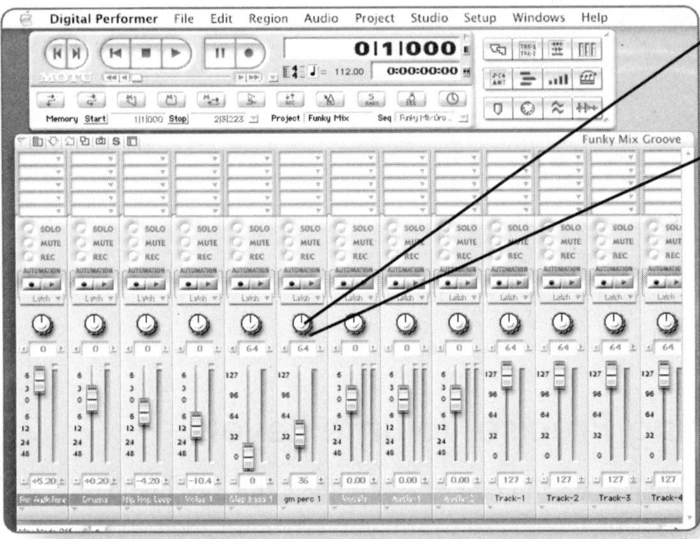

1. **Position** the **mouse pointer** over the panpot for the track that you would like to adjust.
2. **Click** and **drag** to the **right** or **left** to adjust the setting. Alternatively, you can enter a number for pan in the box below the panpot. The setting can be anywhere between 0 for hard left and 127 for hard right.

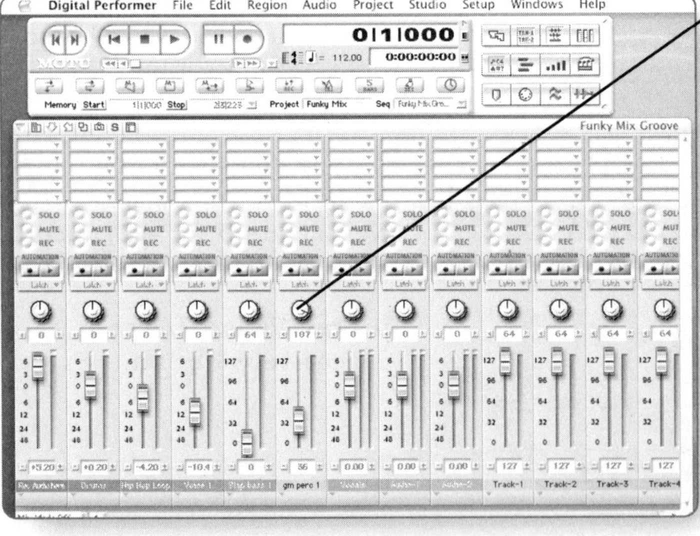

3. **Release** the **mouse button**. The pan settings will be set.

Groups

If you want to apply the same changes to pan knobs or faders for a variety of tracks, Digital Performer allows you to group those tracks together so that any changes made to one in the group will be made to all.

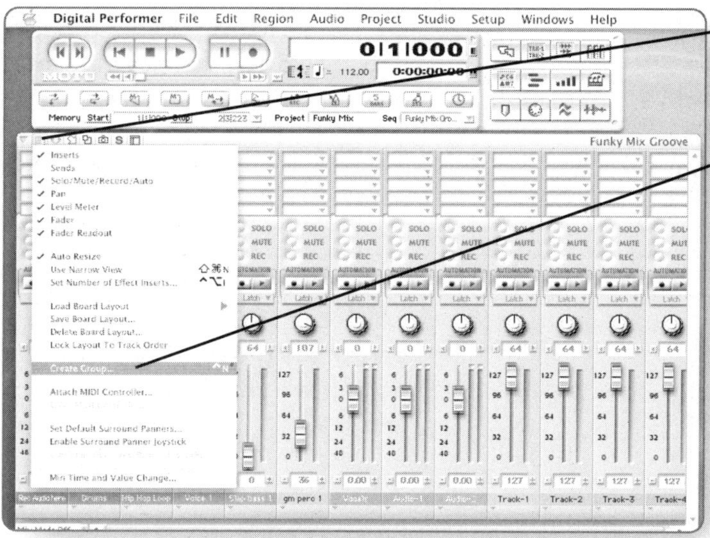

1. Click on the **Mini Menu button**. A list of commands in that menu will appear.

2. Click on **Create Group**. A dialog box will appear in which you can name your group. You can now select which controls you want to be a part of the group. Your mouse pointer will change to a crosshair.

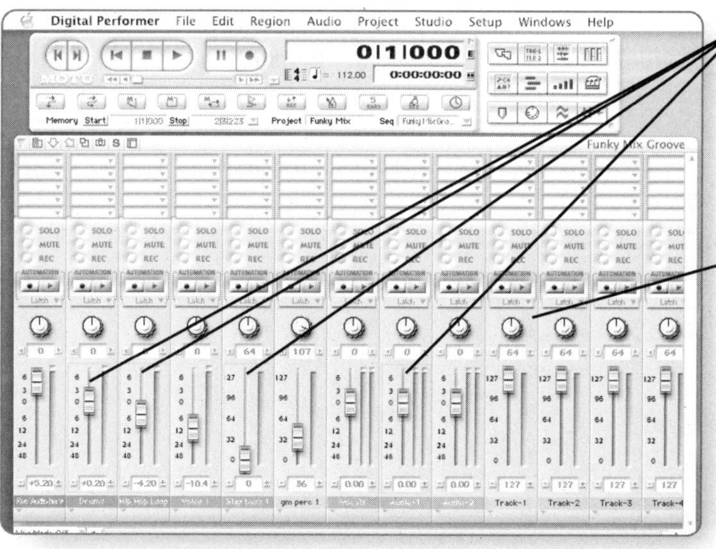

3. Click on the **volume faders** and **panpots** that you would like to be a part of the group. As you click on them, a green box will appear to indicate that they are part of the group.

4. Click in any **blank area** of the Mixing Board window to finish the selection process. The items you selected will now be part of the group.

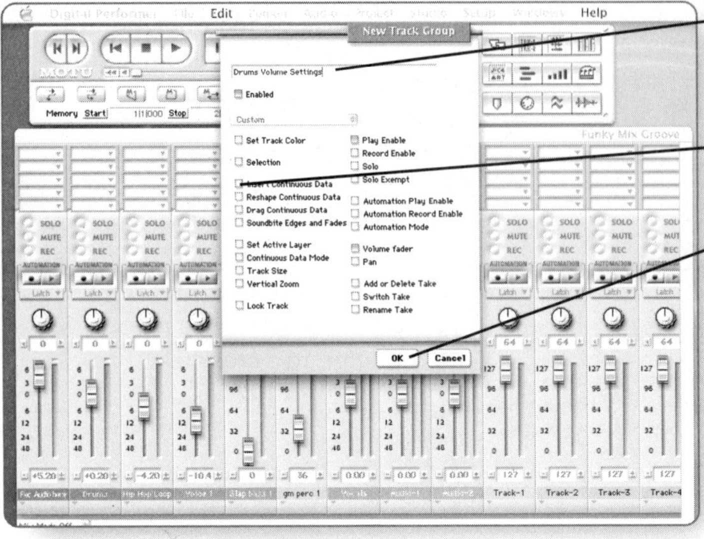

5. **Type** a **name** for your group. You should give it a descriptive name.

6. **Click** on the desired **options** for your group.

7. **Click** on **OK**. The group will be saved and you can now select which controls you want to be a part of the group. Your mouse pointer will change to a crosshair.

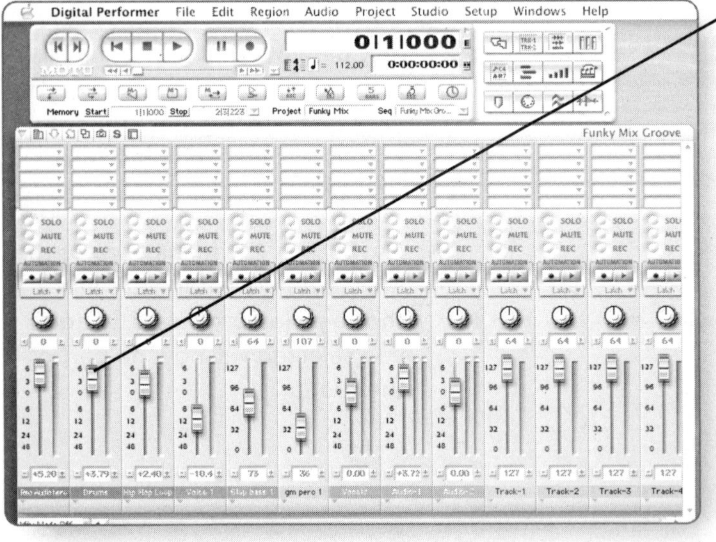

8. **Click** and **drag** a **fader** to adjust the settings of one of the items in the group. All of the other items in the group will adjust simultaneously.

Track Groups Window

If you want to remove or suspend a group that you have created, you can do so by opening the Track Groups window.

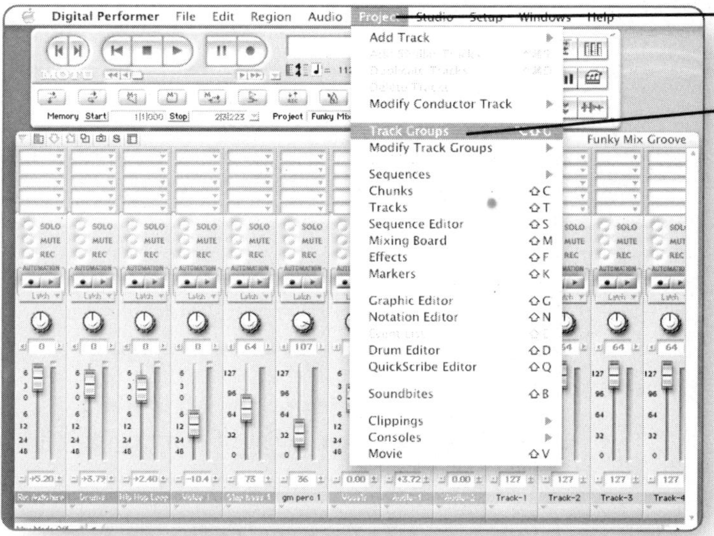

1. **Click** on **Project**. The Project menu will appear.
2. **Click** on **Track Groups**. The Track Groups window will open.

Overriding Groups

There may be occasions when you would like to adjust a setting for a track that is part of a group, without adjusting the settings for other group members. For cases like these, you can temporarily suspend the group to make the desired adjustments.

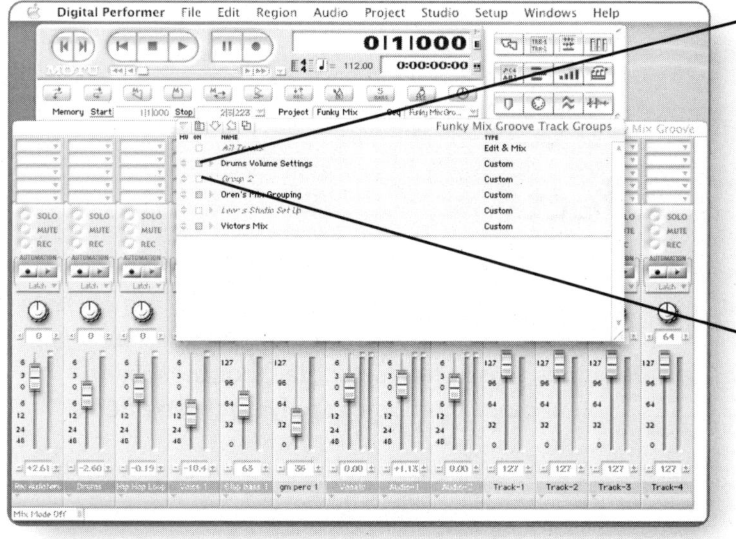

1. **Click** on the **square button** beside the group name. It will no longer be filled in and the name will appear italicized to indicate it is suspended.
2. **Repeat step 1** for any other groups that you would like to suspend.
3. **Click** on an **unfilled square** to remove the suspension.

> **NOTE**
>
> An alternative to suspending the group is to press and hold the Option key and adjust the setting. This will allow you to adjust that setting without changing the settings of the other group members.

Deleting Groups

If you no longer need a group that you have created, you can delete it.

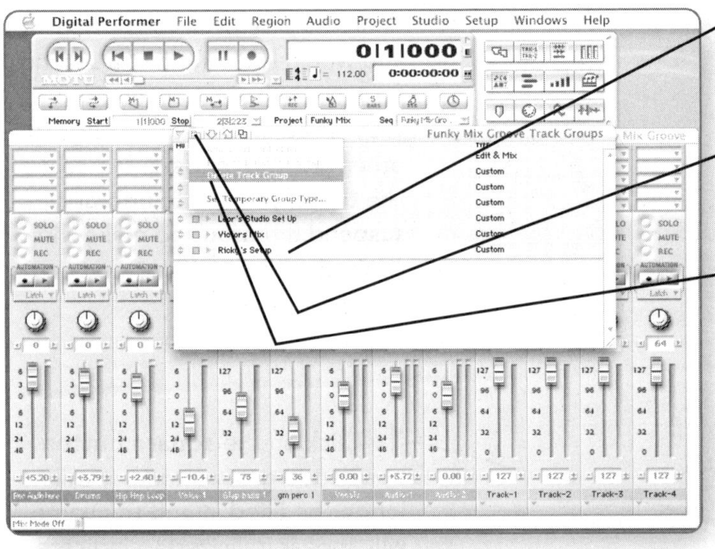

1. **Click** on the **name** of the group that you would like to delete. It will be highlighted.
2. **Click** on the **Mini Menu button**. A list of commands will appear.
3. **Click** on **Delete Track Group**. The group will be removed.

Mix Effects

You can apply many audio and MIDI effects to the tracks in your sequences using the Mixing Board window. Many of these effects are offered as plug-ins. Chapter 13, "Audio Effects and Plug-Ins," describes these effects in detail, but the mixing board offers you another method of applying these effects.

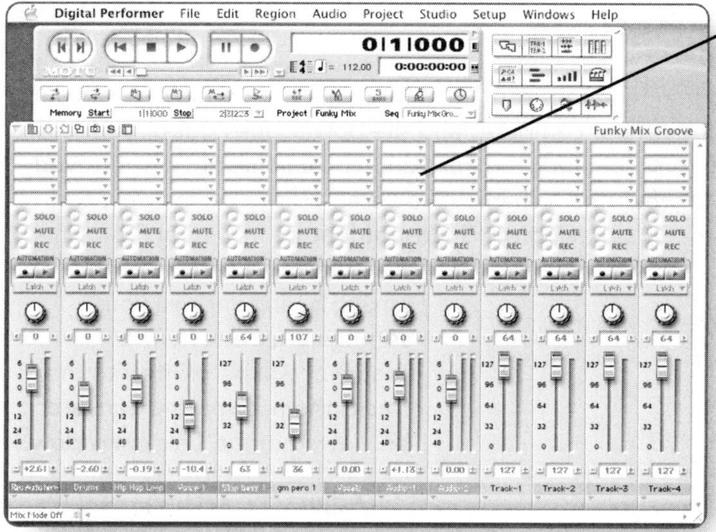

1. Click on an **insert socket**. A menu of different effects will appear. Depending on whether you have chosen an audio track or a MIDI track, different effects will appear.

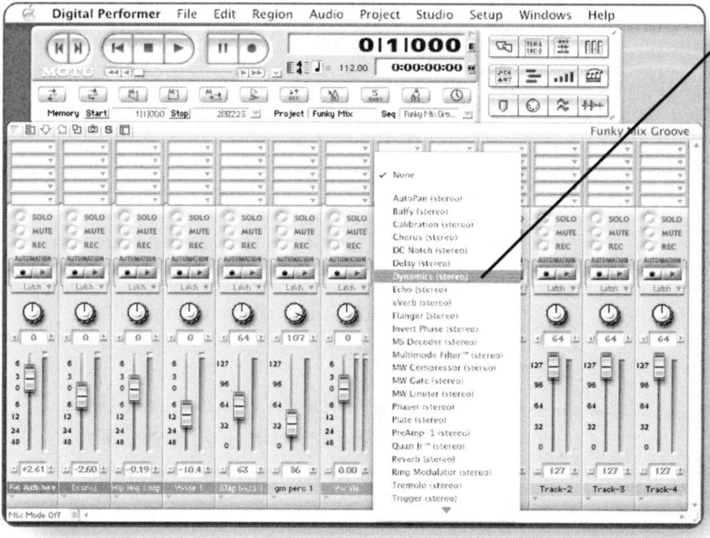

2. Click on the desired **effect**. Depending on the effect you have selected, a dialog box may appear, allowing you to adjust the settings of that effect. You can load additional effects to the track by using the additional inserts.

Snapshots

It has happened to all of us at one time or another. You are working on the computer and the power goes out or your cat accidentally unplugs the cord and you lose all of your unsaved data. It would be a shame if you created the perfect mix and then lost it all. Using the Snapshot feature in Digital Performer is like taking a picture of the mixing board once all your settings are perfect. The snapshot will be printed to the tracks themselves and can later be viewed in the Tracks window.

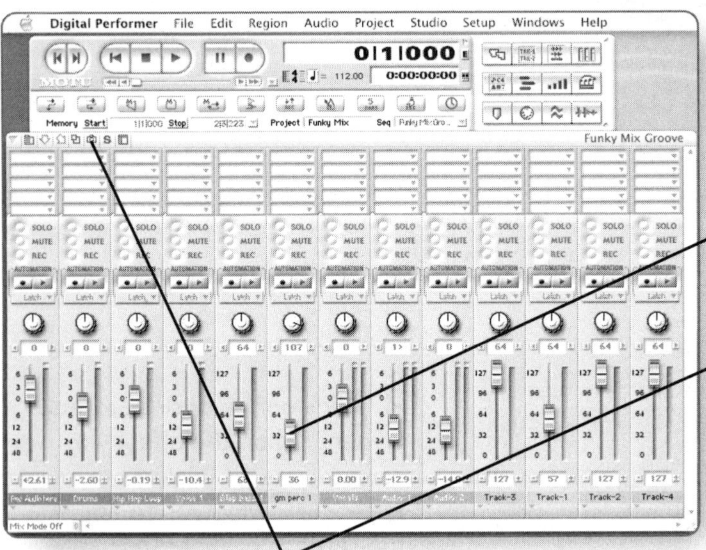

1. **Adjust** the **settings** of the mixing board to the desired levels.
2. **Click** on the **Snapshot button**. The Automation Snapshot dialog box will appear.

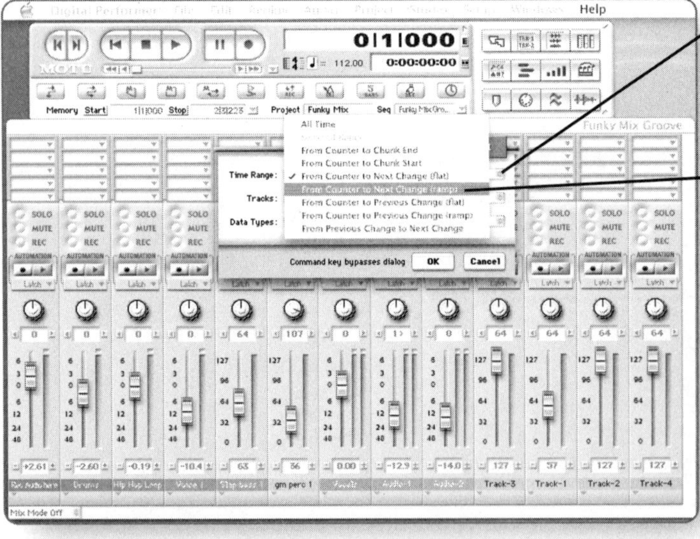

3. **Click** on the **up-and-down arrow** beside the Time Range field. A list of options will appear.
4. **Click** on the desired **time range** for the Snapshot. The option will now be selected.

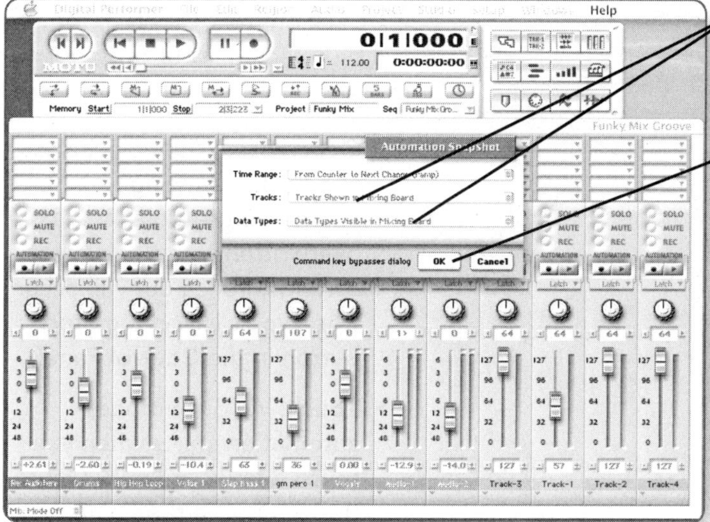

5. Repeat steps 3 and 4 for the Tracks field and the Data Types field.

6. Click on **OK**. The data from the mixing board will be written to the tracks.

Mix Automation

Digital Performer allows you to automate the mixing process so that changes to the mix can be made as the track plays. As you are playing a sequence, you can adjust individual faders and knobs and those adjustments will be recorded. You can then view those changes on playback.

Automation Modes

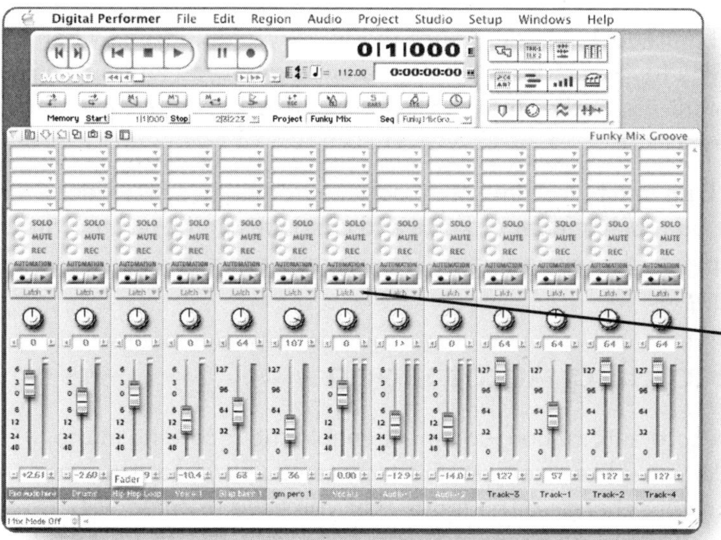

There are five different automation modes that allow you to control how the automation process is handled in Digital Performer. All of these modes can be accessed directly from the Mixing Board window.

1. Click on the **Automation Mode button** in the Mixing Board window. A list of modes will appear.

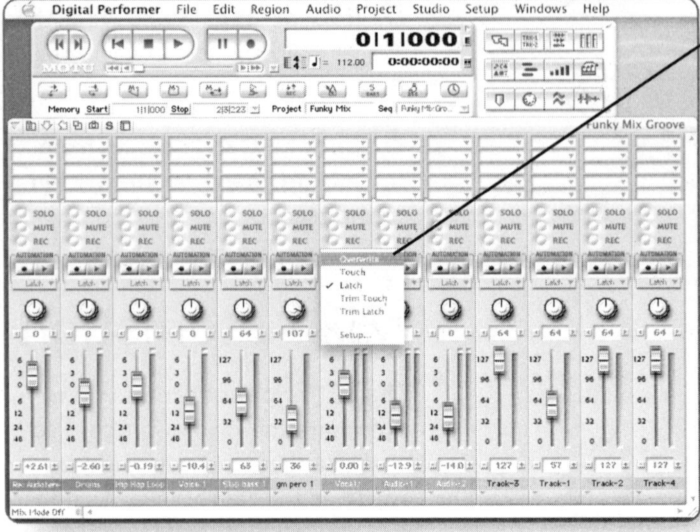

2. **Click** on the desired **mode**. It will be selected. Your options include:

- **Overwrite**. When playback begins, the existing automation setup is overwritten with the current settings. Punch out will occur when you click on the Stop button in the Control Panel.
- **Touch**. In Touch mode, automation starts when you touch a fader or knob. Only the settings in the tracks you adjust are affected. Punch out occurs when you let go of any of the controls.
- **Latch**. In Latch mode, automation starts when you touch a fader or knob and continues until you stop the playback. All of the existing data is replaced.
- **Trim Touch**. In Trim Touch mode, automation starts when you touch a fader or knob and ends when you let go of any controls. Rather than replacing the existing data, the data is scaled.
- **Trim Latch**. In Trim Latch mode, automation starts when you touch a fader or knob and continues until you stop the playback. Existing data is scaled rather than being replaced.

Recording Automation

To record automation, you must enable the recording in the tracks you'd like to adjust. From there you play your track and make your changes. The mode that you have selected will determine how the data is handled.

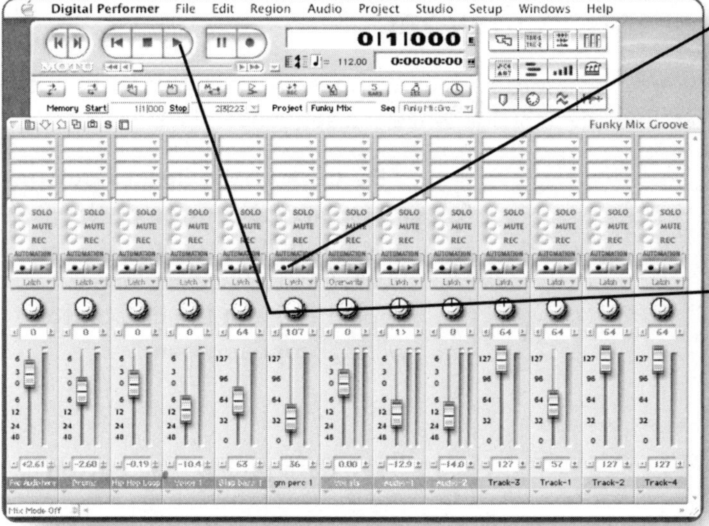

1. **Click** on the **Record button** in the channel strip for the track(s) in which you would like to record automation. The Record button will appear red and the Play button will appear green.

2. **Click** on the **Play button** in the Control Panel. The sequence will begin to play. The Record button in the channel strip will begin to flash to indicate that it will record any adjustments to settings in that strip.

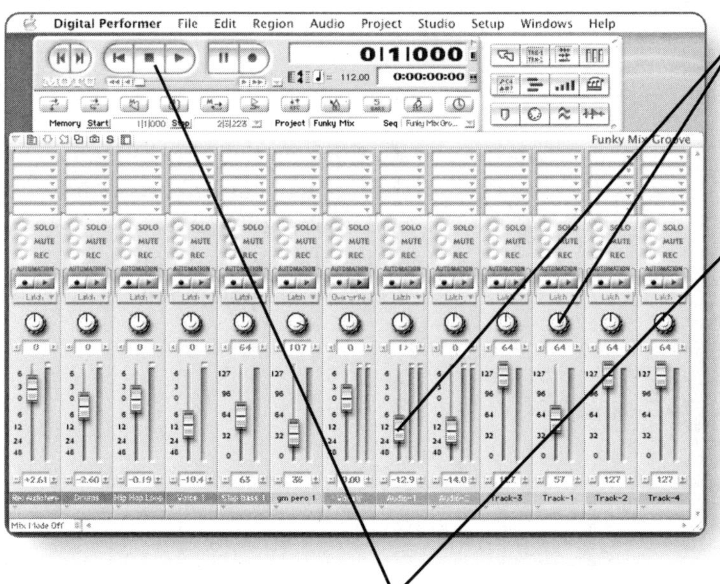

3. **Adjust** any of the **faders** or **knobs** that you have enabled recording on in the channel strips. The changes that you make will be recorded.

4. **Click** on the **Stop button** in the Control Panel to end your sequence and the recording.

Automation Playback

Once you have recorded your changes, you can play them back and watch as they change while the sequence plays.

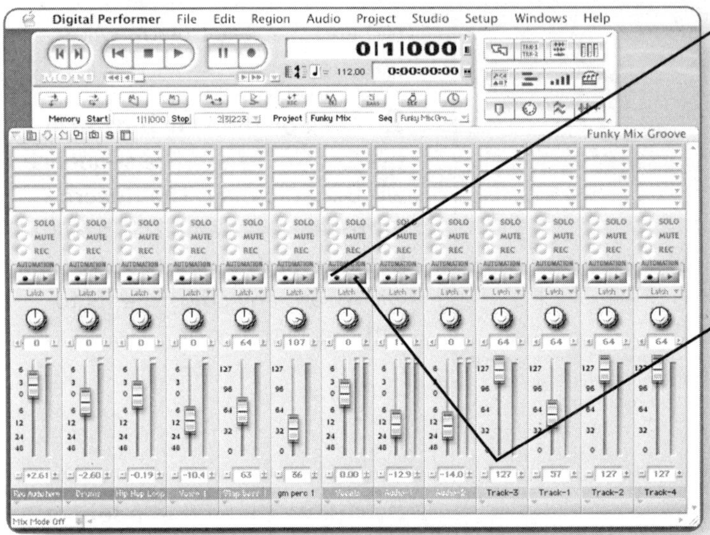

1a. Click on the **Record button** in the channel strip to disable mix automation recording. The Record button will no longer appear red, but the Play button will still appear green.

OR

1b. Click on the **Play button** if the Record button wasn't previously enabled. The Play button will turn green.

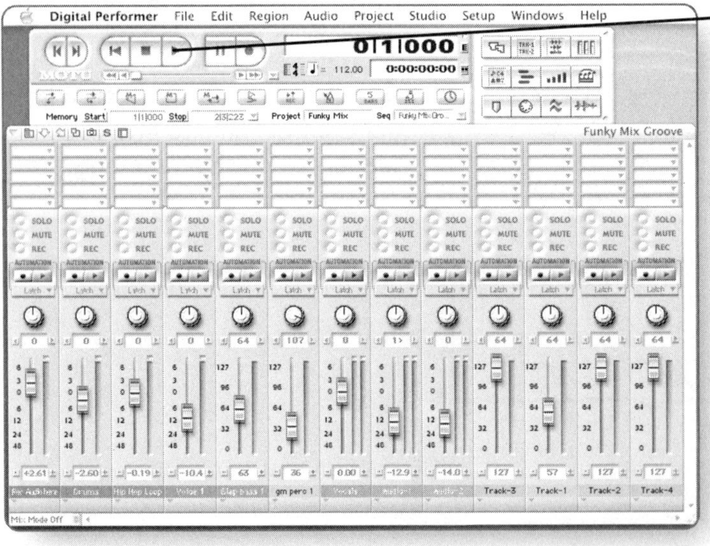

2. Click on the **Play button** in the Control Panel. The faders and knobs will move automatically based on the adjustments you made.

Automation Setup

When using automation, you can change the way Digital Performer handles certain events by adjusting parameters in the Setup window.

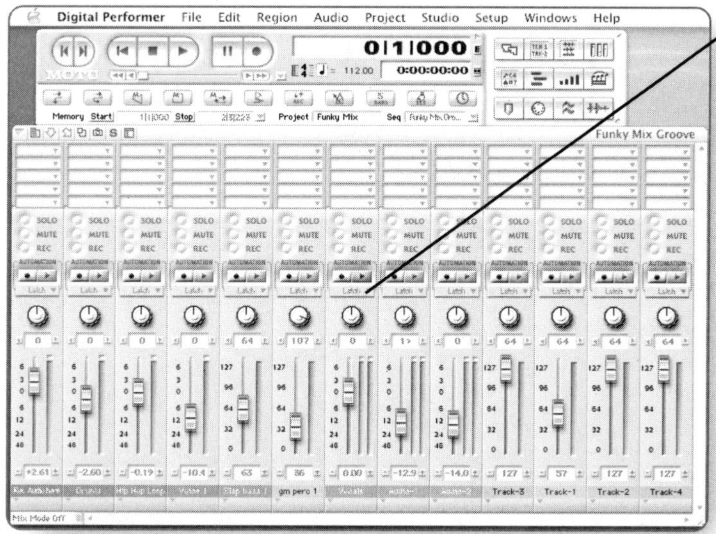

1. **Click** on the **Automation Mode button**. A menu of options will appear.

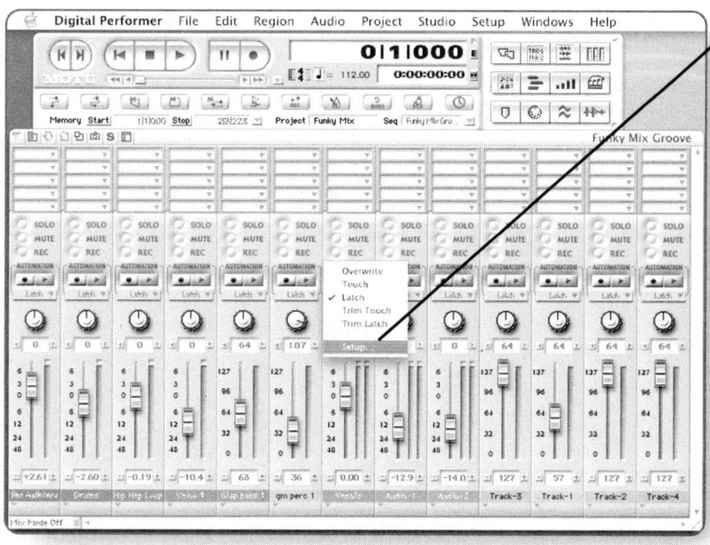

2. **Click** on **Setup**. A dialog box will open which will allow you to adjust the settings for automation.

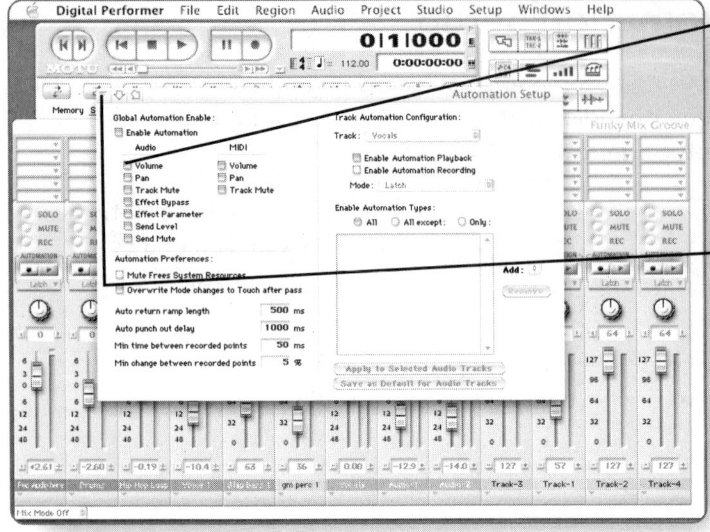

3. Click on the desired **settings**. You can adjust a variety of settings, including which tracks to configure and which automation types to adjust, along with many others.

4. Click on the **Close button** after you've made the desired changes.

15

The QuickScribe Editor

What do some of the biggest music stars have in common? It's sad to say, but many of your favorite performers, who create great music, don't know how to read or write notes. Digital Performer can be your cheat sheet when it comes to scribing music. With the QuickScribe Editor, you play and record your MIDI files and Digital Performer will scribe them for you. You can also use the QuickScribe Editor to modify your music. In this chapter, you'll learn how to:

- Automatically scribe your sequences
- Navigate the QuickScribe Editor
- Edit notes in the QuickScribe Editor
- Adjust score options

Launching the QuickScribe Editor

The QuickScribe Editor will automatically scribe all of the notes in your sequence. It can be launched from the Project menu.

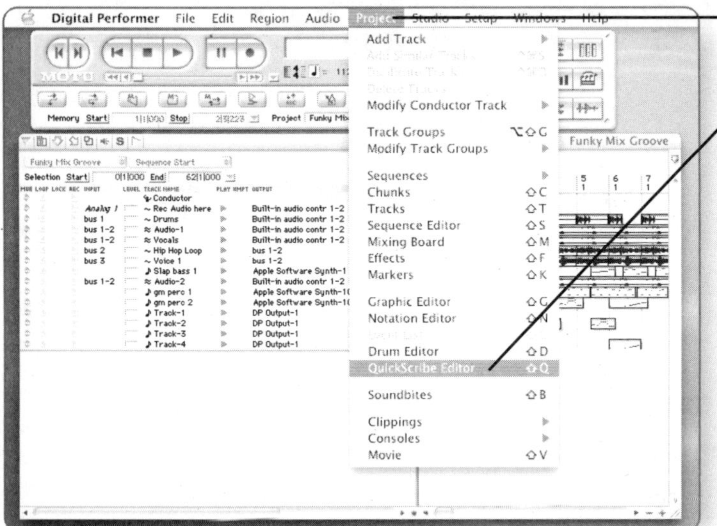

1. **Click** on **Project**. The Project menu will appear.
2. **Click** on **QuickScribe Editor**. The QuickScribe Editor will launch and your sequences will be scribed.

> **NOTE**
>
> If you have a particular MIDI track selected, it will appear in the QuickScribe Editor; otherwise, all MIDI tracks will appear.

Navigating

Because of the length of most sequences, it is almost impossible to view an entire score on one page. Digital Performer provides you with a multitude of ways to navigate around your score.

Changing Pages

Within the Score window, there are several ways to navigate to different pages. You can scroll forward and backward through pages or you can specify a specific page to which to jump.

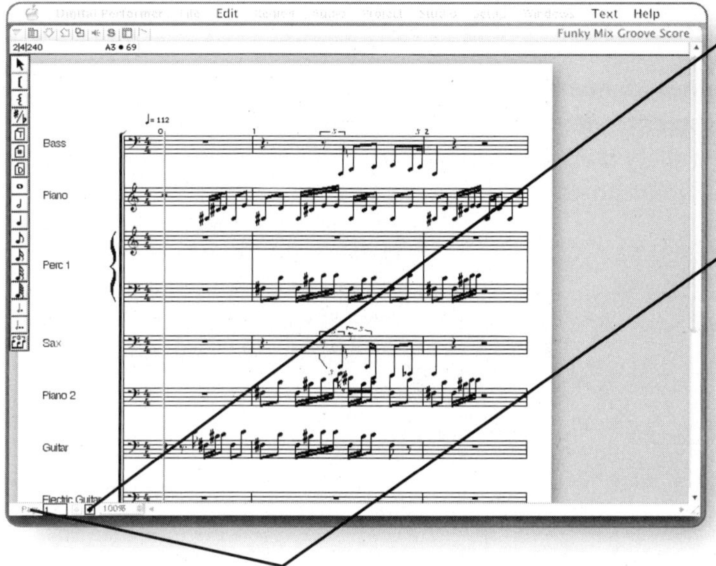

1. **Click once** on a **forward** or **backward arrow** to move one page forward or backward.

2. **Repeat step 1** until you've reached the desired page.

3. **Click once** on the word **Page** in the bottom-left corner of the window. A box will appear around the page number, allowing you to specify to which page to jump.

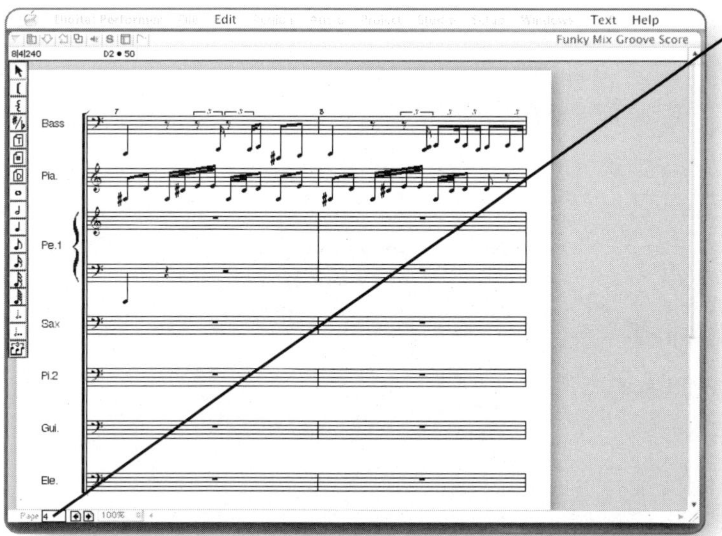

4. **Type** in the desired **page**. The number will appear as you type.

5. **Press Return**. You will jump to the page that you specified.

Changing Views

If you have a number of tracks displayed within a score, it can become difficult to see individual notes. Using the zoom functionality built into Digital Performer, you can zoom in and out of your score.

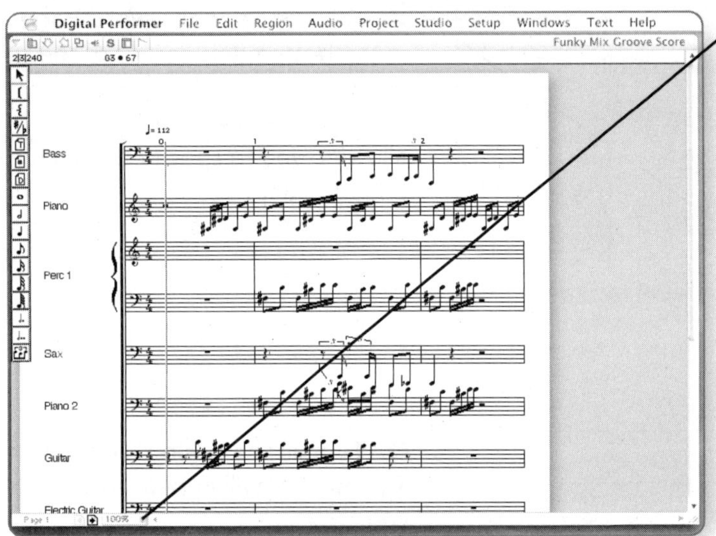

1. Click on the **up-and-down arrow** beside the zoom percentage. A list of different percentages will appear.

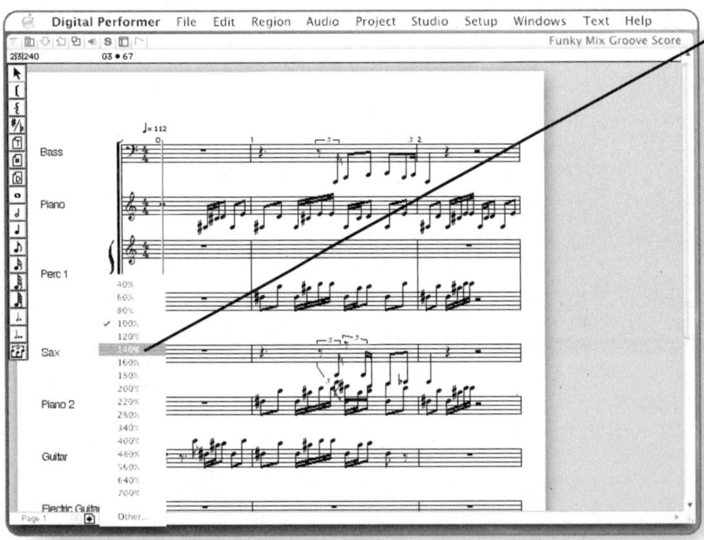

2. Click on the desired **zoom percentage**. The page will zoom in or out based on the percentage you selected.

Jumping to Measures

Rather than having to scroll through pages to get to specific data, you can use the Goto Measures feature. If you know the specific measure that you would like to view, you can quickly jump to that location.

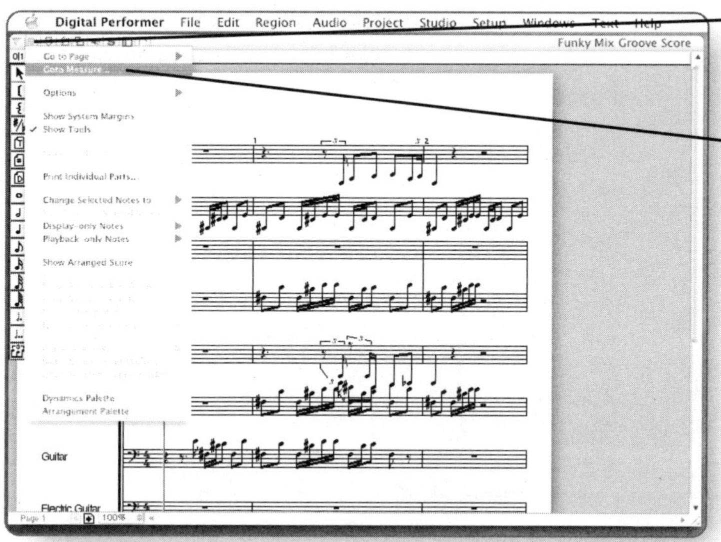

1. **Click** on the **Mini Menu button** in the window. A menu will appear.
2. **Click** on **Goto Measure**. A dialog box will open where you can specify to which measure to jump.

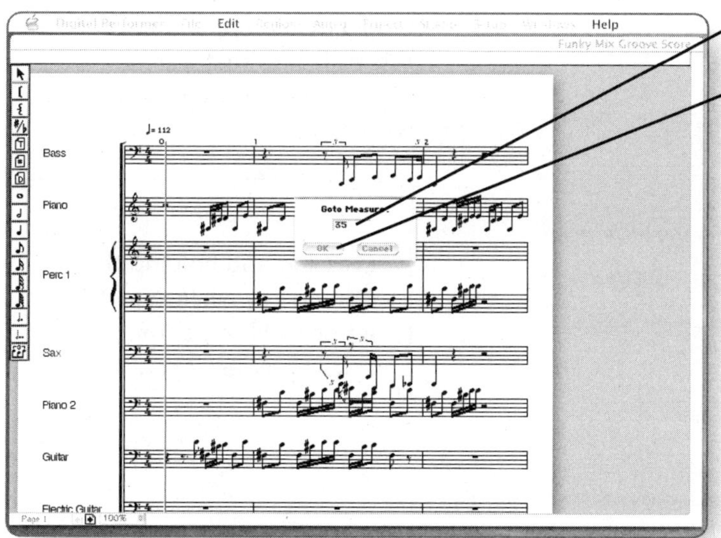

3. **Type** the desired **measure**.
4. **Click** on **OK**. The window will now display that measure.

Showing/Hiding Tracks

You don't have to display all the tracks that are in your sequence in one score. You can select individual tracks, multiple tracks, or all the tracks.

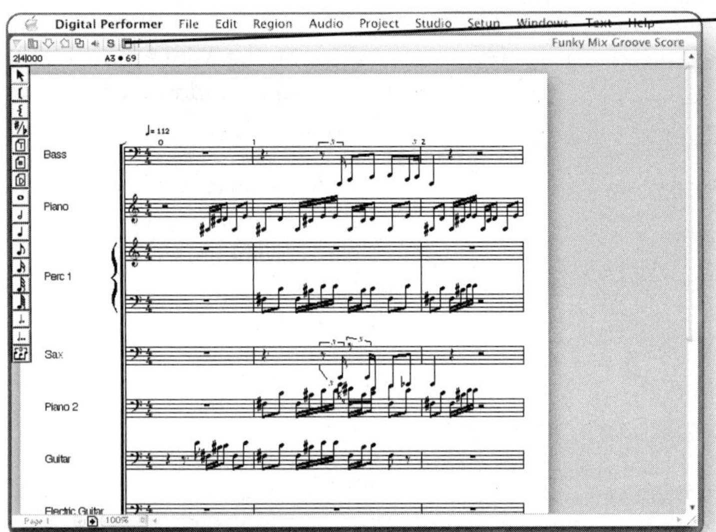

1. Click on the **Show/Hide Tracks button**. A list of all of the tracks in the score will appear.

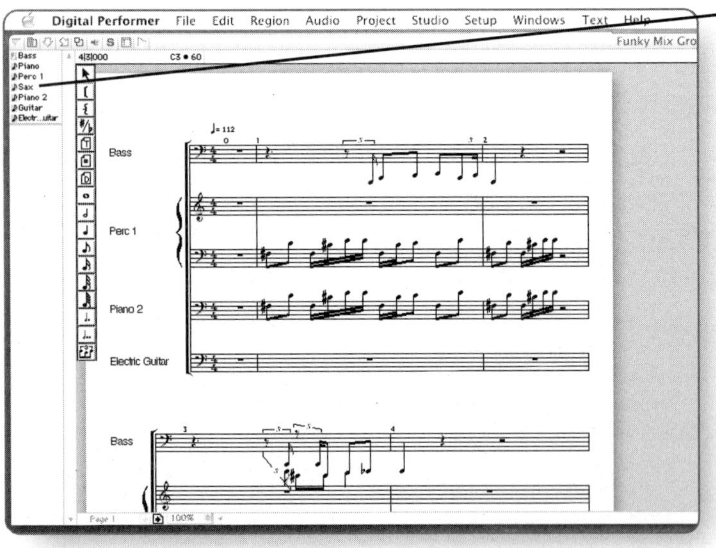

2. Click on the **tracks** that you would like to appear in the score. Tracks that are highlighted will be displayed in the score.

> **TIP**
>
> Pressing and holding the Option key while selecting a track will select that track and deselect all others.

Editing Your Score

The QuickScribe Editor is just that: an editor. This means that it will allow you to insert additional notes into any part of your score, move notes, or deleted unwanted items.

Adding Notes

To add a note to your score, you simply have to select the type of note that you would like to add and then pick a location for it.

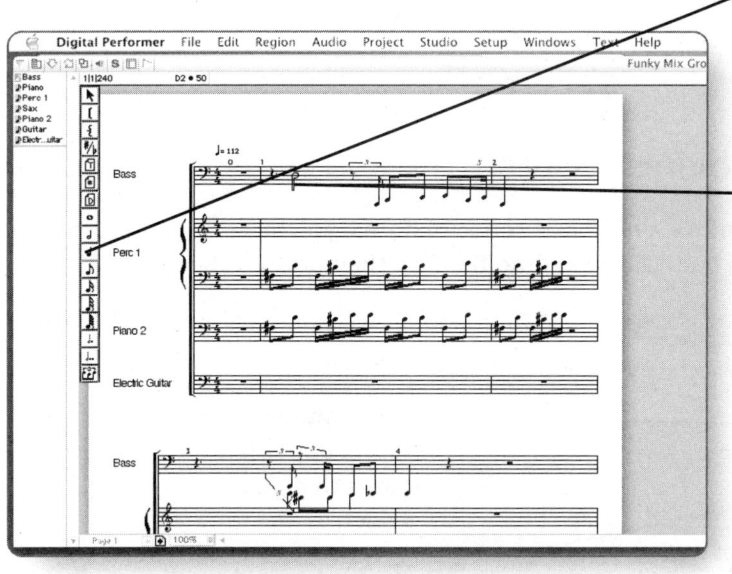

1. **Click** on the desired **note**. The button will be highlighted and the mouse pointer will change to appear like the selected note.
2. **Position** the **mouse pointer** over the location where you would like to insert the note.

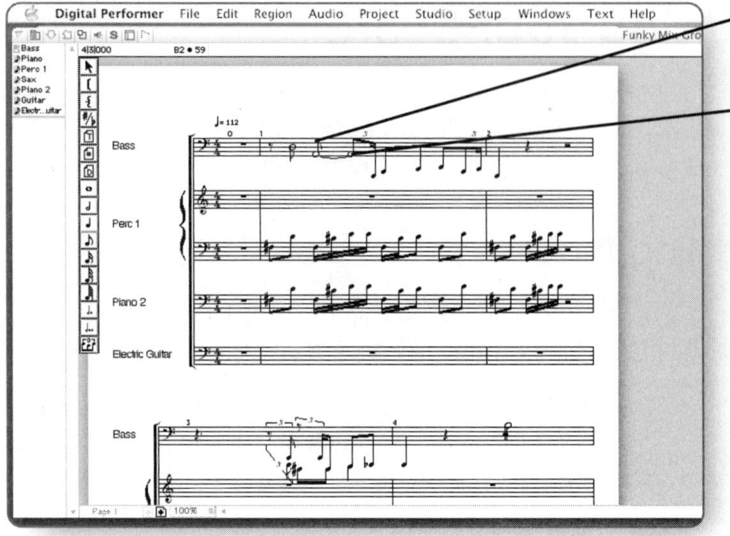

3. Click once. The note will be entered in that location.

4. Repeat steps 1 through 3 until you have finished inserting notes.

Moving Notes

To move a note or a series of notes, you must first select them and then click and drag them to their new location.

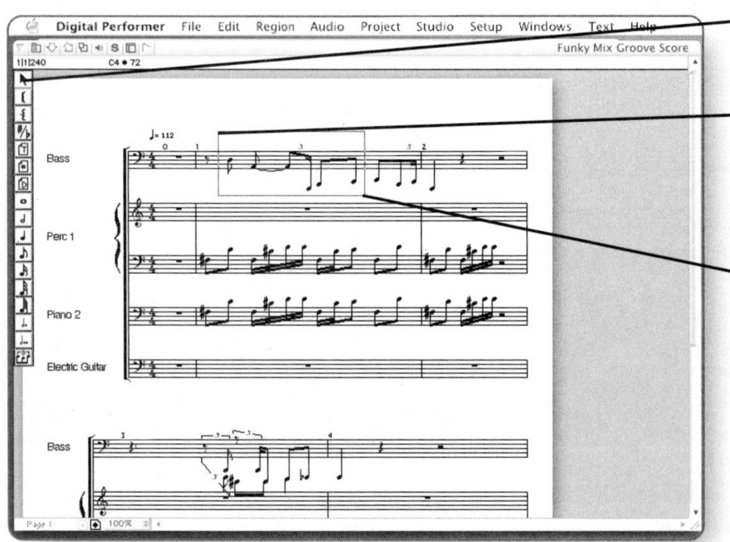

1. Click on the **arrow**. This will allow you to select notes.

2. Position the **mouse pointer** to the upper left of the note or notes that you would like to select.

3. Click and **drag diagonally** to the **right** and **down**. A box will appear as you drag. When you release the mouse button, everything in that box will be selected. Alternatively, if you are just selecting one note, you can simply click on the note.

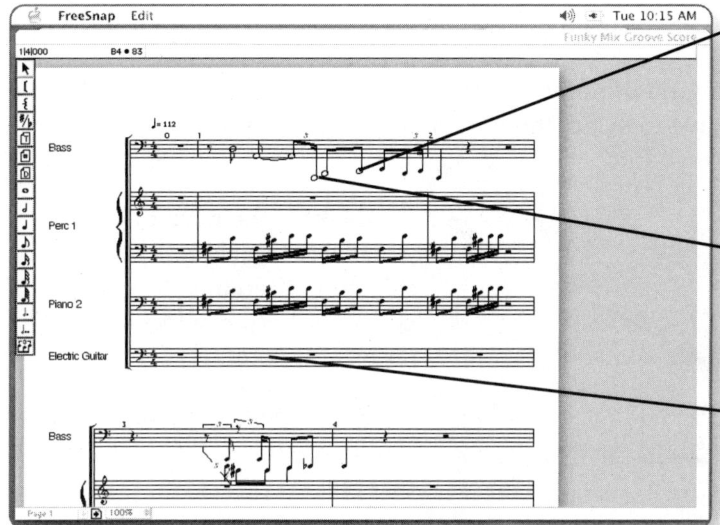

4. Release the **mouse button.** The notes that were encompassed by the box will be selected. They will appear hollow to indicate that they are selected.

5. Position your **mouse pointer** over the selection. The mouse pointer will turn into a small hand.

6. Click and **drag** the **selection** to a new location.

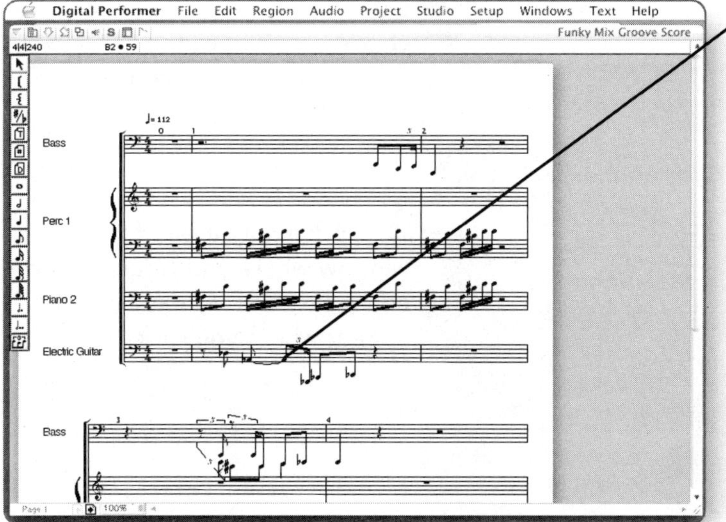

7. Release the **mouse button.** The notes will be moved.

Removing Notes

Getting rid of notes that you no longer want is a breeze. You just have to select the note and then use the Delete key on your keyboard.

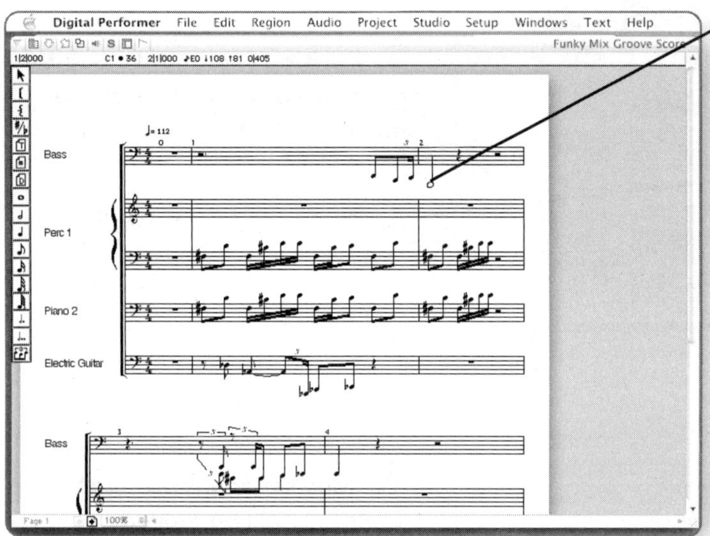

1. Click on the **note** that you would like to delete. It will be selected. Alternatively, you can click and drag to select several notes to delete.

2. Press the **Delete key** on your keyboard. The notes will be deleted.

Inserting Text

The Text tool allows you to add a text box to any location on your score. You can use this to add titles, notes, or comments.

1. Click on the **Text tool**. It will be selected.

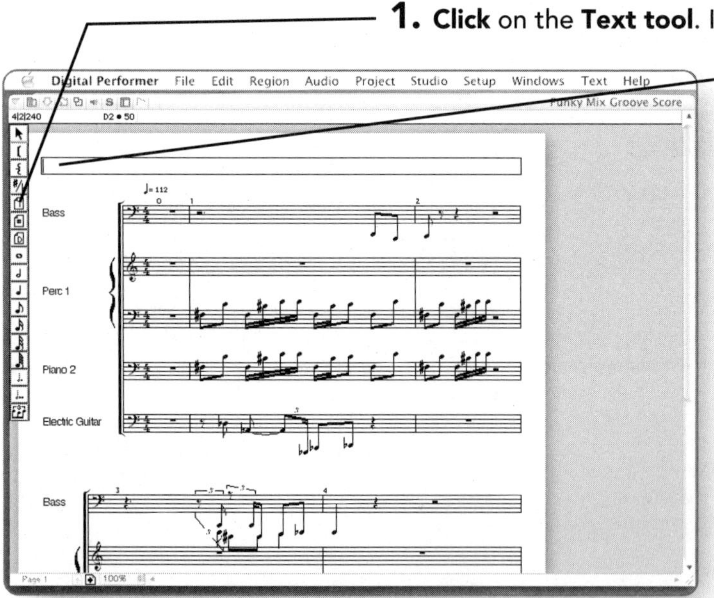

2. Click in **any area** of the window where you would like to add a text box. A text box will appear where you click.

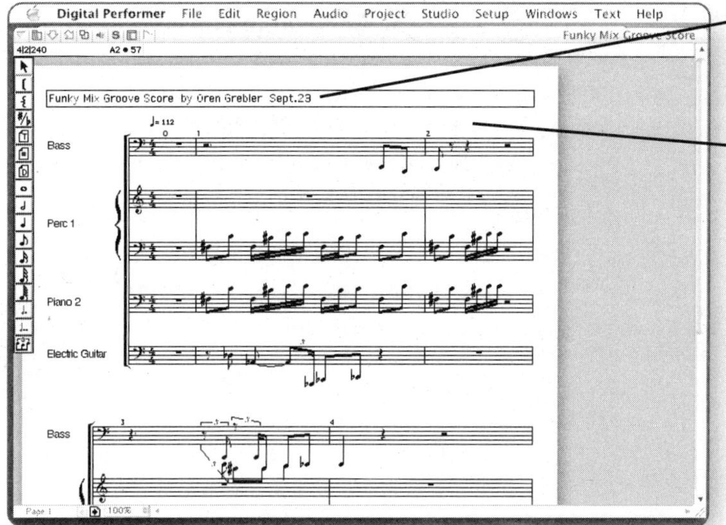

3. **Type** the **text** that you would like to appear on the page. It will appear as you type.

4. **Click** in any **blank area** of the Score window when you have finished entering text.

> **TIP**
>
> After you have entered a text box, you can reposition it by clicking and dragging it to a new location.

Track Options

Digital Performer allows you to adjust settings for how your tracks are displayed in the QuickScribe Editor. These settings can be adjusted in the Track Options dialog box.

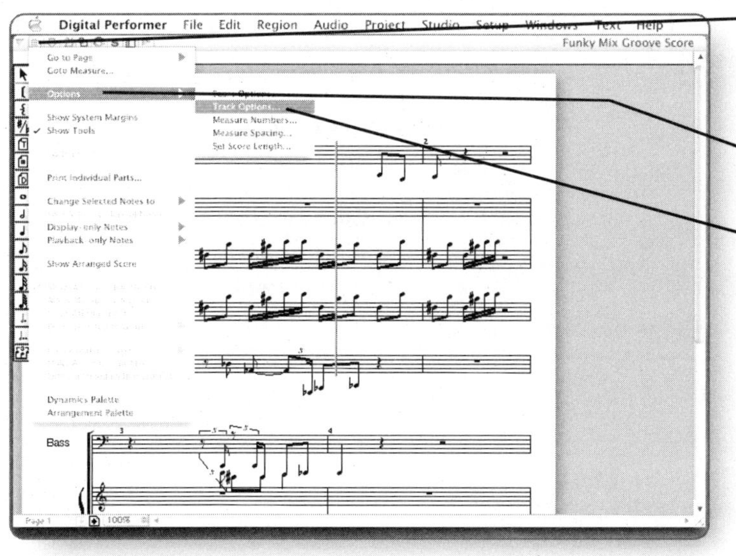

1. **Click** on the **Mini Menu button**. A menu of commands will appear.

2. **Click** on **Options**. A submenu will appear.

3. **Click** on **Track Options**. A dialog box with a variety of options relating to how your tracks are displayed will appear.

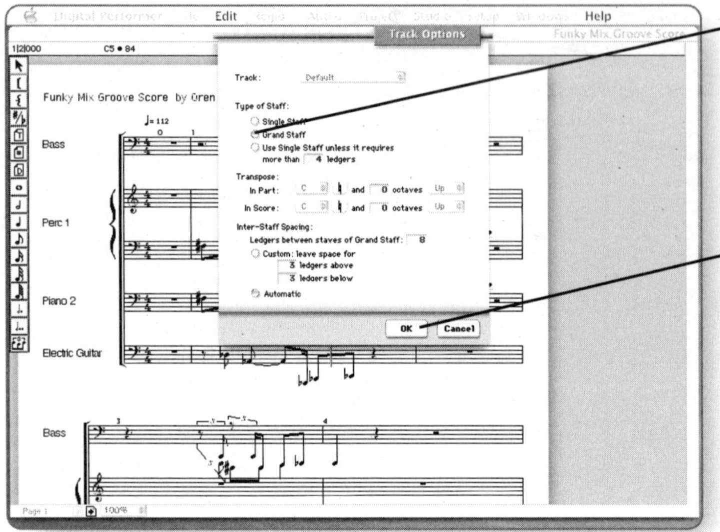

4. Click on the desired **options**. Some options can be selected by clicking directly on the option, some require data input, and others can be accessed from pop-up menus.

5. Click on **OK**. The settings you have adjusted will take effect.

Score Options

The Score Options dialog box allows you to adjust the general look of the score including the appearance of names, markers, rests, and other elements.

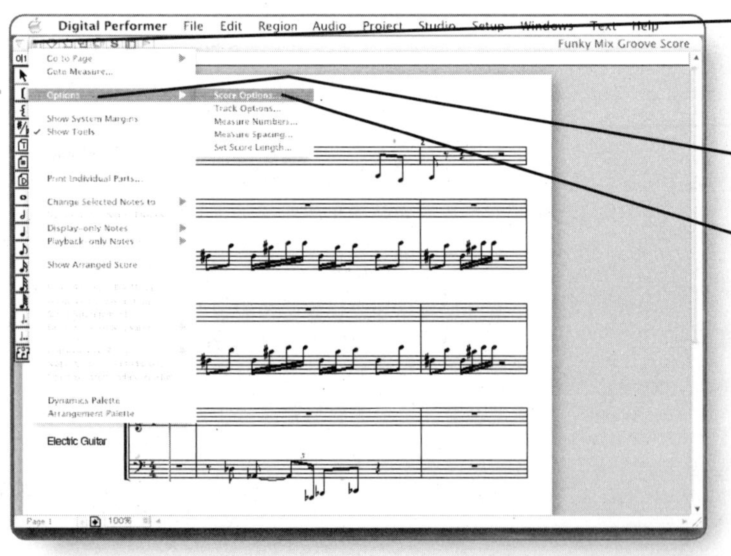

1. Click on the **Mini Menu button**. A menu of commands will appear.

2. Click on **Options**. A submenu will appear.

3. Click on **Score Options**. A dialog box with a variety of options relating to the appearance of the score will open.

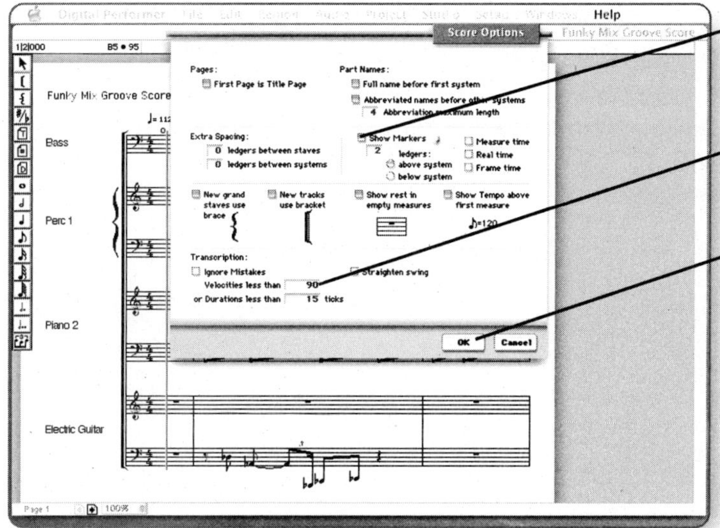

4. Click on the desired **settings**. The box beside the selected settings will be filled in.

5. Type a **number** in any field to change the setting.

6. Click on **OK** to accept and apply the changes that you have made.

16

Searching

It's very easy to accumulate a mountain of data when working in Digital Performer. Simple sequences can contain literally thousands of different notes, a variety of events, audio files, effects, and other elements. Finding specific data would be difficult if it wasn't for the Search functionality built into the program. Digital Performer provides you with a variety of search tools that will find and select data based on the criteria you specify. In this chapter, you'll learn how to:

- Select tracks to search
- Set time criteria
- Set search action
- Search for multiple attributes

Choosing Tracks to Search

One limitation of the search functionality in Digital Performer is that the Search window itself does not allow you to specify what tracks to search. The only option it gives you is to search either all sequences or the sequence that you are currently working with. The Search window selects the tracks from those that are open in the upper-most editing window. In other words, you must open an editing window with the tracks you would like to search before you open the Search window. When selecting tracks, the best editing window to use is the Sequence Editor.

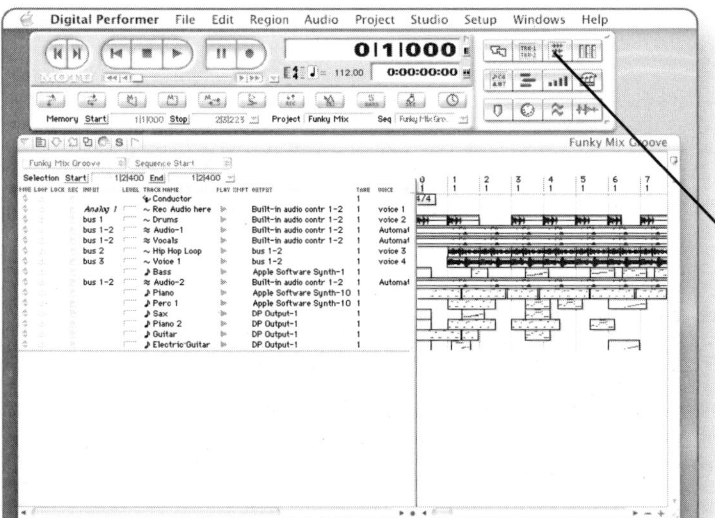

1. **Click** on the **Sequence Editor button** in the Control Panel. The Sequence Editor will launch.

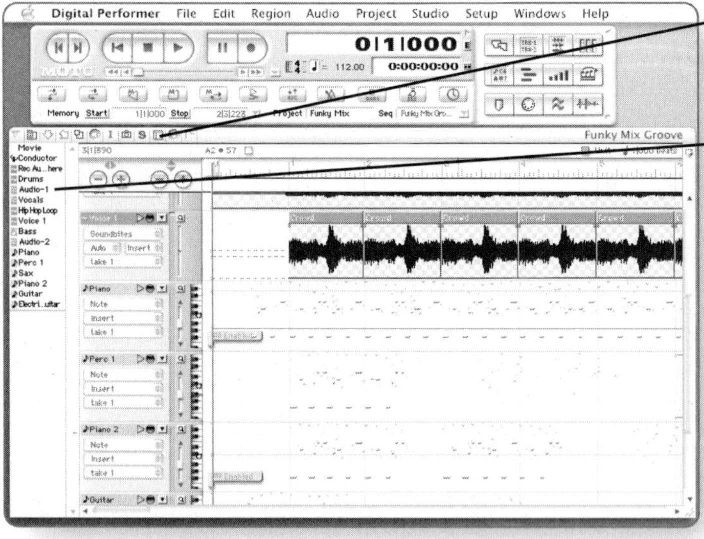

2. **Click** on the **Show/Hide Tracks button** to display all the tracks in the sequence.
3. **Click** on the desired **tracks** to search. Those tracks that are selected will appear highlighted.

Launching the Search Window

The Search window can be accessed through the Edit menu.

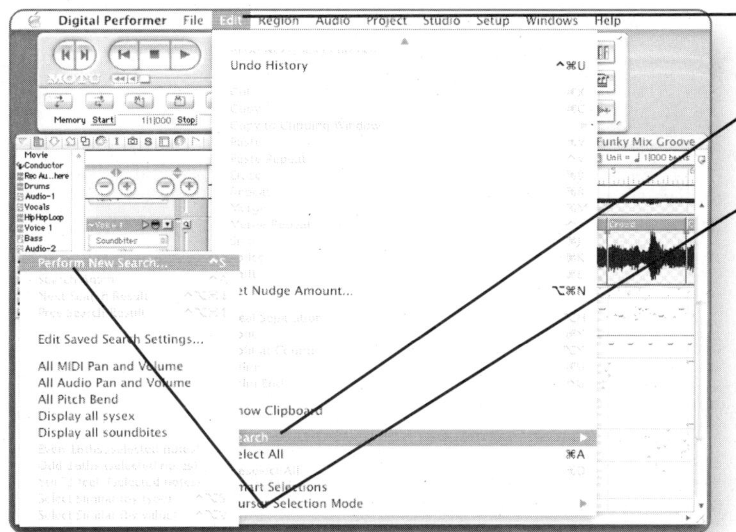

1. **Click** on **Edit**. The Edit menu will appear.

2. **Click** on **Search**. A submenu will appear.

3. **Click** on **Perform New Search**. The Search window will open, allowing you to conduct a variety of searches.

Setting Time Criteria

The Search window is divided into three separate areas. The first area, Time, allows you to specify what timeframe you would like Digital Performer to look in when conducting a search.

Setting Value Criteria

One of the options when selecting the time criteria is to search by value. Using this method, you specify a specific search range.

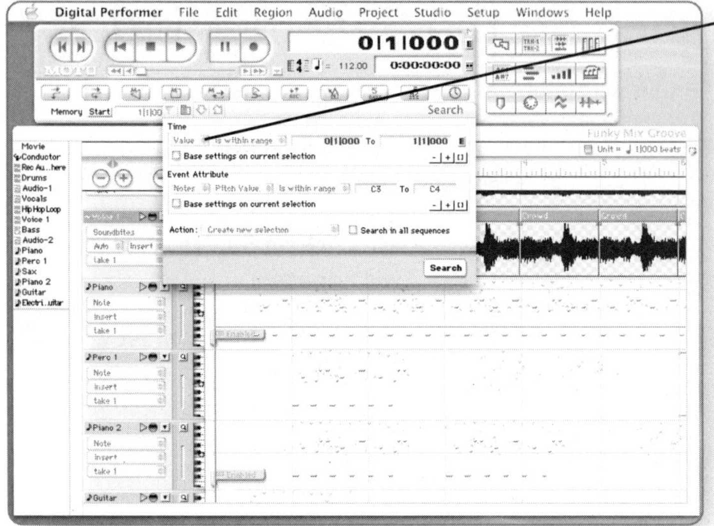

1. **Click** on the **up-and-down arrow** under Time to select the criteria to be used.

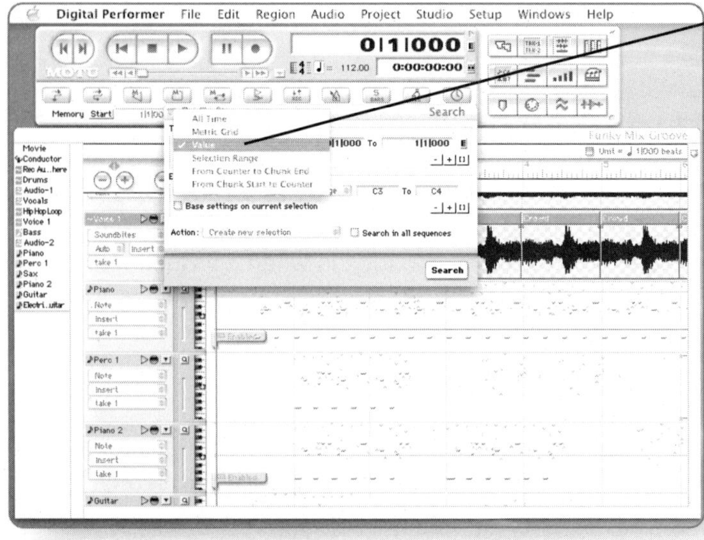

2. **Click** on **Value**, if it is not already selected.

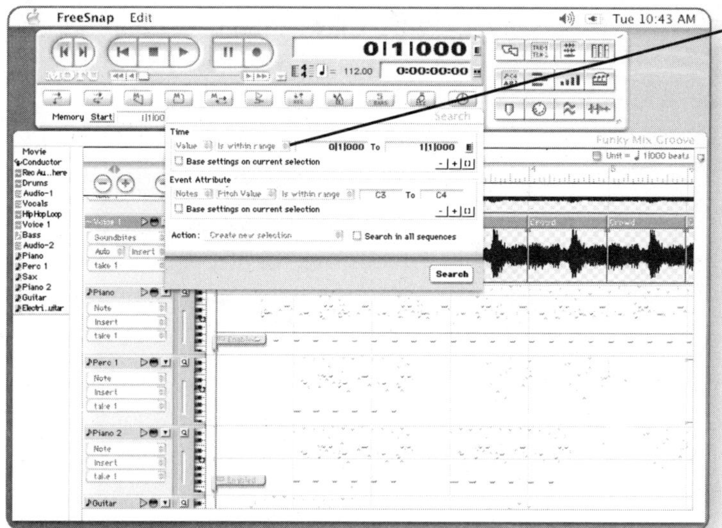

3. **Click** on the **up-and-down arrow** in the next field. This will allow you to set the criteria for the search.

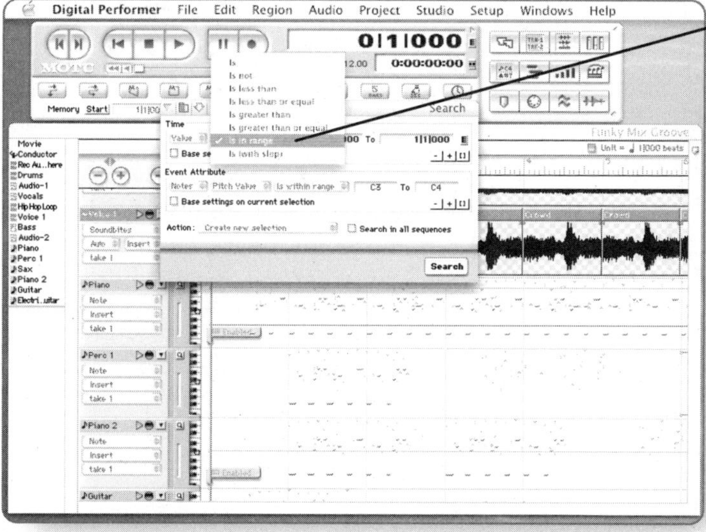

4. **Click** on the desired **criterion**. It will be selected.

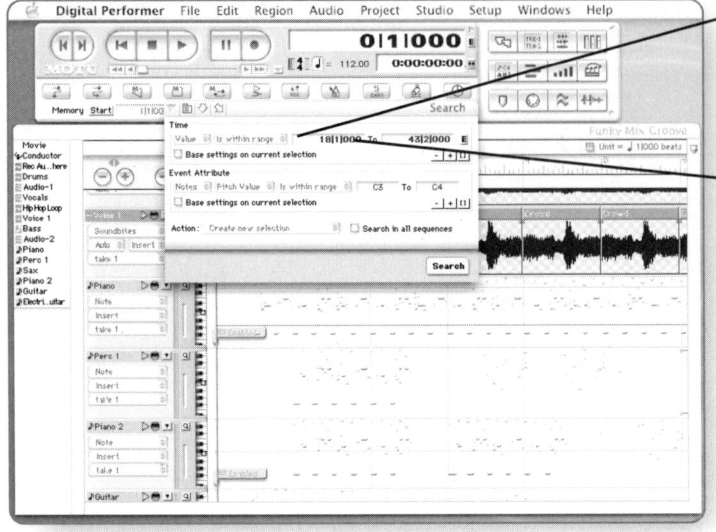

5. Click in the **first time-range box**. This will allow you to set the start time location for your search.

6. Type a **number**. By default, the numbers are displayed as measures, beats, and ticks. You can enter specific numbers for each.

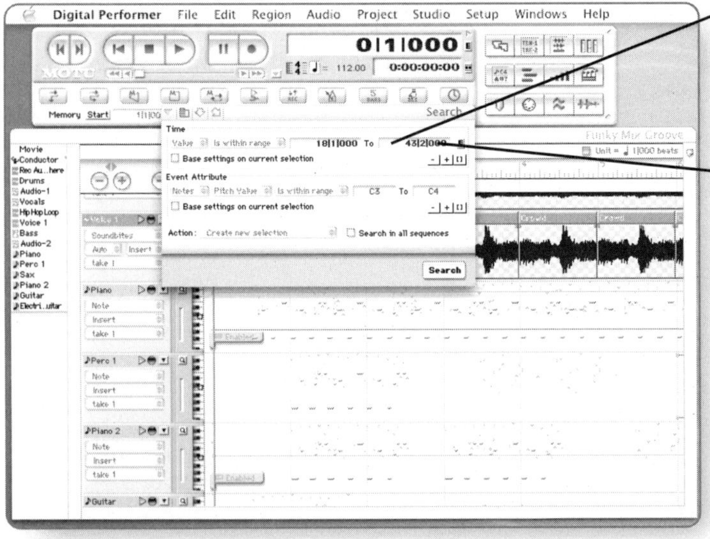

7. Click in the **last time-range box**. This will allow you to set an end time location for your search.

8. Type a **number**. By default, the numbers are displayed as measures, beats, and ticks. You can enter specific numbers for each.

Setting Other Time Criteria

If you don't want to search within a time period that you specify, Digital Performer offers a variety of other Time criteria to select from.

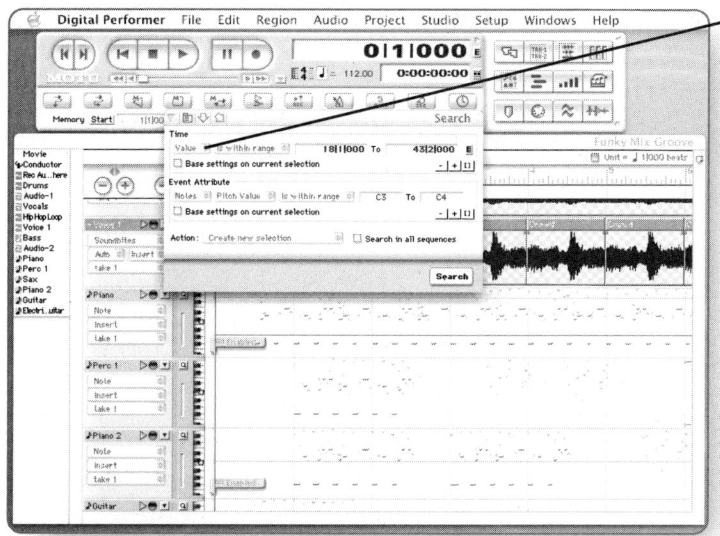

1. **Click** on the **up-and-down arrow** under Time. A menu of options will appear.

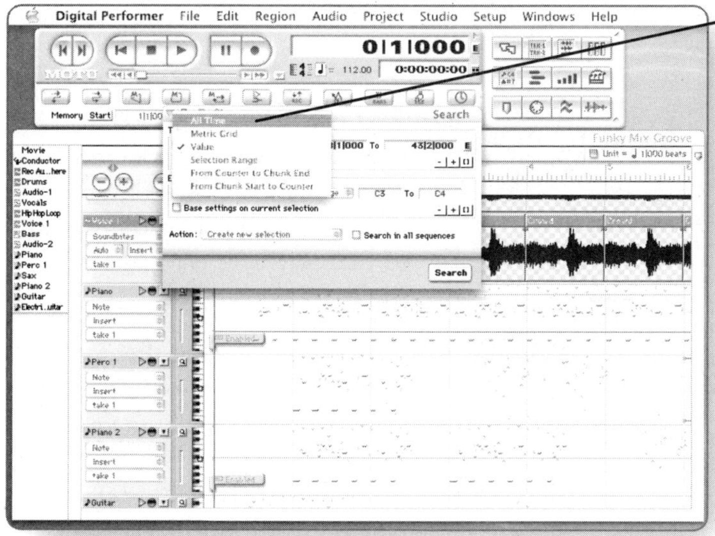

2. **Click** on the desired **option** (see the following descriptions). It will be selected.

- **All Time**. Selecting this will conduct the search throughout the entire track.
- **Metric Grid**. This will allow you to specify certain grid locations to conduct your search.
- **Selection Range**. If you made a selection prior to conducting your search, selecting this option will conduct the search within the selection.

- **From Counter to Chunk End**. This will start the search at the current counter location and continue to the end of the chunk.
- **From Chunk Start to Counter**. This will start the search at beginning of the chunk and continue until it reaches the current counter location.

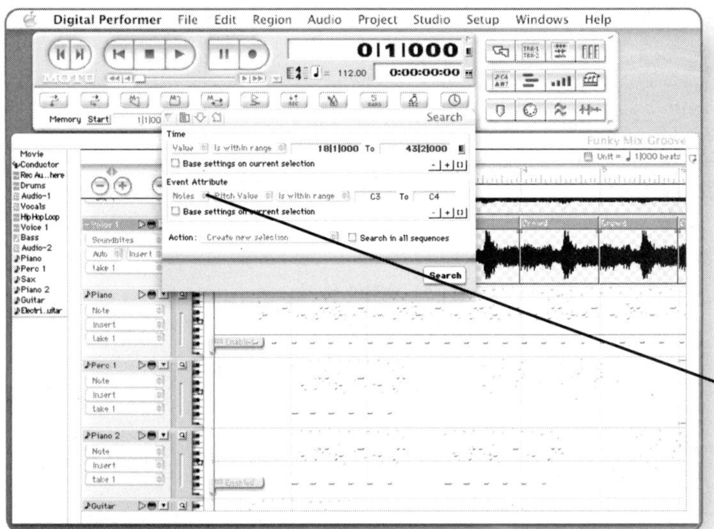

Setting Event Attributes

After you have specified where you would like Digital Performer to search, you must now tell it exactly what to look for. You can select from many attributes for your search.

1. **Click** on the **up-and-down arrow** under Event Attribute. A menu of different attributes will appear.

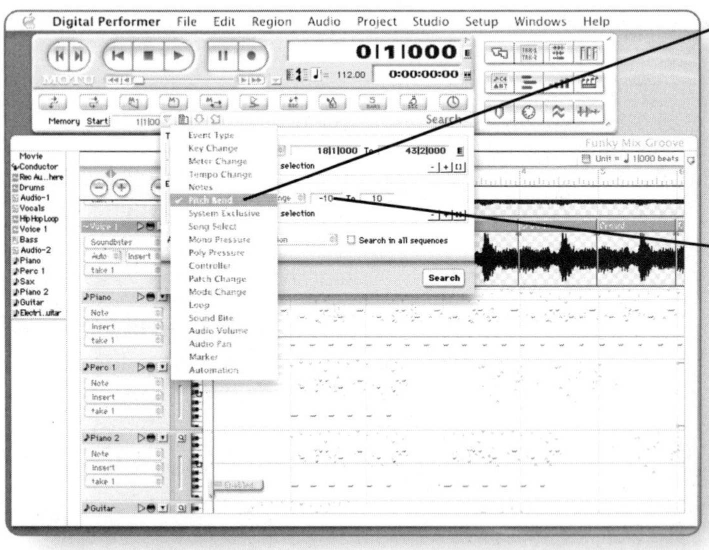

2. **Click** on the desired **attribute**. It will be selected. Depending on the attribute you selected, the options pertaining to that attribute will appear in the window.
3. **Click** on and **set** the desired **option** for the attribute you have selected. Each attribute will have different options associated with it. For example, when you select Notes as your attribute, you will have to select pitch options.

Setting Multiple Attributes

What if you wanted to search for a specific note that is within a certain volume range? It would seem by the setup of the Search window that you could only select one attribute at a time. You can actually select multiple attributes for your search through some creative selecting and saving.

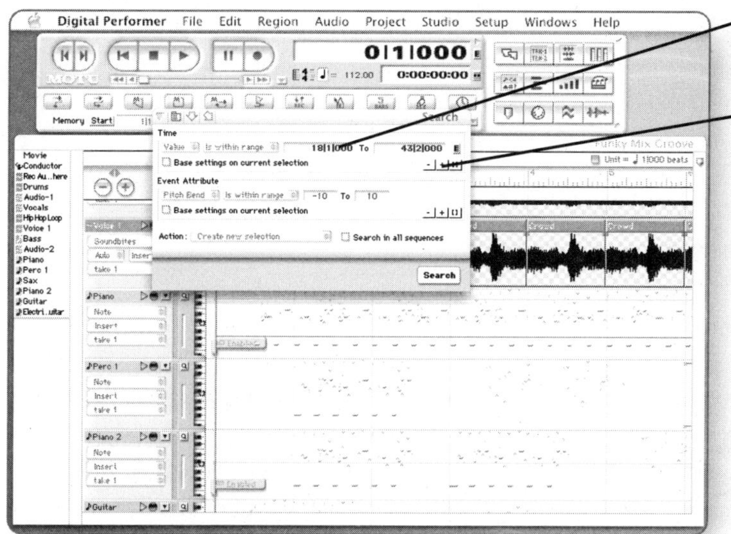

1. **Enter** the initial **criteria** for conducting your search.
2. **Click** on the **+ sign** in the corresponding section. For example, if you are setting multiple attributes for Time, click the + in the sign section of the window. Another line of criteria will open.

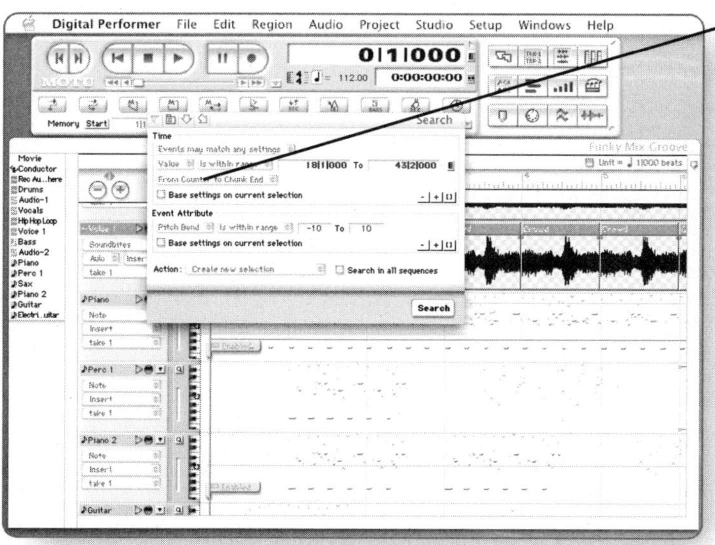

3. **Enter** the **second** set of **criteria** for the search. You can enter it just like the first set.

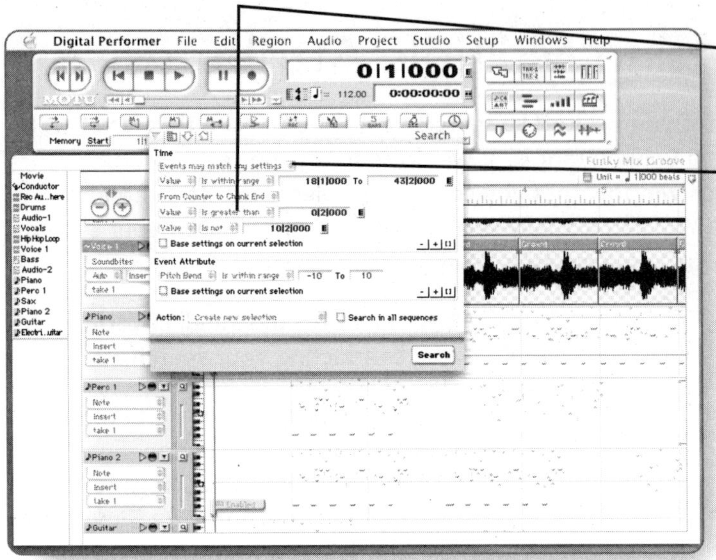

4. Repeat steps 2 and 3 until you have finished entering all of the search parameters.

5. Click on the **up-and-down arrow** at the top of the search parameters. A menu will appear.

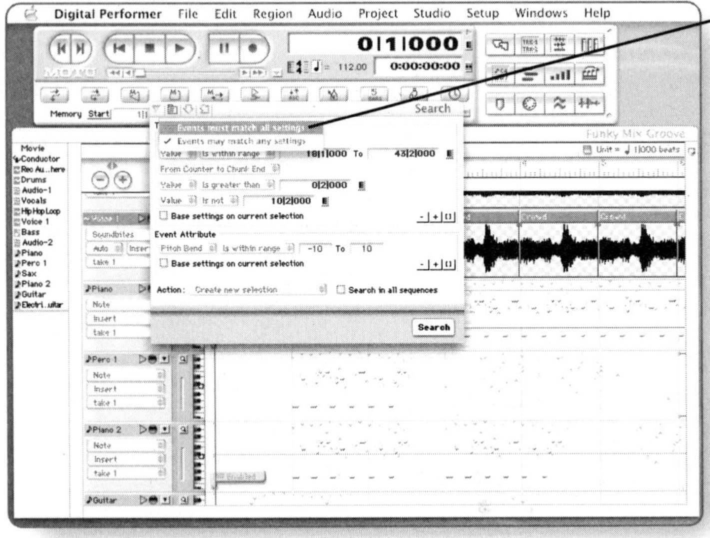

6. Click on the desired **setting**. When the search is conducted, results can include data that meet any or all of the criteria.

Selecting Actions

Once you have all of your criteria specified, you must tell Digital Performer what you want it to do once the search is conducted.

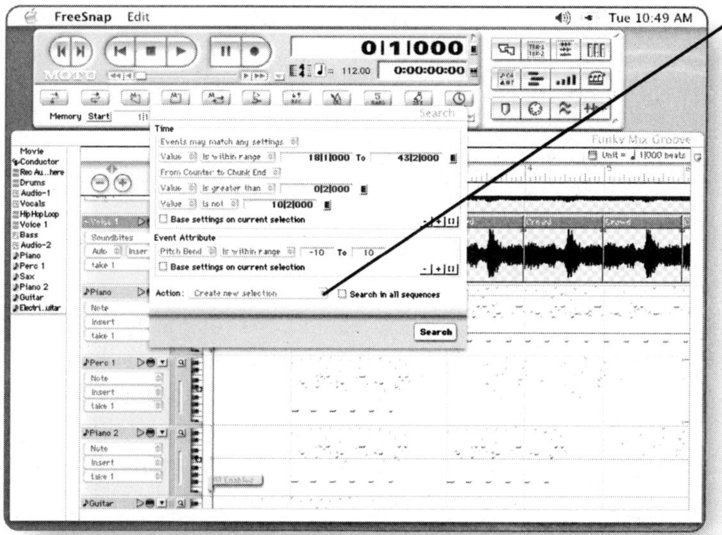

1. Click on the **up-and-down arrow** beside the Action field. A menu of options will appear.

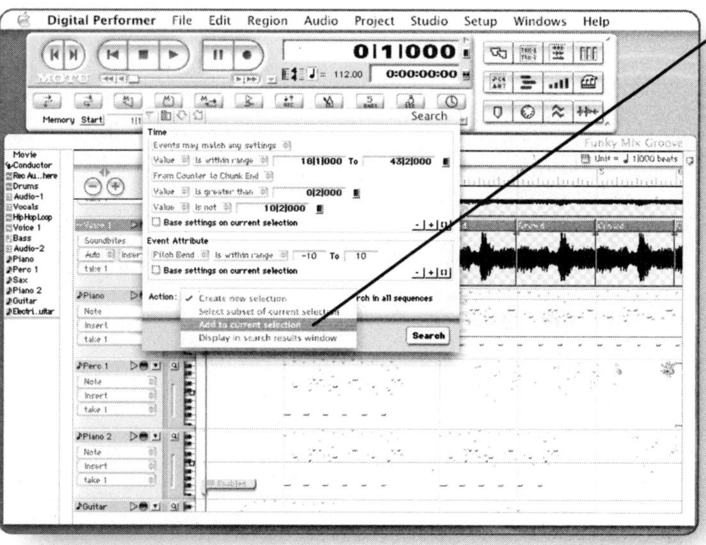

2. Click on the desired **settings**. There are several choices, including:

- **Create new selection.** A new selection will be created from all of the data that matches your criteria.
- **Select subset of current selection.** This will create a new selection that matches your search criteria and is already part of an existing selection.

- **Add to current selection**. This will create a selection comprised of all the data in your current selection plus any other data that matches the search criteria.
- **Display in search results window**. A window will launch that will list all of the data that matched your criteria.

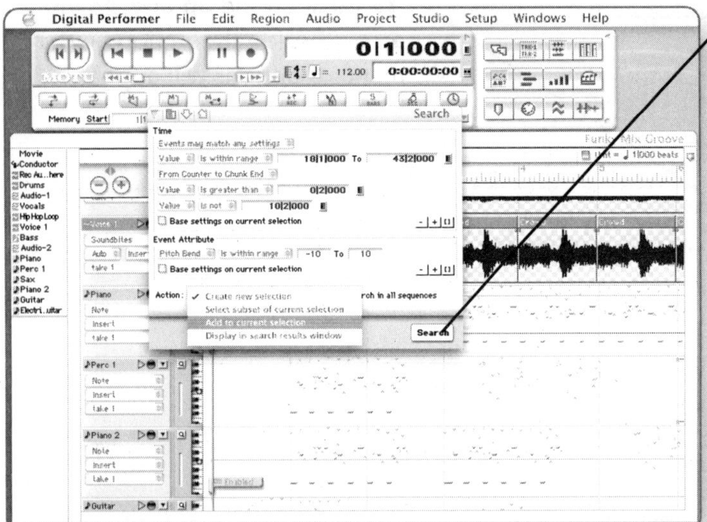

3. Click on **Search**. The search will be conducted and the action that you selected will occur.

The Search Window

Displaying the results of your search in the Search Results window offers you a great deal of control in finding specific data. It allows you to scroll through your results, make selections, and edit specific data found in your search.

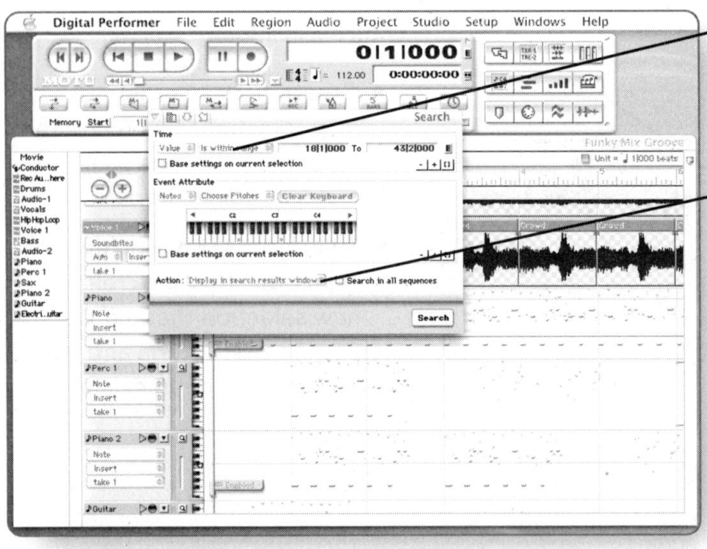

1. Click on the desired **criteria** for your search in the Time and Event Attribute sections of the window.

2. Click on the **up-and-down arrow** beside the Action field. A menu of options will appear.

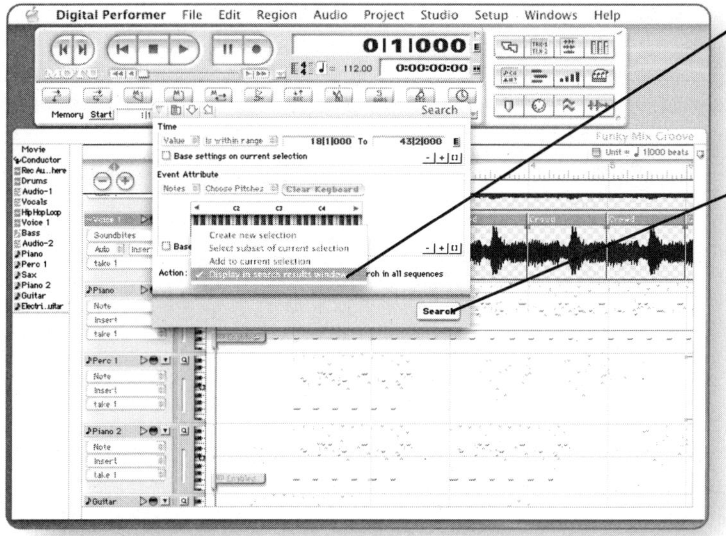

3. Click on **Display in search results window**. This will launch the Search Results window when the search is conducted.

4. Click on **Search**. The search will be conducted and the Search Results window will open.

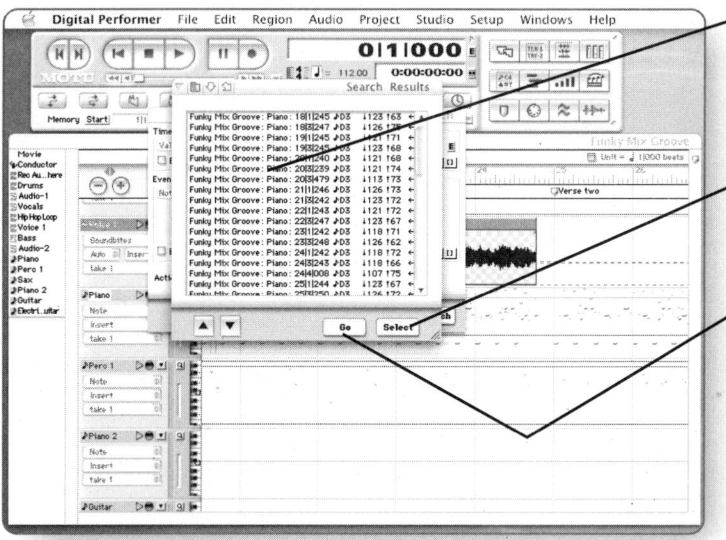

5. Click on an **item** you would like to select. Alternatively, you can click and drag or Shift + select to choose multiple notes.

6. Click on the **Select button**. A selection will be made from the note(s) you have clicked.

7. Click on the **Go button**. An editing window for the note(s) you have selected will open.

17

Getting Help

The purpose of this book is to help you build a solid foundation in Digital Performer so you can begin recording and editing music without having to spend hours reading the encyclopedia of a manual that comes with the program. Should you need help beyond the scope of what is covered in this book, Digital Performer offers built-in Help functionality that will assist you in finding the answers you are looking for. In this chapter, you will learn how to:

- Launch Digital Performer Help
- Search for help
- Get window-specific help

Launching Help

The Help functionality in Digital Performer is integrated with the OS X Mac Help window. Within the program itself there is a Help menu from which you can access help on a variety of topics.

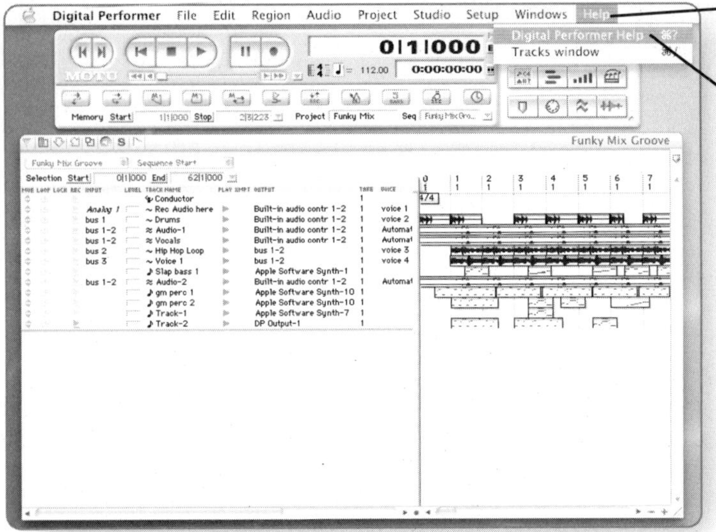

1. **Click** on **Help**. The Help menu will appear.
2. **Click** on **Digital Performer Help**. The Digital Performer Help window will launch.

Help Categories

Digital Performer has grouped the Help topics into a variety of different categories to make it easier to find the particular help you are looking for.

1. **Click** on the **scroll arrows** to scroll through the different Help topics.

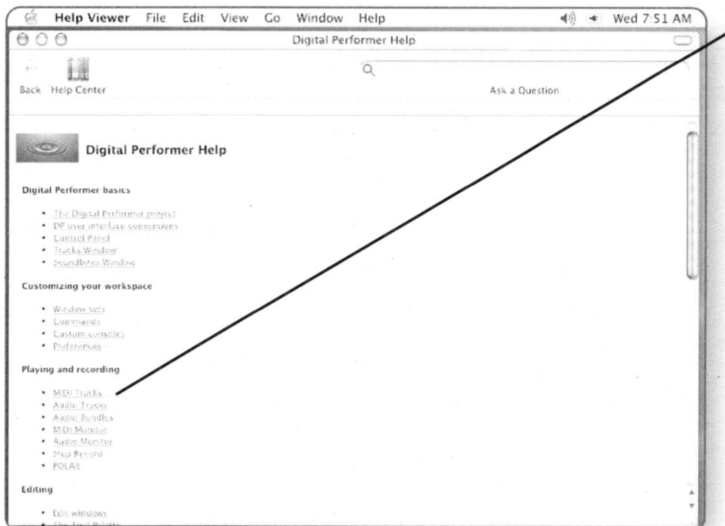

2. **Click** on the desired **topic**. A new window will open with the contents of that topic. You can now read the Help associated with that topic.

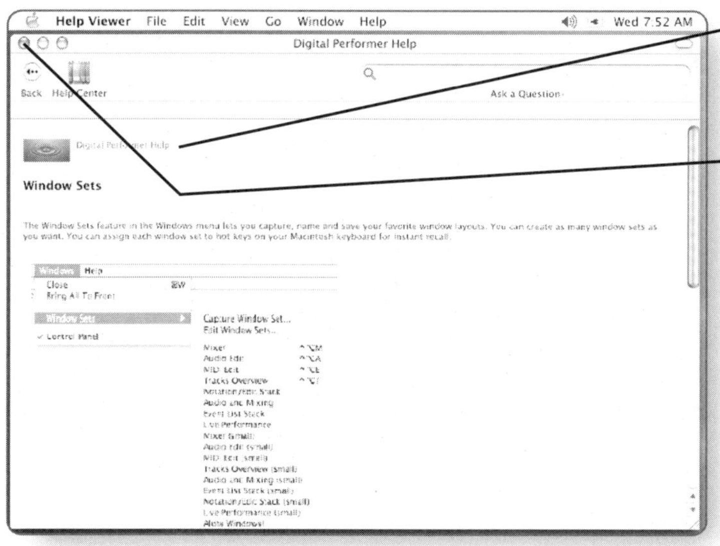

3. **Click** on **Digital Performer Help** to return to the main Help window.

4. **Click** on the **red button** in the top-left corner to close Help and return to Digital Performer.

Searching for Help

Rather than having to sort through a variety of categories looking for assistance, you can search for particular Help topics.

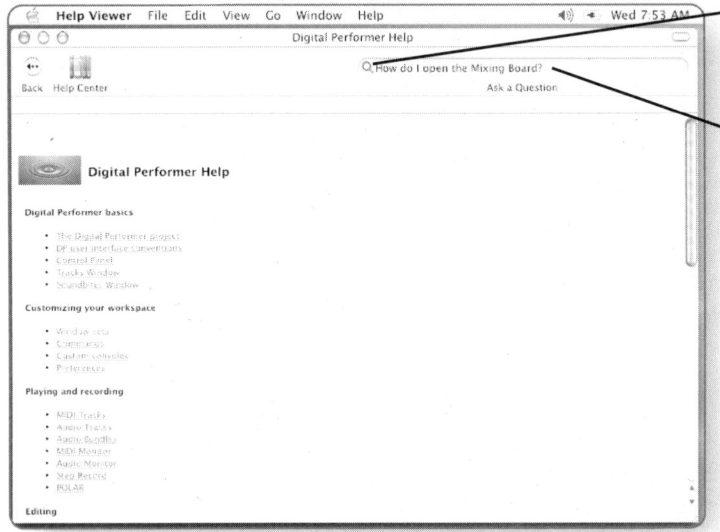

1. Click once in the **Ask a Question field**. Your cursor will flash in the field.

2. Type a **question**. You can pose a question or you can simply enter keywords for your search.

3. Press Return. The search will be conducted and the results will be displayed.

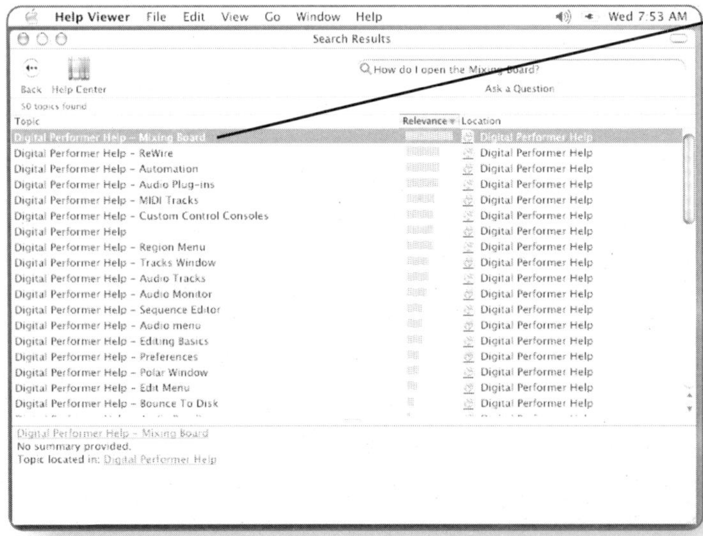

4. Double-click on the **topic** that best covers your search criteria. A new window that explains that topic will open.

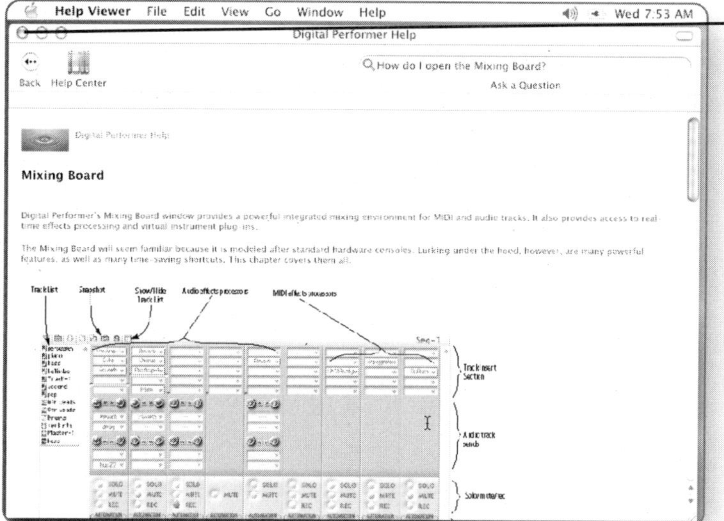

5. Click on the **red button** in the top-left corner to close Help and return to Digital Performer.

Window-Specific Help

With Digital Performer, you can get help associated with the particular window you are working in instantly through the Help menu.

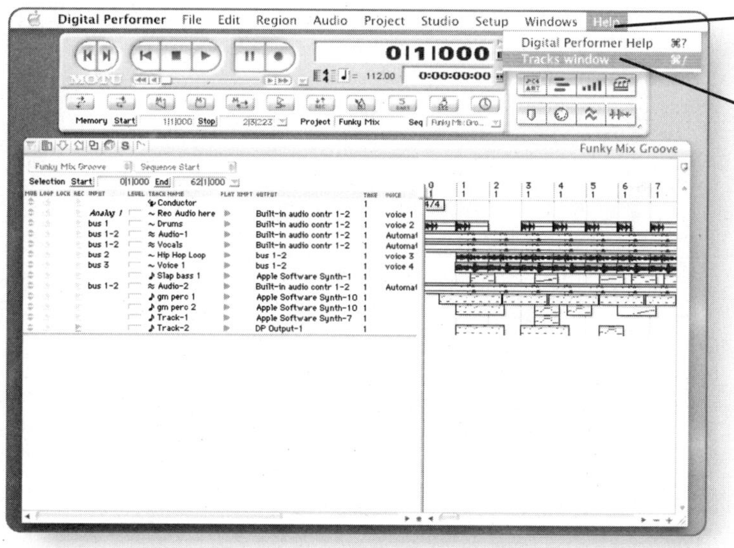

1. Click on **Help**. The Help menu will appear.

2. Click on the **name** of the **window** you are working in. The Help topic associated with that window will open.

> **TIP**
>
> Additional help and support options are available from the MOTU website at http://www.motu.com.

A

Review Questions

Questions

1. What Digital Performer feature allows you to transcribe your MIDI tracks?

2. How can you make your audio seem like it is being played in an auditorium?

3. What keyboard shortcut allows you to copy a selection as you click and drag it?

4. The ________ __________ feature allows you to record one note at a time.

5. What feature allows you to change the pitch, formats, and tempo of a selection all from within one dialog box?

6. What feature in Digital Performer acts as a bookmark, allowing you to jump to specific locations in your track?

7. What are the steps required to loop a selection 10 times?

8. The ________ __________ available in most widows provides you with a list of commands related to that window.

9. What is the difference between audio and MIDI information?

10. How do you set up a MIDI device?

11. What does the Audible Mode feature do?

12. The _______ window is ideal for importing audio into your sequences.

13. How do you insert a new stereo track?

14. The ________ __________in Digital Performer allows you to control the way a sequence is rewound, stopped, and repeated.

15. What is a note's duration?

16. How do you activate the metronome?

17. What feature disables recording until a signal from your keyboard or instrument is received?

18. How do you change the units being displayed in the counter?

19. What does the Snip feature do?

20. What are the steps required to reverse a selection?

21. What feature allows you to add a human touch to your selections?

22. Is it possible to move a selection from a mono track to a stereo track?

23. How do you adjust the volume of a track in the Mixing Board window?

24. In the Mixing Board window, how do you reduce the size of the channel strips?

25. How do you delete a note in the QuickScribe Editor?

26. The ________ tool allows you to graphically manipulate audio events.

27. How do you add a note in the List Editor?

28. How can you change the length of a countoff?

29. A tempo change is indicated in the _________ track.

30. How do you add a comment to a track?

Answers

1. The QuickScribe Editor

2. You can make your audio seem like it is being played in an auditorium by applying the eVerb plug-in and selecting Auditorium as the room type.

3. Pressing and holding the Option key as you click and drag a selection will create a copy.

4. Step Record

5. Spectral Effects

6. Markers

7. To loop a selection 10 times, you must click on Region and then Set Loop. A dialog box will appear. Enter 10 into the dialog box and then click on OK. The selection will now loop 10 times.

8. Mini Menu

9. MIDI information is displayed as little lines in the Tracks window and represents digital information, whereas audio is displayed as waveforms and is actual sound.

10. By clicking on Autoconfigure MIDI Devices from the Setup menu, you can configure your MIDI devices.

11. The Audible Mode feature makes it possible to hear changes as you make them.

12. Soundbites

13. To insert a new stereo track, click on Project > Add Track > Add Stereo Track.

14. Memory bar

15. The duration of a note is defined as the length between its attack and its release.

16. By clicking on the Metronome button in the Control Panel, you can activate the metronome.

17. The Wait button

18. By clicking on the little button to the right of the counter, you can toggle between the different units of display.

19. The Snip feature allows you to delete both phrases and time regions at the same time.

20. After you've created a selection, click on Audio > Audio Plug-ins > Reverse.

21. The Humanize effect will randomize areas of your sequence to give it a human touch.

22. No, mono tracks can only be moved to other mono tracks and stereo tracks can only be moved to stereo tracks.

23. To adjust the volume, position your mouse pointer over one of the faders and click and drag it up or down.

24. Click on the Mini Menu button and then select Narrow View.

25. You must first select the note or notes that you would like to delete and then press the Delete key on your keyboard.

26. Pencil

27. Click on the Insert button and then click on Note.

28. By double-clicking on the Countoff button, you can open a dialog box that will allow you to change the length of the countoff.

29. Conductor

30. Click on the comment box for the desired track in the Tracks window. A dialog box will appear in which you can add a track.

Index

C

D

E

M

T

U

V

W

Z

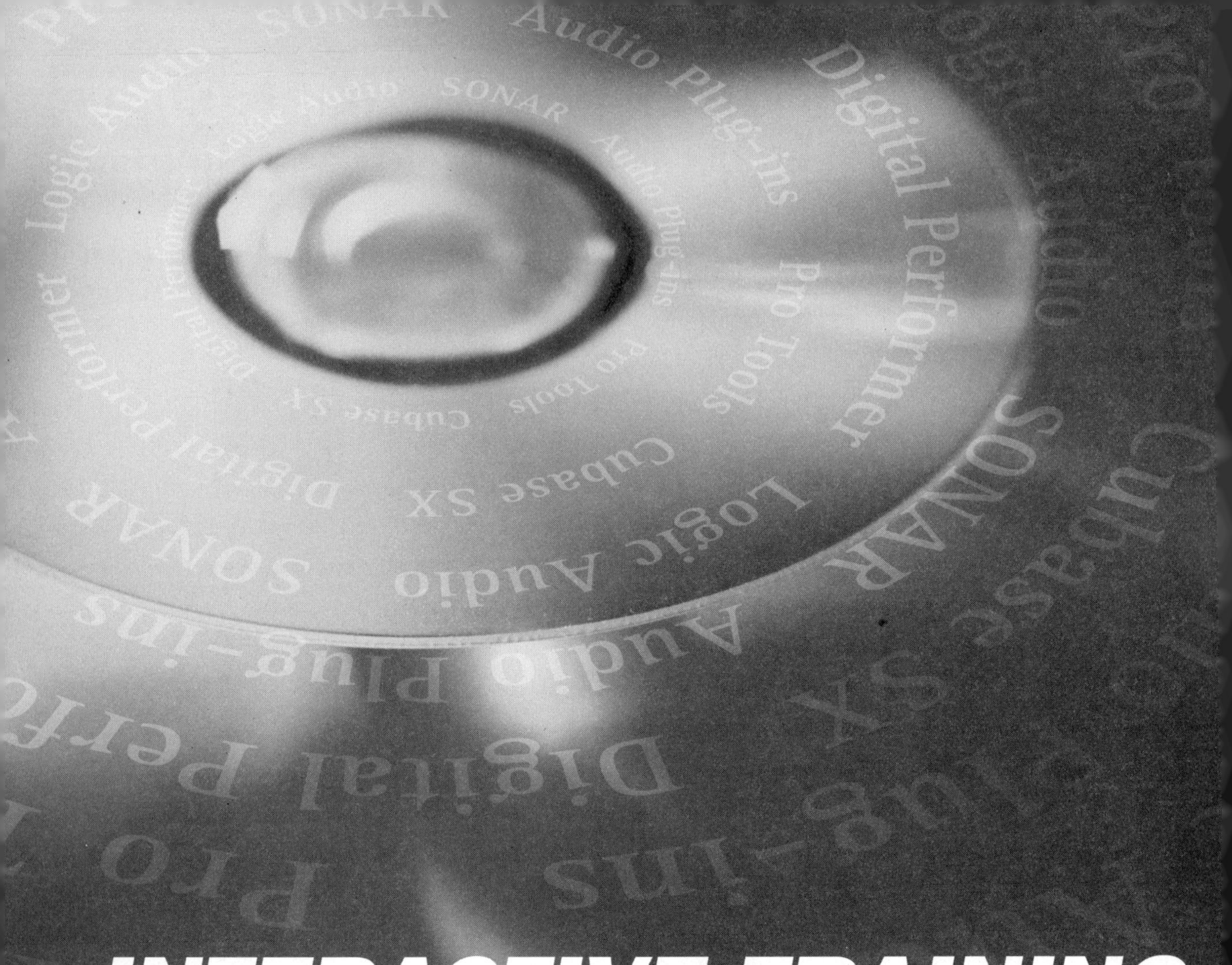